The Roman Empire

Colin Michael Wells ~~~~~~~~~~~~~~~~~~~~~~~~~~~~~~~~~~~~~
School and at Orie~~~~~~~~~~~~~~~~~~~~~~~~~~~~~~~~~~~~~~~
University of Otta~~~~~~
and former Chairm~~~~~~
Studies, and a form~~~~~~~~~~~~~~~~~~~~~~~~~~~~~~~~~~~~~~~
He has also been Vis~~~~~~~~~~~~~~~~~~~~~~~partment of
History in the Uni~~~~~~~~~~~California at Berkeley,
Visiting Lecturer in the Institute of Archaeology at
Oxford, and Visiting Fellow of Brasenose College,
Oxford. He is a Fellow of the Society of Antiquaries of
London. He is the author of *The German Policy of
Augustus* (1972), and since 1977 has been directing
Canadian excavations at Carthage, on the northern edge
of the Roman city astride the Theodosian Wall.

FONTANA HISTORY OF THE ANCIENT WORLD

Editor Oswyn Murray

Colin Wells

THE ROMAN EMPIRE

Fontana Paperbacks

OMNIA SOLITA

The cover shows an early third-century mosaic from
Thysdrus (El Djem), now in the Bardo Museum, Tunis.
Men who are to appear in the amphitheatre the next day
feast before the games and are told to be quiet and not
wake up the bulls they are to fight ('*silentium, dormiant
tauri*' – 'silence, let the bulls sleep'). Thanks are due to
the Bardo Museum for permission to photograph this
mosaic and to reproduce it.

First published by Fontana Paperbacks 1984
Second impression September 1988

Copyright © Colin Wells 1984

Set in Pacesetter Times

Printed and bound in Great Britain by
William Collins Sons & Co. Ltd, Glasgow

Contents

Introduction to the
Fontana History of the Ancient World

No justification is needed for a new history of the ancient world; modern scholarship and new discoveries have changed our picture in important ways, and it is time for the results to be made available to the general reader. But the Fontana History of the Ancient World attempts not only to present an up-to-date account. In the study of the distant past, the chief difficulties are the comparative lack of evidence and the special problems of interpreting it; this in turn makes it both possible and desirable for the more important evidence to be presented to the reader and discussed, so that he may see for himself the methods used in reconstructing the past, and judge for himself their success.

The series aims, therefore, to give an outline account of each period that it deals with and, at the same time, to present as much as possible of the evidence for that account. Selected documents with discussions of them are integrated into the narrative, and often form the basis of it; when interpretations are controversial the arguments are presented to the reader. In addition, each volume has a general survey of the types of evidence available for the period and ends with detailed suggestions for further reading. The series will, it is hoped, equip the reader to follow up his own interests and enthusiasms, having gained some understanding of the limits within which the historian must work.

Oswyn Murray
Fellow and Tutor in Ancient History,
Balliol College, Oxford
General Editor

List of Illustrations

List of Abbreviations

Abbreviations have been avoided as far as possible, but it seemed unnecessarily cumbersome to print in full the titles of the various collections of inscriptions and other documents that are often cited. The following abbreviations have therefore been used:

CIL — *Corpus Inscriptionum Latinarum*

EJ — Ehrenberg and Jones, *Documents Illustrating the Reigns of Augustus and Tiberius*

FIRA — *Fontes Iuris Romani Anteiustiniani*, eds., S. Riccobono and others

IG — *Inscriptiones Graecae*

IGRR — *Inscriptiones Graecae ad res Romanas pertinentes*

ILS — Dessau, *Inscriptiones Latinae Selectae*

LR — Lewis and Reinhold, *Roman Civilization, Sourcebook* II: *the Empire*

P.Oxy. — *The Oxyrhynchus Papyri*, eds., B. P. Grenfell, A. S. Hunt and others

SEG — *Supplementum Epigraphicum Graecum*

Select Papyri — *Select Papyri*, eds., A. S. Hunt and C. G. Edgar (Loeb Classical Library)

Note also:

ANRW — *Aufstieg und Niedergang der römischen Welt*, ed., H. Temporini

JRS — *Journal of Roman Studies*

PBSR — *Papers of the British School at Rome*

The invitation to write this book on the Roman Empire from 44 BC to AD 235 came just as I finished a term as Visiting Professor at the University of California at Berkeley, where I had been lecturing to undergraduates on this period. My lecture notes were in order, I was stimulated by the questions and discussions that the course had evoked, and still drunk on the Berkeley climate in spring. I thought that writing the book would be easy.

Nearly five years later, with most of the book complete, I sat down to write this preface in an Ottawa blizzard. The book has not been easy. The more I thought I knew about a subject, the harder it was to write about it. I could have filled half the book with Augustus alone. It was not easy to do without footnotes. The Fontana History of the Ancient World is aimed at the general reader, but the professional scholar, writing in a field which has seen so much scholarly activity, feels his colleagues looking over his shoulder, and is obsessed with the need to justify himself, to reassure them that he realizes when he is oversimplifying, or when he has passed over in silence a topic generally deemed to be fascinatingly controversial, which generally means hopelessly obscure.

The historian of the Roman Empire must always keep in mind what was happening in the central administration of the Empire and in the entourage of the emperor; but he must also try to reflect how life went on in Italy and the provinces, in the towns, in the countryside, in the army camps, and to ask how far these different worlds impinged on each other. Theodor Mommsen, greatest of all nineteenth-century historians of Rome, wrote of our period:

Seldom has the government of the world been conducted for so long a term in an orderly sequence ... In its sphere, which those who belonged to it were not far wrong in regarding as the world, it fostered the peace and prosperity of the many nations united under its sway longer and more completely than any other leading power has ever done. It is in the agricultural towns of Africa, in the homes of vine-dressers on the Moselle, in the flourishing townships of the Lycian mountains, and on the margin of the Syrian desert that the work of the imperial period is to be sought and to be found ... If an angel of the Lord were to strike the balance whether the domain ruled by Severus Alexander were governed with the greater intelligence and the greater humanity at that time or at the present day, whether civilisation and national prosperity generally have since that time advanced or retrograded, it is very doubtful whether the decision would prove in favour of the present.

Government, however, could only do so much. It could create the conditions of peace and order, but, as has been well pointed out:

The Roman Empire was a very big place. Its economy and its communications were of the most primitive. The great Roman roads passed through little towns which derived most of what they ate, lived in and wore from a radius of some thirty miles. We shall never understand the life of the towns of the Greco-Roman world unless we relive, through the texts, the creeping fear of famine. However we may draw our maps of the grandiose road-system of the Roman world, each small town knew that they would have to face out alone a winter of starvation, if ever their harvest failed ... For many months every year, the 'realities' that have been so confidently invoked in standard accounts of the development of the Roman world – armed force, commerce, fiscal control – were simply washed away. The passes filled with snow, the great flagstones of the Roman roads sunk into the mud, the stores of fodder dwindled at the posting-stations, and the little boats rocked at anchor. The Mediterranean ceased to exist; and the distance between the Emperor and his subjects trebled.

I have tried to keep the balance between the centre and the periphery and, what was harder still, between narrative and discussion. The odd-numbered chapters are meant to provide a more or less sequential account of the development of the central administration of the Empire, the achievements of successive Emperors, the court, and the struggle for power at the top. They could be read as a connected narrative, omitting the intervening even-numbered chapters. These discuss the state of Italy and of the provinces at various phases of development from the Age of Augustus to that of the Severans, with Chapter 2 being devoted to the nature of the sources for this whole period and to some of the problems which they pose.

Translations of passages quoted in the text are usually my own, unless otherwise indicated. I had originally thought to ask permission to use the Penguin translations, especially of Tacitus and Suetonius, since this would make it easier for readers to look up passages quoted in their wider context, but I soon found that these two translations, though excellent in their way and highly readable, often incorporated tacitly in the English version an interpretation of the text which was not mine. On the other hand, I found by experience that I could not improve on Betty Radice's translation of Pliny's *Letters*, while for the *Res Gestae* of Augustus I have used or adapted Brunt and Moore's translation, for the books of the New Testament *The New English Bible*, and for various inscriptions the version in Lewis and Reinhold's invaluable *Roman Civilization, Sourcebook II: the Empire*.

Suggestions for further reading at the end of the book are mostly confined to recent works in English, unless an older work, or a work in another language, seemed the best or the only thing available on an important topic. The selection is highly personal, books which I myself have found useful or stimulating. I have not referred to specific editions of ancient authors, unless hard to find, nor to commentaries, unless of special value to the reader without Greek or Latin. For, translations, there is the Penguin series, readable, reliable, cheap and easy to find. They have done more to keep the interest in the ancient world alive over the last thirty years than all university classics departments put together. Authors not available in Penguin are usually in the Loeb series (Harvard University Press and Heinemann), with Greek or Latin on the left-hand page and the English translation facing, sometimes dated in style or scholarship, but quite invaluable.

Dates are AD unless otherwise stated. Roman legal or technical terms are explained below, or else on their first occurrence in the text. Such explanations can, if necessary, be tracked down through the Index. If a Roman proper name is familiar in an Anglicized form, I have used that form (Mark Antony, Trajan, etc.), while supplying the full name on first meeting, except in chapter 2, on sources, where only the name by which an author is usually known by is given; there is a list of authors' full names and dates on page 309. Towns and cities appear under the ancient or modern name or both, with clarity and ease of recognition being the aim, rather than consistency. Both forms appear in the index. For rivers and other geographical features, I have tended to use the modern name alone (Thames, not Tamesis; Great St Bernard Pass, not Alpis Poenina).

We shall be much concerned with the evolution of social and political institutions in the Early Empire. Some preliminary explanation of technicalities may make things clearer. Under the Republic, ultimate power rested in the body of adult male citizens, meeting in an assembly (*comitia*) under a magistrate. To vote, a citizen had to be present. There were several different types of assembly (Crawford, *The Roman Republic*, Appendix 1), with different systems of voting, according to the type of business to be contracted. Their electoral and legislative functions became progressively less important under the Empire. The last time an assembly is known to have been convened to pass legislation is under the Emperor Nerva. Laws were called after the magistrate who introduced them. Thus a Julian Law (*lex Iulia*) may be the work of either Julius Caesar or Augustus, who bore Caesar's family name by adoption (see Chapter 1).

A resolution of the Senate (*senatus consultum*, abbreviated *SC*, as on coinage from the mint at Rome under the Senate's control) was not technically a law (*lex*), but came to have binding force, although the Senate's authority could be disputed in the troubled times of the Late Republic, especially when it voted virtually to suspend the laws in what it judged to be an emergency (the *senatus consultum ultimum*, cf. Crawford, pp. 123, 183). Under the Empire, the emperor became the fount of law, and increasingly found it more convenient to legislate via the *senatus consultum* rather than the *lex*. The Senate also acquired important judicial functions. By the end of the Republic, it was composed primarily of ex-magistrates, and Augustus systematized the senatorial career (*cursus honorum*) in such a way that 20 men annually were elected quaestor, usually about the age of 25, and thereby entered the Senate. Then they might become aedile or tribune, and at about 30, they could stand for the praetorship (normally twelve posts a year). Quaestors were mostly concerned with financial matters, aediles with municipal administration, praetors with judicial affairs; on tribunes see page 7. Ex-praetors might hold various posts, especially in the provinces, including governorships of smaller provinces and appointments in command of a legion.

At the age of 42, or much sooner for those specially favoured by the emperor, a man might aspire to the consulship. The two consuls who took office each year on 1 January were the nominal heads of state, and the consulship was eagerly sought, even down into the later Empire, when it had become a mere title of honour largely devoid of power. It ennobled one's family: broadly speaking, the descendant of a consul was a *nobilis*, and a man without consular ancestors in the male line, like Cicero or indeed Augustus, was known scornfully as a 'new man' (*novus homo*). The consuls gave their name to the year in the official calendar, so that 44 BC was dated 'in the consulship of Gaius Julius Caesar and Marcus Antonius'. If a consul died in office or resigned, a suffect consul (*consul suffectus*) was appointed to complete his term. Suffect consulships were considered less distinguished, but from 5 BC onwards it became standard for the consuls of the year to resign half way through and let suffects take their place, in order to increase the supply of ex-consuls for the specifically consular posts in the public service, like the governorships of major provinces and, as the Empire went on, an increasing number of administrative jobs at Rome, which were reserved for men of consular rank. The consular lists, known as the *fasti*, survive in various inscriptions (*Fasti Capitolini*, *Fasti Ostienses*, etc.) in various degrees of completeness.

Praetors and consuls, together with ex-magistrates holding a special appointment, such as the governorship of a province, which they were considered to hold as a substitute for a praetor or consul (*pro praetore* or *pro consule*), possessed *imperium*, an untranslatable term signifying the right to command in war, to administer the laws and to inflict the death penalty (subject to a Roman citizen's right of appeal, originally to the people, later to the emperor). The *imperium* of propraetors and proconsuls were normally restricted to the province to which they were appointed (a province, *provincia*, originally meant a defined sphere of action, not necessarily geographical, as we might say in English, 'the interpretation of the law is the province of the courts'; but by the end of the Republic, it normally meant a specific territory, such as the province of Asia or of Gallia Narbonensis, i.e., Provence and Languedoc). In the Late Republic, it occurred that one proconsul might have his *imperium* defined as greater (*maius*) than another's, so that it was clear who prevailed in case of disagreement.

Under the Empire, certain provinces were assigned to the emperor, who governed them through deputies, mostly men of consular or praetorian rank, holding the title of *legatus Augusti pro praetore*, appointed by the emperor for as long as he chose and responsible only to him. Other provinces, of which the most important were Africa and Asia, continued to have proconsuls or propraetors appointed by the Senate for a one-year term. The emperor however always had *imperium maius*, so that he could overrule a senatorial governor at will.

Cognate with the word *imperium* is *imperator*. This was the acclamation traditionally given to a victorious general by his troops. If a victory was won by a commander fighting merely as the legate of a superior, the acclamation belonged to the superior. So the emperors collected imperatorial salutations for all victories won by legates governing the imperial provinces. Octavian in the triumviral period (see Chapter 1) actually adopted Imperator as a forename (*praenomen*), and the number of the emperor's imperatorial salutations regularly appears as part of his official style, for instance on coins, along with the number of years for which he has held tribunician power (see next paragraph), but only with the Emperor Vespasian (AD 69–79) does *imperator*, whence 'emperor', become the usual title by which the emperor is known. Hence, although it is convenient to refer to Augustus and his immediate successors as 'emperor', it is, strictly speaking, anachronistic. Augustus preferred *princeps*, roughly equivalent to 'first citizen'.

Two other Republican magistracies were important for the history of the Empire, both standing outside the regular *cursus honorum*. The first is the tribunate. The tribunes were originally elected to protect the common people against abuse of power by magistrates or by the Senate. They had wide powers of veto, they could initiate legislation, and their persons were sacrosanct. Augustus and his successors were granted tribunician power (*tribunicia potestas*) without actually holding the office. The tribunes themselves became unimportant. The second important office is that of censor. Under the Republic, a pair of censors was elected every five years, primarily to revise the citizenship rolls and the membership of the Senate. They were usually senior ex-consuls. Under the Empire, the emperors came to exercise the censorial powers. This development, and that of tribunician power, are discussed below, especially in Chapter 3. The Republic also knew the office of *dictator*, appointed in emergency with supreme power. The dictatorship was offered to Augustus, but he refused it, and it fell into abeyance.

From Augustus's time onwards, a senator needed at least a million sesterces as capital (on money and monetary values, see next paragraph). Men with at least 400,000 sesterces, though many had more, who did not aim at a political career formed the equestrian order (*ordo equester*). This had evolved from the cavalry of the Early Republic, but the equestrians (*equites* or knights) of the Late Republic had no more in common with mounted warriors than have the successful businessmen, diligent civil servants and distinguished academics raised to the knighthood in modern Britain ('Prince, Bayard would have smashed his sword / To see the sort of knights you dub. / Is that the last of them? O Lord, / Will someone take me to a pub?'). For this reason, I think 'knights' a reasonable translation. The knights were not, as they have sometimes been called, a 'middle class', implicitly or explicitly contrasted with the senatorial aristocracy. The two groups were largely drawn from the same background. One son might choose a political career and end up as consul, another opt for money-making or moneyed leisure and remain a knight. But under the Empire there also developed an equestrian *cursus honorum* whereby men starting at a lower social and economic level could rise through public service (pages 97, 228).

Money and monetary values pose a problem. Sums of money were generally reckoned and are generally quoted in sesterces (*sestertii*), there being 4 sesterces to the *denarius*. The smallest coin in common use was the *as*; in the Early Empire there were 16 *asses* to the *denarius*. The Greek *drachma* was equivalent to the *denarius*. Any attempt to relate ancient monetary units to modern ones, as used to be done, is nugatory in an age of inflation. Let it suffice to point out that the Emperor Tiberius is said to have left a fortune of 2700 million sesterces (Suetonius, *Caligula* 37); that the richest men known to us under the Empire, outside the imperial house, allegedly had 400 million apiece (Gnaeus Cornelius Lentulus, consul 14 BC, and the Emperor Claudius's freedman, i.e., ex-slave, Narcissus); that an ordinary legionary under Augustus received 900 sesterces a year in pay, less deductions for food, clothing, etc.; and that the unskilled labourer at Rome at this time received about 3 sesterces a day as his wage. This subject is discussed further in Chapter 8 (pages 203–4).

This book has been much delayed. One reason is my preoccupation with the Canadian (University of Ottawa) excavations at Carthage which I am directing. They were to have finished in 1980, but the richness of the site has encouraged us to continue. We now range from a Punic cemetery, through Roman, Vandal, Byzantine and Arab phases, to a British army dump, *circa* AD 1944, overlying the remains of the late Roman city wall. Running a dig on this scale without administrative help is a time-consuming business.

I am therefore grateful to Oswyn Murray, as general editor of this series, and to Helen Fraser of Fontana, for their superhuman patience, unfailing encouragement and valuable comments. My former Ottawa colleague, now, alas, at Stanford, Susan Treggiari, and my Ottawa graduate student and Carthage assistant, Marianne Goodfellow, have read the entire book as it was written, and I have adopted almost all of their suggestions. They both kept up my faith in the book and in myself when I was in danger of losing it.

To Susan Treggiari, as a result of many years' friendship and teaching together, and to Peter Brunt, formerly Camden Professor, once my tutor and subsequently a fellow Fellow of Brasenose, I owe a lifelong debt for shaping the way I think about Roman history, although they may feel that this book is a poor way of repaying it. Professor Brunt's comments on an earlier article of mine saved me from many errors, and I have since derived many ideas from discussion with him.

Others to whom I am grateful for discussion and ideas are

Shimon Applebaum, on the Jewish sources; Simon Ellis, on the transition to Late Antiquity; and David Cherry, also an Ottawa graduate student, on soldiers and citizenship. My wife Kate and my son Dominic read certain chapters from a non-specialist viewpoint and helped me to clarify points that were obscure. I have tried out drafts on successive Roman history classes at the University of Ottawa and benefited from discussion of particular points in graduate seminars.

The book comes out of my teaching and is therefore dedicated to the students who have helped to shape it. My thanks are due to them, as well as to all the persons named. The book was actually finished in Oxford, between two visits to Carthage. I am grateful to the staff of the Ashmolean Library for their kindness, which makes it still an agreeable place to work, despite the ravages occasioned by the Fire Marshal, and above all to the Principal and Fellows of Brasenose College, whose exemplary hospitality to a former Fellow makes my visits to Oxford so pleasant and rewarding.

For permission to reproduce figures and plates, the author and publisher gratefully acknowledge the following: (figs. 2a, 4 and 5); Weidenfeld and Nicolson (figs. 2b and 6); Methuen (fig. 3); Benn (fig. 7); Oxford University Press (fig. 8); Ashmolean Museum, Oxford (plate 1a, 1b and 8a); M. S. Goodfellow (plate 3b, 7a and 8b).

1 *The New Order*

The future Emperor Augustus was born in Rome on 23 September, 63 BC, on the morning of the great Senate debate on Lucius Sergius Catilina's projected coup d'état. The child's father was an ambitious and rising young senator named Gaius Octavius, who died however, four years later, before he could stand for the consulship. He was a 'new man' (page 5), indeed the first of his family even to enter the Senate. The family came from Velitrae (modern Velletri), a small town in the Alban Hills near Rome. Gaius Octavius is said to have been 'from the beginning of his life a man of wealth and standing' (Suetonius, *Augustus* 3). His wife came from nearby Aricia; her family had held senatorial rank for many generations and was connected with both Pompey (Gnaeus Pompeius Magnus) and Caesar (Gaius Julius Caesar). The Octavii are typical of the sort of small-town family from that part of Italy, long established, rich and well connected, but traditionally aloof from politics at Rome, which Cicero (Marcus Tullius Cicero), who came from just such a family himself, called 'nobles in their own place' (*domi nobiles*, Cicero, *For Cluentius* 23; also Sallust, *Catiline* 17).

Octavius's only son (there were two daughters, one by an earlier marriage) grew up in a world dominated by the ruthless struggle for personal aggrandisement which characterized the last decades of the Republic (Crawford, *The Roman Republic*, chapters 14 and 15). He was only thirteen when Caesar crossed the Rubicon and led his legions on Rome, whereupon Pompey abandoned Italy, to meet eventual defeat at Pharsalus in Greece and ignominious death when he sought refuge in Egypt. Caesar made his peace with those of Pompey's supporters who were willing to swallow their pride and accept the 'clemency' (*clementia*) that Caesar boasted of. The others were hunted down. By the end of 46 BC, Caesar was master of the Roman world, dictator for ten years (for life from 44 BC) and consul for 46, 45 and 44, an autocrat who did not even try to hide his contempt for the cherished forms and institutions of the Republic. For this he paid the price, murdered on the Ides of March (15 March 44 BC), by senators who could not stomach the affront to their oligarchic dignity that Caesar's personal supremacy and quasi-monarchical attitudes represented.

Had Pompey, not Caesar, won the Battle of Pharsalus, we might have heard no more of the young Octavius. But the boy's maternal grandmother was Caesar's sister, and Caesar, who had no son, was impressed by his great-nephew's energy and abilities. Consequently, when the civil wars were over,

> Caesar planned an expedition against the Dacians and then the Parthians, and sent him [Octavius] on ahead to Apollonia, where he spent his time studying. As soon as Octavius heard that Caesar had been killed, and that he himself was his heir, he hesitated for some time whether to appeal to the nearest legions, before rejecting the idea as rash and premature. He did however return to Rome and take up his inheritance, despite his mother's doubts and the strong opposition of his stepfather, the ex-consul Marcius Philippus. (Suetonius, *Augustus* 8)

Adopted by Caesar's will, Octavius in the usual Roman style took his adoptive father's name, with his own name added in a modified form, becoming Gaius Julius Caesar Octavianus. For clarity's sake, modern writers generally refer to him henceforth as Octavian, but contemporaries usually called him Caesar. He was not yet nineteen, but 'felt that there was nothing more important for him than to avenge his uncle's death and uphold his enactments' (Suetonius, *Augustus* 10). Caesar's fellow-consul, Antony (Marcus Antonius), had laid his hands on Caesar's papers and some of his money, and seemed unwilling to recognize the lawful

heir. Octavian's version of what happened next is preserved
in the *Res Gestae* (see Chapter 2, page 35):

.At the age of nineteen on my own responsibility and at my
own expense I raised an army, with which I successfully
championed the liberty of the republic when it was
oppressed by the tyranny of a faction. On that account the
Senate passed decrees in my honour enrolling me in its
order in the consulship of Gaius Pansa and Aulus Hirtius
[i.e., 43 BC], assigning me the right to give my opinion
among the consulars and giving me *imperium*. It ordered
me as a propraetor to provide in concert with the consuls
that the republic should come to no harm. In the same
year, when both consuls had fallen in battle, the people
appointed me consul and triumvir for the organization of
the republic. I drove into exile the murderers of my father,
avenging their crime through tribunals established by law;
and afterwards, when they made war on the republic, I
twice defeated them in battle. (*Res Gestae* 1–2)

'Liberty' and 'faction' are stock words of the political
vocabulary. *I* am always for liberty, *you* are always a faction.
Like 'democracy' today, 'liberty' could mean anything you
wanted it to mean, and nobody was ever against it. Apart
from that, the account in the *Res Gestae* is quite accurate, as
far as it goes. It tells the truth, but by no means the whole
truth. What is remarkable is how much it omits, such as any
mention of Antony. The Senate in fact, with Cicero to the
fore, took up Octavian, hoping to use the magic of his name,
Caesar, to win the soldiers and people away from Antony.
Octavian let himself be used, for his own purposes. He got
what he could out of collaboration with the Senate, including
the consulship before he was twenty, and then made a deal
with Antony. The two of them brought in another of Caesar's
old supporters, Marcus Aemilius Lepidus, now governor of
Gallia Narbonensis and Hispania Citerior, and as such commander of an important army, and got a friendly tribune to
convene an assembly, which met in the Forum, ringed by troops,

to vote them supreme power as a 'Commission of Three for the Organization of the Republic' (*triumviri reipublicae constituendae*, 23 November 43 BC). Imitating Sulla's proscriptions forty years earlier (Crawford, *The Roman Republic*, p.151), the triumvirs promptly took vengeance on their enemies, at the same time raising money to pay their troops: at least 130 senators and an unknown number of knights were outlawed and their property confiscated. Many went into exile. The only man of consular rank actually killed was Cicero, and that was largely because he was slow and indecisive in escaping.

Octavian had shown himself, as he was to show himself again, ruthless and tenacious in pursuit of his aims. 'Although for some time he opposed his colleagues' idea of a proscription, yet once it was begun, he carried it out more ruthlessly than either of them' (Suetonius, *Augustus* 27). As we shall see, he would be equally ruthless in eliminating each of them in turn, until the defeat and disgrace of Antony at the Battle of Actium in 31 BC left Octavian master of the Roman world. In his youth, he had merited the label once applied to Pompey, 'the teenage butcher'. After Actium, taking the name Augustus, with solemn, quasi-religious overtones, learning from Julius Caesar's fate to veil his power beneath traditional forms, he ruled for forty-five years, and when he died, 'father of his country' (*pater patriae*) and full of honours, the transfer of power to his stepson Tiberius, tardily and reluctantly adopted and groomed for the succession, went almost without a hitch. By then, as Tacitus pointed out, hardly anyone was left who even remembered the Republic (*Annals* i.3). And of those that did, few would have preferred the chaos and violence which followed Caesar's death to the continuity of administration which Augustus's own death scarcely troubled.

Before tracing the history of the Triumvirate, we may ask ourselves why Augustus succeeded where Caesar had failed in establishing a dictatorship. It was not only that he played his cards more skilfully, but that Italy was sick of war and sick of 'liberty' which seemed only to mean oligarchic licence.

From the lynching of Gaius Gracchus onwards (Crawford, *The Roman Republic,* p.98), violence was flagrantly used in Republican politics, and to the destruction wrought by violence must be added the horrors of proscriptions and confiscations, whereby whole communities might suffer. Poverty, hardship and unrest were widespread. Men raised private armies. We have seen that Augustus in the *Res Gestae* boasts of doing so, and Marcus Licinius Crassus (consul 70 BC) is credited with the remark that nobody could call himself rich unless he could afford to maintain an army from his own resources. Senators travelled between their numerous estates guarded by a strong retinue. Even in Rome, they might need an armed escort to go down to the Senate. Their houses might be attacked and virtually besieged. Public order and respect for the laws sank so low that the consular elections for 52 BC could not be held, and the Senate resorted to the quite irregular expedient of naming Pompey sole consul. Then came open war between Caesar and Pompey, Caesar's victory, and war again after his assassination. Before Actium, Octavian claimed to have 'the whole of Italy' supporting him (*Res Gestae* 25). Probably he did; his growing authority offered the best hope for peace and stability. The greatest literary work of the period (some would say the greatest in all Latin literature) was Vergil's *Georgics*. Vergil himself had suffered in the confiscations after Philippi (see below). The *Georgics* are filled with love of Italy and longing for peace. Vergil laments 'so many wars throughout the world ... the fields going to waste in the farmer's absence' (i.505–7). No contemporary could fail to get the message when Vergil, discussing bees with an imagery that consistently suggests human society as well, stresses their fidelity to one single king (the ancients thought the queen bee a male) and advises that, where there are two rivals, described with their followers in terms like those used elsewhere of Octavian and Antony and *their* followers, 'the one who seems the worse, him ... give over to death, let the better reign in his vacant place' (iv. 88–102, 206–14). No wonder that Octavian so appreciated the poem that on his return to Italy after

Actium he had it read to him over four consecutive days.

There can be little doubt that in the decade after Actium only Augustus stood between the Roman world and a return to civil war and anarchy. He nearly died in 23. Thereafter, having made other provision to secure all necessary legal powers, he ceased to stand each year for the consulship, which he had held annually since 31 (see Chapter 3). Significantly, the people of Rome, fearing any diminution of his authority, rioted to try to force him to accept the office. His rule in fact rested on a broad popular consensus. Periods of disorder, like the last decades of the Republic, often lead to a reaction in favour of strong centralized government. The Wars of the Roses ushered in the Tudors, the excesses of the French revolution led to the autocracy of Napoleon, the Russian Revolution produced Stalin. This is equally true in other spheres of life: Yehudi Menuhin is quoted as saying, 'An orchestra that has let itself go, not having a strong enough conductor to hold it together ... usually welcomes a more authoritarian conductor who will restore a sense of unity and cohesion' (Robin Daniels, *Conversations with Menuhin*, Futura Paperbacks, 1980, p.91). Augustus was that conductor which Rome needed.

Let us now go back to 42 BC to trace in more detail the history of the Triumvirate. After the proscriptions, the triumvirs turned to deal with the main army of their opponents, commanded by Marcus Junius Brutus and Gaius Cassius Longinus, whom they met and defeated in two engagements at Philippi in Macedonia (October 42 BC). Both Brutus and Cassius committed suicide. Octavian's part in the fighting was inglorious: among the less happy events of his life we read of 'his flight from the Battle of Philippi while ill and three days' hiding in a marsh, although he was diseased and, according to Agrippa and Maecenas, swollen with dropsy' (Pliny, *Natural History* vii.148). In his absence, Brutus captured his camp. The official line was that Octavian had been warned to escape in a dream vouchsafed to his doctor (Velleius ii.70). He got his revenge after the battle:

He showed no moderation in following up the victory, but sent Brutus's head to Rome to be cast at the feet of Caesar's statue, and raged against the most distinguished captives, not sparing them his insults. For instance, when one of them begged humbly for proper burial, he is said to have replied that that would be a question for the birds . . . This is why the other prisoners, including Marcus Favonius, the well-known disciple of Cato, when they were being led off in chains, saluted Antony respectfully as *imperator*, but attacked Octavian to his face with the foulest abuse. (Suetonius, *Augustus* 12)

Now it is a problem to know which stories of this sort to believe. Rome had a lively tradition of political invective and invention. After they had fallen out, Octavian and Antony swapped insults with enthusiasm, and since surviving accounts of the period naturally reflect the victor's editing of the record, Antony generally comes out badly. But here, Pliny's story should be above suspicion: Marcus Vipsanius Agrippa and Gaius Maecenas were two of Octavian's closest advisers from the start. Presumably his absence from the scene when his camp was captured was known to too many people to be hushed up, and the best that Octavian's advisers could do was to make plausible excuses. Similarly, the conduct of Favonius and his fellow captives must have been fairly public, and the fact that Antony comes out of the story so well is itself an argument for authenticity.

Despite the allegations of cruelty, which did not stop with Philippi, Octavian himself claimed to have 'spared the lives of all citizens who asked for mercy' (*Res Gestae* 3), and subsequently flaunted 'clemency' as one of his cardinal virtues along with 'courage', 'justice' and 'piety' (*Res Gestae* 34). But clemency came later, when he could afford it. For the moment, the deaths of their opponents in battle, by suicide or by execution were just what the triumvirs needed: 'No other war was bloodier with the deaths of the most distinguished men' (Velleius ii.71). The irreconcilables, the survivors of Philippi and of the proscriptions who scorned to ask for clemency, took refuge with Sextus Pompeius, Pompey's son, whom the Senate had earlier put in command of the fleet and the coastal districts (April 43), and who had now occupied Sicily and was blockading Italy and supporting his fleet and army by what his opponents considered piracy.

Antony and Octavian now proceeded to divide the spoils. A reallocation of the provinces, excluding Lepidus, fore-shadowed the later division between East and West. Antony however took all Gaul, except Cisalpina, which became part of Italy:

> Antony undertook to restore order in the East, Octavian to lead the veterans back to Italy and settle them on lands belonging to the Italian towns. He got no thanks either from the veterans or the former landowners; the latter complained that they were being driven out, the former that they were not getting as much for their services as they had hoped. (Suetonius, *Augustus* 13)

The silence of the *Res Gestae* on this subject is all the more significant in that the disbursement of 600 million sesterces is recorded on two later occasions (30 and 14 BC) to pay for land for soldiers (*Res Gestae* 16). After Philippi, however, eighteen towns were simply stripped of their land, which was resurveyed and reassigned to new owners. One town which suffered was Cremona, where the new survey also brought in land belonging to the neighbouring towns of Mantua, 'alas, too close to unhappy Cremona' (Vergil, *Eclogues* ix.28), and perhaps Brixia (Brescia). Archaeological fieldwork suggests that the basic allotment was of 35 *iugera* (just under 10 hectares or 25 acres), and that Cremona might have provided for 3000–4000 veterans. One understands the resentment of the former landowners.

Relations between Octavian and Antony were strained. While Octavian incurred the odium of the confiscations, short of money and with Italy short of food because Sextus Pompeius was intercepting the food ships, Antony was able to tap the resources of the eastern half of the Empire, which he proceeded to reorganize, making and breaking client princes. Of these, one of the most important was Cleopatra of Egypt, whom Antony summoned to meet him; she arrived spectacularly ('The barge she sat in, like a burnished throne, Burned on the water . . . ,' says Shakespeare whose *Antony and Cleopatra* follows Plutarch closely.) Antony confirmed her in her possessions and subsequently joined her in Egypt for the winter of 41/40. This was a grim winter in Italy, where Antony's brother, Lucius Antonius, as consul for 41, waged open war on Octavian. Outmanoeuvred and trapped with his army in Perusia (Perugia), he surrendered early in 40. The city was burned and Octavian

> condemned large numbers of men, giving the same reply to all who tried to beg for pardon or make excuses: 'You must die.' Some writers claim that he picked out 300 senators and knights from among the prisoners and slaughtered them on the Ides of March like sacrificial victims at an altar built to the Deified Julius. (Suetonius, *Augustus* 15)

Lucius Antonius was spared and even sent off to Spain as governor, where he died soon after.

It cannot be proved that Antony knew what his brother was doing, and after he had failed, it suited both Antony and Octavian not to make too much of the episode. Gossip, however, or Octavian's propaganda, focused on the debauched and luxurious life that Antony was said to be leading with Cleopatra, 'too besotted with lust and drink to think either of his friends or of his enemies' (Dio xlviii.27). His conduct was at least imprudent. Octavian tried at this point to make an agreement with Sextus Pompeius, and as part of the diplomatic negotiations married one of Sextus's connections by marriage, a certain Scribonia, a much older woman and allegedly very difficult to live with. Neither the marriage nor the proposed alliance lasted, but the marriage produced the only child that Octavian was ever to have, his daughter Julia.

By the summer of 40, Octavian and Antony had come to open hostilities. Antony sailed for Italy, with Sextus Pompeius's support, and tried to land at Brundisium, which closed its gates to him. But the soldiers on both sides did not want to fight, and the triumvirs patched up their differences. By the Treaty of Brundisium (September 40) Antony took the eastern provinces from Macedonia eastwards, while Octavian took Illyricum and the West, and Lepidus, that 'slight unmeritable man, Meet to be sent on errands', in Shakespeare's phrase, was fobbed off with Africa. Peace was made with Sextus Pompeius, who kept control of Sicily and Sardinia, and there was an amnesty for all who had taken refuge with him. The treaty was sealed by the marriage of Antony, whose wife Fulvia had just died, to Octavian's sister, the virtuous Octavia, whose first husband, Gaius Marcellus, had died the previous year, leaving her with a son of the same name, later to marry his cousin Julia. Octavian himself subsequently divorced Scribonia, once she had served her turn, politically and biologically, to marry Livia, already pregnant for the second time by her first husband, Tiberius Claudius Nero. Livia was connected with two of Rome's oldest and most powerful families, with the Claudii by birth and marriage, and with the Livii through her father's adoption into that family. Livia has fascinated writers, from Tacitus to Robert Graves, and she fascinated Octavian, remaining 'the one woman he truly loved until his death' (Suetonius, *Augustus* 62); but the marriage connection with the Claudii and Livii was also to his political advantage.

The Treaty of Brundisium saved Italy from invasion and from renewed civil war. In the general feeling of relief, Antony and Octavian were each voted the sort of minor triumph called an ovation (*Fasti Triumphales Capitolini, EJ* p.33), and Vergil's fourth *Eclogue* probably expresses the universal feeling of relief, foretelling the coming of a child who will 'rule over a world given peace by his father's virtues' (*Eclogues* iv.17). The identity of the child is one of the puzzles of scholarship, but it is probably the expected child of Antony and Octavia. Antony was still the senior member of the Triumvirate; only gradually, over the next decade, did Italy's hopes for lasting peace come to focus on Octavian instead.

Meanwhile, during Antony's absence from the East, the Parthians had invaded the Roman provinces, led by the renegade Labienus, Caesar's old general from the days in Gaul, who had 'gone across to the Parthians from Brutus's camp' (Velleius ii.78). They actually penetrated as far as Jerusalem, deposed the ruling high priest, the pro-Roman Hyrcanus, cut off his ears to make him ritually unfit for the office, and installed their own nominee. Antony got the Senate to recognize Hyrcanus's son-in-law Herod as King of Judaea, and sent his best general, Ventidius, to drive out the Parthians, which he did so effectively that he was awarded the first ever triumph over the Parthians. This was a dramatic reversal of fortune. Ventidius himself, 51 years earlier, had been exhibited as a captive in Pompeius Strabo's triumph over the rebellious Italian allies in the Social War (Dio xlix.21). It shows to what extent some Italians had since prospered in Roman society.

Octavian now set out to consolidate his position in the West. His chief general, Marcus Vipsanius Agrippa (he soon dropped the ultra-plebeian 'Vipsanius', which betrayed his obscure origin), was sent to govern Gaul, which had remained more stable than might have been expected over the past decade. Julius Caesar had done the job of pacification well (page 139). Agrippa put down disturbances, laid out a strategic road system based on Lugdunum (Lyon), and permitted the Ubii, a tribe which had crossed over from the right bank of the Rhine under pressure from migrating Germans, to remain in possession of the lands which they had occupied around the site of the future Cologne (Oppidum Ubiorum, later Colonia Claudia Ara Agrippinensium, hence Köln or Cologne). The Ubii were good farmers and could be relied on to defend their new lands against other would-be invaders.

Nearer home, the peace with Sextus Pompeius did not last. Octavian was presented with Sardinia through the defection of one of Pompeius's lieutenants, and planned to invade

Sicily, but Pompeius and a storm shattered his fleet and his hopes (38). Octavian's chief diplomatic agent and adviser, the Etruscan Gaius Maecenas, helped to persuade Antony to send reinforcements; Lepidus agreed to bring his legions over from Africa. When the attack was finally launched (1 July 36), Octavian himself was defeated, but Agrippa saved the day. Sicily fell, and Pompeius fled to the East, where Antony's generals hunted him to death. Lepidus thought Sicily should be his and ordered Octavian to leave the island. Octavian, 'though unarmed and dressed in a civilian cloak, bearing nothing but his name' (Velleius ii.80), entered Lepidus's camp, and Lepidus's soldiers came over to him *en masse*. Velleius omits to mention that Octavian had already been tampering with their loyalty (Appian, *Civil Wars* v.124). Lepidus begged for mercy, was magnanimously allowed to retain his property and the office of *pontifex maximus,* and departed to twenty-four years of inglorious retirement at Circeii, a small town in Latium famous for its oysters.

It was already the common talk of the army (the combined forces totalled some forty legions), that the next war would be between Octavian and Antony, and they mutinied:

> Shouting angrily, they demanded to be discharged from service, on the grounds that they were worn out, not because they really wanted to be released (most of them were in their prime), but because they suspected that the war with Antony was coming and so valued themselves highly ... Caesar [i.e., Octavian], even though he certainly knew precisely that the war would take place and clearly understood their intentions, nevertheless did not give in to them. (Dio xlix.13)

In fact, he discharged all those with ten or more years of service, announced that nobody would henceforth be allowed to re-enlist, and then offered land on discharge, 'not to all, except among the most senior, but to those who had most deserved it'. He added a gratuity of 2000 sesterces each, made other promises to the rank and file, and 'gave the centurions to hope that he would enroll them in the senates of their native cities'. We shall see that hope of social advancement was to be one of the mainsprings of army recruitment over the next century (pages 99, 138). The mutiny collapsed. More land for the veterans was found, this time by purchase. Capua, for instance, suffering from depopulation, gave up large tracts for settlement, in exchange for lands in Crete which it still held in the third century, and for the construction of a splendid new aqueduct, the Aqua Iulia. It was a sign that things in Italy were getting better, and that Octavian's fortunes were also looking up.

At Rome, the victors received a delirious welcome. The defeat of Pompeius opened the seas and drove away the spectre of famine. 'I made the sea peaceful and freed it of pirates', was the official version (*Res Gestae* 25). The civil wars seemed at an end (Appian, *Civil Wars* v.130, 132). Octavian received a second ovation, statues, an arch and various ceremonial distinctions, such as the front seat at the theatre, the right of entering the city on horseback, a crown of laurel at all times, a house at public expense, an annual victory banquet in the temple of Jupiter on the Capitol. Probably at this time too he received the personal immunity of a tribune, as Dio says (xlix.15), rather than *all* a tribune's power, which is Appian's version (*Civil Wars* v.132). Dio, however, records the grant of tribunician power in 30 and again, confusingly, in 23 (li.19, liii.32). The whole question has long been a historian's delight, and we shall return to it in Chapter 3.

In this welter of honours, Agrippa, to whom Octavian owed the victory, was not wholly forgotten. He was awarded a golden crown adorned with ships' beaks in place of the traditional laurel wreath; it appears on his portrait on coins. Another of Octavian's successful generals, Lucius Cornificius, took to arriving at his host's house on an elephant when he went out to dinner. One can imagine what the old nobility thought of these new honours and this vulgar display. Octavian's earliest supporters were almost all from outside the traditional ruling class and Octavian himself was, as we have seen, for all his Julian connection, a 'new man', but his increasing success gradually brought to his side ambitious nobles. Dio and Appian name eight recent or future consuls actively involved on Octavian's behalf in the Sicilian campaign. Three were Italians of non-Latin stock, definitely 'new men' (Marcus Vipsanius Agrippa, Gaius Calvisius Sabinus and Titus Statilius Taurus), and so probably was another (Quintus Laronius), while a fifth, Lucius Cornificius, the elephant-rider, came from a family of no particular distinction, though possibly senatorial. The other three, however, were great nobles: Appius Claudius Pulcher, Paullus Aemilius Lepidus and Marcus Valerius Messalla Corvinus. They were still exceptional. Most of the nobles, most of those who had fought for Pompey, and again for Brutus and Cassius, now preferred Antony, if they were still alive. But Octavian controlled Italy, and thus was better placed than Antony to dispense patronage. It must rapidly have become apparent that sooner or later men in public life would have to choose sides, unequivocally, and that the stakes would be high.

After the defeat of Pompeius and the euphoria of Rome, Octavian went off to the wars again. In 35 and 34 he campaigned in Illyricum, on the northeastern frontier of Italy, one of the areas from which ambitious generals had long been accustomed to bring home triumphs. Partly, he wanted to train and feed his army at the natives' expense: 'At this time, lest idleness, the worst thing of all for discipline, should spoil the soldiers, he conducted several campaigns in Illyricum and Dalmatia, thus hardening his army by endurance of danger and experience of war' (Velleius ii.78; so too Dio xlix.36). In part also, he wanted to acquire personal glory, which had signally eluded him at Philippi and against Pompeius; in Illyricum he is said to have exposed himself rashly and been honourably wounded, in a way suitably reminiscent of Alexander the Great. But the main aim was to strengthen his position for the coming showdown with Antony. The territorial acquisitions were modest, comprising the upper Sava valley to as far down as Siscia (Šišak), which propaganda described as a good base for a future campaign against the Dacians, and the Dalmatian coast up to the line of the Dinaric Alps, but they were strategically important, securing the eastern approaches to Italy. Italy was duly grateful, and Octavian also got the credit for having far reaching plans of future conquest, inherited from Caesar. He even put it about at this time that he proposed to invade Britain (Dio xlix.38). This sounded romantic. Britain was at the end of the earth, or beyond it; Horace later in the twenties was to harp on the glory to be won there. So was another unknown poet: 'There awaits you the Briton, unconquered by Roman Mars' (*Panegyric on Messalla* 150). Nothing, however, is less likely than that Octavian seriously considered turning his back on Italy at this particular moment.

What was Antony doing all this time? He had spent the winter of 37/6 at Antioch in Syria, planning an invasion of Parthia. He also sent for Cleopatra, Queen of Egypt, and married her. Roman law did not recognize the marriage of a citizen with a foreigner, but this marriage was accepted in the East. It was in the tradition of Hellenistic monarchs, and Alexander the Great, whose legend capivated both Antony and Octavian, had a Persian as well as a Macedonian wife. The new marriage was of course an insult to the legitimate Roman wife, Octavia, who already had two children by Antony and was pregnant again. She stayed virtuously at home in Italy, looking after not only her own children, but also Antony's two sons by his former marriage to Fulvia. Naturally Octavian made capital out of the situation, and Suetonius give us one of Antony's coarsely worded letters in reply:

What's come over you? That I'm screwing the queen? We're married. Is it anything new? It's been going on for nine years. Is Livia Drusilla the only one you're screwing? Good luck to you if you haven't screwed Tertulla or Terentilla or Rufilla or Salvia Titisenia or all of them by the time you read this. Does it matter when you have it away, and who with? (Suetonius, *Augustus* 69)

Of course the story of Antony's relationship with Cleopatra is distorted by Octavian's propaganda. Nor is there any doubt that she was politically important to him, supplying men, money and supplies, and that she in turn received political benefits. But some modern scholars have stressed this aspect to the virtual exclusion of the romantic element, the Shakespearean picture of 'The triple pillar of the world transformed Into a strumpet's fool', which is, however, precisely the picture in the ancient sources (most vividly in Plutarch, *Antony* 36). Antony certainly kept Cleopatra by him later, when she had become a disastrous political liability. Perhaps the scholars cannot imagine themselves being carried away and sacrificing all for love, like Antony.

The Parthian Empire was the only organised power on Rome's borders. Elsewhere her neighbours were petty kings or barbarian tribes. But the Parthians had wiped out a Roman army under Crassus in 54, and a strong Parthia threatened Rome's rich eastern provinces. Rome always had to watch her eastern frontier, but the task was lightened by the dynastic quarrels to which the polygamous Parthian royal family was prone. There was one of these going on in the summer of 36, when Antony marched via Armenia into Parthia. He had with him several of Rome's client kings (page 141), and his forces are estimated at 60,000 Roman infantry, with 10,000 Iberian and Celtic cavalry, and 30,000 allied troops. And yet, comments Plutarch:

All this preparation and power, however, which terrified even the Indians beyond Bactria and agitated the whole of Asia, was of no benefit to Antony, they say, because of Cleopatra. He was in such a hurry to spend the winter with her, that he began the war before things were ready, and got the administration into a mess, as if he were not in his right mind, but under the influence of drugs or magic, gawping after her the whole time and thinking more of how soon he could get back to her than of defeating the enemy. (Plutarch, *Antony* 37)

We again note in passing the echo of Alexander's magic, in the reference to 'the Indians beyond Bactria'. The passage as a whole, however, sounds like army gossip and grumbling. We can imagine the soldiers, from the generals downwards, as one thing after another went wrong, making coarse jokes about their commander's evident preoccupation. If Cleopatra was all she is reputed to have been ('Age cannot wither her, nor custom stale Her infinite variety'), every man in the army must have envied him; but .Cleopatra herself, with her imperious temper and insatiable ambition, cannot have been widely popular.

And one thing after another did go wrong. The exact chronology, the intended plan of campaign and the route followed have been much discussed. The ancient accounts are vivid but often imprecise. Antony reached the Median capital, Phraaspa, and besieged it in vain, having abandoned his siege train, all 300 wagons of it, including an 80-foot battering ram, because they slowed him down. The Parthians captured the lot and cut to pieces two legions. Antony's chief vassal-ally, the King of Armenia, deserted with 16,000 cavalry, on which Antony was relying heavily. As summer came to an end, Antony was forced to retreat, under a pledge of safe conduct which the Parthians broke. The army got back, but the casualties were horrendous. Velleius puts them at over a quarter of the army (ii.82), Plutarch (*Antony* 50) at 20,000 infantry and 4000 cavalry, over half of them by sickness. It was a disaster from which Antony could never recover. Cut off from Italy and the West, he could not replace seasoned Roman legions, and Octavian would send him only token reinforcements. These he accepted, though when Octavia tried to join him, he sent her back to Rome. Her ostentatiously dutiful conduct made Antony look bad: 'he was hated for wronging a woman like this' (Plutarch, *Antony* 54).

In the autumn of 34, Antony celebrated a triumph at Alexandria, sitting on a golden throne at Cleopatra's side in the gymnasium, distributing kingdoms and titles to her, to the three children he now had by her, and to her son by Julius

Caesar, officially called Ptolemy Caesar but nicknamed Caesarion, whom Antony declared legitimate. This last act was clearly intended to undercut Octavian's position, but failed. Even if we allow for Octavian's propaganda, it is clear that Roman opinion was scandalised. The triumph was a cherished piece of Roman public ceremonial (page 53), and to celebrate it except at Rome was to strike at Rome's dominant position. The gymnasium moreover was a thoroughly un-Roman institution, the hallmark of Greek culture, especially at Alexandria, where communal hostility between Greeks, Jews and Egyptians was endemic (page 117). The episode showed how out of touch Antony was getting with Roman opinion.

Few doubted that a new civil war was imminent, and it was subsequently counted among Antony's greatest errors of judgement that he did not force it as early as 32, since Octavian's position was getting stronger all the time, while Antony's was weakening. It would appear that the powers voted to the triumvirs expired at the end of 33; the question has greatly exercised modern scholarship. But Octavian, in Italy, whatever his legal position, had public opinion on his side. The consuls for 32 were Antony's supporters, but after a public altercation with Octavian in the Senate, they abandoned Rome for Antony's headquarters. Probably a quarter of the senators followed them. On Antony's side, the question was whether to go to war with Cleopatra's help (she had men, money and ships), thus giving Octavian a propaganda trump, or to send her home. She stayed. Instead, Lucius Munatius Plancus, consul in 42, one of the most trusted of Antony's supporters (he had charge of Antony's seal in 35, Appian, *Civil Wars* v.144), deserted to Octavian. He was alleged to have treachery like a disease (Velleius ii.83), which is another way of saying that he was good at recognising a sinking ship.

His desertion of Antony was thus a portent; moreover, he knew or guessed what was in Antony's will, and advised Octavian to open it. Octavian took it from the Vestal Virgins, who had it in their custody, and read it to the Senate and people. Though he incurred some odium for doing so, the will made a bad impression, particularly the clause directing that Antony be buried in Egypt, even if he died in Rome. It lent credence to the rumour, no doubt fostered by Octavian's agents, that Antony planned to give Cleopatra Rome as a present (she was alleged to swear oaths, 'As surely as I shall dispense justice on the Capitol...'), and to transfer his capital to Alexandria. Dio has a long list of Antony's indiscretions, exaggerated, no doubt, and to our eyes often trivial, many of them things which Antony might have done without thinking, for the pleasure of the moment, living in Cleopatra's ambiance and surrounded by her entourage. The court of the Ptolemies had its own etiquette, its own traditions; but they accorded ill with Roman *gravitas,* and sober stay-at-home citizens were duly shocked. Antony had not been to Rome himself for seven years, and emissaries who came from Rome were not made welcome, because the advice they brought was not welcome: it was to get rid of Cleopatra.

The publication of the will brought matters to a head. Antony was deprived of the consulship for 31, to which he had been designated eight years earlier, when he and Octavian were arranging such things (Dio l.4, cf. xlviii.35, l.10), and war was declared with ancient ritual and Octavian as presiding priest, 'theoretically against Cleopatra, but in practice against Antony as well' (Dio, l.4 preferable to Suetonius, *Augustus* 17, clearly muddled). Octavian and his advisers knew that Antony would inevitably put himself outside the law by supporting her, 'and wished to put this additional reproach on him, of having voluntarily taken up the war on behalf of the Egyptian woman against his own fatherland, when no wrong had been done to him personally by the people at home' (Dio l.6). The support of Italy and the western provinces was assured by patronage or threats: 'The whole of Italy of its own free will swore allegiance to me and demanded me as the leader in the war in which I was victorious at Actium. The Gallic and Spanish provinces, Africa, Sicily and Sardinia swore the same oath of allegiance'

(*Res Gestae* 25). The conflict of East and West was a theme for poets:

> On this side Augustus Caesar leading the Italians into battle, with senate and people, with the household deities and the great gods ... Elsewhere Agrippa, the winds and gods abetting ... On the other side, with barbaric wealth and multicoloured armour, Antony, victor over the peoples of the dawn and the Red Sea shore, with Egypt and the men of the East and farthest Bactria in his train, and following (the shame of it!) his Egyptian wife. (Vergil, *Aeneid*. viii.678–88)

In the spring of 31, Octavian took the offensive, blockading Antony's base at Actium, at the mouth of the Ambracian Gulf in northwest Greece. Antony was weakened by further desertions, supplies ran short, disease set in, morale was low. Finally a council of war seems to have decided that Antony and Cleopatra would run for Egypt (Dio l.15), although naturally enough their intentions were concealed by preparations as if for a decisive battle (this version is more plausible than the alternative in Plutarch, *Antony* 66 and Velleius ii.85, that Cleopatra's sudden flight during the battle (2 September 31) took Antony by surprise, and that he simply abandoned everything to follow her). Once they had gone, setting sail for the south and not seriously pursued, resistance quickly collapsed, the Antonian fleet surrendered, and the army, after some bargaining, followed suit a week later. Details of the battle and subsequent negotiations are obscure, perhaps designedly so: Octavian had every reason to exaggerate the severity of the fighting and hence the glory of the victory. Perhaps some of Antony's officers were already in touch with him before battle was joined. In any case, casualties were relatively light.

During the winter of 31/30 Octavian discharged many of the troops, incorporating what remained of Antony's army into his own, and reorganized the eastern provinces and client kingdoms. Most of Antony's clients, including Herod,

hastened to change sides. Not until the summer did Octavian
invade Egypt. Antony's fleet and cavalry deserted *en masse,*
Antony committed suicide, and Octavian entered Alexandria
as a conqueror (1 August 30). Cleopatra was captured, but
escaped being led in Octavian's triumph by taking poison.
Her son by Julius Caesar was put to death, as was Antony's
eldest son by Fulvia, who been with his father over the past
few years. In striking contrast, Antony's and Fulvia's second
son, who had stayed in Rome with Octavia, subsequently
married Octavia's eldest daughter by her first marriage, rose
to the consulship and to be proconsul of Asia, only to die for
his part in the affairs of Julia (page 70). Octavia now also
took and brought up Antony's children by Cleopatra.

Octavian boasted of his clemency (*Res Gestae* 3). Velleius
was impressed: 'The victory [of Actium] was indeed marked
by great clemency and no one was put to death, except a very
few who could not bring themselves actually to plead for
mercy' (Velleius ii.86, where the text is mildly corrupt, and
the Loeb edition, for instance, prints and translates unjustified conjectures which radically change the sense: 'no
one was put to death, and but few banished . . .'). And again
after the double suicide at Alexandria, 'It was in keeping with
Caesar's [Octavian's] good luck and clemency that none of
those who had borne arms against him was put to death by
him or by his orders' (Velleius ii.87): palpable exaggeration,
but it is true that very few were killed. Most Romans of any
note had deserted Antony and come to an arrangement with
Octavian before the last act was played.

The downfall of Cleopatra was celebrated by Horace in a
famous ode, *'Nunc est bibendum . . .'* ('Now is the time to
drink . . .') (i.37). Coins were struck to commemorate the
conquest of Egypt (AEGYPTO CAPTA); Octavian claimed to
have 'added Egypt to the empire of the Roman people' (*Res
Gestae* 27). So too in the decree of the Senate over twenty
years later (8 BC), when Octavian, now Augustus, was to be
honoured by having the month Sextilis called August, one
reason is that 'Egypt in this month was brought into the
power of the Roman people, and in this month the

civil wars were brought to an end' (Macrobius i.12.35 = *FIRA* 42 = *EJ* 37). Actium and the subsequent conquest of Egypt were conclusive. Octavian was now ruler of the Roman world. Of his career so far, there were two possible views: had he taken power because 'there was no other remedy for the state's divisions' (Tacitus, *Annals* i.9)? Or were 'filial duty and national crisis merely pretexts' and Octavian's motive simply 'the lust for power' (*Annals* i.10)? Most people did not care. Peace was everything.

Octavian celebrated a spectacular triple triumph (13–15 August 29; cf. Vergil, *Aeneid*. viii.714–23), for the fighting in Illyricum in 35–34, for Actium, and for Egypt. He was still only 33, the age at which Alexander the Great died. Octavian, more fortunate and more prudent, had another 43 years to live. They enabled him to consolidate his power (see Chapter 3), to outlive the unsavoury image of his youth, to end as 'father of his country' (*pater patriae*), the great exemplar for all later emperors. By the time he died, the new order which he had brought about was so firmly established that no alternative seemed possible; as Tacitus was to say, 'Actium had been won before younger men were born. Even most of the older generation had come into a world of civil wars. Practically no one had ever seen truly Republican government' (*Annals* i.3).

The first half of our period has traditionally been more studied and written about than the second half. The reason lies in the nature of the sources. The old-fashioned approach to history, based primarily on the reading of literary sources, found four writers to hand dealing with the emperors, their personalities, their policies, their impact on their court and on the Senate, from Augustus to Trajan. Three of them wrote at the very end of the first century or in the early decades of the second: Tacitus, the younger Pliny, and Suetonius. Tacitus and Pliny were senators, and very conscious of the fact. Suetonius was of equestrian rank, secretary to the emperor Hadrian, with access to the imperial archives. The fourth writer was again a senator, writing a century later, Cassius Dio. It is easy to view this period through their eyes and hence to see it from the perspective of senators and courtiers, with Rome and Italy in the forefront of the picture. Tacitus in particular brings to the presentation of his material such a powerful intellect, so individual an interpretation and so memorable a style, that no one reading him can wholly escape his influence. No other historian of antiquity except Thucydides has so successfully imposed his own framework on the historiography of the period he is dealing with. So the history of the first century AD still tends to be seen in terms of the personality and actions of the reigning emperor, stressing as Tacitus did, his relations with the Senate, the court intrigues and the dynastic imbroglios. The world-picture is that of the Italian upper classes, the sources imbued with the senatorial ethos.

For the second half of our period, however, once Pliny's letters peter out (the latest dates from 108, apart from his official correspondence as governor of Bithynia, contained in Book X), we simply do not have the sources to study such topics in as much detail, even if we wanted to. We cannot know the personalities and the gossip of Hadrian's court, for instance, as we know those of Nero's. We also lack for most of this period the annalistic framework which Tacitus and Dio provide for much of the earlier period. Chronological precision, for instance in the field of legislation, becomes even harder to achieve. Rome and Italy no longer dominate our picture to the same extent. The emperors Trajan, Hadrian and Marcus Aurelius spent much of their time outside Italy. The balance has shifted. We now tend to have more and better evidence for social and economic conditions, for the life of the poorer classes, and for the provinces. Greek literature from the movement known as the Second Sophistic gives information on the East, Christian sources show us life and death in the prisons and arenas. There is more evidence from inscriptions or papyri – not that such evidence, particularly epigraphic evidence, is lacking for the first century, but there is more of it later. Epigraphy and papyrology tell us about people whom senatorial writers like Tacitus and Pliny would have thought beneath their notice. The archaeological record for the second century is also generally richer than for the first, apart from such spectacular exceptions as Pompeii and Herculaneum, destroyed by the eruption of Vesuvius in 79.

This present volume inevitably reflects the imbalance of the sources. It would be perverse to neglect Tacitus and Suetonius, although we shall try not to limit our perspective to theirs. It would be equally perverse, in discussing the second- and third-century emperors, to devote as much space to family history as Tacitus and Suetonius enable us to do for the first century. For the whole period, we must try to give the provinces their due, to consider social and economic factors, and to present the evidence for life outside the governing classes.

In all of this, notwithstanding the bipartite division of the period set out above, the age of Augustus stands slightly apart. The only connected narrative covering the period in any detail is that of Dio, who becomes *faute de mieux* a major source. Tacitus offers a summary of Augustus's career. Appian covers the history of the civil wars down to 35 and the campaign in Illyricum the following year, while Plutarch's life of Antony is also of great value for the triumviral period. Velleius Paterculus gives us an eyewitness account of some of the later military campaigns, fascinating in its detail, although his evidence and interpretations where he is not an eyewitness are to be used with care. Suetonius's biography is particularly rich, the longest of all his biographies. Augustus's own memorial of his achievements, originally inscribed on bronze in front of his mausoleum, the *Res Gestae Divi Augusti* (*The Achievements of the Divine Augustus*), has no parallel in our sources for any of his successors. The poets, especially Vergil and Horace, tell us a great deal about the image of Augustus in the earlier phases of his career. The Greek geographer Strabo conveys much incidental information on Italy and the provinces under Augustus. Other writers deal with particular topics or regions, like the elder Seneca on oratory and Flavius Josephus, *Jewish Antiquities,* valuable for the history of Judaea and the eastern provinces. Since Augustus dominated the Roman world for 45 years, from the Battle of Actium in 31 BC to his death in AD 14, a longer period than any of his successors reigned, and since he shaped that world for generations to come, it will be clear why his work is so important and why two whole chapters are devoted to his work and to the Augustan Age.

The predominance of Tacitus in the historiographical tradition has already been alluded to. In the introduction to the *Annals*, the last of Tacitus's works to be written, he criticizes previous historians of the period after Augustus's death, as follows:

For relating the period of Augustus, there was no lack of honest talents, until they were put off by the growth of flattery. The history of Tiberius, Gaius, Claudius and Nero was falsified from fear while they were in power, and after their death was influenced by recent hatreds. Hence it is my intention to write little about Augustus and that on the end of his life, and then to deal with Tiberius's principate and the rest, without anger or partiality, whose causes are remote from me. (i.1)

It is generally agreed that Tacitus fails in his declared intention of avoiding anger and partiality. He exercises considerable selectivity in choosing what facts to present, and will for instance devote to episodes which lend themselves to dramatic treatment an amount of space disproportionate to their historical importance. He has heroes and villains, and, because he does not recognize to what an extent people's characters can change or be inconsistent, his heroes, like Germanicus, tend to be all white, and his villains, like Tiberius, all black (see Chapter 5). He sees Tiberius, for instance, as fundamentally evil, and explains away any good deeds which he feels bound to record by attributing them to hypocrisy or dissimulation. History, he thinks, has a moral purpose, 'that virtues may not be passed over in silence, and that for evil words and deeds the blame of posterity may be a deterrent' (*Annals* iii.65). Some facts are not 'worthy of record', such as the building of an amphitheatre (*Annals* xiii.31, cf. Suetonius, *Nero* 12). Most of all, he projects back into the past the preoccupations, the interests and the animosities of his own day. Although he may be dealing with things that happened two or three generations earlier, the occasions of 'anger and partiality' in the interpretation of them lie within Tacitus's own experiences.

His earliest works were apparently the biography of his father-in-law, *Agricola,* and the *Germania,* useful because it preserves much that would otherwise have been lost, but influenced by the desire to present the German as the 'noble savage' in contrast with the degenerate Roman. Both works date from around 98, and it is now generally held that they were followed by the *Dialogue on Orators,* though some would put the *Dialogue* first. The *Histories* were composed between 100 and 110 (only the opening books devoted to the events of 69 and 70 survive), and lastly came the *Annals,* tracing events from Augustus's death down to the beginning of the *Histories*. For the historical works, Tacitus consulted an impressive range of sources. Among earler historians, he mentions specifically the elder Pliny's history of the German wars and his general history, as well as Cluvius Rufus, Fabius Rusticus and Domitius Corbulo. All are now lost. He consulted the memoirs of Agrippina, Nero's mother, where he says that he found one fact omitted by all other historians, namely that Agrippina's mother in 26 asked Tiberius for another husband (*Annals* iv.53). How much more court scandal, often of doubtful accuracy, may come from the same source?

Tacitus also used biographies, funeral orations and other speeches. He consulted the minutes of the Senate (*Annals* xv.74), the official gazette (*acta publica*), the emperor's archives (*commentarii principis*), and drew information from inscriptions and from pamphlets. He records material derived from oral tradition, specifically contrasting this with the literary record, *fama* opposed to *auctores*. What he uses, he adapts to his own stylistic ends: we can compare the exact text of a speech delivered by Claudius at Lyon (*ILS* 212) with Tacitus's idiosyncratic version of it (*Annals* xi.24). But he was diligent in his research, and his facts are often corroborated by other evidence, especially that of inscriptions. If we have to treat Tacitus's account of events with caution, it is not because he gets his facts wrong, but because of the interpretation he puts upon them and the things he leaves out.

Cassius Dio does not have Tacitus's intellect or power of expression, but he is, after Tacitus, the most important single source for the whole of our period, deriving his value from his assiduity as a compiler of facts, rather than from any general ideas or interpretations. His work, written early in the third century, originally went down to his own second consulship in 229. It survives whole or in substantial fragments for the period 68 BC–AD 46, and again becomes valuable for parts of Dio's own lifetime, providing an annalistic record whose value can best be measured by how much we miss it where it has not survived, or has survived only in Reader's Digest versions (*epitomes*) by the eleventh- and twelfth-century epitomators, Xiphilinus and Zonaras. Dio, like Tacitus, is inclined to read the problems of his own day back into the past, and his lengthy speeches in particular tend to be pure invention, often wholly anachronistic.

There are many other works of historical value which are not themselves histories. To Pliny's *Letters* we can add his *Panegyric* addressed to Trajan in 100 when Pliny became consul. There are works of geography, not only Strabo, but also the Latin Pomponius Mela, the Greek Ptolemy, and such curiosities as Pausanias's guidebook for the second-century tourist in Greece, and an unknown sailor's handbook on the *Circumnavigation of the Red Sea*. Pliny's uncle, the elder Pliny, left 37 books of *Natural History,* a mine of information and misinformation, since Pliny wrote too fast to bother with accuracy. There are also two Senecas, the elder who wrote on oratory, and his son, Nero's tutor, valuable for his anecdotes and for the insight which he gives into the intellectual history of the period. Technical treatises also give valuable information. Vitruvius wrote *On Architecture* probably in the hope of securing commissions, but it became for the Renaissance the standard handbook on classical architecture. Columella, Spanish by birth but with extensive properties in Italy, wrote on agriculture under Nero. Quintilian, another Spaniard, professor of rhetoric at Rome, wrote twelve books on *Oratorical Training,* valuable social history and literary criticism. Frontinus, consul for the third time in 100, a former governor of Britain and the man in charge of Rome's water supply, wrote on *Stratagems* and a highly technical work *On the Aqueducts*.

Of prose writers not yet mentioned, the greatest from every point of view is Petronius, to be identified with Nero's 'arbiter of elegance' (Tacitus, *Annals* xvi.18), whose novel, almost universally known as *The Satyricon,* since Fellini's film, was probably originally called *Satyrica* or *Satyricon libri*. A bawdy, picaresque tale, its longest surviving episode describes a dinner party of gross vulgarity and ostentation given by the self-made freedman millionaire Trimalchio. Clearly the elegant Petronius exaggerates the grossness and vulgarity to amuse his sophisticated audience, but the satire would lose its point unless based on some reality, and the novel can be seen as a source for the social history of the period. It gives us an insight into circles far below those of the senatorial aristocracy whose standards and way of life inform the writings of most of the writers so far mentioned. Even more valuable, as documents for social history, are the books of the New Testament, which show us aspects of Roman provincial administration and of everyday life from below. If the life style of a rich landowner like the younger Pliny suggests eighteenth-century Whig opulence and leisure, if Roman imperialism and ideals caused nineteenth-century imperialists, like the British and the French in India and North Africa respectively, to see themselves as Romans, then the world of the gospels, the milieu, for instance, of Jesus's parables, is very close in many essentials to the day-to-day existence of the labourers on our excavations at Carthage, late in the twentieth century.

The Jewish world is in fact well represented in our sources. In addition to the New Testament books, we have mentioned already Flavius Josephus, who published under Domitian his 20 books of *Jewish Antiquities* and who wrote, from the point of view of a Jew who had changed sides, the *Jewish War,* culminating in the Roman capture of Masada (page 174). Then, too, Philo Judaeus, a Hellenized Jew from Alexandria, went on an embassy to Caligula in 39 and tells us something of the racial and cultural conflicts in his native city. There is also much incidental information to be derived from later Jewish tradition: the Mishnah, a codification of rabbinical opinions and rulings on Jewish law compiled in the late second century; the Talmud, a later development and extension of the Mishnah; and the *midrashim* or commentaries often enshrined in the Mishnah and the Talmud. A knowledge of Hebrew helps.

Finally among prose authors we should mention the anthologists and collectors of anecdotes, such as Valerius

Maximus, Macrobius and Aulus Gellius; the second-century Florus, whose outline history of Rome suggests that he was a man of egregious stupidity; Aurelius Victor and Eutropius in the fourth century; and the Christians Eusebius and Orosius, who preserve information otherwise lost; and the author of the so-called *Apocolocyntosis* or *Pumpkinification of the Divine Claudius,* a wicked satire, blackly humorous, usually and perhaps rightly ascribed to Nero's tutor Seneca.

So far, prose: what now of poetry? The Augustan poets, such as Vergil (70–19 BC) and Horace (65–8 BC), tell us a great deal about how Augustus was perceived and wished to be perceived in the decades before and after Actium (see Chapters 1 and 3). Ovid, (43 BC–AD 18) writing later in the reign and in the early years of Tiberius's, offers enough historical material for a recent book to have been wholly devoted to it. Phaedrus (*c.* 15 BC–AD 50), a freedman of Augustus, wrote fables with enough satirical bite in them to get him prosecuted by Sejanus. On the other hand, the satires of Persius, who died in 62, have little relevance to real life. Lucan, grandson of the elder Seneca and nephew of the younger, forced to commit suicide in 65, wrote an epic on the civil wars that contains much historical material, although mostly relating to the period before ours. But of the post-Augustan poets the two who interest us most are undoubtedly Martial and Juvenal, especially for the light they cast, lurid and not wholly trustworthy though it is, on life at Rome under the Flavians.

Martial was yet another Spaniard, who was born at Bilbilis, moved to Rome in 64, in his middle · twenties, returned to Spain in 98, and died there six years later (Pliny, *Letters* iii.21). He wrote back from his retirement, claiming to have been received with honour in his home town and commiserating with Juvenal, stuck in crowded Rome, courting the great in a sweaty toga (xii.18). In Carcopino's vastly influential *Daily Life in Ancient Rome,* the entries under 'Martial' occupy considerably more lines of the index than those for any other writer, with the younger Pliny beating Juvenal into second place by a short head, and the rest of the field nowhere. Juvenal was still writing in 127 (*Satires* xv.27), but his subject matter is largely the same as Martial's, namely the personages and the scandals of Juvenal's youth but Martial's maturity, the age of Domitian. It is all fine and powerful stuff, but it does not do to forget that both poets are satirists, and that satirists exaggerate. They need checking against other evidence.

With Juvenal, classical Latin literature is conventionally considered to come to an end. Certainly there is a decline in the quantity and the quality of what has survived. Greek literature, in contrast, was due for something of a revival, but Latin had to await the advent of the Christians, with something new to say. From this point on, the historian is badly served by literary sources. For the second century and the early third, the only approximation to a continuous narrative is that provided by the eleventh- and twelfth-century epitomators of Dio, Xiphilinus and Zonaras, supplemented from 180 onwards by the history of Herodian, a Syrian Greek. The actual text of Dio is however lost, except for considerable portions of the books covering the death of Caracalla, the reign of Macrinus, and the rise of Elagabalus (217–19).

To confuse the issue, from Hadrian onwards, we have biographies of each emperor which go collectively by the name of the *Augustan History* (*Historia Augusta*), and purport to be the work of several authors writing under Diocletian and Constantine. They are now generally agreed to form a single work by a man writing at the end of the fourth century, who ascribes them to earlier writers and inserts bogus 'contemporary' allusions appropriate to the supposed date of composition, in the manner still common to writers of historical fiction. The author used genuine source material now lost, including the biographies written as a sequel to Suetonius by Marius Maximus (consul AD 223), whose works were fashionable in fourth-century Rome; but he also embroiders freely. The problem is to know how much of what he says is true. It is as if Tacitus and Suetonius were lost, and our main source for the Julio-Claudian period was

Robert Graves's *I, Claudius*. In general, scholars tend to agree that the earlier lives contain more reliable material than the later, and the lives of the emperors themselves are less fictitious than those of the secondary figures (pretenders and heirs to the throne), but the uncorroborated testimony of the *Augustan History* must always be regarded with grave suspicion, even though it sometimes preserves information found in no other writer. For instance, it is the only ancient source which credits Hadrian with building Hadrian's Wall (*Hadrian* 11), a fact now corroborated by epigraphic and archaeological evidence. But it is often the most vivid and therefore oft-quoted detail that is likely to have been invented, in the spirit of Pooh-Bah in *The Mikado,* 'merely to give artistic verisimilitude to an otherwise bald and unconvincing narrative'.

Other writers, Greek and Latin, cast light on specific topics, regions or periods. The main Greek writers of the first century are Plutarch, with his biographies and other works, the Stoic philosopher Epictetus, with anecdotes of the court, and the orator Dio Chrysostom, who prefigures the personalities of the Second Sophistic discussed in Chapter 10 (page 256). Philostratus, the historian of the Second Sophistic, also wrote a life of the first-century philosopher and wonder-worker Apollonius of Tyana, which preserves stories about Tigellinus and Vespasian, and other material useful to the historian. Letters between Marcus Aurelius and his tutor Fronto give an insight into the imperial household, and Marcus's *Meditations* have great autobiographical value. Apuleius, author of the ancient world's second great picaresque novel, *The Golden Ass,* and Lucian with his dialogues and other works, are valuable for social history in the provinces in the second century. Galen, the great physician, provides medical texts with interesting case histories. More information about communal tensions at Alexandria comes from the *Acta Alexandrinorum,* usually but somewhat misleadingly called in English *Acts of the Pagan Martyrs*. The latest incident which it records dates from Commodus's reign. Christian sources tell about relations between

Christians and their pagan neighbours and their relations
with the authorities; Christian writers include Justin Martyr,
Irenaeus, Minucius Felix, Tertullian, Cyprian, Lactantius, to
which we must add the various accounts of Christian martyrdoms. Then again there are the legal sources, like Gaius's
Institutes and the *Digest* and *Institutes* of Justinian, which
preserve much second- and third-century material, and the
works of later writers like Libanius, some of whose material
is equally valid for our own period, and it becomes clear that
the amount of literary material for the second and third
centuries is not necessarily less than for the first, but it is
different in kind, less traditionally historical, less concerned
with how the Empire was governed, but capable of casting
light on how life was lived lower down the social scale. Nor
do Rome and Italy hog so much of the limelight: Apuleius
and the Christians, like the Greek orators and Pausanias,
bring the provinces into the forefront of the picture. Justin
Martyr was from Palestine, Lucian from Samosata on the
Euphrates, and Irenaeus a native of Asia Minor who became
Bishop of Lyon, while Minucius Felix was apparently from
Africa, Tertullian and Lactantius both came from Carthage,
where Apuleius was educated and of which Cyprian was
bishop.

Let us now turn from the literary sources to the epigraphic
evidence. The main categories of inscriptions in our period
are as follows. Firstly, public documents: texts of laws,
municipal charters, calendars and official records, copies of
important speeches (especially the emperor's), inscriptions in
honour of important personages, dedications and building
inscriptions. Secondly, private records: tombstones and
epitaphs, military discharge certificates (*diplomata*), curses
(generally written on sheets of lead), and letters, receipts and
other writings on wooden tablets or the like. The two
categories naturally overlap, and we ought perhaps to
consider graffiti as a third: everything from election slogans
to lists of prices in a shop to the amatory and excretory
scribbles so well represented at Pompeii.

Some epigraphic texts are of considerable length: the *Res*

Gestae fills nearly ten pages in Brunt and Moore's edition. Other famous and substantial documents from our period include the five edicts from Cyrene, in Greek, which constitute invaluable evidence for Augustus's direct intervention in what was technically a senatorial province (page 143); the inscription from Lyon with Claudius's speech already referred to (page 123); the law conferring on Vespasian the same legal powers as his predecessors (the *lex de imperio Vespasiani*) (page 172); the records of the public child support programme (*alimenta*) from two Italian municipalities under Trajan (page 201); Hadrian's address to the troops at Lambaesis in Africa after he had inspected their manoeuvres in 128 (page 254); the regulations governing the operation of the mines at Vispasca in Lusitania under Hadrian (page 204). The list could be prolonged indefinitely. Many dedications, building inscriptions and epitaphs reveal valuable information about public policy, as well as private ambition. At the other end of the scale, other tombstones and graffiti give us 'the short and simple annals of the poor': 'Here lies Vitalis, slave of Gaius Lavius Faustus and also his son, a slave born in his home. He lived 16 years' (*ILS* 7479, near Philippi); 'the muleteers urge the election of Gaius Julius Polybius as *duovir*' (graffito from Pompeii); 'yours for twopence' (also from Pompeii, referring to a prostitute).

To the evidence of inscriptions we must add that of coins and papyri. Coins were used for propaganda, to advertise notable events or official programmes, as modern governments use postage stamps. So we get Augustus commemorating the return of the Parthian standards (page 76) or the establishment at Lyon of the altar of Rome and Augustus, and towards the end of his reign sharing the altar series of the Lyon mint with Tiberius to accustom people to the idea of Tiberius as his successor. Nero's coinage emphasises his benefactions in a way which helps us to understand his undoubted popularity with the ordinary people. Vespasian's coin types hark back to those of Augustus; we remember that the *lex de imperio Vespasiani* keeps referring to Augustus's powers as a suitable precedent for those conferred on

Vespasian (page 172). Hadrian, the great traveller, celebrated his tours of the provinces. Antoninus Pius, who pushed the Roman frontier in Britain northwards to the line of the Forth and the Clyde (page 234), issued a coin with the legend BRITANNIA and a seated woman representing the province; Charles II borrowed the idea, and Britannia remained on British pennies right down to decimalization. Coins also show us what famous buildings looked like, and provide magnificent portraits of the emperors and their wives.

Now for papyrus: unlike inscriptions and coins, the papyrus documents which we have were not designed for posterity. Only in the dry Egyptian desert or in similar conditions elsewhere has papyrus survived (there are three famous find spots outside Egypt, at Dura-Europus on the Euphrates, Nessana in the Negev, and in a villa at Herculaneum, where the papyrus had been carbonized in the eruption of AD 79). Almost all our papyri are written in Greek; the main exception is official army records, which were kept in Latin, even in the Greek-speaking East. We have private letters, financial records, wills, official memoranda, petitions to authority, legal decisions, tax cases. Much of what we learn may strictly relate only to Egypt, which was administered differently from other provinces. The personal documents, however, to an even greater extent than inscriptions, show vignettes of daily life, like the sailor Irenaeus on one of the ships of the Alexandrian grain fleet (page 152), writing home from Puteoli to his brother that he and the rest of the fleet are stuck in port but 'daily awaiting our discharge'; he has been to Rome and 'the place received us as the god willed', which suggests that the visit was not an unqualified success (*Select Papyri* 113 – *LR* p.142). Or the slave boy Epaphroditus, eight years old, who leaned out of an upstairs window to see the castanet players at a festival and fell to his death, and now there must be an inquest (*P. Oxy.* iii.475).

Also within the sphere of the papyrologist are ostraca, bits of broken pot on which people wrote brief notes, and which were commonly used for receipts; for instance, tax receipts or receipts for military rations. Again, but more rarely, we get writing on wooden tablets, which it may take a papyrologist to read, but which are generally reckoned to belong to epigraphy not papyrology. The two most important deposits of such documents are the financial records of Lucius Caecilius Jucundus at Pompeii, and the letters and military records found in the 1970s at Vindolanda, just south of Hadrian's Wall.

Finally, we come to the unwritten archaeological record, the evidence of buildings and structures surviving above ground from antiquity, or excavated by archaeologists, together with the artefacts and other finds associated with them. Until after the Second World War, archaeology in the Mediterranean lands concentrated mostly on the great monuments and urban ensembles. In Rome itself the Palatine and the Forum naturally attracted attention; elsewhere in Italy Pompeii and Herculaneum were excavated, sometimes with more enthusiasm than scientific precision. Where shifts of population and prosperity since antiquity had left whole town sites vacant, as in North Africa or Asia Minor, these towns were cleared, with undeniably impressive results. But what was not monumental or impressive was often neglected or even destroyed in the archaeologists' preoccupation with uncovering remains that would be visually and emotionally satisfying.

In the northwestern provinces of the Empire, especially in Britain and along the Rhine, opportunities for this type of archaeology were limited. Roman towns had generally been less rich than in Italy and the Mediterranean provinces. Such great cities as could compete with the grand ones (if not with the grandest) further south were inaccessible beneath the modern city which still occupied the Roman site: so London, Cologne, Lyon. But what Britain and Germany had in abundance was military installations. Britain and France also had many prominent hill-forts, the Celtic *oppida* which the Romans found when they invaded. Neither military installations nor Celtic hill-forts provided monumental remains like those of Domitian's palace on the Palatine or even those of so many towns in North Africa, such as Timgad, Djemila or Dougga. Excavation required great care, if traces of rotted wooden buildings were not to be overlooked and lost for ever. In the last decades of the nineteenth century, General Pitt-Rivers in Dorset was founding scientific archaeology, Joseph Déchelette excavating the Celtic *oppidum* of Bibracte in France (Mont Beuvray), the Aeduan capital, and the German Limes-Kommission setting to work to trace the Roman frontier and its associated forts. The nature of the sites, the objectives of the excavators and the techniques they developed were different from their counterparts in Italy, Africa and the East.

It is important to be aware of these differences between one country and another because they affect both the amount and the nature of the archaeological evidence available, and if we are not aware of this, we may interpret data as evidence of ancient phenomena when really they derive from the idiosyncrasies of modern research. The relationship between town and country in Roman Britain can be studied as it cannot in Roman Spain; a book can be written on Augustan military sites in Germany and along the Rhine, but there is no certain Augustan site in the middle or lower Danube area or in Moesia, although few later military sites in this region have been so excavated that one could actually disprove the possibility of Augustan occupation. On the eastern frontier, archaeological evidence is scantier still; sites are known from air photography or are even visible on the ground, but in default of excavation dating is often the merest guesswork.

Historians who are not themselves also archaeologists tend often to accept the conclusions of an excavation report without evaluating the evidence; more often, perhaps, they take their archaeology from summaries prepared largely for the historian's benefit. From this a number of dangers arise. An archaeologist claims for instance to have found 'no evidence' for, shall we say, Augustan occupation at a particular site; the earliest pottery and coins were Flavian. The unwary historian repeats, 'This was not an Augustan site, but was first occupied in Flavian times', and uses this to elucidate Flavian strategy. Fuller study of the excavation report might however show that the archaeologist only dug in narrow

trenches and over a very limited area of the site, and stopped
when he got to the earliest stone buildings, with which he
found Flavian pottery associated. He is thus entitled to say
that he proved Flavian occupation. But if he did not go down
beneath the buildings to look for possible traces of earlier
timber structures, it cannot be proved that there *was* no
earlier occupation; it is in fact a common pattern in Roman
military architecture to find a phase of timber buildings and
earth ramparts with timber revetments subsequently rebuilt in
stone. On the Rhine and Danube, stone comes in under
Claudius; many are the sites where pre-Claudian occupation
was not at first recognised, but where improved techniques of
excavation and a better knowledge of the find material have
pushed the date of first occupation back earlier.

The converse may also happen. In North Africa, for
instance, the early French archaeologists saw themselves as
the heirs of Rome. They wanted to find the works of their
predecessors. On a very practical level, there was great
interest in Roman aqueducts and irrigation works. Could the
country again be made to produce as abundantly as it had in
the Roman period? So, at a time when Déchelette was
excavating the wooden huts of the Aedui, his compatriots in
Algeria and Tunisia were laying bare the great urban centres,
digging down to the well-laid streets and the paved forum,
clearing out the theatres, restoring the public buildings. In the
process, they often ignored the flimsier structures, the
resurfacing of streets with packed earth instead of stone, the
squatters' huts overlying the monumental remains which had
been abandoned – all the evidence, in fact, for what happened
to the cities once their prosperity declined and municipal
government apparently collapsed.

The evidence derived from excavation must continually be
reappraised as new knowledge becomes available. This can
best be exemplified from studies of pottery. Pottery is a
crucial dating tool. Some types of Roman pottery have been
intensively studied since the last century, others have
attracted interest only recently and are imperfectly known.
But even types of pottery which appear to have been well

worked over by scholars may have surprises in store. The commonest tableware in the West in the period covered by this book is what British archaeologists traditionally call 'samian' and others 'terra sigillata'. It is a glossy red ware, sometimes plain, sometimes with designs in relief, produced in Italy from the middle of the first century BC onwards and in Gaul, so it was supposed, from the beginning of the first century AD, the Gaulish centres of production rapidly supplanting the Italian in the export markets and in supplying the Roman army in the western provinces. Not until the 1960s was it shown by excavations at Lyon and by laboratory analyses of the chemical composition of the clays used, that 'Italian' sigillata was also made in Gaul, and that the main Italian production centre, Arezzo (whence the pottery is also called 'Arretine'), played a lesser role in supplying the army than had been assumed. The basic typology of 'Arretine' sigillata was first worked out and published in 1909 on the basis of the material from the Augustan legionary base at Haltern in northern Germany. It was then assumed that it all came from Arezzo. We now know that most of it came from Lyon or from another workshop at Pisa. The consequences of this discovery for the dating of Augustan sigillata have still not been fully worked out.

The relationship between literary and archaeological evidence is not that of mistress and 'handmaid', as used to be said. The archaeological data are as much a primary source as the text of Tacitus or an inscription. The historian must recognize that they may complement the literary evidence (cf. page 79); contradict it (Casear claims the Rhine as a major ethnographic and cultural boundary between Gauls and 'Germans', but archaeology gives him the lie); or provide us with information about matters on which the literary record is wholly silent. But we must also beware of the limitations of the archaeological evidence. Archaeology deals with material remains. It tells us, ideally, what was physically present at a given place at a given time. To argue from what was there to who put it there and for what purpose may be hazardous if no written record exists; and to go on from there to try to establish the builders' or users' spiritual state is more hazardous still. Certain religious symbols are clear, the Christian ones, for instance, such as the cross, the chi-rho sign (XP, the initial letters of Christ's name in Greek), the fish, but they are clear because we have Christian writings to explain them. Without that, would archaeologists know what they meant?

Worth special mention, in conclusion, is the value of archaeological air photography. Air photographs can show up hidden buildings, roads and ditches by revealing the differential growth of crops in shallow soil above a road or a line of stone foundations, or conversely in deeper soil where a ditch or the rotted foundations of a wooden building lay. Systematic air survey of Britain and of northern France has revealed a far greater density of rural settlement in Roman times than was previously suspected; the dry summers of the mid-seventies provided what may be a once-in-a-lifetime opportunity. In North Africa, Colonel Baradez of the French Air Force was able to map part of the Roman frontier system, with its associated communications network and settlement pattern, to a quite remarkable degree. Elsewhere Roman centuriation patterns (page 162) have revealed themselves. This is particularly valuable, since rural archaeology in most areas of the empire lags well behind urban, and air photography helps to fill a serious gap in our knowledge.

Finally, let it be stresssed that all our sources for the history of the ancient world, without exception are grossly incomplete, and their survival and recovery due to chance. Only one manuscript stood between Tacitus's *Annals* and oblivion, and it is, for instance, pure chance that we possess his account of the accession of Tiberius, but not of Claudius, because of a gap in the manuscript. It is chance that sent Tacitus's father-in-law out to govern Britain, so that Tacitus's family piety in writing his biography gives us so much detail on the conquest of Britain: he might have been sent to the East instead. It is chance which preserves and brings to light inscriptions, and it is therefore perverse to argue, as even great scholars have done on occasion, from the mere absence of some institution in the epigraphic record, that it did not, or did not yet, exist. An illustration will make this clear: the emperor's financial interests in any province were looked after by an imperial procurator. The system was established by Augustus, and in several provinces Augustan procurators are attested on inscriptions. This is the case in Spain, for instance; in fact the survival of one single inscription attests that one and the same man was procurator in Raetia, Spain and Syria successively (*ILS* 9007 = *EJ* 224, see page 98). Yet the first epigraphic record of a procurator in Aquitania, Gallia Lugdunensis and Germany comes only under Domitian. The first epigraphic record in Britain is about 80, though the presence of a procurator is attested in the literary sources earlier. We cannot say that no epigraphic record means no post. Yet this is precisely what scholars have argued in other cases, where it is an obscurer appointment in question, of which the date is open to doubt. Fashions moreover change: under the Republic, it was not the fashion to commemorate one's whole public career on an inscription, in the first century AD it was common for senators to do so, by the second century equestrians have adopted the practice, in the third century commemorative inscriptions decline quite drastically. Towns in Italy and Africa were more generous with inscriptions to benefactors or successful native sons than those in other provinces – or is this again due at least in part to the chance of survival and recovery?

We have already said enough to show that what is true for inscriptions is still more true for papyri. We have made the same point for archaeology. The rate of destruction of archaeological sites by modern development and by intensive farming, at least in western Europe, is so rapid, and the funds available for excavation are by comparison so scarce, that the present situation has been likened to being in a library, knowing that it was about to be destroyed, and allowed only to take one book in ten – and having to choose them by the colour of the binding, without looking inside. The historian, like the archaeologist, must naturally be selective. What he considers important and how he shapes his material and his conclusions depend on his objectives and his preconceptions. We must not forget, in dealing with the ancient world, that much of the selection has been done for him. There is much that we should like to know, and many questions that we can ask, to which there is no answer. The evidence is simply not there.

III *The Work of Augustus*

After Actium and the conquest of Egypt, Octavian returned in the summer of 29 to Rome, where he celebrated his triple triumph (see Chapter 1). The spoils of war enabled him to spend lavishly on public works and other benefactions. His position for the moment was unassailable. Each year, beginning in 31, he was consul, and in 28, when Agrippa was his colleague, the two consuls spent the whole year of office together at Rome, for the first time in twenty years. Octavian, warned by Caesar's fate, was concerned to conciliate potential opposition by deference to traditional forms. 'In my sixth and seventh consulships (28 and 27)', by his own account, 'after I had extinguished civil wars and at a time when with universal consent I was in complete control of affairs, I transferred the affairs of state from my own power to the control of the Senate and people of Rome' (*Res Gestae* 34). Other sources refer to this as 'the restoration of the Republic' (*respublica restituta*), or with similar phrases. What did this mean?

It was not a single act; in fact we are told that it took two years. Let us take one example: the Romans had a highly developed and theatrical sense of public ceremonial (cf. page 277). Crucifixion is one facet of it. The Roman triumph is another. Yet another is the ceremonial surrounding the higher magistracies. Consuls, for instance, were attended by twelve lictors carrying *fasces,* bundles of rods and axes which were not only symbolic of the consul's power of corporal and capital punishment, but which could actually be used to inflict it. By Republican precedent, the two consuls each had the twelve *fasces* in alternate months. Octavian had arrogated to himself permanent possession of the *fasces,* to the exclusion of his colleague. Now, in 28, he chose to share them. On 1 February, Agrippa paraded behind the *fasces*. It was a very public demonstration that the emergency was over.

Apart from such propaganda gestures, Octavian also needed to find legal forms, preferably backed by good Republican precedents, under which he could exercise the real power which he already held. Earlier generations of scholars have been unduly concerned about 'the constitutional position of Augustus'. This is a legacy of the nineteenth- and early twentieth-century obsession with constitutional forms and constitutional history. Augustus was not a German lawyer dreaming of 1848 or a British civil servant drawing up an impeccably liberal constitution for a new African state. Cicero, it is true, in his work *On the Republic* discusses what is 'the best constitution', *optimus civitatis* or *rei publicae status* (i.39–71), but Augustus was not a theoretician. He simply wanted to legalize and at the same time to veil his virtual monarchy.

The first attempt at a comprehensive legal settlement came in 27. At a meeting of the Senate on the Ides of January (13 January), by prearrangement with his chief supporters, he resigned all extraordinary powers and placed all his provinces at the disposal of the Senate (Dio liii.11–19 is our chief source for this). He was still consul, and was to go on holding the consulship annually until 23. This gave him *imperium* (page 6) and made him superior to all proconsuls. He was also promptly offered, and accepted with apparent reluctance, the provinces of Syria, Cilicia, Cyprus, Gaul and Spain (excluding peaceful Baetica, in the south). They were to be held for ten years, and comprised most of those which needed an army, although Africa, Illyricum and Macedonia, with their legions, were still left for the time being to senatorial proconsuls. Augustus also retained Egypt as successor to the Ptolemies in his own right (see Chapter 6, page 141). Among other honours voted to him were an oak wreath over his door, a shield inscribed with his virtues and, most important, on the motion of that Munatius Plancus who had so opportunely deserted Antony five years earlier, the new name of Augustus, the word applied to 'sanctuaries and all places consecrated by the augurs' (Suetonius, *Augustus* 7).

There were good Republican precedents for most of this. Pompey, for instance, had accumulated provinces in the 60s, and in the 50s had governed Spain through deputies while himself staying in Rome, and what better precedent than Pompey, the champion of the Republic against the tyrannical self-aggrandisement of Caesar? Caesar had served his turn in Augustus's propaganda. But the cumulative effect was unprecedented, and we must agree with Dio, who saw that Augustus's control of finances and of the army gave him complete final control (liii.16). Indeed Dio reverses the formula used by Augustus and suggests that by the settlement of 27 'the whole power of people and senate passed to Augustus and from this time there existed what was really a monarchy' (liii.17).

The main disadvantage of the settlement of 27 was that holding the consulship each year made Augustus's predominance too blatant and halved the number of consulships available for others. It was not yet the custom for the consuls to resign early so that replacements, *suffecti*, could be appointed. Indeed, in the 22 years from 27 to 6 BC, it happened only four times that there was a suffect. Augustus stopped holding an annual consulship in 23, when he resigned halfway through the year. He was consul again in 5 BC to introduce his grandson to public life, and promptly resigned when the office had served its purpose. That year there were three suffects, and thereafter it became normal practice, so that, down to Augustus's death in AD 14, there was only one year without any. This represents a striking change and a subtle cheapening of the office.

In 23, therefore, to give Augustus the legal status he required without his holding the consulship, a new package was devised. The crucial element was the granting of tribunician power (*tribunicia potestas*). So important was it, that emperors came to date their rule by the number of years they had held it (so, for instance, commonly on coins and inscriptions), and the grant of this power to a second person came to be regarded as equivalent to designating him as the successor. Thus, when Tiberius in AD 22 asked for it to be conferred on his son Drusus, Tacitus comments:

> This title of supreme dignity Augustus invented, so as not to take the name of king or dictator and yet to stand out from other office-holders by some appellation. He subsequently chose Marcus Agrippa to be partner in this power, and after Agrippa's death Tiberius Nero, so that his successor should not be uncertain. (*Annals* iii.56)

It seems likely that Augustus had in fact received certain specific powers associated with the tribuneship on previous occasions, for instance in 36 (page 23, cf. Appian, *Civil Wars* v.132, followed by Orosius vi.18.34) and in 30 (Dio li.19). A great deal of confusion surrounds the question, but Dio's account of the proceedings in 23 (liii.32) makes it clear that this was when Augustus for the first time received tribunician power as a whole. Personal immunity (*sacrosanctitas*) and appellate jurisdiction (*ius auxilii*), which had belonged to tribunes under the Republic, Augustus probably had already. To these were now added the tribune's right to convene the Senate and the popular assembly and to submit measures to either (he subsequently received the right to put a motion at any time during a meeting of the Senate); to veto any item of public business or the action of any other magistrate; and the right of *coercitio,* that is, the right of any magistrate to compel obedience to his orders and punish the recalcitrant (see Chapter 10 on the status of Christians, page 266). Some of these powers were redundant. For instance, Augustus's *imperium* already gave him *coercitio.* But it is clear that, if he used his tribunician power to the full, it enabled him virtually to block any development he disapproved of, and to initiate legislation as he wished.

Moreover, as Dio indicates, although he now ceased to have *imperium* as consul, he received a grant of proconsular *imperium* for life, to be valid even in the city of Rome (where normally proconsular *imperium* lapsed), and to be superior to that of all other proconsuls (*imperium maius*). Again, a Republican precedent could be found for the grant of *maius imperium,* but the cumulation of powers was unprecedented. The new settlement was very skilfully put together. It immeasurably strengthened Augustus's position, and by freeing him from the routine obligations of the consulship no doubt lightened his workload. This was important, because earlier in the year he had been gravely ill and not expected to live.

About this time, there was a major challenge to the regime. Suetonius calls it simply 'Murena's conspiracy' (*coniuratio Murenae*) (*Augustus* 65–6). The details are uncertain. It looks as if Augustus and his advisers tried to hush the matter up, and that more than one version of what really happened was current. The only ancient evidence sets the conspiracy in 22, most explicitly Dio, who links it with the trial of a certain Marcus Primus, otherwise unknown, who had made war without instructions when proconsul of Macedonia:

> Not a few voted for Primus's acquittal, and others formed a plot against Augustus. Fannius Caepio started it, but others joined in. Even Murena was said to be in the conspiracy ... They did not wait to stand trial, but were convicted *in absentia* as if intending to escape and killed not long afterwards, nor was there any help for Murena either from Proculeius his brother or from Maecenas, his sister's husband, although they were most highly honoured by Augustus. (liv.3)

Although he does not expressly say so, Dio certainly implies that the Murena of the conspiracy is the same Licinius Murena who he has previously told us defended Primus. Velleius calls the conspirator Lucius Murena (ii.91), Suetonius calls him Varro Murena (*Tiberius* 8). Both name Fannius Caepio as his associate. Maecenas's wife was Terentia, so her brother should be called Terentius. Dio elsewhere records a Terentius Varro in 25 conquering the Salassi of the Val d'Aosta in northen Italy (liii.25, cf. Strabo iv.205–6). Another Varro was governor of Syria at the same time, according to Josephus. Strabo says that the conspirator, whom he calls simply Murena, had recently held a governorship in the East (xiv.670). The problem is to know how many men we are dealing with, and which was which. It is complicated still further by the fact that the Capitoline *fasti*, or register of magistrates, record an Aulus Terentius Varro Murena as Augustus's colleague in the consulship for 23, replaced by Gnaeus Calpurnius Piso, whom all other surviving *fasti* make Augustus's sole colleague at the start of the year, ignoring Varro Murena completely. Unfortunately the Capitoline inscription is fragmentary, and the phrase which records why Varro Murena had to be replaced is missing. The simplest explanation is that he was consul designate but died before taking office, which is why all other *fasti* just make Piso the regular consul, taking office on 1 January. .

Perversely, in my opinion, the weight of published scholarship on the question in the 1960s and 1970s has favoured redating the conspiracy to 23, with no support from the ancient evidence. It is possible to darken the plot by filling out the gap in the Capitoline *fasti* with the phrase 'Murena *was condemned during his magistracy*' (so printed in *EJ*, without comment), or '. . . *was removed from his magistracy*'. But this is historical fiction. Sometimes disputes about the precise date, though interesting in themselves, do not affect the wider interpretation of the period, but the question of 22 or 23 does. If you opt for 23, then the revision of Augustus's legal powers in the middle of that year can be seen as a response to the crisis. This interpretation is favoured by those who for some reason do not see Augustus and his advisers planning far ahead. If you accept 22, as I believe we must (apart from Dio's evidence, we do not have the space to deploy the other arguments here), then the conspiracy becomes the result, not the cause of these changes. Contemporaries could see, as we can, that the new settlement strengthened Augustus's position, and opposition may have crystallized on a 'now or never' basis. That the conspiracy touched the inner circles of the regime is clear. We hear that the conspirator Murena was brother of Maecenas's wife Terentia; Maecenas let her know that the plot had been discovered, and his relations with Augustus were never again as close as they had been.

Whatever the date and the motivation of the conspiracy, the people of Rome were wholly loyal to Augustus. This was sufficiently demonstrated early in 22, when they rioted to force him to accept the dictatorship. It seems that floods, an epidemic and a food shortage were all ascribed to Augustus's withdrawal from the consulship, which to the politically unsophisticated meant that he was no longer in charge. Augustus went to great lengths to avoid the dictatorship that was thrust upon him, 'For since he already had power and honour above that of a dictator, he was right to take precautions against the envy and hatred which the title would arouse' (Dio liv.1). He also refused to accept the censorship for life, for the same reasons, appointing instead two men of irreproachably Republican antecedents as censors, the last private citizens ever to hold that office together. Augustus, however, carried out various measures himself which more properly belonged to the censors. He did accept responsibility for the grain supply (there was a Pompeian precedent for such action), delegating responsibility to annual commissioners of praetorian rank. Rome, as had been shown when Sextus Pompeius was intercepting the ships bringing grain from overseas (page 18), was wholly dependent on imported supplies, and the grain supply is the constant preoccupation of the emperors.

The popular misunderstanding of Augustus's position continued. In the winter of 22/1, when he was out of Rome, only one consul was elected, with Augustus, though he was not a candidate, being acclaimed to the other consulship. The year 21 began with only one consul in office, and when Augustus refused to change his mind, the election to fill the second place caused more rioting, so that Agrippa had to be sent to restore order. Two years later there was the same trouble, but worse. Augustus, bowing to the popular will, thereupon accepted a five-year appointment as supervisor of morals (*praefectus moribus*) and censor, along with consular authority for life, at least if we are to believe Dio (liv.10), who records another five-year term as supervisor of morals in 12 BC (liv.30). Augustus did not want to go on being consul, and did not need the consular authority, but the outward and visible signs of it sufficed to reassure the people.

Augustus's own version is as follows:

> The dictatorship was offered to me by both Senate and people in my absence and when I was at Rome in the consulship of Marcus Marcellus and Lucius Arruntius (22 BC), but I refused it. I did not decline in the great dearth of wheat to undertake the charge of the grain-supply, which I so administered that within a few days I delivered the whole city from apprehension and immediate danger at my own cost and by my own efforts. At that time the consulship was also offered to me, to be held each year for the rest of my life, and I refused it. (*Res Gestae* 5)

He then goes on to record that three times (in 19, 18 and 11) Senate and people offered him the post of 'supervisor of laws and morals without a colleague and with supreme power', and that he refused it as being inconsistent with ancestral custom (*mos maiorum*); instead, 'the measures that the Senate then desired me to take I carried out in virtue of my tribunician power' (*Res Gestae* 6). This appears at first sight to contradict both Dio, in the passage just quoted, and Suetonius, who says that, in addition to tribunician power, 'he further received control of morals and laws, also for life, in which capacity, though without the title of censor, he nonetheless thrice held a census of the people, the first and third times with a colleague, the second time alone' (*Augustus* 27). The emphasis in the *Res Gestae* however is on the phrase 'without a colleague and with supreme power', which would have made him virtually dictator. This invidious position he wished to avoid, but to be 'supervisor of morals' for a limited term, acting on the advice of the Senate and carrying out some of the traditional censorial functions, might be thought a legitimate device not inconsistent with Republican precedent.

In 8 BC, he held a full-scale census, updating the citizenship lists which had last been revised by Augustus and Agrippa 20 years before (and the last one before that had been in 70 BC, 41 years earlier), and again in AD 14 with Tiberius as colleague (Suetonius, *Tiberius* 21). Revisions of the membership list of the Senate were carried out independently, thrice by Augustus himself, in 29, 18 and 11 BC (*Res Gestae* 8; Dio lii.42, liv.13–14, liv.35), and once by a senatorial commission in AD 4 (Dio lv.13). Dio also records one in 13 (liv.26), but wrongly, since this was rather a revision of the equestrian rolls (Suetonius, *Augustus* 38).

The legal forms were observed. The people, as we have seen, were willing to vote Augustus whatever powers he wanted; the problem was rather to avoid having thrust upon him powers and offices which might prove invidious. The army was loyal, the higher commands were given to men whom Augustus could trust, the provinces had every reason to be grateful, not only for peace and the increasing prosperity which it brought, but for release from a system of government which in the late Republic had been 'looked upon sceptically as a matter of sparring dignitaries and extortionate officials. The legal system had provided no remedy against these, since it was wholly incapacitated by violence, favouritism and – most of all – bribery' (Tacitus, *Annals* i.2). Tacitus, though he tries to paint Augustus's motives as black as possible, recognizes that his position became unshakeable, because based on genuine gratitude and on a general recognition of where everyone's interests lay, 'He seduced the army with bonuses, and his cheap food policy was a successful bait for civilians. Indeed, he attracted everybody's goodwill by the enjoyable gift of peace ... Opposition did not exist' (Ibid.).

Augustus himself in a famous phrase sums up the position as follows: 'After this time (27 BC) I excelled all in influence (*auctoritas*), although I possessed no more official power than others who were my colleagues in the several magistracies' (*Res Gestae* 34). This is why, in the last resort, the magistracies were arranged, not to give Augustus power, but

The Roman Empire

to clothe his power in decent and traditional formal garments. At the trial of Marcus Primus, in Dio's account which we have already quoted, when Augustus's right to intervene in the case was challenged ('What are you doing here, and who summoned you?'), he replied simply, 'The public interest' (liv.3). One reason why the story is told is that the challenge was clearly unexpected. But it is only when such a challenge is made that a precise justification of actions in terms of legal authority is required. Someone whose authority is not challenged can make arrangements, give instructions which other people comply with, without their asking by virtue of what precise clause in what document he is acting. As early as the 20s, and even right after Actium, Augustus's authority was so overwhelming that for most of the time he got his own way simply by making his wishes known, and others hastened to comply without stopping to ask or to analyse whether Augustus was acting by virtue of consular or proconsular *imperium,* or maybe, perhaps, tribunician power?

The years 19 and 18 saw the last major changes in Augustus's legal position, though his power and influence continued to increase. The creation of special commissions to oversee particular aspects of the administration of Rome and Italy eroded the authority of the Senate and the elected magistrates. For instance, whereas the water supply of Rome had once been the responsibility of the aediles, Agrippa became special curator of the water supply system, and after his death in 12, 'Augustus by an edict determined the rights of users according to Agrippa's records, making the whole system dependent on his own benefactions', while a contemporary decree of the Senate (11 BC) records that Augustus had appointed 'with the Senate's approval' a board of three commissioners, chaired by an ex-consul, to have the same status, signs of rank, and staff as the commissioners for the grain supply (Frontinus, *On the Aqueducts* ii.99–100 = *FIRA* 41 = *EJ* 278).

Particularly after Agrippa's death, Augustus was a towering and lonely figure. Horace writes to him: 'When you bear so many and such great responsibilities, you alone protect Italy's concerns with your arms, adorn them with manners, correct them with laws, I should sin against the public weal, if by a long discourse I occupied your time, Caesar' (*Epistles* ii.1.1–4). What Augustus at this time meant to the ordinary Italian is again expressed by Horace, especially in the magnificent odes of his fourth book, which we can now show to have been published in 8 BC, just before his death, rather than in 13, as generally believed. Read Ode 5 regretting Augustus's absence in Gaul (16–13 BC) and celebrating the peace and prosperity which he has brought ('Safely the ox plods around the fields . . . over the sea freed from war fly the sailors . . .), and the two final odes, 14 and 15. Read in full the letter to Augustus just quoted (*Epistles* ii.l), in order to appreciate the extent to which Augustus, for all his power, remained approachable, human, very much *primus inter pares*, even if a long way *primus*; as Fraenkel says, historians should 'ask themselves whether a letter such as this could possibly have been written, let us say, to Louis XIV'.

Augustus's impact on the social and economic life of Rome and Italy will be more fully examined in the next chapter and his reorganization of the army in chapter 6. It remains for us in the rest of this chapter to consider what steps he took, firstly, to ensure the continuance of his work after his death, and secondly, to extend and secure the frontiers and to stabilize the provinces. The relevance of these questions to the security of Augustus's own position and the stability of the regime will be readily apparent.

Augustus owed his own position ultimately to his being Julius Caesar's adopted son; 'you, boy, who owe everything to your name,' as Antony once said (quoted by Cicero, *Philippics* xiii.24). The whole structure of Roman aristocratic society was dynastic. The perpetuation of the family was both politically desirable and enjoined by religion. The network of mutual obligations implied by the words *amicitia* (friendship, but often signifying political alliance), and *clientela* (the relationship of patron and dependent) was familial as well as personal and nobody outside the family could could count on inheriting it, even in default of a family heir. Apart from this, what did Augustus have to pass on? His *auctoritas* was his own, and could not survive him. His various legal powers were a heterogeneous packet, each the subject of a special grant. At the time of Vespasian's accession (AD 69), one single law provided for him to receive all of the powers which Augustus and his successors had held (page 172). But it is scarcely conceivable, in view of the care which Augustus took in the decade or so after Actium to veil his supremacy and conciliate republican sentiment, that any such blunt law would have been proposed if he had died during that period, as indeed he nearly did in 23. In the early stages of the principate, the most that Augustus could do was to arrange for certain people to receive certain specific powers or privileges: so his nephew and son-in-law Marcellus, Octavia's son by her first marriage and the husband of Augustus's only child, Julia (his daughter by Scribonia), elected aedile in 24 for the following year, was at the same time granted honorary rank among the expraetors and the right to stand for the consulship ten years earlier than the legal age, while Tiberius, Augustus's stepson, was elected quaestor for 23 and allowed to stand for all subsequent offices five years ahead of time (Dio liii.28). Augustus was now nearly 40, and he had been married to Livia for over fourteen years without having a child, and must have come to despair of having one, in which case his only descendants would be the children of Marcellus and Julia. What more natural than that he should exert his power and influence to further his son-in-law's career? Nor does one need to see in Livia the implacable intriguer, set only on furthering her own children's careers (the picture popularized by Robert Graves, with some support from Tacitus and other ancient writers), in order to suppose that she will at least have encouraged her husband to do something for his stepsons.

But this is very far from designating Marcellus as a successor. On what then seemed his deathbed in 23, he gave his fellow-consul of the year all the military and financial details, and handed his signet ring to Agrippa (Dio liii.30). In other words, if one consul (Augustus) died in office, his colleague would continue to administer the affairs of state, while Agrippa was entrusted with Augustus's personal seal and would no doubt use it at his discretion in confidential matters and in winding up Augustus's own personal and family affairs. Gossip, intrigued and perhaps shocked by the favour shown to Marcellus the previous year, speculated on the possibility of his further advancement. But Augustus, even if he ever thought of it, knew how far he could go; there was no hope that such powerful figures as Agrippa and the other generals and ex-consuls would defer to an untried young man, and indeed there is no evidence that Augustus ever tried to push him on further.

After he had recovered, Augustus offered to read out his will 'to show people that he had not designated any successor to his power, though in fact he did not read it, because no one allowed him to. Everyone was amazed, however, because, although he loved Marcellus both as son-in-law and as nephew ... he had not entrusted the monarchy to him, but had actually preferred Agrippa to him' (Dio liii.31). No doubt the charade of offering to read the will actually took place. The death of Augustus at that moment, only four years after the settlement of 27, would have caused such an upheaval that many leading senators must have been calculating how it would affect them personally. But Dio's own interpretation is coloured, as so often, by the situation of his own time: he had seen the emperor Severus designate his son, the future emperor Caracalla, partner in the Empire with the title Augustus at the age of eight (page 284).

It seems likely that, had Augustus died in 23, civil war would sooner or later have broken out again. Horace reflects the concern for Augustus's health: 'I shall not fear civil strife nor death by violence as long as Caesar rules the earth' (*Odes* iii.14.14–16); or 'as long as Caesar is unharmed' (*Odes* iv.5.27). In fact it was Augustus who recovered and Marcellus who died. Gossip accused Livia, because she was jealous that Marcellus had been advanced over her own sons, but rational people discounted the gossip. There was an epidemic, and no need to suspect foul play (Dio liii.33). In any case, rumours of poison must have been common, when the causes of disease and the use of antibiotics were equally unknown. The death of Germanicus provides a parallel (page 108). And in 1917 a British general captured Baghdad and died there; an account based on contemporary sources records, 'Officially it was put down to cholera, but there were many who believed that he was a victim of the traditional Eastern method of disposing of enemies, by poison.'

Within two years, the widowed Julia was remarried to Agrippa, who divorced Augustus's niece, Octavia's elder daughter by her first marriage, to marry her first cousin, who was also her sister-in-law; he already had a daughter by a still earlier marriage, to the heiress daughter of Cicero's friend Atticus. Dynastic marriages were expected in the Roman ruling class. Julia will not have been surprised at her new match, though she need not necessarily have been pleased. Agrippa was, quite literally, old enough to be her father, and a boor, 'a man closer to rusticity than to elegance' (Pliny, *Natural History* xxxv.26). She promptly had five children by him in less than ten years. These grandchildren of Augustus were in their turn inevitably destined for rapid advancement (the boys) or useful marriages (the girls).

Meanwhile the two stepsons, Livia's boys, were growing up. Even without their mother's remarriage, they would have been political figures in their own right through their connection with two of the most powerful families in Rome, the Claudii and Livii. They also showed a natural aptitude for warfare. Tiberius, the elder, was married to Agrippa's daughter, Vipsania; thrust into prominence as Augustus's personal representative in the East in 20, when he accepted the return of the Roman standards which the Parthians had captured (page 76), he was to be consul in 13. But before that he had shared with his younger brother Drusus the command of all the Roman forces assembled for a great converging invasion of the Alpine regions in 15. No doubt much of the credit for the success goes to other generals, unhonoured and unsung (literally; it is Drusus and Tiberius who get the odes:

Horace, *Odes* iv.4 and 14), who had prepared the ground and planned the overall strategy. But the two young men went on to command in the Balkans and in Germany, and did well. Drusus died in 9, after a fall from a horse; Tiberius went on to become, by sheer merit, the best general of his age, much loved by his men (Velleius ii.104, 114).

Drusus, the younger brother, married another daughter of Octavia: the younger of her daughters by Antony. Two of their sons were to be important in the history of Rome: Germanicus, adopted by his uncle Tiberius, and his younger brother the emperor Claudius (see chapter 5). The latter had an unhappy and unhealthy childhood. His mother used to say of people, 'He's an even bigger fool than my son Claudius', and his formidable grandmother, Livia, 'never failed to treat him with the deepest scorn, and seldom addressed him personally; her reproofs came in the form of brief, bitter letters or oral messages' (Suetonius, *Claudius* 3). Suetonius also quotes an exchange of letters between Livia and Augustus making clear the thought that went into planning the children's careers, with Augustus writing,

The public ... must not be given a chance of laughing at him and us. I fear that we shall find ourselves in constant trouble if the question of his fitness to officiate in this or that capacity keeps cropping up. We should therefore decide in advance whether he can or cannot be entrusted with offices of state generally.

Tiberius had a son by Vipsania; he was named Drusus, like his uncle, and died, allegedly poisoned, in AD 23. Tiberius was very fond of Vipsania, and it was a personal tragedy when he was made to divorce her in order to marry Julia on Agrippa's death (Suetonius, *Tiberius* 7). By this marriage he became stepfather to her five children; she herself was his stepsister, as well as being his father-in-law's widow and the stepmother of her new husband's ex-wife. Even by Roman upper-class standards, this was a relationship of unusual complexity, reflecting Augustus's

The Family of Augustus: Forming a Dynasty

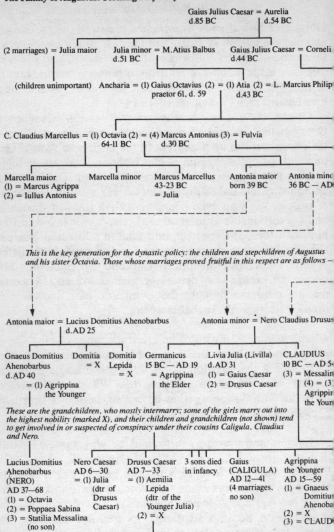

Gaius Julius Caesar = Aurelia
d.85 BC | d.54 BC

(2 marriages) = Julia maior | Julia minor = M. Atius Balbus | Gaius Julius Caesar = Corneli
d.51 BC | d.44 BC

(children unimportant) | Ancharia = (1) Gaius Octavius (2) = (1) Atia (2) = L. Marcius Philip
praetor 61, d. 59 | d.43 BC

C. Claudius Marcellus = (1) Octavia (2) = (4) Marcus Antonius (3) = Fulvia
64-11 BC | d.30 BC

Marcella maior | Marcella minor | Marcus Marcellus | Antonia maior | Antonia mino
(1) = Marcus Agrippa | | 43-23 BC | born 39 BC | 36 BC — AD
(2) = Iullus Antonius | | = Julia

*This is the key generation for the dynastic policy: the children and stepchildren of Augustus
and his sister Octavia. Those whose marriages proved fruitful in this respect are as follows —*

Antonia maior = Lucius Domitius Ahenobarbus
d. AD 25

Antonia minor = Nero Claudius Drusus

Gnaeus Domitius | Domitia | Domitia | Germanicus | Livia Julia (Livilla) | CLAUDIUS
Ahenobarbus | = X | Lepida | 15 BC — AD 19 | d. AD 31 | 10 BC — AD 5
d. AD 40 | | = X | = Agrippina | (1) = Gaius Caesar | (3) = Messalin
= (1) Agrippina | | | the Elder | (2) = Drusus Caesar | (4) = (3
the Younger | | | | | Agrippi
| | | | | the Youn

*These are the grandchildren, who mostly intermarry; some of the girls marry out into
the highest nobility (marked X), and their children and grandchildren (not shown) tend
to get involved in or suspected of conspiracy under their cousins Caligula, Claudius
and Nero.*

Lucius Domitius | Nero Caesar | Drusus Caesar | 3 sons died | Gaius | Agrippina
Ahenobarbus | AD 6—30 | AD 7—33 | in infancy | (CALIGULA) | the Younger
(NERO) | = (1) Julia | = (1) Aemilia | | AD 12—41 | AD 15—59
AD 37—68 | (dtr of | Lepida | | (4 marriages, | (1) = Gnaeus
(1) = Octavia | Drusus | (dtr of the | | no son.) | Domitius
(2) = Poppaea Sabina | Caesar) | Younger Julia) | | | Ahenoba
(3) = Statilia Messalina | | (2) = X | | | (2) = X
(no son) | | | | | (3) = CLAUD

5 children, including Junia Calvina, the only one of Augustus's
descendants still alive late in Vespasian's reign — at the death of Ne
NO MALE MEMBER OF THE DYNASTY SURVIVED

Note: 'maior' and 'minor' mean elder and younger, of sisters, and are part of
normal Roman usage; mothers and daughters are here distinguished as
'the Elder' and 'the Younger', e.g., Julia, Agrippina

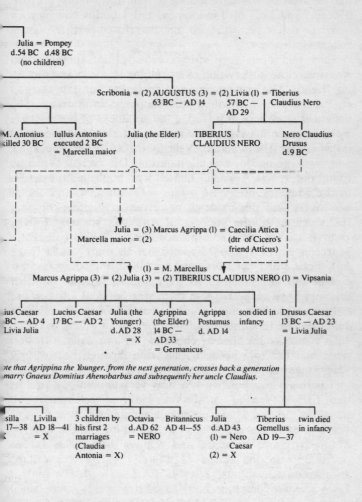

single-minded manipulation of the private lives of his family and associates for dynastic ends. The only child born to Tiberius and Julia died in infancy, and Tiberius had by then come to detest her so much that he refused further marital relations.

Julia had been very strictly brought up: spinning and weaving, close supervision of everything she said and did, no boyfriends. The same regime was applied to her daughters as well. Poor Julia had found little happiness in marriage. She sought it elsewhere, 'measuring the greatness of her position by the licence it gave for sin and considering that she could do whatever she wanted' (Velleius ii.100). Everyone knew what was going on, except Augustus (Dio lv.10). When he found out, it was Augustus himself who published the details to the whole senate (2 BC). Julia was banished, and one of her lovers was put to death or driven to suicide; this was Iullus Antonius, the younger of Antony's sons by Fulvia, Octavia's ward, who had married Octavia's eldest daughter Marcella when Agrippa divorced her to marry Julia (page 66). Four other senators were banished, including one ex-consul and three men of the very noblest families. Modern scholars have suspected that there was political intrigue, not only sexual indiscretion. Augustus forced Tiberius to divorce Julia; despite their incompatibility, he was unwilling to do so. Julia's mother, Scribonia, chose to go into exile with her; what had her role been in Julia's life through nearly forty years since her own supplanting by Livia?

Tiberius's own position was now very anomalous. In 7 he had held a second consulship. He had celebrated two triumphs. In 6 he was granted tribunician power for five years. Clearly marked out as the second man in the state, he promptly chose to retire and remove himself as far as possible from the centre of affairs; his motives excited speculation (Suetonius, *Tiberius* 10, Dio lv.9). His mother Livia tried to dissuade him, Augustus openly complained about his desertion in the Senate, but in vain. Leaving Julia in Rome, he retired to Rhodes, an island whose charm and healthful climate he had remembered from many years before. Four years later the scandal about Julia broke. The next year, Tiberius's tribunician power expired and was not renewed. In his absence from Rome Augustus's grandsons, the children of Julia and Agrippa, and hence Tiberius's stepsons, came of age. Gaius Caesar in 5 and Lucius Caesar in 2. Augustus, who had adopted them, was inclined to be worried about their behaviour: they showed signs of the unthinking arrogance that came naturally from their birth into what was virtually a royal house (Dio lv.9). When people wanted to elect Gaius consul before he was even of military age, Augustus put a stop to it – though Tacitus alleges that secretly he was pleased (Tacitus, *Annals* i.3). The way he records what happened in the *Res Gestae* suggests that Tacitus is right (*Res Gestae* 14).

The tradition that Tiberius retired to Rhodes in protest against this blatant dynastic promotion is probably correct. His first consulship had been only four years earlier, and he had earned it by his military achievements. This cult of the two grandsons was something different. Augustus admitted to them that he hoped they would succeed him (letter of AD 1, quoted by Aulus Gellius, xv.7). By then Augustus was 64, and so secure (he had become *pontifex maximus* on Lepidus's death in 12, 'father of his country', *pater patriae,* in 2 BC), that he could now hope for a quasi-monarchical succession, as he could not have done in 23. Yet within three years, both young men were dead, Lucius in AD 2, Gaius in AD 4. Meanwhile, Tiberius had been allowed back to Rome, largely through Livia's influence, but had been given no honours or responsibilities. The death of Gaius changed that: Tiberius, though both privately and publicly expressing unwillingness, received once more the tribunician power and was also adopted by Augustus. From now on, it was plain sailing. He was marked out for the succession, and Augustus never changed his mind again. There was, however, one further twist: Tiberius had to adopt his brother's son Germanicus, who took precedence by age over his own son Drusus. Germanicus was related by blood to Augustus: his maternal grandmother was Octavia. Drusus was not: his maternal grandparents were merely Agrippa and Atticus's daughter. But more important perhaps than the blood was the need to avoid a disputed succession. Germanicus, if left out of the line of succession, might not have acquiesced. His wife Agrippina was one of Augustus's granddaughters. The adoption satisfied both their claims.

Agrippina had an elder sister, called Julia, like her now-disgraced mother, and a younger brother, born after his father's death, Agrippa Postumus. Both finished up in exile. Agrippa Postumus, though the brother of the late and adored Gaius and Lucius, was 'devoid of liberal qualities and brutishly savage in his physical strength' (Tacitus, *Annals* i.3), inclined to violent rages and always quarrelling with his grandfather Augustus and with Livia (Dio lv.32). Since he *was* Augustus's grandson, his character made him impossible, his birth politically embarrassing. In 7 he was exiled to an island and eventually on Augustus's death, probably by Augustus's orders, put to death. The alternative to having Tiberius adopt Germanicus would have been to get rid of *him* as well. Also exiled, to a different island, was the elder sister Julia (AD 8). Her husband, Lucius Aemilius Paullus, a man of the highest nobility, was executed, now or earlier, for conspiracy, her lover or lovers banished, the child she bore after exile exposed to die (Suetonius, *Augustus* 19, 65; Tacitus, *Annals* iii.24, iv.71). As in her mother's case, the cause of the disgrace was adultery, but Paullus's execution suggests something more. Did he and Julia aim to supplant Tiberius? Julia was after all the eldest surviving grandchild. If so, he (or they) had miscalculated.

This left two other males in the family, in the same generation as Germanicus and Tiberius's son Drusus. One was Germanicus's brother Claudius. He was, as we have seen, thought to be a fool and simply excluded from public life. The other was their first cousin, Gnaeus Domitius Ahenobarbus, also a grandson of Octavia; his mother, like theirs, was one of her two daughters by Antony, and had married Lucius Domitius Ahenobarbus, a successful general but 'notorious for his arrogance, extravagance and extreme rudeness'. The son took after the father, and is recorded as having killed one of his own freedmen for refusing to drink too much, deliberately run over a boy in his chariot, gouged out a knight's eye in the forum, and as having also been remarkably dishonest. Augustus does not appear to have considered him promising material for his dynastic schemes, but he was to marry the daughter of Germanicus and Agrippina (also called Agrippina), by whom he begot the future emperor Nero (Suetonius, *Nero* 4–5), while Agrippina, his widow, eventually married her uncle Claudius, whom Nero succeeded.

This incredibly complicated family tree has in fact three main branches: that which springs from Augustus through Julia, that which derives from Octavia through her various children, and that which goes back to Livia, grafted on to the Julian stock by marriage. The Claudii Marcelli and the Antonii are involved at the start through marriage to Octavia; in the next generation the Aemilii and Domitii Ahenobarbi become involved; in the third generation, that of Augustus's, Octavia's and Livia's grandchildren, the Valerii and Quinctilii; in the fourth generation, the most important new connection is with the Junii Silani, from which sprang Junia Calvina, a merry and dissolute lady, who, in the 70s AD, had the distinction of being the only person still alive descended from Augustus.

Which then were the families of equal distinction that did not intermarry? Above all, the Cornelii, whose various branches flourished: the Cornelii Lentuli have no consul after AD 26, but their blood passed by adoption into the Cornelii Pisones, while the *fasti* in the 50s and 60s AD still exhibit the evocative names of Scipio and Sulla. The Cornelii Pisones came to be the nearest thing there was to an alternative dynasty: linked by adoption or by marriage to the descendants of Pompey and Crassus, they furnish three men who died for their prominence between 65 and 70, including the conspirator against Nero, a proconsul of Africa, and L. Calpurnius Piso Frugi Licinianus, adopted by the emperor Galba (page 169). Still later, Gaius Calpurnius Piso Crassus Frugi Licinianus, whose very name is a dynastic affirmation, conspired against Nerva and Trajan, was exiled, and was killed under Hadrian, while another branch of the family is still to be found in the *fasti* in the second half of the second century.

The quasi-monarchical superiority of Augustus did not stop the nobles from continuing their old mutual rivalry; indeed, a new generation coming into public life after Actium and especially after the settlement of 23 found it easier to accept the dominance of Augustus, a semi-divine arbiter above the strife for honours, than they would have done to accept the supremacy of an equal. Hence the story that, when Gnaeus Cornelius Cinna Magnus, a grandson of Pompey, consul in AD 5, was suspected of conspiracy against Augustus, Augustus calmly deterred him by pointing out that, even if Augustus himself were out of the way, the other great families would never put up with him (Seneca, *On Clemency* i.9.10). As under the Republic, for nobles and new man alike, the great prize was still the consulship, for which Augustus's favour was required, and Augustus also controlled access to the great military commands. No one might outshine Augustus himself, but his legates could win the glory which the aristocratic ethos demanded and which career inscriptions still commemorate. Cicero's dictum still held, that 'the glory of military achievement is superior to all other' (*For Murena* ix.22).

The great military commands after 19 were along the northern frontier; before that, during the 20s, the main fighting was in Spain. Syria had an important army, but its legates did relatively little fighting. Africa was a special case: a senatorial province whose proconsul not only had troops under him (reduced by the end of Augustus's reign to one legion), but could expect to use them in battle. Certain military specialists could expect prolonged and repeated employment as Augustus's legates: Marcus Lollius (consul 21 BC) and Marcus Vinicius (suffect consul 19), for instance, were both new men who later served on the Rhine and in the Balkans, and Lollius also had experience in the East; Gaius Sentius Saturninus (consul 19) was in Syria and Germany;

the aristocratic Lucius Domitius Ahenobarbus, (consul 16), married to one of Augustus's nieces, commanded in the Balkans and in Germany, as well as being proconsul of Africa; Lucius Calpurnius Piso (consul 15) and Publius Sulpicius Quirinius (consul 12) were eastern specialists; and of course Agrippa and Tiberius were everywhere.

It is a mistake to suppose that Augustus's frontier policy was basically defensive, nor was the army employed in the basically defensive role that it later assumed. After Actium and the takeover of Egypt, Augustus reorganized the army, retaining 28 legions (see Chapter 6, page 133), and set out to complete the conquest of Spain which, as Velleius eloquently points out, for 200 years had absorbed so much Roman energy and blood, and destroyed so many Roman commanders (Velleius ii.90). Augustus in the 20s had at least seven legions there, and the final conquest of the northwest by Agrippa in 19 freed troops for operations elsewhere. The twenties had also seen Roman armies conducting limited campaigns elsewhere, pushing forward the limits of Roman control. So for instance in 25 the Terentius Varro, whom we discussed earlier, subdued the Salassi of the Val d'Aosta and opened up the Great and Little St Bernard Passes, founding a colony (Augusta Praetoria) at Aosta itself (Dio liii.25, Strabo iv.205–6). In the same decade, two triumphs and two imperatorial salutations were earned in Gaul and along the Rhine. In the Balkans Marcus Licinius Crassus and the unfortunate Marcus Primus made or tried to make conquests. In 19 Lucius Cornelius Balbus celebrated the fifth triumph from Africa in fifteen years, suggesting steady fighting to maintain and extend Roman control in the south and southwest of the province against the nomadic tribes. Balbus's triumph was the last ever to be celebrated by a person outside the imperial house and the last ever by the proconsul of a senatorial province. In Egypt the frontier was pushed as far south as was considered practicable, and from Egypt was launched in 25 an attack on southern Arabia, led by Aelius Gallus, prefect of Egypt, whose object, according to Strabo, was simply plunder (Strabo xvi.780).

Meanwhile in the far east and northeast, on the frontier with Parthia and Armenia, diplomacy secured the great propaganda triumph of 20, when Phraates, King of Parthia, weakened by dynastic rivalries, agreed to surrender the Roman standards captured from Crassus and Antony. 'Augustus received them as if he had conquered the Parthian in a war; for he took great pride in the achievement, declaring that what had previously been lost in battle, he had recovered without a struggle' (Dio liv.8). Phraates also acquiesced in the elimination of the King of Armenia and his replacement by his brother, Tigranes, who had spent ten years in Rome, and who now received the crown from Tiberius's hand, just as it was Tiberius to whom the standards were actually handed over (Suetonius *Tiberius* 9). Augustus's coins celebrated 'the return of the standards' (SIGNIS RECEPTIS) and 'the conquest of Armenia' (ARMENIA CAPTA), and the return of the standards, with Tiberius and Phraates, is the central event depicted on the breastplate of the famous but enigmatic Prima Porta statue of Augustus.

Armenia as a client kingdom was to prove less tractable than most. It never graduated to full provincial status, and was to be fought over again and again (see Chapter 6 for the affairs of Parthia and Armenia in Nero's day). It was on the eastern frontiers that Augustus in fact made most use of client kings (*reges socii*), of whom the most important after 20 BC were Herod of Judaea, Archelaus of Cappadocia, and Polemo of Pontus, the former client kingdom of Galatia having been made a province in 25 when its king Amyntas died. Suetonius rightly stresses that he treated them as 'members and parts of the Empire,' encouraging ties of marriage and friendship amongst them, appointing regents for such as were minors or incapacitated, and bringing up their children with his own (*Augustus* 48). It suited Augustus to minimise direct Roman military intervention in the East so that he could concentrate resources elsewhere (on client kingdoms, see further Chapter 6, page 141).

From 19 onwards the main concern and the bulk of the legions were concentrated on the northern frontiers. Further campaigns in the Alpine valleys and the establishment of new Roman bases prepared the way for the decisive conquest of the Central Alps under the command of Augustus's stepsons, Tiberius and Drusus, in 15 BC. The Maritime Alps were overrun the next year, and Augustus's grandiose trophy still stands on the hillside at La Turbie above Monaco:

> To the Imperator Caesar Augustus, son of the deified, *pontifex maximus, imperator* for the 14th time, holding tribunician power for the 17th year, the Senate and People of Rome, because under his leadership and auspices all the Alpine peoples from the Adriatic across to the Mediterranean have been brought beneath the Empire of the Roman People. (There follows a list of 45 conquered tribes in rough geographical order, *CIL* v.7817 = *EJ* 40, also recorded in Pliny, *Natural History* iii.136–7.)

Also in 14 BC began a push down the Sava valley, initiating a series of campaigns which brought the whole Balkan peninsula under Roman control, right up to the Danube. The first year saw Marcus Vinicius in command, then Agrippa, then, after Agrippa's death, Tiberius. Later troubles in Pannonia and a rebellion in Thrace were suppressed and the work of pacification completed:

> The Pannonian Peoples, whom the army of the Roman people never approached before I was *princeps,* were conquered by the agency of Tiberius Nero, who was then my stepson and legate. I brought them into the Empire of the Roman people, and extended the frontier of Illyricum to the banks of the Danube. (*Res Gestae* 30)

Augustus himself, meanwhile, from 16 to 13 was in Gaul, while plans were laid for a massive advance across the Rhine into Germany. Most of the soldiers who had begun their service in the civil wars were used up in the wars of the 20s, especially in Spain (cf. Dio liv.11), and will have earned their discharge before the great campaigns in the Alps, the Balkans and across the Rhine began (15 BC onwards). Many were in fact discharged in 14, when there was a clear-out like that after Actium: in the two years 30 and 14, Augustus paid out 860 million sesterces for land in Italy and the provinces to settle veterans on (*Res Gestae* 16). For the new generation of recruits that were to serve in the new campaigns, Augustus standardized rates of pay, length of service and discharge bounties. In 13 BC new regulations were published which fixed the period of legionary service at sixteen years, with twelve years for the praetorians (Dio liv.25; cf. Suetonius *Augustus* 49). Annual pay for a legionary was 900 sesterces, payable in three instalments; this is probably what it had been fixed at by Caesar, and was double the amount previously customary (Suetonius, *Julius Caesar* 26). It had to pay for food and equipment, and was to remain unchanged for over a century, until Domitian increased it by one-third (Dio lxvii.3). In AD 5 the period of service was raised to twenty years (sixteen for the praetorians), and the discharge bounty was fixed at 12,000 sesterces, the equivalent of over thirteen years' pay (Dio lv.23; *Res Gestae* 17). The following year Augustus established a special military treasury (*aerarium militare*) to assume responsibility for these payments (Dio lv.24–5), whether in cash or in the form of land allotments. Other Augustan measures affecting soldiers' legal status are discussed in Chapter 6 (page 136).

It was probably during these years of Augustus's sojourn in Gaul that the first permanent legionary bases were established on the left bank of the Rhine. When all was ready and Drusus in 12 invaded Germany, he used three main invasion routes: from the lower Rhine via a specially dug canal and up the North Sea coast to the mouths of the River Ems, Weser and Elbe, and then up the rivers; due east from the base at Vetera (near Xanten), up the Lippe Valley; and east and northeast from Moguntiacum (Mainz) up the Main and the Wetterau. A supply base with large granaries at Rödgen in the Wetterau, some 56 km from Mainz, suggests the scale and thoroughness of Roman preparations. An unusually large permanent base at Oberaden on the Lippe,

90 km east of Vetera (60 hectares in area, enough for two legions and strong auxiliary forces), established in 10 or at least 9 BC, shows that the Roman forces were settling down to occupy the land. Both Rödgen and Oberaden were given up after the initial phase was over (neither has yielded coins of the Lugdunum altar type, first issued in 10 BC, which otherwise is the commonest of all issues at Augustan military sites in Germany). But they were replaced by other bases, Oberaden in particular by Haltern, an impressive legionary base 36 km further west, which went on being occupied until destroyed in the aftermath of Varus's defeat in AD 9.

By the time Drusus died after his riding accident in 9 BC Roman troops had reached the Elbe and some degree of Roman administrative structure was in force. Tiberius, brought from Illyricum to replace him, 'carried on [the war] with his usual courage and success, and after passing victoriously through every part of Germany without any loss to the army in his charge . . . he so thoroughly conquered it as to reduce it to the status of a virtually tributary province' (Velleius ii.97). It is a salutary reminder of the incompleteness of the archaeological record, that of the hundreds of marching camps that must exist from Drusus's and Tiberius's campaigns only a handful have been found, and those relatively close to the Rhine.

In 6 BC, as we have seen, Tiberius retired from public life: 'the whole world felt the departure of Nero (Tiberius) from his guardianship of the city' (Velleius. ii.100). For ten years, until Tiberius's return and reappointment to the German command in AD 4 (Velleius ii.104), Velleius's account is brief and uninformative. For the same ten years, by unhappy coincidence, the full text of Dio has perished and we have to be content with his epitomators. We cannot therefore fully reconstruct the history of those years. In the Balkans, Gnaeus Lentulus and Marcus Vinicius crossed the Danube, 50,000 Getae were transplanted to the south bank, and the Dacians were forced 'to submit to the Empire of the Roman people' (*Res Gestae* 30). In Germany, Lucius Domitius Ahenobarbus crossed the Elbe and concluded a pact of friendship with the tribes beyond the river (Dio lv.10a). Succeeding him, Marcus Vinicius had enough fighting to justify the award of triumphal insignia. Overall, by AD 6, the situation in both Illyricum and Germany seemed stable enough to justify another great advance.

Two armies were assembled to invade Bohemia, where Maroboduus had established a centralized monarchy of a type new among the Germans. One army under Tiberius was to cross the Danube at Carnuntum and march north and north-west, the other under Sentius Saturninus to invade Bohemia from the west. Tacitus makes Maroboduus claim that there were twelve legions against him, which may indicate the total garrison of Germany, Raetia, and Illyricum at the time, the attacking force being composed of some whole legions with detachments (*vexillationes*) from the rest. Germany was left under the command of Publius Quinctilius Varus. He came from a patrician family that had been in eclipse for centuries, but married well, into circles of power, first of all a daughter of Agrippa, then a grandniece of Augustus. Consul in 13 BC, subsequently proconsul of Africa and governor of Syria, he was not primarily a military man, as all his predecessors in the German command had been, but 'a man mild by nature and peaceable in his behaviour, more accustomed to the leisure of the camp than to active military service' (Velleius ii.117). The governor of Illyricum, Marcus Valerius Messalla Messalinus and most of his army were with Tiberius at Carnuntum. It looks as if no trouble was expected. This was a fatal miscalculation.

First, Illyricum: native levies from Dalmatia assembled to take part in the invasion of Bohemia revolted; an early success provoked a general uprising; some of the Pannonians joined in; the Roman garrison in Sirmium on the Sava was attacked, and the whole Dalmatian coast ravaged. The governor of Moesia to the east intervened to save Sirmium, but subsequently had to withdraw because Dacians and Sarmatians crossed the Danube to invade Moesia in his absence. Tiberius abandoned the plans for invading Bohemia and hurried back to suppress the rebellion. It took three years of hard fighting, and required extraordinary measures at Rome, such as the forced enlistment of freedmen, the introduction of a new war tax (a two-per-cent sales tax on slaves) and other financial measures. In the initial stages, Tiberius had at one time assembled an army of ten legions, with numerous auxiliaries (Velleius ii.113, an eye-witness account: Velleius was one of Tiberius's senior officers, and testifies to Tiberius's military skill, and to his care for his men, putting at the disposal of the sick his own transport, doctors, cooks and mobile bath unit).

The summer of AD 9 brought the end of the rebellion, with a triumph decreed to Augustus and Tiberius and triumphal insignia to Germanicus, Tiberius's nephew and adopted son, who had distinguished himself. But 'within five days of the completion of so great a task, disastrous dispatches from Germany brought the news that Varus was dead and three legions massacred, with three cavalry regiments and six cohorts' (Velleius ii.117). The consequences of the Varian Disaster are clear: the lost legions, 18th, 19th and 20th, were not replaced, no attempt was made to reconquer the territory between the Rhine and the Elbe, and the legionary bases went back to the left bank of the Rhine, to stay there for centuries. New tribes from the north and the east, from beyond the Elbe, moved swiftly into the territory from which the Romans had been driven out (that was one reason why the territory could not be reconquered), and over the next century or so cultural differences developed between the western German tribes, independent of Rome but with constant trade and other contacts, and the more easterly tribes who remained relatively unaffected. What is less clear, however, is why the disaster happened.

The ancient sources blame Varus.

He thought the Germans were people with no qualities but speech and limbs, and that those who could not be conquered with the sword could be tamed by law. With this in mind, he entered the heart of Germany as if amongst men who rejoiced in peace, and he spent the summer season in the pleasures of holding assizes and in observing correct legal etiquette ... he came to see himself as the city praetor giving judgement in the forum, not as a general commanding an army in the middle of Germany. (Velleius ii.117–8)

A plot was formed against him by Arminius, a Cheruscan chief's son, 'very intelligent for a barbarian, a constant participant in our earlier campaigns', who had attained Roman citizenship and equestrian rank (Velleius ii.118) – in fact, Gaius Iulius Arminius, presumably a former prefect of a Cheruscan cohort in Roman service. Varus was warned of the plot, but did not believe it. Marching to suppress a revolt whose outbreak the conspirators had reported to him, Varus was ambushed in deep forest, his army wiped out and all Roman garrisons east of the Rhine overwhelmed.

In fact the blame falls less on Varus than on those who appointed him. Rebellion had not been foreseen. By AD 9 'the Romans were holding parts of it [Germany] ... and their soldiers were wintering there and cities were being founded; the barbarians were adapting themselves to Roman civilization and establishing centres for trade and coming together in peaceful assemblies' (Dio lvi.18). The legionary base at Haltern shows signs of some adaptation to peaceful purposes in its latest phase, and there may have been civilian occupation outside the defences. The one Roman garrison that escaped the massacre and broke through to the Rhine had women and children with it (Dio lvi.26). Varus was in fact doing what he had been appointed to do: establishing the regular administration of justice and taxation in a province that was felt to be ready for it.

The news of the disaster caused panic measures in Rome, but the Germans failed to invade Gaul, and Tiberius, having reinforced the Rhine frontier, began to restore morale (AD 11) by cautiously invading Germany. But the lost territory was not recaptured, the great Haltern base was never reoccupied, and even Germanicus's more extensive campaigns into Germany in 14–16 were 'more for wiping out the disgrace of losing an army with Quinctilius Varus than with the desire of extending the Empire or for any worthwhile return' (Tacitus, *Annals,* i.3). Augustus at his death left the Empire 'fenced in by Ocean or far-off rivers' (Tacitus, *Annals* i.9), but the Rhine was not his own choice as one of these 'far-off rivers'; it was imposed on him by Arminius.

Augustus was a great conqueror in the Republican tradition. The *Res Gestae* stresses this (26–33). If he *had* conquered Bohemia, would he or his successors have stopped there? There is no reason to think so, nor that he aimed at placing the frontier on the Elbe because the Elbe-Danube line was a 'natural frontier' or particularly easy to defend. Livy, Vergil and Horace emphasise Rome's divine mission to rule. 'I have given them Empire without end', Vergil makes Jupiter say (*Aeneid* i.279). And again, 'You, Roman, remember to rule the nations by your empire (these will be your skills), and impose the way of peace, spare the submissive and war down the proud' (*Aeneid* vi.851–3). So too Livy:

> Go, he said, tell the Romans that it is the gods' will that my Rome shall be the capital of the world; therefore let them cultivate the arts of war and let them know and pass on to their descendants that no human forces can resist Roman arms. (Livy i.16)

There is reason to think that Augustus failed to realise how much land lay east of the Rhine and north of the Danube. Barbarians had no rights. They were better off anyway with the blessings of Roman civilization: Florus later was to dismiss scornfully the nomadic Sarmatians, 'They are such barbarians, they do not even understand what peace is' (Florus ii.29). Suetonius says Augustus never fought 'without just and necessary causes' (Suetonius, *Augustus* 21), but the Romans were past masters at arranging this.

It was the will of our ancestors that the gateway of Janus Quirinus should be shut when victories had secured peace by land and sea throughout the whole empire of the

Roman people; from the foundation of the city down to my birth, tradition records that it was shut only twice, but while I was *princeps* the Senate resolved that it should be shut on three occasions. (*Res Gestae* 13)

The emphasis is on the victories that had secured peace, not just on peace itself. In other contexts it is clear that the words 'peace' and 'pacify' (*pax, pacare*) have this connotation.

Next to the immortal gods he honoured the memory of the generals who had increased the empire of the Roman people from its smallest to its greatest extent. And so he restored the public works of each of them, leaving the original inscriptions, and dedicated statues of them all in triumphal regalia in the two porticoes of his forum, announcing moreover in an edict that he had done so, in order that he himself, while he lived, and the leading citizens of future ages should be forced by the citizens to live up to the standard set by the lives of these men. (Suetonius, *Augustus* 31)

The *Res Gestae* themselves open with the words, 'The deeds of the divine Augustus, by which he brought the world under the empire of the Roman people ...' Cicero tells us that 'this praise is inscribed on the statues of the greatest generals, "He extended the bounds of empire"' (*On the Republic* iii.24). It is not the least of Augustus's achievements that he added more territory to the Empire than anyone else who ever lived, and he was proud of it. When he bequeathed to his successor the advice to keep the Empire within its present frontiers (Tacitus, *Annals* i.11), he was not only preaching what he had not practised, but was perhaps reacting belatedly to the realization forced upon him by the revolts in Illyricum and Germany that Rome's power was not as unlimited as he had once supposed.

*Italy under Augustus:
the Social and Intellectual Climate*

In 32 BC, records Augustus, 'the whole of Italy swore allegiance to me and demanded me as the leader in the war in which I was victorious at Actium' (*Res Gestae* 25). Twenty years later, when Lepidus at last died and Augustus was elected *pontifex maximus,* 'such a multitude poured in from all of Italy to my election as had never been recorded at Rome before that time' (*Res Gestae* 10).

Italy had much to be grateful for. The end of the civil wars brought an economic boom. Rome itself was transformed by the Augustan building programme:

I built the Senate house, the Chalcidicum adjacent to it, the Temple of Apollo on the Palatine with its porticoes, the Temple of the Divine Julius ... [here follows a list of thirteen other major temples or other structures]. I restored the Capitol and the Theatre of Pompey, both at great expense, without having my name inscribed on either. I restored the channels of the aqueducts, which in several places were falling into disrepair through age, and I brought water from a new spring into the aqueduct called Marcia, doubling the supply. I completed the Forum Julium and the basilica between the Temple of Castor and the Temple of Saturn, works begun and almost finished by my father, and when that same basilica was destroyed by fire, I began to rebuild it on an enlarged site, to be dedicated in the name of my sons, and in case I do not complete it in my lifetime, I have given orders that it should be completed by my heirs. In my sixth consulship [i.e., 28 BC] I restored 82 temples of the gods on the authority of the Senate, neglecting none that required restoration at that time ... I built the Temple of Mars the Avenger [Mars Ultor] and the Forum Augustum on private ground from the proceeds of booty. I built the theatre adjacent to the Temple of Apollo on ground in large part bought from private owners, and provided that it should be called after Marcus Marcellus, my son-in-law. (*Res Gestae* 19–21)

The text goes on to list Augustus's gifts to temples, his remission of customary contributions to Italian municipalities, and his giving of gladiatorial games and other shows, culminating in a naval battle 'across the Tiber at the place where the grove of the Caesars now stands, where a site 1800 feet long and 1200 feet broad was excavated; there 30 beaked triremes or biremes and still more smaller vessels were joined in battle, and in these fleets about 3000 men fought, apart from the rowers' (*Res Gestae* 23).

The scale of the operation is vast. The studied moderation with which Augustus records that in some cases he did not have his name inscribed on buildings which he restored suggests that usually he did. The buildings listed were spread throughout the city. No major public space was without some impressive monument to Augustus's power, wealth and munificence. Others of his family and associates also built, especially Agrippa. Not only did Augustus 'find Rome built of brick and leave it built of marble' (Suetonius, *Augustus* 28), but he also provided a lot of work for contractors, purveyors of building supplies, and ordinary labourers. The opening of new quarries at Carrara made the extensive use of marble possible. Greek craftsmen were imported to work it, since there was no local tradition of marble working. Land-owners near Rome who had suitable clay beds on their land, including some of the great senatorial families, went into brick production on a large scale. This apparently did not offend against the traditional prohibition of senators' engaging in trade (page 211): it was acceptable to exploit one's estates, and brick-making seems to have counted as an offshoot of agriculture. Architects were also coming increasingly to use concrete, and were learning how to produce concrete of better quality, slow-drying and fusing into a solid mass, although they were not as yet exploiting the revolutionary possibilities in the use of concrete which we began to find under Nero (page 129). Techniques and styles were still strictly traditional. Brick and concrete were covered over. The first great public building to expose its brick-faced concrete construction was probably the barracks of the praetorians, the *castra praetoria,* in the 20s AD.

A motif of Augustan propaganda was the restoration of stability. Just as his legal powers were based on Republican precedent, just as he revived obsolete or obsolescent religious ceremonial, just as those who shared his views, like Livy and Horace, looked back to the good old days of uncorrupted simplicity, so too Augustan art and architecture followed traditional models, and indeed went back for their inspiration beyond the late Republic to classical Greece. No Augustan building is so radical, so outrageous for its day, as Sulla's Temple of Fortuna Primigenia at Praeneste.

In the long extract just quoted from the *Res Gestae,* we notice the emphasis on completing Julius Caesar's unfinished projects (the same emphasis as we find in Augustus's political and military activities of the 30s). The classicizing revival had indeed begun already under Julius: his statue of Venus Genetrix, ancestress of the Julian house, was commissioned from late fifth-century models. His own statues were classical in style, with idealized body and realistic head. It was Julius who had had the Carrara marble quarries developed. The Roman state gods were now depicted in forms indistinguishable from their Greek counterparts. Classical allegories were freely used, and new ones freely invented. Augustus took this process further. His portraits were still more classical, more idealized, than those of Julius. His forum, though Roman in basic conception and layout, a forum, not an agora, is Greek in the style and details of the architecture, even to the use of reduced copies of the Erechtheum caryatids. Roman again is the shrewd practicality of the firebreak wall separating the forum from the slums of the Subura, while the use of coloured marbles from Africa, Greece and Asia Minor, as well as white Carrara marble for the centrepiece, the Temple of Mars the Avenger, exemplifies Augustus's supremacy. The master of the world calls the world to pay tribute. One detail reminds us that the master of the world, when at home, veiled his power and behaved like an ordinary citizen under the law: Augustus could not get the owners to sell all the ground he wanted, and the forum is asymmetrical at the east corner.

Apart from the Forum of Augustus and the Theatre of Marcellus, the most impressive remains of the Augustan period still visible in Rome are, first, Augustus's mausoleum, surpassing in grandeur or grandiosity any Republican antecedent, but recognizably in the same tradition as, for instance, the Late Republican tomb of Caecilia Metella on the Appian Way; and, second, the Altar of Augustan Peace (*ara Pacis Augustae*), now recreated, though not on its original site. Built between 13 and 9 BC, it comprises an almost square enclosure surrounding a monumental altar approached by steps, the whole lavishly decorated with sculpture. The friezes on the enclosure wall and on the altar depict processions. All the family and associates of Augustus are there. The portraits are recognizable, conforming to the iconography which will have been familiar to everyone from statues and coins; the proportions and the draperies are strictly classical, although the grouping of the figures is more naturalistic than on the Parthenon frieze, from which the Altar friezes derive, via Hellenistic intermediaries, just as Trajan's column over a century later looks back to the Altar. The Theatre of Marcellus has the same fusion of elements: classical orders on a stone theatre reminiscent of Pompey's, which was the first stone theatre in Rome. The theatre also provided a public park and an open-air museum. It set a fashion, which was to be followed throughout the Empire.

Augustus and his friends built for use, not just for show. Augustus records how he improved the water supply, but the most important work in this area had been done by Agrippa, who restored and enlarged Rome's four existing aqueducts and built two more. He adopted the new material, concrete, instead of cut stone, although his concrete is still crude, its rough aggregate being laid with little care in loose friable mortar, while the facing is of coarse, poor quality, reticulate with wide, irregular joints. He was also the first to have several channels carried on a single series of arches. Agrippa's own gang of slaves, trained to maintain the supply system, passed into the hands of Augustus on his death and became the basis of the imperial aqueduct service. Agrippa also overhauled the entire drainage system of the city, repaired the retaining walls of the Tiber, and built a new bridge. He was also responsible for a monumental quarter in the Campus Martius, including the original Pantheon, later totally rebuilt by Hadrian (page 225), although the core of Agrippa's podium survives, incorporated into Hadrian's foundations.

Much of this construction work was paid for out of war booty. Not only does Augustus specifically record the fact for several of his buildings, but we find Cornelius Balbus, the last *triumphator* from outside the imperial house, dedicating his theatre in 13 BC from the spoils of Africa. In this way Augustus repaired, or saw to it that his generals repaired, the roads of Italy (Suetonius, *Augustus* 30; Dio liii.22). Among Augustus's own booty was the accumulated treasure of the Ptolemies (not that he was poor without it; as we have seen (Chapter 1), he started his career by raising a private army, and subsequently enriched himself from confiscations and legacies). But the spoils of Egypt were exceptional: they enabled Augustus to put so much new money into circulation that interest rates fell from 12 to 4 per cent, and the value of property rose accordingly (Suetonius, *Augustus* 41; Dio li.21). The whole of Italy was affected. Much property had of course changed hands during the civil wars, through confiscations, or through donations to veterans and others with a claim on the generosity of the new men in power. Now with peace assured and the economy booming, landed proprietors set out to develop their estates, whether as revenue-producing operations or as country retreats, or a combination of both (page 93).

Throughout Italy roads were repaired, bridges built

and the communications network developed. We see the same process at work in the provinces, as numerous milestones attest (page 162). 'In my seventh consulship (27 BC) I restored the Via Flaminia from the city as far as Rimini, together with all the bridges except the Mulvian and the Minucian' (*Res Gestae* 20), and an arch at Rimini confirms and supplements this statement:

> The Senate and people of Rome to the Imperator Caesar Augustus, son of the deified, seven times *imperator*, seven times consul and consul designate for an eighth time, because he paved the via Flaminia and the other most travelled roads of Italy on his own initiative and at his own expense' (*ILS* 84 = *EJ* 286).

Milestones and coins reinforce the message: Italy owed this to Augustus (cf. *EJ* 287–8). Augustus also made travel safer by instituting military guard posts at key points on the road network (Suetonius, *Augustus* 32).

The towns of Italy were also endowed by Augustus and his family or by local benefactors with public buildings, with monumental arches, with gates and walls suitable to their dignity, and with new or augmented supplies of water. A lengthy inscription with the text of an edict of Augustus governing the provision and maintenance of the water supply to Venafrum shows the importance attached to such matters (*ILS* 5743 = *EJ* 282). There are cities, especially in the north of Italy, which preserve to this day the basic Augustan street layout, for instance Turin (Augusta Taurinorum), Verona and Aosta. Aosta (Augusta Praetoria) was founded in the territory of the Salassi after their conquest in 25 BC. It lies at the point in the Val d'Aosta where the road coming up the valley divides, one branch going over the Great St Bernard pass into the *vallis Poenina* (the Swiss canton of Valais, *the* valley), the shortest route from Italy to Helvetia and the Rhine, the other crossing the Little St Bernard into Gaul. Another pair of key Alpine passes, the Mont Cénis and the Mont Genèvre, also had a town at their foot on the Italian

side. This was Susa, (Segusio) capital of a Celtic chieftain
turned Roman prefect governing the tribes through whose
territory the passes ran. An inscription on the arch at Susa,
built in 9–8 BC, refers to him as 'Marcus Julius Cottius, son
of King Donnus, prefect of the communities listed below,'
and the names of fourteen tribes follow (*ILS* 94 = *EJ* 166).
In the northeastern corner of Italy, Aquileia prospered
solidly, a supply base for the troops in Illyricum. Augustus
spent time there, and Tiberius's son by Julia was born there
(Suetonius, *Augustus* 20; *Tiberius* 7). It was also a natural
base for trade with Noricum and indeed with the faraway
tribes beyond the Danube; for centuries already it had been
the terminus of the amber route to the Baltic, the route which
a Roman knight would take in person under Nero to bring
back an extraordinary quantity of amber (Pliny, *Natural
History* xxxvii.45). These towns on the edge of Italy were
centres of Romanization. The tribes of the Alpine valleys
were 'attributed' to them. At Aosta the Salassi who had been
permitted residents of the colony 'from the beginning' set up
an inscription (*ILS* 6753 = *EJ* 338). Tribes around Trent
(Tridentum) were allowed to usurp citizenship and used it to
such effect that Claudius agreed to confirm them in it (*ILS*
206). Cisalpina, in general, and especially the regions north of
the Po, proved the most fertile recruiting ground for the
legions in all Italy.

The Apennine regions of central Italy were relatively
backward. They too produced their quota of recruits, and
some notable examples of social mobility. We shall return to
look more closely at the Paeligni later. Samnium remained
poor and somewhat isolated. But it provides us with one
classic example of Augustan prosperity and urban development, in the town of Saepinum, today a tiny hamlet (Sepino),
in the valley 1300 feet below its Samnite predecessor, set
down to be a centre for the whole region, endowed with 'a
wall, gates and towers at their own expense' by Tiberius and
his deceased brother Drusus (*ILS* 147 = *EJ* 79, between 2
BC and AD 4). Transhumance was an essential feature of the
local pastoral economy, and Saepinum lay across one of the

great transhumance routes along which flocks of sheep were driven up into the mountain pastures in the spring and down again in the autumn. The practice is still common. You see it in Wales, although now the farmers often use lorries. A second-century inscription from Saepinum, however, containing a letter from the imperial secretariat to the magistrates of Saepinum, enables us almost to see and smell the sheep on the move:

> Since the lessees of the flocks of sheep . . . are now repeatedly claiming to me that they frequently suffer injury along the drove roads into the mountains at the hands of the military guards and the magistrates at Saepinum and Bovianum, inasmuch as they detain in transit draught animals and shepherds that the lessees have hired, saying that they are runaway slaves and have stolen draught animals, and under this pretext even sheep belonging to the emperor are lost . . . (*CIL* ix.2438 = *LR* p.186)

No region of Italy benefited more from Augustan prosperity than Campania. Augustus himself built a great aqueduct 96 km long to supply Naples and the other towns of the Bay, such as Puteoli and Cumae. Puteoli was the great port for trade with the East. It was where the Egyptian grain fleet put in, and members of an important local family are to be found being honoured by traders connected with Alexandria, Asia and Syria (Suetonius, *Augustus* 98; *ILS* 7273). Only after Trajan built his new harbour off the Tiber mouth did Puteoli decline (cf. *IG* xiv.830). Wealthy men vied with each other to build luxurious villas on the Bay of Naples. Baiae enjoyed a building boom, and there was an unbroken succession of houses and vegetation from Misenum to Athenaeum (Strabo v.246–7). Such seaside villas were chiefly for pleasure and relaxation. Many produced no income and were empty for much of the year, although it was the custom to lend one's house to a friend, since inns were poor and renting property was considered rather dubious.

The rich also had villas in the hills around Rome, in

Latium and Etruria. These were not only for recreation, but were also expected to pay for themselves. Latium was reputed to produce the best wine, and Horace makes it clear that it was a matter of pride to have produce from one's own estates (*Epistles* ii.2.160). Estates near Rome also had orchards and market gardens, and might be a source of building materials, as mentioned above, such as bricks, stone and timber. But it would be a mistake to think of Latium and Etruria as wholly given over to great estates. Horace had a small estate in the Sabine hills: a home farm with eight slaves under a slave manager and five other tenant farms with vineyards, an orchard and vegetable garden, cornfields, pastureland and woods (*Satires* ii.7.118; *Epistles* i.14.1–3). He tells a story of a client who gets a farm worth 14,000 sesterces from his patron. Catullus in a previous generation had a property in the Sabine hills near Tibur (Tivoli) mortgaged for 15,200 sesterces (xxvi.44), and Cicero speaks of a certain Hippodamus, possibly his brother's freedman, who expects to be given the price of a suburban farm (*Letters to his brother Quintus* iii.1.9).

Throughout Latium and Etruria, as in Cisalpina, we find that the towns also flourished under Augustus. Sutri for instance in Southern Etruria derived its prosperity from its position as the first town out of Rome on the Via Cassia; its rock-cut amphitheatre is probably Augustan. In fact most of the towns of Etruria and Umbria benefited from the building boom. Etruria had been particularly affected by the disturbances of the past two or three generations. Men dispossessed by Sulla's confiscations were an important element in Catiline's support, including 'many from the colonies and municipalities, who were nobles in their own place' (*domi nobiles*, Sallust, *Catiline* 17). The triumvirs followed Sulla's example, probably because land in Etruria was particularly fertile and desirable. Again, when Augustus purchased land for veterans in 30 and again in 14 BC, and later was proud of his 28 flourishing Italian colonies (*RG* 16, 28, cf. Suetonius, *Augustus* 46), Etruria and Campania were more affected than any other part of Italy. Some Etruscan families which survived the proscriptions and confiscations not only prospered under Augustus but entered the ranks of the Roman nobility, no longer content to remain merely *domi nobiles*. Such were the Caecinae of Volaterrae, who provided a suffect consul in 1 BC, and who built a theatre for their native town (*AE* 1957, 220). They had deep roots there; the family tomb, discovered in 1739, had many urns, all with inscriptions in Etruscan. There were the Spurinnae and Caesennii at Tarquinii, and the Seii of Volsinii, who provided a prefect of Egypt, father of Sejanus, Seius Strabo. In Southern Etruria especially there were rich villas, but agriculture was not the only source of prosperity. Luna had its marble quarries, Arezzo its potteries which exported all over the world, even to India and the Yemen, as well as establishing branch workshops at Pisa and in Gaul for the lucrative army-supply contracts. Even Veii, bypassed by the main roads, seems to have shared briefly in the boom, before declining into obscurity.

This contrasts strongly with the situation in the South of Italy, where there is little evidence of wealth in the towns. Here much of the land was given over to ranching, though there is evidence for grain, wine, oil, fruit and vegetables. The landowners were mostly non-resident. If they were senators, for instance, it was too far from Rome and the countryside lacked the obvious attractions of the Bay of Naples or the hills around Tivoli and Praeneste. Transhumance was practised, but here the animals included pigs, which fed in the extensive oak forests, as well as sheep, bred for their wool. Horace refers to a man from Calabria feeding spoiled fruit to his pigs as if the association of the area with pig-breeding was well known (*Letters* I.vii.14–19). The herdsmen were slaves. Writers comment on the depopulation of the countryside; the evidence suggests that this is only relative. There may well have been less people living on the land than there were a century or two earlier, and many of these will now have been slaves. But each district continued to produce enough food for its own requirements, even if large stretches of the south were given over to grazing.

Land remained not only the best investment, but probably the main source of profit (see chapter 8). Gaius Caecilius Isidorus had lost property in the civil wars, but nevertheless, when he died, he left estates with over 4000 slaves, 3600 pairs of oxen, over a quarter of a million sheep and other animals, and 60 million sesterces in cash (Pliny, *Natural History* xxxiii.135). The boring and greedy Gnaeus Cornelius Lentulus, though poor in his youth, is said to have amassed a fortune of 400 million sesterces, the largest private fortune recorded (Suetonius, *Tiberius* 49; Seneca, *On Benefits* ii.27). Nobody, of course, could compete with Augustus himself, and the imperial properties continued to grow, and were to be passed on even through changes of dynasty. The villa at Posilippo that passed to Augustus from his disreputable friend Vedius Pollio was still in the imperial domain, administered by a freedman procurator, under Hadrian. In AD 37 Tiberius died in a villa that had come down through Marius, Sulla and Lucullus to the imperial house.

A recent estimate puts the adult male citizen population of Italy at not more than $1\frac{1}{2}$ million at the end of Augustus's reign. The number of slaves is anybody's guess. The total population of Rome itself must have been getting on for a million: little wonder that Augustus himself accepted responsibility for the all-important grain supply from 22 BC onwards, trying out various administrative formulae and finally towards the end of his reign putting an equestrian prefect in charge (*Res Gestae* 5, cf. Tacitus, *Annals* iii.54). Africa was the most important source of supply, Egypt next. Rome needed at least six million sacks of grain a year, and such quantities could be transported only by water. Even so, conditions in the city for the poor were grim. A physician early in the second century says that rickets were common among children in Rome. Probably no other city in the Empire provided so sharp a contrast between rich and poor (page 213).

Some of the rich, like Augustus himself, affected the frugality that Roman tradition lauded. But standards of luxury were rising (this could hardly be avoided with so much 'new' money around), and standards of behaviour had fallen. Several of Augustus's own close associates were notorious for their luxury and laxity, none more so than Maecenas. Horace and the elegiac poets present a society much given to parties and love affairs with women and boys of charm and elegance, belonging to what the nineteenth century would have called the demi-monde; and if the expression 'demi-monde' is unfamiliar to modern readers, it is because modern Western society has lost in the course of this century a recognizable sub-culture of easy virtue with its own rules and conventions, catering outside marriage to the pleasures of 'respectable' society. All the evidence shows that such a demi-monde, deeply penetrated by Greek influence, existed in Rome; the poets were not just indulging in literary fancies.

Augustus tried to restore a higher standard of respectability in upper-class behaviour, and at the same time to check a falling birthrate. A series of laws stretching from 18 BC and AD 9 made adultery a criminal offence, governed the legality of marriages between different classes (in particular, marriage with freedwomen was permitted, except for senators and their families), and prescribed penalties, especially with regard to legacies, for the unmarried and childless. It is often difficult to tell which clause preserved by the later jurists came from which law, nor is it clear that the laws were effective or indeed much enforced, though they could be used savagely against highly-placed offenders if necessary, as Admiral Byng was shot, *pour encourager les autres*. Other social legislation included laws giving statutory freedom but without full citizen rights to slaves freed without due process, and restricted the number of slaves whom an owner might free. Slaves formally freed ('manumitted') continued to receive full citizenship, while still owing certain duties and services to their former owners. The patron-client relationship was fundamental to the way Roman society worked. To be attended by many clients was a status symbol, and by turning slaves into freedmen one increased the number of one's clients. Society was governed by a network of reciprocal obligations, at all levels, most clearly visible in the letters of Cicero and Pliny. Seneca enjoys the paradox of the freedman Callistus (page 124) who has become so rich and powerful that his former master, who had once put him up for sale, now waits on him as one of his clients, and is refused admittance (*Letters to Lucilius* xlvii.14). Few slaves could hope to draw such a prize in life's lottery, but the mere possibility was a factor which helps to explain why the majority, at least of household slaves, must have accepted their lot. There is evidence enough that slave-owners lived in fear of violence; we need go no further than Tacitus and Pliny on the murders by their slaves of two senators, Pedanius Secundus in 61 and Larcius Macedo in the first years of the second century (*Annals* xiv.42–5; *Letters* iii.14, respectively). We shall return to the question of slavery in chapter 8 (page 216).

For all its peace and prosperity, perhaps indeed because of it, the reign of Augustus was a period of rapid and irreversible social change affecting all levels of society and all parts of Italy. The composition of the senatorial class changed radically by comparison with the late Republic, the equestrian order expanded, new men moved up into municipal prominence. Even the remoter and more backward parts of Italy, as we shall see in a moment, began to move into the mainstream of Roman life. A study of the family origins of the consuls of the period shows what was happening. Down to 19 BC, the new men who had done well in the wars predominate. Then we start to find a new generation of nobles, often men whose fathers had missed the consulship because of the civil wars. From 5 BC onwards, as we have already noted, suffect consulships become normal and so the number of men attaining consular office greatly increases; they include representatives of the great Republican houses, others from families ennobled by the successful generals of the previous generation, and still some new men, mostly from the municipalities of Italy. The culmination of this process is discussed in Chapter 8: the old aristocracy virtually dies out, and a new aristocracy of office develops, within which the turnover is surprisingly rapid.

A few examples of how men from one of the remoter regions of Italy made their way into the mainstream under Augustus will illustrate what was happening. The Paeligni were an Italian people from the Abruzzo, in the Apennines of Central Italy. Under Augustus they produced their first senator, a certain Quintus Varius Geminus, who rose to be a proconsul and to hold two separate appointments as legate of Augustus. We should not know about him, unless his towns-folk had been so proud of him that they set up an inscription at public expense to commemorate him recording that 'he first of all the Paeligni' became a senator and held these honours' (*ILS* 932 = *EJ* 205). Of course another man *ought* to have been the first senator from the Paeligni, if he had not turned his back on 'these honours' and become a poet: this is Ovid (page 101). Varius Geminus also became 'patron' of the municipality, an arrangement to his credit and the town's advantage.

The Paeligni were in fact just starting to take their place in Roman life. The town of Superaequum Paelignorum, now Castelvecchio Subequo, which gives us the inscription to Quintus Varius Geminus, also gives one recording an equestrian career, that of Quintus Octavius Sagitta, who had been *praefectus fabrum*, which meant a sort of honorary *aide-de-camp,* had then commanded a cavalry regiment, and then served as a staff officer, *tribunus,* in a legion (*ILS* 9007 = *EJ* 224). After this military service, he went on to a successful career as a financial administrator looking after Augustus's interests for a total of sixteen years in three different provinces, starting in the Alps, moving to Spain, and ending up in the rich and important post of Syria. After his retirement he was three times *duumvir,* that is one of the two joint mayors of the municipality, each time in the special fifth year, when the *duumvirs* exercised censorial powers. He was clearly a man of substance.

So was Sextus Pedius Lusianus Hirrutus, again known to us from a Paelignian inscription (*ILS* 2689 = *EJ* 244), who not only held high municipal office, but also presented the town with an ampitheatre built at his own expense. In his

military career he had risen to become the senior centurion
(*primus pilus*) of the 21st Legion, and had then moved into
the equestrian post of prefect of that same Alpine province
where Octavius Sagitta served as financial administrator.
Since the commander of a legion was always a senator, only
a province with no legionary garrison could be governed by
an equestrian prefect (Egypt was the exception, page 144), and
Sextus Pedius gives his full title as 'prefect of the Raeti, the
Vindolici [*sic*], the *vallis Poenina*, and the light-armed troops,'
who presumably represent the only garrison that the province
had. This province covers the upper valleys of the Rhine and
the Rhône, joined by the Furka Pass; Sextus Pedius probably
served here with his legion during the conquest in 15 BC, and
stayed on as governor afterwards. Once the conquest of the
Alps was complete and the area organized, the legions moved
forward. All that the rear areas needed was guard posts at
intervals along the roads.

There is no way of telling whether Sextus Pedius rose from
the ranks, or came from a higher social and economic level
and actually entered the army as a centurion. But we do have
one case from Tiberius's reign where we can identify a
ranker. This is Marcus Helvius Rufus, who distinguished
himself in fighting in Africa early in Tiberius's reign during
the revolt led by Tacfarinas (Tacitus, *Annals* iii.21). He was
awarded the civic crown, *corona civica,* the Roman VC, for
saving a comrade's life. He turns up again on an inscription
from a small town near Rome (*ILS* 2637 = *EJ* 248). He has
added Civica to his name to commemorate his early feat,
risen to the rank of *primus pilus,* and is found presenting
public baths to the town. Considering that the *primus pilus*
made sixty times the ordinary legionary's pay, with various
bonuses in proportion, we can understand why Sextus Pedius
could afford to build an amphitheatre and Helvius Rufus
public baths on their retirement. Even if such substantial
success was the exception, any soldier could feel that he had,
if not a marshal's baton, at least a centurion's vine-wood cane
in his knapsack. The cane, it may be pointed out, was the
centurion's badge of office, and was also used to encourage

the laggards, so that one unpopular martinet, who was always breaking his stick on the men's backs, was nicknamed 'Fetch another' (Tacitus, *Annals* i.32); when they got the chance, the men lynched him. Numerous centurions are attested, wealthy and distinguished in the Italian municipalities after retirement, and men of established municipal families must have felt about the military career as Jane Austen's Sir Walter Elliot felt about the Navy in the Napoleonic Wars, that it was 'the means of bringing persons of obscure birth into undue distinction'.

The Augustan Age is the age of Italy. The participation of provincials in the administration and in the profits of the Empire is still largely in the future. It will be one of our main themes in subsequent chapters. Augustus was consciously aiming to create a new order and to perpetuate it, institutionally and dynastically, but he was also concerned to placate conservative sentiment by appeals to precedent and by maintaining and restoring traditional values, ceremonies, and procedures. Not for nothing was one of his favourite maxims, 'Make haste slowly' (Suetonius, *Augustus* 25). Nor is it coincidental that the writers closest to him in the first part of his reign, Vergil and Horace, not only show how much was seen to depend on Augustus himself, but also reflect a strong sense of identification with Italy. Nowhere in literature do we see the Italian countryside more vividly than in the *Eclogues* and *Georgics*: 'And now the rooftops of the houses in the distance smoke and longer fall the shadows from the high mountains' (*Eclogues* i.82–3), or from the praises of Italy in the *Georgics,* 'So many notable cities, the fruit of toil, so many towns heaped up by man's labour on the steep crags and the rivers gliding past beneath the ancient walls' (ii.155–7). Equally vivid is the city of Rome in Horace, as in the poem where the bore meets him strolling down the Sacred Way and sticks to him like a leech half way across town (Satires i.9). Rome and Italy and the old values were things that Augustus too cared about. It was a sad irony, for which he took an implacable revenge on the unhappy poet, that the successor of Vergil and Horace, the inextinguishable voice of the second half of his reign, should be the Paelignian dropout, Ovid.

Augustus in the last years of his life began to show his age. In AD 12 he asked senators to stop calling at his house and to excuse him from public dinners (Dio lvi.26); the following year Dio records that he no longer attended the Senate 'except very rarely', and that he conducted public business from his couch (lvi.28). Tacitus records gossip about his possible successors, 'idle talk about the blessings of freedom', and widespread fear of civil war (*Annals* i.4).

As Augustus's health deteriorated, so steps were taken to ensure a peaceful transition of power. Throughout the summer of 14 the Rhine legions were kept in camp on the left bank of the river 'with nothing to do or on light duties' (Tacitus, *Annals* i.31), presumably ready to keep order in Gaul if there were any unrest. Augustus visited Campania with Tiberius, and they parted at Beneventum (Benevento), Tiberius to go to Illyricum and Augustus to return to Rome. But he was already unwell, got worse, and died at Nola on 19 August. Messengers had been sent to recall Tiberius. When he reached Nola, says Suetonius, Augustus 'kept him a long time in private conversation, and after that paid no further attention to any important business' (*Augustus* 98, cf. *Tiberius* 21). Velleius also records a touching deathbed farewell (ii.123). Dio on the other hand accepts the version that Augustus died before Tiberius got there, as having the support of 'the majority of writers' and the more reliable ones' (lvi.31). Tacitus registers perplexity: 'It is not clearly established whether he found Augustus alive or dead, for efficient guards had closed off the house and streets on Livia's orders and favourable reports were published at intervals until the precautions which the situation required had been taken, and Augustus's death and Tiberius's accession to power could be announced simultaneously' (*Annals* i.5).

Tacitus then continues, characteristically, 'The first crime of the new reign was the murder of Agrippa Postumus', thus creating a prejudice against the new reign from the start. The Postumus affair caused much scandal. Suetonius actually says that Tiberius 'delayed announcing Augustus's death until young Agrippa had been killed' (*Tiberius* 22). Nobody knows who gave the order. Tacitus suspects Livia, but says that Tiberius himself 'pretended that Augustus's orders to the tribune commanding Agrippa's guard were to put him to death immediately Augustus himself departed this life' (*Annals* i.6). In any case, he accuses Sallustius Crispus, Augustus's closest confidant in his latter years, of actually sending the orders (*Annals* i.6. cf. iii.30). Crispus, like Maecenas in Augustus's earlier years, was a knight, not a senator. Suetonius also knows of written orders, but not 'whether Augustus had left them when he died ... or whether Livia had written them in his name and, if so, whether or not Tiberius knew about it', though Tiberius in any case denied all knowledge (*Tiberius* 22).

Rumour alleged that Augustus had visited Agrippa some months earlier, with only one attendant, and effected a tearful reconciliation (Tacitus, *Annals* i.5, Dio lvi.30). But even Tacitus seems sceptical, and Dio's story that Livia, who had known nothing about the voyage at the time, subsequently heard of it and promptly poisoned Augustus, is distinctly implausible. But then so is the whole notion that Augustus would wreck everything he had worked for by entrusting power to a successor as unsuitable as Agrippa Postumus. Sallustius Crispus's warning was evidently well heeded, 'that family secrets, the advice of friends, and the services done by the soldiers should not be made known' (*Annals* i.6).

Tiberius convened the Senate by virtue of his tribunician power. He had also taken command of the praetorian cohorts and sent out orders to the armies. Tacitus suggests that he was afraid lest Germanicus, commanding on the Rhine, 'in whose hands were so many legions and huge forces of allied auxiliaries', might 'rather have power than the prospect of it' (*Annals* i.7). To what extent is Tacitus anachronistically interpreting events of an earlier period in the light of his own experience? When Nero died and Galba at first succeeded him, it was the Rhine legions who rose against Galba and marched on Rome (see Chapter 7), thus precipitating the course of events which led to the revelation of the secret that 'emperors could be made elsewhere than at Rome'. Thereafter, every emperor knew that he had to watch the Rhine legions and their commander. In 97 civil war was averted only by Nerva's decision to adopt as his successor the then commander of these legions, Trajan (page 185). Little wonder if Tacitus credits Tiberius with similar apprehensions. Suetonius and Dio support Tacitus, and there is no doubt of Germanicus's enormous popularity. Moreover, both the Illyrian legions and those of Lower Germany mutinied for better conditions when they heard of Augustus's death. But the army felt a great personal loyalty to Tiberius, and the older soldiers had served under his personal command, although the Rhine legions were admittedly diluted by 'a mass of recent slave-bred recruits from the city' (*Annals* i.31, referring to the men hastily recruited in the panic of AD 9, page 81). Even if Germanicus were tempted to disloyalty, however, the legions of Upper Germany were not involved in the mutiny, while Tiberius's own son, Drusus, who was with the legions of Illyricum, could hardly be expected to stand aside and watch Germanicus try to seize power. Tacitus is surely guilty of exaggeration, if nothing more; but his version enables him to praise his hero, Germanicus, for loyalty to a man who Tacitus says hated him.

Tacitus, that unmilitary man, clearly expects us to admire his hero's handling of the mutiny. In fact, any soldier must find Germanicus weak, theatrical and incompetent. Drusus did better in Illyricum, but it does not suit Tacitus to say so. The mutineers show admirable trade-union solidarity, organising a workers cooperative (*Annals* i.32, 'neither tribune nor camp prefect any longer had authority; patrols, sentries, and whatever else military order required were organised by the men themselves'), and sending a flying picket to bring out their brethren of the Upper Rhine army (i.36). Tacitus seems to want to show them as good men on the whole, apart from the new recruits whom welfare handouts at Rome had corrupted, led astray by irresponsible and even deliberately lying agitators like the inflammatory Vibulenus who tried to get the legate in Illyricum lynched for having ordered the murder of Vibulenus's brother, who proved never to have existed (*Annals* i.22–3).

While the mutinies were taking place in Illyricum and Germany, 'not for any new reasons, except that the change of emperor offered a chance for mob action and hope of profit from civil war' (*Annals* i.16), Tiberius was settling into Augustus's place at Rome. Again our main source is Tacitus, again Tacitus's own sympathies colour his whole presentation. The first meeting of the Senate convened by Tiberius heard Augustus's will and discussed arrangements for the funeral. Among those remembered in the will were the leading senators; Tacitus sneers that Augustus really hated most of them and was leaving them money out of ostentation and a craving for posthumous popularity. Some of the honours proposed struck Tiberius as excessive, for instance the proposal that the body should be carried on the shoulders of senators; Tiberius 'excused them, with arrogant restraint' (*Annals* i.8). Poor Tiberius can do nothing right.

After the funeral Augustus was declared a god. Then everyone turned to Tiberius, who addressed the Senate, contrasting the greatness of the Empire with his own unworthiness:

> Only the deified Augustus had an intellect capable of such a burden. He himself, when asked by Augustus to take on a share of the responsibilities, had learned by experience how hard and how chancy was the task of ruling the whole Empire. Besides, in a state able to rely on so many distinguished men everything should not be entrusted to a single person: a group could more easily carry out the duties of government by pooling their efforts. (*Annals* i.11)

At the same meeting Tiberius also had read out a report in Augustus's own hand on the financial and military state of the Empire, to which Augustus had added 'the advice to keep the Empire within its present limits.' This reading of the report may have been intended to prove the point that the scope of activities was now so vast that wider delegation of power was desirable. Tiberius specifically said that 'although he was not equal to the whole responsibility for public affairs, he would accept any part that might be entrusted to him'.

The Senate continued to urge him to take on the whole, to 'succeed to his father's position' (*statio*), as Velleius puts it (ii.24). Tacitus and Suetonius both record expressions of senatorial impatience, which Tiberius took amiss. Tempers were getting frayed. Finally Tiberius gave way: 'he saw that whatever he did not undertake would be ruined' (Velleius ii.24); 'as though against his will, and complaining that a wretched burden of slavery was being imposed on him, he accepted the Empire, but in such a way as to leave open the hope that he would one day lay it down – his actual words were, 'Until I reach the time when it may seem right to you to grant some rest to my old age' (Suetonius, *Tiberius* 24). He was now two months off his fifty-fifth birthday.

For Tacitus, the whole debate was a farce, and Tiberius a hypocrite, marking down for later destruction those who took him at his word. But Tiberius might legitimately shrink from taking on so enormous a burden. He knew that he lacked Augustus's affability and skill at managing people, and he was naturally suspicious and afraid of plots against him. He had led a strenuous life, with many years away from Rome, in exile at Rhodes or on campaign. He was a good soldier, liked by his men, and presumably happy in that role, but he had never had to bear the supreme responsibility before, and may have felt ill-at-ease in the political intrigues of the court and the Senate. He inherited the austere code of a great Roman noble, which, unlike Augustus, he was by birth. Like that humbler Roman officer, the centurion in the gospel, he had always been 'a man set under authority'; he had done what he thought his duty, and Augustus, required of him. If he now felt unequal to sole power, the sequel proved him right.

Much of Tacitus's account of the first three years of Tiberius's reign is devoted to events in Germany, where Germanicus, having settled the mutiny, conducted campaigns across the Rhine each year. Tacitus himself says that they were merely intended to restore Roman prestige, and not to lead to any accretion of territory (*Annals* i.3), and the archaeological evidence seems to support this interpretation, since the key base at Haltern was not reoccupied. It is hard to escape the conclusion that Tacitus's purpose in giving these campaigns so much emphasis is to build up his tragic hero, Germanicus. Where Tacitus in these years does discuss affairs at Rome, Tiberius is seen behaving with sense and moderation. Dio concurs.

At the end of the campaigns of 16, Germanicus was recalled to celebrate a triumph. He asked for another year in Germany 'to finish what had been begun' (*Annals* ii.26). Since he was still fighting the same tribes in 16 as he had been in 14, and nothing suggests that he had made any real progress in the meantime, either Germanicus or Tacitus is being over-optimistic. There is no reason to think that another year would have brought the Germans to submission. Germanicus had achieved two bloody massacres of unarmed tribesmen. Twice his own army had come close to disaster. One pitched battle, at Idistaviso on the Weser, had been a great Roman victory. Germanicus showed himself given to theatrical gestures, nauseatingly self-satisfied (cf. *Annals* ii.13), and insensitive to Tiberius's susceptibilities. His ambitious wife Agrippina, daughter of Agrippa and of Augustus's daughter Julia, cultivated popularity with the army and paraded their little son, the future emperor Gaius, in miniature uniform, whence his nickname, Caligula, 'Bootikins'. Again, Tacitus seems to think that everything he relates is to Germanicus's credit. A reader who tries to see things from Tiberius's side, and who is attuned to military matters, will find Tacitus a damning witness against his hero.

The best of the Roman generals comes out as the veteran Caecina.

Germanicus returned, unwillingly, to a splendid triumph (16 May 17), and was promptly sent out to the east with *maius imperium*. Armenia needed attention again, the Parthians having expelled the king appointed by Rome. In any case, it was clearly desirable for the heir to the throne to get to know the eastern provinces, and to be known there. Tiberius would surely not have sent him if he distrusted his loyalty, but he had more reason to distrust his judgement. So he appointed a new governor of Syria, Gnaeus Calpurnius Piso, consul with Tiberius as long ago as 7 BC, to advise and restrain Germanicus, and no doubt to report on him independently to Tiberius. Germanicus and Piso quarrelled. Germanicus illegally visited Egypt without Tiberius's permission, which was needed by any senator, and there issued a typically smug and pompous edict (*Select Papyri* 211 = *LR* p.562). Returning to Syria, he ordered Piso to leave. Soon after, Germanicus died, accusing Piso of having poisoned him. Agrippina dramatically conveyed the ashes to Rome. Piso re-entered Syria by force, but was expelled by the new acting governor.

Germanicus's ashes were received at Rome with passionate demonstrations of grief. Tiberius offended by his characteristic moderation. Tacitus naturally puts the worst possible construction on it. Piso was tried before the Senate, with Tiberius urging respect for correct procedures and a decision on the evidence presented. Piso cleared himself of the poisoning charge to the satisfaction even of Tacitus, but Tiberius pressed for conviction on the charge of having made war on the province. This would seem to have been unanswerable. Piso anticipated the verdict by committing suicide. The result satisfied few people. Most seem to have gone on talking as if Germanicus had been poisoned, despite the evidence. Piso's wife was also acquitted on the poisoning charge; Tacitus attributes this, unreasonably, not to lack of evidence, but to her friendship with Livia. Tiberius appears to have behaved rather well, but he got no credit for it.

Tiberius's own son Drusus was now next in line for the succession. He had done well in the mutiny in Illyricum, but had a reputation for violence, cruelty and drunkenness. Germanicus's death did not affect Tiberius's way of governing, which earned praise even from Tacitus at this period; indeed Tacitus makes him sound like the perfect constitutional monarch:

> To begin with, public business and the most important private business was carried out in the Senate, and its leading men were allowed to debate, and anyone who slipped into flattery was restrained by the emperor himself. In conferring office, he took account of the family's nobility, military distinction and eminence in civil life, so that it was generally agreed that no better appointments could have been made. The consuls and praetors maintained their prestige. The lesser magistracies too still had their authority. The laws, if one leaves out the treason court, were judiciously enforced. Grain levies, indirect taxes and other public revenues were managed by associations of Roman knights. His own affairs the emperor entrusted to the most competent people, some of whom he knew by reputation only, and once they were engaged they were kept on indefinitely, most of them growing old in the same jobs. The ordinary people were oppressed by high grain prices, but the emperor cannot be blamed for that. He did all that he could to combat bad harvests and difficulties of navigation, sparing neither expense nor effort. He took steps to see that the provinces were not harassed by new burdens, and that the old ones which they had to bear were not aggravated by the greed or cruelty of officials. Beatings and confiscations did not occur. Few were his estates in Italy, his slaves respectful, his household limited to a few freedmen. And if he had disputes with private citizens, they were settled in the lawcourts. (*Annals* iv.6)

In 23, Drusus died. Nobody at the time suspected foul

play. Tacitus specifically states that this marked the end of Tiberius's good government, and then promptly contradicts himself by saying that Tiberius found distraction in attention to public affairs (iv.13), and gives examples, for instance Tiberius's insistence later in 23 that the Senate hear a case brought by the people of Asia against Tiberius's own financial agent in the province (iv.15). In 26 Tiberius left Rome for good to live on the island of Capri. It was 'a plan long considered and several times deferred' (iv.57). Tacitus is inclined to attribute it to the influence of Sejanus, the praetorian prefect; but he notes also the rumour that Tiberius wanted to escape his mother's interference, a story repeated with much dramatic detail by Suetonius (*Tiberius* 51). Other alleged motives include over-sensitiveness to his appearance (in old age he had become scrawny, bent, bald, and disfigured by a skin disease which covered his face with sores and plasters), and a wish to indulge secretly in cruelty and lust. Apart from Sejanus, his only companions (certainly not chosen to pander to cruelty and lust) were a distinguished jurist of consular rank, a knight known for his literary interests, and scholars and literary men, mostly Greeks, 'whose conversation cheered Tiberius up' (*Annals* iv.58).

Nothing in Tacitus's own narrative justifies the belief that Tiberius's administration had degenerated over the three years since Drusus's death, although it is a gloomy account, full of trials in the Senate, deaths of eminent men and growing dissension in the imperial house. Tacitus has a long complaint about how dull the period is: 'peace was unbroken or scarcely troubled, affairs at Rome depressing, and the emperor not interested in extending the Empire', so that Tacitus has no heroic stories to 'interest and stimulate' his readers, but 'cruel orders, continual accusations, treacherous friendships, the ruin of the innocent, causes and consequences the same, the monotony and tedium readily apparent' (iv.32–3). In fact he records over twenty legal cases in these three years, roughly a third of which end in acquittal. Some of the others are in the normal course of justice: extortion, judicial corruption, perjury, wife-murder. In one case, a husband and wife (Gaius

Silius and Sosia Galla), who Tacitus says were undoubtedly guilty of extortion, were instead prosecuted for treason (*maiestas*), which seems evidence of a tendency attested in other cases unduly to extend the scope of the treason law. The worst example of this was in the trial of Aulus Cremutius Cordus, accused at Sejanus's instigation of having praised Brutus in a published historical work and of having called Cassius 'the last of the Romans' (iv.34). Crematius committed suicide and the Senate ordered his books to be burnt. If Tiberius can be blamed for not intervening, the Senate's complicity is clear, and it is interesting to note that in two trials Gaius Asinius Gallus, elsewhere described as a personal enemy of Tiberius, argues for a harsher penalty than Tiberius's close associate or Tiberius himself (iv.20, 30).

Apart from the trials of prominent Romans, various administrative measures are recorded during these years, affecting public order at Rome, the state religion or (the most numerous category) the affairs of provincial communities. In every case Tiberius appears to good advantage. Delegates from Spain arrive seeking permission to erect a temple to Tiberius and Livia. Tiberius refuses, saying that he is 'a mortal man performing human tasks and content with first place among men.' He kept up this attitude even in private conversation. One might have expected Tacitus to approve. Not a bit of it: 'Some people thought it [Tiberius's attitude] a sign of degeneracy'. He was not setting himself high standards: 'contempt for fame is contempt for virtue' (*Annals* iv.37–8; the final phrase, *contemptu famae contemni virtutes,* is typical of Tacitus, succinct, memorable, dismissive – and the narrative swiftly goes on to something else, leaving the victim of the epigram pinned to the board).

The death of Drusus had intensified the rivalries within the imperial house. Who was now to succeed Tiberius? Germanicus had left three sons, and his widow, Agrippina, was an imperious character. By traditional Republican standards, she was a parvenue beside the noble Claudii, but she was Augustus's granddaughter, and so thought herself superior to the Claudii, not only to the late Drusus and his widow Livia

Julia, generally known as Livilla, but to Tiberius himself. She advertised her merits and her grievances incessantly. Sejanus warned Tiberius that she was forming her own party of supporters, and invoked the spectre of civil war (*Annals* iv.17). Her behaviour lent credence to the charge. When she came to Tiberius with a complaint and found him sacrificing to the divine Augustus, she burst out that 'his divine spirit had not passed over into dumb statues; she herself was his true image, born of his heavenly blood' – which moved Tiberius to take her hand and quote to her a line of Greek poetry, asking 'Do you think a wrong is done you because you do not reign?' (*Annals* iv.52; Suetonius, *Tiberius* 53). She asked for another husband, or so her daughter's memoirs said (page 37), one who 'would welcome Germanicus's wife and children', and publicly demonstrated her suspicion that Tiberius was trying to poison her. Tiberius felt it would be safer to let her stay unmarried.

Livilla for her part hoped to marry Sejanus, who was already her lover. Sejanus actually wrote to Tiberius for her hand, which Tiberius refused, partly on the grounds that this would intensify Agrippina's hostility and make the family divisions irreparable. Livilla's twin sons by Drusus were only three years old when their father died, and one of them died shortly after. The survivor, Tiberius Gemellus, was seven years younger than even the youngest of Agrippina's three sons, the future emperor Gaius (Caligula), while Gaius's two elder brothers had already entered public life and were commended to the Senate by Tiberius on Drusus's death in terms that clearly marked them out as potential successors. Agrippina also had three daughters, who could be relied upon to make influential marriages. Her position seemed secure. Nobody could have foreseen that Gaius's two elder brothers were in fact to die in prison; Agrippina committed suicide; Livilla, charged with Drusus's murder, committed suicide or was put to death; Gaius as emperor killed Gemellus. One can make all possible allowance for scandal and exaggeration; the reality is stark enough. The ruling family had not come to terms with its power and its members' ambitions.

Although Sejanus is credited with stirring up hostility and suspicion against Agrippina, her own actions were, as we have seen, imprudent. Livia strongly disliked her, and had a natural preference for her own granddaughter, Livilla. But Livia's relations with Tiberius were also strained. She was said to keep harping on how much Tiberius owed to her influence with Augustus (*Annals* iv.57), and Tiberius had repeatedly to warn her 'to keep out of important affairs that were not a woman's business' (Suetonius, *Tiberius* 50), a phrase that has the true ring of the old-fashioned, slow-moving, unbending Tiberius. Their relationship degenerated to the point where they met only once in three years after Tiberius retired to Capri, before Livia died in 29. It is not surprising that Tiberius wanted to get out of this happy family circle, nor that he should have turned so much for advice to someone outside the family, namely, Sejanus.

Tacitus consistently depicts Sejanus as the evil genius of the imperial house, single-minded and long-sighted in his ambition. He was Seius Strabo's son, a knight from Volsinii in Etruria (page 94). Tacitus sneers at Livilla for disgracing her noble family by taking 'a small-town lover' (*Annals* iv.3), where the sting is in the 'small-town'. But Sejanus's father was successively praetorian prefect and prefect of Egypt; his mother's sister was Terentia, wife of Maecenas, Sejanus himself was adopted by Aelius Gallus, a former prefect of Egypt, and had brothers, cousins and an uncle of consular rank (Velleius. ii.127). With his ability and connections, he could have made a successful senatorial career himself. That he chose not to do so suggests that he found more scope for his energies and ambitions in an equestrian career. His father was already praetorian prefect when Augustus died. The son was appointed co-prefect, to take over as sole prefect when Seius Strabo was promoted to Egypt. He subsequently enhanced his power by concentrating all the praetorian cohorts in a single camp on the edge of Rome, whereas Augustus had never allowed more than three cohorts in Rome together, with no regular camp, the other cohorts being billetted in neighbouring towns (Suetonius, *Augustus* 49). He made himself indispensible to Tiberius, largely by his efficiency and capacity for work, so that Tiberius referred to him as 'my partner in toil' (*Annals* iv.2). Drusus was jealous, and their mutual ill-feeling brought them, quite literally, to blows.

Drusus had shown great competence when sent to suppress the mutiny of the Illyrian legions in 14 (on which occasion he had Sejanus on his staff); and when he held the consulship with his father (21) and was left to handle things alone at Rome when Tiberius retired to Campania for his health early in the year, he again showed good sense and earned good opinions. Although he had two sons himself, he was 'friendly, or certainly not hostile' to Germanicus's boys (*Annals* iv.4). Tiberius took pleasure in having him as colleague in the consulship (*Annals* iii.31), and appears to have been distressed by his death. But Drusus was not the efficient and indefatigable 'partner in toil' that Sejanus was.

Tiberius's retirement to Capri in 26 vastly strengthened Sejanus's position. As Sejanus had foreseen, 'he himself would control access [to Tiberius], and would to a large extent control his correspondence also, since it would be carried by soldiers; gradually the emperor, as old age grew apace, would be softened by the seclusion of the place and would more readily delegate the duties of his office' (*Annals* iv.41). So it turned out. For five years Sejanus had things all his own way. The Senate resorted to outrageous flattery. The death of Livia in 29 removed a moderating influence; perhaps significantly, it was followed almost immediately by the denunciation of Agrippina and her eldest son, who were declared public enemies. Livia had disliked her grandson's wife, Agrippina, but the children were her own great-grandchildren, and she would have stood by the family in a crisis. The next year Agrippina's second son (another Drusus) was also imprisoned; the third son, Gaius (Caligula), was summoned to Capri. Sejanus was to be consul for 31 with Tiberius, which forced him to return to Rome, leaving Tiberius on Capri. He now received the proconsular *imperium*. In May, when he and Tiberius both resigned the consulship in favour of suffects, as had now become the regular practice, he was still confidently expecting the crucial grant of tribunician power. But in fact Tiberius's suspicions had been awakened, partly at least by a letter from his sister-in-law Antonia, the widow of his brother Drusus and the grandmother of Agrippina's children. Tiberius's despatches from Capri grew increasingly enigmatic: 'at one moment he would warmly praise Sejanus and at the next warmly denounce him' (Dio lvii.6). He was testing the wind. Finally, two letters arrived in Rome simultaneously, carried by Sutorius Macro, former prefect of the *vigiles*, the Roman fire-brigade. One, 'wordy and ample,' was given to the consuls to be read to the Senate at its meeting of 18 October. Sejanus had been led to believe that it contained his tribunician power. In fact, it was his death warrant.

The other letter contained Macro's commission to replace him as praetorian prefect and the promise of a donative to the praetorians. While Tiberius's rambling letter was being read in the Senate, Macro had had time to put a guard of *vigiles* on the building where the Senate was meeting, and to hurry to the praetorian barracks to take command. When the unexpected denunciation of Sejanus came at the end of the letter, nobody raised a finger to save him. He was arrested on the spot, condemned to death that afternoon, and executed immediately. His body lay exposed for three days while a mob tore down his statues and lynched his agents. His children were put to death (page 278). His supporters turned on one another in their haste to disassociate themselves from him. Many were tried and condemned. Even two years later Tiberius ordered a mass execution of 'all those who were being held in prison accused of association with Sejanus' (*Annals* vi.19).

Sometime before Sejanus's fall, but when Tiberius already suspected him, Agrippina's oldest son had been put to death. Not until 33 was his brother Drusus killed. Their mother then committed suicide. The next years saw more trials and executions, with Macro proving as ruthless in eliminating opposition as Sejanus had been. Attempts have been made to exonerate Tiberius, or at least to suggest that Tacitus exaggerates. Perhaps he does. And it is easy to forget when reading him that the circle affected by the executions and suicides was relatively limited. But two things are clear and indisputable: the demoralization of the senatorial class, collectively and for the most part individually; and the fact that whenever Tiberius made his wishes clear, for leniency or the reverse, he was obeyed. In theory, he could have stopped the denunciations and the useless deaths; in practice, of course, isolated, scared, increasingly cynical, he lacked the will to do so. Both Suetonius and Tacitus quote the opening of a letter to the Senate which seems to have impressed both of them as showing him at the end of his tether: 'What I shall write to you, fathers, or how I shall write, or what I shall not write at all at the present time, may the gods and goddesses afflict me worse than I feel myself suffer every day, if I know' (Suetonius, *Tiberius* 67; Tacitus, *Annals* vi.6).

He died unmourned on 16 March 37. His personality continues to puzzle historians, because Tacitus made it into an enigma. No other emperor, apart from Augustus, has been so much written about. Yet his reign is not notable for innovation. As to his death, rumour alleged, probably without foundation, that he was poisoned or smothered with a pillow. He had made Caligula and Tiberius Gemellus joint heirs, but the Senate voided the will, alleging that Tiberius had been of unsound mind when he made it, and handed everything over to Caligula, who underlined Gemellus's youth and inferior position by adopting him and giving him the honorary title, appropriate to a youngster, of *princeps iuventutis*. He was to have no legacy and no share in the Empire; within a year he had been murdered. Caligula's accession to sole power had been carefully stage-managed by Macro. In any case, Caligula, as Germanicus's last surviving son, was 'the emperor most desired by the majority of the provincials and soldiers, many of whom had known him as a child, as well as by the whole citizen body at Rome because of his father Germanicus's memory and their pity for a family that was almost wiped out' (Suetonius, *Caligula* 13). He set out to increase this popularity by a shrewd mixture of theatrical gestures and sound practical measures. Even his extravagances, his parties, shows and circuses, endeared him to the people who had been starved of such things under Tiberius; but, ominously, in less than a year he ran through the entire fortune of 2700 million sesterces which Tiberius had left, and more besides (Suetonius, *Caligula* 37).

Suetonius devotes only 9 chapters of his biography to 'Gaius as emperor', 39 to 'Gaius as monster' (*Caligula* 22). Tacitus's account is lost. Caligula had never been a paragon of virtue. He was caught in incest with his sister Drusilla while still in his teens, and on Capri is said to have combined the utmost obsequiousness towards Tiberius and his household with delight in watching tortures and executions, and in feastings, adultery, dancing and singing. Within a month and a half of his accession he brought about the death of his grandmother Antonia. A serious illness later in the year is generally thought to have affected his reason, and some contemporaries thought so, but there is no evidence that he was much better even before the illness, and his increasingly erratic and tyrannical behaviour afterwards may be due only to a wider realization of just what the emperor could get away with. Drusilla's death the year after (38) removed the one person who probably did have real influence over him. In the autumn of that year, Macro was made to kill himself and many of his supporters executed. Shortage of money led to other indiscriminate executions and confiscations. Caligula showed little interest in the administration of the Empire, and the impact of his disordered personality was largely confined to Rome. On the other hand, his increasing conviction of his own divinity set him against the Jews, who refused to recognize it. This led to anti-Jewish outbreaks in Alexandria and elsewhere in the East, and we have the record of an embassy which the Alexandrian Jews sent to Caligula asking to be excused from worshipping him. This document, Philo's *Embassy to Gaius,* gives a vivid picture both of Caligula as tyrant, and of the endemic violence between religious communities in the East, just as if it were Lebanon in the 1980s. Philo charitably dismisses Egyptians as 'a worthless breed whose souls were infected with the poison and bad temper of their native crocodiles and asps' (*Embassy to Gaius* 26). On the Greeks at Jamnia in Judaea, who have 'wormed themselves into the town', he comments that they did in fact build an altar to Caligula, but 'of the most shoddy material, sun-dried brick', and with the sole intention of provoking the Jews to tear it down, so as to get them into trouble (ibid. 30).

In the autumn of 39 there were farcical operations on the Rhine, for which Caligula was saluted as *imperator* seven times, and next spring a projected operation to Britain, never carried out. By now Caligula was losing no opportunity to terrorize and humiliate the Senate. He also upset the urban populace by new taxes, and made the palace freedmen and the officers of the praetorian guard afraid for their own safety. On 24 January 41, he was killed in a well-planned ambush, and his uncle Claudius, found hiding behind a curtain, was rushed off to the praetorian barracks and proclaimed emperor. The Senate debated, some senators invoking the catchword 'liberty' (page 13), but they could not agree what to do, there was a popular demonstration in Claudius's favour, and the Senate accepted the praetorians' *fait accompli*. Claudius began by executing Caligula's murderers, but recalled Caligula's exiles, restored confiscated property and abolished the new taxes. This too was a sort of liberty, and coins duly proclaimed LIBERTAS AUGUSTA.

Claudius was of course Germanicus's younger brother, now fifty, who had been carefully excluded from public life because of physical disabilities and disconcerting eccentricities. Almost predictably, the literary tradition emphasizes his oddities and depicts him as a slave to gluttony and lust, wholly under the thumb of his freedmen and his successive wives, to whose influence Suetonius attributes the execution of thirty-five senators and over three hundred knights (*Claudius* 9). His relations with the Senate were often tense and he had to deal with several conspiracies, the most dangerous being that in 42 led by Lucius Arruntius Camillus

Scribonianus, governor of Dalmatia and a descendant of Pompey, who was however killed by his own troops. There were more plots in 46 and 47, and in 48 a mysterious affair involving Claudius's third wife Messalina, who actually went through a form of marriage in public with the consul Gaius Silius. Silius is said to have planned to murder Claudius, adopt his son Britannicus, and presumably rule through him. The story of the marriage ceremony, says Tacitus, 'reads like a novel', but he specifically vouches for the truth of it (*Annals* xi.26–7).

Claudius inherited a war in the client kingdom of Mauretania, where Gaius had put to death the last king, Ptolemy, grandson of Antony and Cleopatra, 'king, ally, and friend of the Roman people' for his help in suppressing Tacfarinas's revolt (page 162). It was quickly settled and Mauretania reorganized as two provinces with capitals at Iol-Caesarea (Cherchel), 100 km west of Algiers, and Tingis (Tangiers). Claudius returned a moderate and judicious reply to another embassy from Alexandria (*Select Papyri* 212 = *LR* p.366). Various changes were made in the eastern provinces and client kingdoms, notably in Judaea, which Claudius first added to the kingdom, consisting of Galilee and southern Lebanon, ruled by Herod's grandson, Marcus Julius Agrippa (the Herod Agrippa of *Acts* 12), and then on his death in 44 made it into a province again. Agrippa, like his grandfather was a notable builder, specially favouring the Roman colony of Beirut, which he presented with a theatre, amphitheatre, baths and porticoes, celebrating the opening of the amphitheatre with a show in which 700 pairs of gladiators fought (Josephus, *Jewish Antiquities* xix.335–7). It was Julius Agrippa's daughter Berenice who became Titus's mistress (page 180). There was also Roman intervention in Armenia and in the Bosporus kingdom in south Russia, and in the West fighting on the Rhine, in which Gnaeus Domitius Corbulo, later the best of Nero's generals, distinguished himself. But the major initiative was the invasion of Britain.

Southeast England had submitted to Julius Caesar, and although the Romans had never exercised effective control,

they could claim that it belonged to them. Britain also carried
the glamour of being outside the known world (page 25).
Claudius and his advisers realised how necessary it was for
him to acquire military prestige. Where better than Britain?
The invasion force comprised four legions with Aulus
Plautius in command. It fought its way to a Thames crossing
near London, waited for Claudius to arrive, bringing elephants, and then advanced to capture the main centre of
opposition, Camulodunum (Colchester), capital of the
Trinovantes, the dominant tribe of the southeast, whose chief
Caratacus fled westwards to continue the fight. Neighbouring
tribes which had chafed under Trinovantian domination, the
Iceni in what is now Norfolk and the people in the Sussex
region, submitted and their chiefs were allowed to stay on
as Roman clients. Cogidubnus, whose Roman-style palace
has been excavated at Fishbourne, near Chichester, was
honoured with the title 'king and legate of Augustus,' whence
his people were called Regni or Regnenses, probably to be
explained as 'those of the kingdom (*regnum*)'; rather than as
coming from some Celtic root.

Claudius himself spent only sixteen days in Britain and
then 'hastened back to Rome, sending ahead the news of his
victory' (Dio lx.22). The Senate voted him a triumph and an
arch erected later in his reign recorded that it was 'because he
received the surrender of eleven kings of Britain conquered
without any loss and because he was the first to subject to the
sovereignty of the Roman people barbarian tribes across the
ocean' (*ILS* 216 = *LR* p.113). Triumphal insignia were
distributed to Claudius's staff with a generous hand. All had
been stage-managed to give Claudius his triumph with a
minimum of risk and effort on his part. He also acquired the
name Britannicus, which he did not use, but gave to his son.

The army advanced in three columns, northwards towards
Lincoln, northwest across the Midlands, and southwest
through Hampshire and Dorset. The third of these columns
was under the future emperor Vespasian. It saw hard fighting,
and among the native strongholds which it captured were two
which have since been the sites of notable excavations,

Maiden Castle and Hod Hill. By the time Aulus Plautius handed over the new Province to his successor, Publius Ostorius Scapula, in 47, the Roman advance had taken them right across the lowland area to the line of the Fosse Way, which Ostorius laid out from Exeter (Isca Dumnoniorum) to Lincoln (Lindum), thus providing lateral communication along the line of advance. Caratacus was then driven out of South Wales, where he was inspiring resistance among the Silures, and took refuge with the Brigantes of Yorkshire and Lancashire, whose queen Cartimandua handed him over to the Romans (51).

It will be convenient to follow through this account of operations in Britain to the end of Nero's reign. After a period of consolidation, during which Roman merchants established themselves in considerable numbers at St Albans (Verulamium) and London (Londinium), apart from the veteran colony at Colchester, the next major advance was undertaken in 59 by Suetonius Paulinus through North Wales towards Anglesey, a Druid stronghold, where the excavation of the dried-up lake, Llyn Cerrig Bach, has produced evidence for the extent of trade or exchange relations in the Celtic world at this period. In 60 or 61, however, Prasutagus, king of the Iceni, died, and the Romans decided to incorporate his kingdom in the Roman province. When his queen Boudicca protested, Roman troops flogged her and raped her daughters. Boudicca raised the tribe in revolt. Joined by the Trinovantes, they sacked Colchester, defeated the 9th Legion which marched down from Lincoln to oppose them, while Suetonius Paulinus marching back from Anglesey found himself unable to save London and St Albans, the 2nd Legion which he had summoned from its base at Gloucester failed to arrive (its acting commander later killed himself), and 70,000 Romans are said to have been massacred in the three towns. Suetonius, however, then brought the British tribesmen to battle somewhere in the Midlands, totally defeating them. One cause of the revolt was British indebtedness to Roman moneylenders, Seneca among the foremost. Punitive measures by Suetonius were so severe that the imperial procurator, responsible for the finances of the province, protested to Rome, and Suetonius was recalled. There followed a period of peace until after Vespasian's accession (page 175). The garrison was reduced to three legions in 67 when the 14th was withdrawn for service in the East.

Claudius's reign was marked by solid achievements, and the inscriptions and papyri give a more favourable impression of his personal contribution than the literary tradition. His dependence on his wives and freedmen is probably exaggerated, even if their influence increased in his last years. It is probable that his third wife Messalina systematically deceived him and used her position to destroy those she disliked. Claudius was also unfaithful to her. When she was put to death after her 'marriage' to Silius in 48, Claudius married his niece Agrippina, daughter of Germanicus and *his* wife Agrippina. Suetonius says that he was motivated by sexual attraction, but Agrippina also had a son, the future emperor Nero, by her former marriage to Gnaeus Domitius Ahenobarbus (page 73). Nero was older than Claudius's only surviving son, Britannicus, and would inevitably have been a rival for the succession when Claudius died. It was like Caligula and Tiberius Gemellus over again; in three successive generations, starting with Germanicus and Tiberius's son Drusus, there had been two likely candidates for the succession, and in each case the actual son or grandson of the reigning emperor was the younger of the two. Claudius may have realised, or been advised, that he should either marry Agrippina and adopt her son, thus giving him precedence over Britannicus, or have them killed. He chose the former alternative. The two most powerful freedmen Narcissus and Pallas, were split, one against the marriage, the other for it. Claudius can at least be credited with deciding for himself between their conflicting advice.

But there is other evidence that he played a greater role in policy-making than the tradition gives him credit for. One of the most striking initiatives was the Senate's decision in 48 to admit to membership men from the Gallic provinces, apart

from Gallia Narbonensis, which already enjoyed this
privilege. Tacitus tells us that the decision followed
Claudius's personal intervention, and gives us what purports
to be his speech (*Annals* xi.24). A bronze plaque from Lyon,
discovered in 1528, preserves a large part of Claudius's
actual text (*ILS* 212 = *LR* p.133). The crabbed style, the
sudden irrelevant digressions, the clumsy breaking-off in the
middle when Claudius suddenly addresses himself – 'The
time has now come, Tiberius Caesar Germanicus, for you to
reveal to the members of the Senate where your speech is
leading to', and we can imagine the senators inwardly
thinking, 'At last!' – all is so typical of the peculiarities which
the tradition attributes to Claudius that we seem to have
Claudius's own words, and so probably his own policy. Were
he just a mouthpiece for others, we should expect them at
least to draft his speeches.

Other incidents also show Claudius's personal involvement
in government. For instance, among the steps he took to
improve the all-important supply of grain (see Chapter 3, page
60) was the building of a new harbour to supplement that at
Ostia:

> Although virtually all the grain used by the Romans was
> imported, the region near the mouth of the Tiber had no
> safe landing places or suitable harbours ... This being the
> case, Claudius undertook to construct a harbour, and
> would not be deterred even when the architects, when he
> asked what it would cost, answered, 'You don't want to do
> that,' because they so fully expected the huge expenditures
> necessary would deter him, if he learned the cost
> beforehand. But he conceived this undertaking worthy of
> the dignity and greatness of Rome, and carried it through.
> (Dio lx.11)

Claudius adopted other measures to improve the grain
supply, including government insurance for winter sailings.
He also replaced the *quaestor Ostiensis* by an imperial
procurator portus Ostiensis, while the senatorial prefects in

charge of grain distribution probably ceded practical responsibility to the emperor's *praefectus annonae*. Distribution was reorganized and centralized at the Porticus Minucia, under the supervision of an imperial freedman. Later evidence shows how the system developed (page 250). All of these measures no doubt contributed to greater efficiency, but they also encroached further on the position of the Senate. In this they were typical of what is perhaps the most far-reaching development of Claudius's reign, the establishment of what, in modern terms, formed a cabinet of ministers in charge of the great departments of government, outside the Senate and responsible only to the emperor, whereas the administrative responsibilities which Augustus had taken away from the Senate or from individual magistrates had at least been delegated to senators (see Chapter 3).

Paradoxically, Claudius seems genuinely to have wanted to collaborate with the Senate as Augustus had done. Several measures aimed at restoring its outward dignity after the open degradation it had suffered under Caligula. He urged senators to show more independence in debates. But he also, like Augustus, found it more efficient to work through permanent non-senatorial officials than through senatorial magistrates. His chief ministers were four freedmen: Narcissus, in charge of all official correspondence (*praepositus ab epistulis*); Pallas, in charge of the imperial finances (*a rationibus*); Callistus, responsible for petitions to the emperor (*a libellis*) and probably also for legal matters (*a cognitionibus*); and Polybius, librarian and archivist (*a studiis*). Narcissus and Pallas in particular 'he willingly permitted to be honoured by a decree of the Senate not only with huge financial rewards but even with the insignia of quaestors and praetors; and he also allowed them to acquire such wealth legally and illegally that one day when he was complaining of shortage of funds, someone answered quite wittily that he would have plenty if his two freedmen made him a partner' (Suetonius, *Claudius* 28). Narcissus is credited with a fortune of over 400 million sesterces, the largest private fortune recorded (Dio lxi,34).

Claudius reorganized the finances of the state and of the imperial possessions. The *procurator patrimonii* reported to Pallas and had under him imperial procurators in all provinces, even senatorial ones; from 53 onwards they exercised financial jurisdiction independently of the proconsul. The administration of the public treasury, the *aerarium Saturni,* was transferred to quaestors whom Claudius himself appointed. By the end of the next century, the distinction between the emperor's funds, the *fiscus,* and the public *aerarium* becomes negligible. A special procurator controlled the tax on legacies, and there were other encroachments on senatorial authority, for instance in connection with the grain supply already mentioned, in taking care of the roads in Rome, and above all in the institution of trials before the emperor and his advisors (*intra cubiculum*) instead of before the Senate. Such trials speeded up the administration of justice, but were, or appeared to be, more open to bias and corruption, and the Senate disliked them. Other legal measures show Claudius genuinely interested in the law, and responsible for developments tending to greater humanity as well as greater efficiency. Nor does this exhaust the record of Claudius's activities: we might also notice his programme of public works, particularly on the Roman aqueducts, for which there is copious epigraphic evidence, and his measures to strengthen traditional state religion.

In Claudius's last years, his fourth and last wife Agrippina achieved extraordinary prominence. Claudius adopted her son early in 50; he took the name Nero Claudius Drusus Germanicus Caesar, though his new stepbrother Britannicus continued to call him, to his great annoyance, Ahenobarbus. Agrippina received embassies and appeared at public ceremonies in a way that no previous empress had done. She manoeuvred men loyal to her and to her son into key positions, in particular Afranius Burrus to be praetorian prefect. Nero came of age in 51, was named *princeps inventutis,* next year became prefect of the city (*praefectus urbi*), and the year after entered the Senate and married Octavia, Claudius's daughter by Messalina and Britannicus's sister. If Claudius died, Nero's succession was assured. If Claudius lived longer, something might go wrong. Accordingly, on 13 October 54, Agrippina had him poisoned. There were different versions of how it was done, but little doubt that mushrooms came into it. Tacitus talks of 'poison poured over a delicious mushroom' (*Annals* xii.67), Suetonius of 'a doctored mushroom' (*Claudius* 44); Dio, Pliny, Martial and Juvenal also refer to a mushroom or mushrooms. Claudius was deified; Nero joked that mushrooms were 'the food of the gods'. The modern literature is extensive and inconclusive. Many rumours of poisoning are suspect (see page 66), but this one is surer than most.

'The first death of the new reign,' goes on Tacitus (*Annals* xii.1), in an obvious reminiscence of the way he introduces Tiberius's reign ('the first crime . . .'), was that of the inoffensive Marcus Junius Silanus, known as 'the golden sheep'. He was idle, but in the prime of life, blameless, noble, and, like Nero, Augustus's great-great-grandson. The next death was that of Narcissus. Both were Agrippina's work. But her influence was checked by Burrus and by Lucius Annaeus Seneca, Nero's tutor:

> These controllers of the emperor's youth, men who (as is rare among those who share power) agreed with each other, were in different ways equally influential, Burrus by a soldier's attention to detail and strictness of behaviour, Seneca by his lessons in eloquence and his combination of dignity with affability, helping each other so that they might more easily confine the emperor's dangerous adolescence to acceptable indulgences, if he was going to reject virtue. They were united in opposing Agrippina's violence. (Tacitus, *Annals* xiii.2)

So began the famous *quinquennium Neronis,* the first five years of Nero's reign, which Trajan is said to have picked out as a golden age of good government (Aurelius Victor, *Epitome* 5). Nero, following Seneca's advice, said all the things that the Senate wanted to hear. Pallas was removed from office, Britannicus poisoned, Agrippina herself driven out of the palace. If she had hoped to rule through her son, she in fact found herself with less power than when Claudius was alive. Nero took to music, lavish shows and various nocturnal escapades. Seneca and Burrus apparently exercised effective power. The new harbour started by Claudius was completed and celebrated on the coinage. There was a new, efficient and honest *praefectus annonae* (Faenius Rufus, later to be praetorian prefect). Several provincial administrators were charged with corruption. Centralization of the administration continued with the replacement of the quaestors in charge of the treasury by imperial prefects of praetorian rank. But there were few innovations. If the system worked well, much of the credit is due to Claudius.

So far, so good. The year 58, however, saw 'the beginning of great evils for the state' (Tacitus, *Annals* xiii.45). First, Nero fell in love with Poppaea Sabina, the dissolute and ambitious wife of one of his drinking companions. The husband, Marcus Salvius Otho (the future emperor, eleven years later), was got rid of, sent out to govern Lusitania (modern Portugal). Poppaea wanted Nero to divorce Octavia and marry her, which Agrippina opposed, until the following year, when Nero, egged on by Poppaea, had her murdered. Officially it was alleged that she had plotted to kill him, but nobody believed the official version.

Another ominous sign in 58 was that Nero took a sudden interest in the state finances. He was persuaded that his plan to abolish all indirect taxes was impractical, and it was withdrawn, but the episode suggested that he might not be content to leave public affairs in other people's hands indefinitely. Also in 58 came an attack on Seneca in the Senate: 'By what wisdom, by what philosophical precepts had he made 300 million sesterces in four years of friendship with the emperor?' (Tacitus, *Annals* xiii.42). It was a valid, damning and unanswerable question, and suggested that Seneca might be falling out of favour.

The following year, 59, was marked not only by Agrippina's murder, but also by Nero's institution in his own gardens of the *Ludi Iuvenales,* public competitions, gymnastic and artistic, in which senators and knights were to take part. Conservatives were as shocked by the gymnastics as by the murder. The year after, there were more games, in which Nero appeared as both musician and charioteer. In 62, Burrus died and of the two men who replaced him, one, Ofonius Tigellinus, was prepared to encourage Nero in any crime. Seneca was forced into retirement, Octavia divorced and then executed. Trials and executions began again on trumped up charges. Anyone at all related to the imperial house was at risk. There was by this time serious fighting both in Britain (page 121) and in Armenia under Corbulo (page 119); Nero does not appear to have been very much concerned. He never visited a frontier or an army camp, and there was no change in established policy.

The Senate was now alarmed. Soon a great fire in Rome (July 64) caused Nero unpopularity among the ordinary people of the city. The fire totally destroyed three of the fourteen districts into which Rome was divided and left only four untouched. Looters helped it to spread and obstructed fire-fighting efforts. Nero promptly took generous and efficient relief measures. These however 'brought him no thanks, since a rumour had gone round that at the very time when the city was burning he had mounted his private stage and sung the fall of Troy, making present evils like ancient disasters' (Tacitus, *Annals* xv.39). Nero was also credited with the desire to found a new city named after himself. He tried to divert suspicion to the Christians, many of whom were condemned to the beasts or burnt alive (see Chapter 10), but his cruelty was such that it discredited him still further, and people felt sympathy for the Christians, even though they deserved what they were getting (Tacitus, *Annals* xv.44).

Excellent measures were taken to facilitate rebuilding, and a new building code regulated the width of streets and the height of buildings, which had to be at least partly built of fireproof materials. On the other hand,

Nero profited from his country's ruin to build a residence

where it was not so much jewels and gold that were the wonder, since they were already common and cheapened by luxury, as fields and lakes and, as if it were a wilderness, woods on this side and open spaces and views on that . . . (*Annals* xv.42)

Suetonius tells us that it was called 'the Golden House,' *domus aurea*, and adds such details as a triple colonnade a mile long, an entrance hall with a statue of Nero 120 feet high, and a revolving dining-room or more probably a dining-room with a revolving ceiling. The palace and its grounds covered an area the size of Hyde Park in London, or one-third that of Central Park, New York. Contemporaries were impressed by the sophisticated engineering and constructional techniques involved. But the real importance of the Golden House, like that of Nero's baths in the Campus Martius, finished just before the great fire ('What worse than Nero, what better than Nero's baths?' asked Martial, vii.34), was the use they made of the new techniques of construction in concrete (page 87). Nero's most lasting contribution to Roman civilization may have been as a patron of architecture.

His taste for building was however expensive, like his taste in everything else. Money was short. This was perhaps the reason for a debasement of the gold and silver coinage; but there was also a considerable outflow of precious metals to pay for luxury imports from India and the far east (page 144). Nero also resorted to confiscations, for instance by putting to death six rich men who were reputed to own between them half the province of Africa and confiscating their land (page 195).

The year after the fire came a major conspiracy aiming to replace Nero by Gaius Calpurnius Piso, a great noble unconnected with the imperial family (page 73). It had been hatching for three years, was overblown, inefficient and betrayed. Among those executed or forced to commit suicide were Piso, Seneca, the poet Lucan, and Tigellinus's colleague as praetorian prefect Faenius Rufus. Tigellinus was empowered to hunt down more victims. Those of the year 66 included the novelist Petronius, Nero's 'arbiter of elegance' (page 38), and the Stoic philosopher Publius Clodius Thrasea Paetus (consul in 56). Thrasea had made a show of independence in the Senate, had ostentatiously abstained from religious ceremonies for Nero's benefit, and for the past three years had refused to attend the Senate at all. He had considerable influence. Tacitus's account of the trial is the last of his great rhetorical set-pieces (xvi.21–35, where the *Annals* break off in mid-sentence). Thrasea and his friends objected to tyranny on good Stoic principles and celebrated the memory of Brutus and Cassius. They provided a striking example of moral courage, but had little impact on policy and government.

A few months later three provincial governors were recalled and killed, including Corbulo. Nero's war on the Senate had virtually wiped out the imperial family and the old nobility. He no longer trusted the army. When rebellion broke out in Judaea, the command was entrusted to a man, one of whose chief qualifications was that he seemed of too low birth to aspire to the throne. He was the future emperor Vespasian (Chapter 7). Nero's megalomania increased. Poppaea, who had some influence over him, was dead, killed by a kick from Nero in a temper while she was pregnant. A tour to Greece in 67 won him 1808 first prizes in the various games, which were all celebrated that year to allow him to compete. He even won competitions in which he did not compete, and a chariot race in which he fell out of the chariot. Reports sent back to Italy lost nothing in the telling. Helius, the freedman whom Nero had left to govern Rome, urgently summoned him to return, which he did reluctantly, only to leave Rome again for Greek-speaking Naples. Here in March 68 he heard that Vindex, governor of Gallia Lugdunensis, was in revolt. The last act had begun. The secret was about to be revealed, that emperors could be made elsewhere than at Rome (Chapter 7).

Nero was the last emperor of the Julian and Claudian families, and the first not to have been born while Augustus was alive. His permanent achievements were threefold: first, that he ended the Julio-Claudian monopoly of the throne (not that this was intentional); second, that he left an imperishable reputation, not a salubrious one, perhaps, but he is the one emperor who is 'utterly memorable', in the sense of *1066 and All That*; third, as a patron of the arts. Of architecture we have already spoken, and in literature it is no coincidence that the age of Nero produced a small renaissance after the relatively barren years since the deaths of Livy and Ovid. Nero himself was a writer, his tutor Seneca was enormously prolific, the court circle included two other great writers, Petronius and Lucan and we have already noted that it was a magnet for the aspiring poet Martial, hoping for patronage from his fellow-Spaniards, Seneca and Lucan. Other writers of the time include the satirist Aulus Persius Flaccus, the writer of pastorals Titus Calpurnius Siculus, the polymath Gaius Plinius Secundus (the elder Pliny), the agricultural writer Columella, and Caesius Bassus, whose works are lost, but whom Quintilian thought the only Latin lyric poet fit to be compared with Horace. Silius Italicus, although he wrote his boring epic on the Second Punic War in retirement under the Flavians, had been a member of Nero's circle; the younger Pliny, who says 'he took great pains over his verses, but they cannot be called inspired,' also records that 'he damaged his reputation under Nero – he was believed to have offered his services as an informer' (*Letters* iii.7). Other literary figures of the Flavian period, like Statius and Valerius Flaccus, and the great and influential teacher Quintilian, passed formative years under Nero's reign. In literature as in architecture, we should give Nero credit for inspiring a climate where these things were possible.

Let us sum up: the emperor's real power, as in Augustus's day, was still veiled as far as possible in Republican forms. The Senate debated, the magistrates still held office. But Tiberius's seclusion, Gaius's autocracy, Claudius's instinct for centralized efficiency, the five-year administration of Seneca and Burrus, and the terror and executions of Nero's last years, all had tended to put power in the hands of the emperor and his advisors and to leave nobody in doubt that this was so. Individual senators might be competent and ambitious, but the more ambitious they were, the less they could trust one another. The Senate as a body had proved incapable of concerted action, except when safety, profit and inclination all converged in one single course of action, as when Sejanus fell or on the death of Tiberius. The emperors at their best and most conscientious, like Tiberius and Claudius early in their reigns, again and again expressed exasperation at the Senate's inability to accept collective responsibility, but found themselves driven to reduce still further that responsibility by giving authority to officials outside the Senate, thus exacerbating the problem. It was to remain acute under the Flavians, and one may wonder to what extent it was solved in the second century, or indeed was soluble.

In the last resort, the peace and stability of the Empire depended on the army. So did the emperor's own security. Augustus was aware of this, Nero seems to have forgotten it. Not only was the army responsible for the frontiers, but for internal security as well, and in some provinces the latter took precedence over the former. The two legions in Dalmatia were at hand to intervene in Italy if needed (Tacitus, *Annals* iv.5), and throughout the first century Egypt had two legions whose presence was required, not by any external threat to the province, but by the need to keep order, particularly in Alexandria, at that time the second largest city in the empire and subject to outbreaks of communal violence because of the mutual hatred of its Greeks and its Jews. The army also played an important social and economic role, as an agent of social mobility among its recruits and its officers, as a powerful influence for Romanization, and as an economic stimulus to the areas in which it was stationed.

The army had been reduced in size and reorganized after Actium. Out of his own and Antony's legions, Augustus seems to have retained 28 as a permanent standing army. For although there is no direct evidence for the number 28, Tacitus tells us that there were 25 legions in AD 23 (*Annals* iv.5), and 3 had been lost with Varus in Germany in AD 9 and not replaced. No new legions had been raised in the latter part of Augustus's reign, and it is generally agreed that there were 28 as far back as 14 BC, when the first big campaigns of expansion were launched in the north. Although a legion, probably 5th *Alaudae*, lost its eagle-standard on the Rhine in 17 BC, the eagle was recovered and the legion was not disbanded; and although another legion 22nd *Deiotariana*, originally raised by King Deiotarus of Galatia, is often said to have been incorporated in the Roman army when Galatia became a province in 25 BC (which would imply only 27 legions from 31 to 25 BC), I think it likely that it already formed part of Antony's army, having been incorporated on Deiotarus's death (Dio xlviii.33). This gives us 28 legions from 30 BC to the Varian Disaster, each with a nominal strength of some 5400 men, making 150,000 in all. The total stayed at 25 until two more legions were raised, either by Caligula, or at the start of Claudius's reign in preparation for his invasion of Britain, and after some fluctuation in numbers at the end of Nero's reign and under the Flavians Trajan brought the total up to 30.

We may conveniently step beyond the chronological limit of this chapter to complete this account: 2 legions disappear from the record after Hadrian's reign, but Marcus Aurelius raised 2 more to bring the number back up to 30, and Septimius Severus increased it to 33. Thus for over a century and a half between 27 and 30 legions were judged sufficient for the needs of the whole Empire. Individual legions maintained their identity and traditions for centuries. A legion might be disbanded for cowardice or disloyalty, or struck off the list when destroyed in action: not only were the three legions lost in Germany under Varus in AD 9 not replaced, but their numbers, 17th, 18th and 19th, disappear from the army list. But 19 of Augustus's original legions still existed in Dio's time (Dio lv.23), and 16 are still found in the late fourth-century document known as the *Notitia Dignitatum*.

Augustus also created a permanent praetorian guard, like the bodyguard which Republican commanders had had in the field, with special pay and privileges, nine cohorts strong (equivalent to a legion and a half). He also built on Republican precedent in establishing on a regular basis auxiliary regiments (infantry cohorts and cavalry *alae*) recruited from the subject peoples of the Empire, commanded sometimes by Roman officers and sometimes by their own tribal leaders. Arminius, for instance, the destroyer of Varus and his army, had commanded a cohort of his tribesmen in the Roman service.

Tacitus tells us where the 25 legions which existed in AD 23 were then stationed (*Annals* iv.5): there were 8 on the Rhine and 6 in the Balkans and on the Danube (i.e., 2 apiece in Moesia, Pannonia and Dalmatia); Spain had 3, Africa and Egypt 2 apiece, and Syria 4, to watch over the eastern frontier. There were also, he notes, 9 praetorian and 3 urban cohorts; fleets at Misenum and Ravenna in Italy and at Fréjus in the south of France; client kingdoms in Mauretania, on the eastern frontier, and in Thrace; other allied fleets in various provinces; and auxiliary cavalry and infantry regiments whose numerical strength was about the same as that of the legions. He excuses himself from a detailed account of the auxiliaries, however, because they are moved from place to place as required, and their number fluctuates.

The legions too might be moved around. Tacitus's list has 2 legions in Africa, but this was because the war against Tacfarinas was then at its height, and an extra legion had been drafted in from Pannonia, to which it was to return the following year (*Annals* iv.23). This was to leave Africa with 1 legion, the 3rd *Augusta*, stationed successively at Ammaedara (Haidra), Theveste (Tebessa) and Lambaesis, where we find it under Hadrian (see Chapter 9), and where it stayed for centuries. The legions under Augustus had changed their bases whenever Augustus's aggressive strategy required it, and the Augustan legionary bases on the Rhine show evidence of frequent modification to accommodate greater or lesser numbers of men. But they were already more permanent than the winter quarters, which were literally that and nothing more, of Caesar's army in Gaul, and we find the Rhine and Danube bases rebuilt in stone instead of wood under Claudius, a belated recognition that Augustus's forward policy had been abandoned and that the legions were there to stay.

Under Augustus, until the Varian Disaster broke his nerve, there were no permanent frontiers, except with Parthia. The permanent frontiers which developed thereafter were more administrative than military. They permitted the authorities to control trade, to collect customs duties, to check smuggling and cattle rustling. Philostratus has the mystic philosopher Apollonius arrive at Zeugma on the eastern frontier, and the customs official asks him what he has to declare. 'Prudence, Justice, Temperance, Courage, Perseverance,' replies Apollonius – all are nouns in the feminine gender; the official thinks they are female slaves and wants to charge duty (*Life of Apollonius,* 20). The linear barriers which were put up along frontiers not otherwise demarcated, such as the German *limes* and Hadrian's Wall, channelled movement across the frontier, rather than seeking to prevent it. Legionary transfers might still be required by policy changes or to meet emergencies, but the processes whereby the army became sedentarised were accelerated by a growing tendency throughout the first and second centuries towards local recruitment, which was in its turn a factor in persuading veterans increasingly to settle in the areas where they had served and where in many cases they had raised a family.

Legionaries were Roman citizens, auxiliaries usually not. In the West, in the first century, most legionaries came from Italy or increasingly, as the century went on, from the more Romanized provinces, especially southern Gaul and Spain. The eastern legions recruited heavily in Asia Minor, especially in Galatia. East and West alike found likely recruits among soldiers' and veterans' sons. Many recruits give their place of origin as a veteran colony, others simply as 'from the camp'. The auxiliary units took non-citizens from whatever local area was able to provide tough but reliable men. Many auxiliary regiments bore in their title a reference to the tribe or the area from which they had originally been raised, such as the 1st Cohort of Thracians, but they did not continue to recruit there, except for some specialist units requiring recruits with a special skill, such as archery, which was found only among certain peoples with whom it was a tradition, like the Syrians (page 177).

In discussing Augustus's regulations promulgated in 13 BC (page 78), we referred to other important measures affecting the life and legal status of soldiers. It was certainly Augustus who ruled that a soldier whose father was alive and who was therefore by Roman law subject to that father's authority was nonetheless allowed to dispose as he wished of his pay and booty; and that a soldier's will was valid if its intent was clear, independently of legal niceties. More important still was the ruling that soldiers were not allowed legally to marry, and this too seems likely to go back to Augustus. It may have been meant to keep the soldier free from family ties, in the interests of military efficiency; but soldiers formed such ties anyway, though their children were illegitimate, with all the disadvantages which that entailed (page 230). They could enlist in the legions only if given citizenship on enlistment to make them eligible to do so. This certainly happened, both in the West and still more, it would seem, in the East, sparingly perhaps at first, but quite commonly by the Antonine period. Auxiliaries on the other hand received citizenship on discharge, perhaps not yet under Augustus (the first certain example falls under Tiberius), but it becomes standard from Claudius onwards. Until about 140 the standard formula on the *diploma* given at discharge ran 'citizenship for themselves, their children and descendants, and the right of legal marriage with the wives that they had at the time citizenship was given or, for those who are bachelors, with those they married later, as long as there is only one wife per man'; but thereafter existing children are not mentioned, so that they in their turn have to enlist in order to qualify, whereas children born after the father got citizenship and the right of legal marriage (*conubium*) would be born citizens. The same happened in the families of ex-slaves, like Titus Flavius Felicio of Aquincum (Budapest), of whose children only the youngest was born free, and the proud father named him Titus Flavius Ingenuus (*ingenuus* meaning 'free-born') to celebrate (*AE* 1939, 10, on the family tombstone).

During the civil wars, conscription had been common, but it was naturally unpopular, and Augustus was therefore unwilling to enforce it in Italy, except in emergencies, such as those of AD 6 and AD 9 (page 81), while Tiberius appears to have done away with it completely in Italy, though not in the provinces. Despite allegations of harsh discipline and complaints that soldiers were kept on beyond their term and then given allotments on poor, marginal land (Tacitus, *Annals* i.17), the rewards of an army career were nevertheless considerable, especially for those who rose to the higher ranks of the centurionate (page 99). The centurions were the career officers, some directly commissioned from civilian life, but most promoted from the ranks of the legions or the praetorian guard. Within the centurionate itself, there were many graduations of rank. Junior centurions, commanding a 'century' of 80 men, were like modern company commanders. The senior centurion of a legion, the *primus pilus*, had some 5400 men under him; we might equate him with a brigadier. The youngest *primus pilus* known is one Blossius Pudens, who died at 49 on the verge of promotion (*ILS* 2641). The *primus pilus* reported to the legionary legate, a senator and not a career soldier at all. Even junior centurions were paid 15,000 sesterces a year, and the *primus pilus* 60,000, or nearly seventy times the ordinary legionary's pay, with allowances and a discharge bonus in proportion. It was this that made the career prospects attractive, and the retired *primus pilus*, as we have seen, was a man of some standing in his municipality.

The army was a great avenue for social mobility. To the Italian examples already discussed we may add examples of provincials bettering themselves in the same way, but through the auxiliary units rather than the legions. There are two men, both called Gaius Julius, from Saintes (Mediolanum Santonum) in western France. One of them served for 32 years in a cavalry regiment, became an NCO (a *duplicarius*, someone getting double pay), was recalled to serve with an Alpine unit, and was presented with awards, presumably for valour, by his fellow soldiers. He got the citizenship, possibly under Tiberius, although Augustus is not excluded, and finished up on his tombstone as Gaius Julius Macer, a name which we might think wholly Roman, except that his non-citizen father has the purely Celtic name of Agedillus (*CIL* xiii.1041 = *ILS* 2531).

Our other case is again a man with a Roman name, Gaius Julius Victor, also from a Celtic background: his father was called Congonnetodubnus and his grandfather Acedomopas (*CIL* xiii.1042–5). Victor comes from a much higher social class than Macer. His family was wealthy and doubtless of the pre-Roman tribal nobility. Victor achieved the ultimate social distinction for a Romanized Gaul in the early Empire, the priesthood of Rome and Augustus at Lyon. His son gave him a grandiose tomb, and other members of the family are also known. Victor, however, interests us particularly in this context because he began his public career as *praefectus fabrum,* which by this period meant an honorary *aide-de-camp,* reminding us of Indian princes in the British service under the Raj, and he went on to command an auxiliary cohort, perhaps the 1st Cohort of Belgians. For a parallel, we might cite the case of Colonel His Highness Shri Sir Ranjit-sinjhi Vibhaji, Maharajah Jam Sahib of Nowanagar (known to all cricketers as the immortal 'Ranji'), Honorary ADC to the Viceroy, Lord Elgin, and in 1914, initially to be ... an Honorary Major, but before long word came through that he was to join Field Marshal Sir John French as ADC'.

It is convenient at this point to emphasize how many cases there are of Gallic notables who had done well out of Roman rule. We can reconstruct the history of another family from the same tribe of the Santones. An inscription from Lyon records the construction of an amphitheatre by Gaius Julius Rufus, also priest of Rome and Augustus, at his own expense, near the sanctuary. It is broken, but appears to mention also his sons and a grandson. The same man dedicated in AD 19 an arch at Saintes itself, from which we learn that he too was Honorary ADC (no mention of a military command, however, unlike Victor), and it gives his father's name as Gaius Julius Otuaneunus, his grandfather's as Gaius Julius Gedomo, and his great-grandfather's as plain Epotsorovidus (*CIL* xiii.1036; the very first priest had been an Aeduan, Gaius Julius Vercondaridubnus, Livy, *epitome*

139). All these men called Gaius Julius got the citizenship, or descend from ancestors who got the citizenship, from Caesar or Augustus. If Gaius Julius Rufus in AD 19 was of an age to have a grandson, then by counting back at 25–30 years to a generation, we find that his grandfather Gedomo, the first of the family to receive the citizenship, will have been in his prime during Caesar's campaigns in Gaul, and it seems likely that Caesar was rewarding him for his support of the Roman cause. It is clear from Caesar's own account that he profited from and exploited divisions between pro- and anti-Roman factions in most tribes. The main benefit of the citizenship in Gaul will have been to bring the new citizen under the Roman law of property, which probably meant that they could now be held to own wholly and in perpetuity land which probably under Celtic tribal law belonged to the tribe, although in some way assigned to the chief or one of the other tribal nobility. Centuries later, the coming of English law, first to Wales, and later to the Scottish highlands, produced a similar effect.

If we now turn to look at where the army was stationed, we see that from the Varian Disaster in AD 9 to the start of the Flavian period, the Rhine was the most heavily garrisoned frontier. Over the next quarter of a century the preponderance shifted irrevocably to the Danube. In the intervening period, the main changes had been the reduction of the garrison of Spain from 3 legions to 1, the sending of 4 legions to Britain, and temporarily, after the outbreak of the Jewish Revolt in 66, the presence of 3 legions in Judaea, to be reduced to 1 when the Revolt was over. But by the end of Trajan's Dacian Wars, a few years into the second century, the Rhine was down to 4 legions, while the Balkans and the Danube, including the new province of Dacia, had 12 or 13. The eastern frontier, with 4 legions under Augustus, all in Syria, had now gone to 6, divided between Syria, Judaea, and Cappadocia in the north. The pattern, incidentally, was to change very little through the third century. Once they had gone over to the defensive, the Romans had little room to manoeuvre. The basic geophysical and strategic imperatives remained constant. In the East, for instance, where Roman territory was effectively protected by the impenetrable desert in the south and the almost equally impenetrable mountains of Armenia in the north, the key was the route across the Euphrates from northern Mesopotamia into Syria and Anatolia. Augustus had left this largely to clients, later emperors took it under direct control. But at all times, it was this route that the legions had to watch, whether centrally based at Antioch under Augustus or more widely deployed, as later.

Tacitus, as we have seen, in his enumeration of the forces of the Empire in 23, mentions client kings, and Strabo says that Augustus treated them as 'members and parts of the Empire' (*Augustus* 48). They were a striking element in the strategic plan of the Julio-Claudian period, and the gradual incorporation of their territories into the Empire as regular provinces marks a distinct change in strategical thinking. Client kings were expected to keep order in their own domain, to guard their frontiers (though they were not left exposed to major external threats, unless we count Armenia). If Roman intervention were needed, it could be limited to protecting Roman assets and keeping the client-ruler in control; it would have required much greater effort to bring the client kingdom up to provincial standards of tranquility. In a client kingdom Roman prestige was not so directly involved. The actual term 'client king' is a modern metaphor drawn from the patron-client relationship so basic to Roman social relationships (page 96). The Romans usually called such kings 'friends' and 'allies'.

Armenia was a true buffer state. Whatever its juridical status in Roman eyes, it in fact fulfilled the role of a neutral 'no-go area' keeping Roman and Parthian forces apart. Other client states were there to absorb external thrusts and internal unrest. The model is one of a central zone of direct control, surrounded by an inner zone of client states under diplomatic control and subject to direct Roman military intervention in time of crisis, with an outer zone of influence. The model which superseded this, once the client states had been absorbed, required the Roman forces to be stationed on the perimeter of Roman control to repel any attack, unbuffered by clients. In the first case, the Roman authorities were ready to meet aggressors on the territory of clients, in the second they were committed to preventing potential aggressors from penetrating the perimeter at all. The distinction today dictates NATO strategy: NATO has to take the second option, because it is unacceptable to West Germany, not unnaturally, to let the Russians cross the frontier and then fight them on German soil.

At all times the majority of the legions were in the frontier provinces, and these were almost wholly under the direct authority of the emperor. The basic distinction between 'imperial' and 'senatorial' provinces goes back to the settlement of 27 BC. The former were those entrusted to the emperor, to which the emperor appointed as governor his own legate (*legatus Augusti pro praetore*). The legate was directly responsible to the emperor and held office at the emperor's pleasure. Tiberius left one man to govern Moesia for twenty years. Legates of the more important provinces would be ex-consuls, but it was the emperor who was technically acting *pro consule,* on behalf of the consuls, so that his deputies were considered as being subordinate in rank, acting *pro praetore*, with praetorian power. In the senatorial provinces, on the other hand, governors were appointed annually by lot, following the old Republican practice, and they reported to the Senate, not to the emperor, although it is clear that as early as the reign of Augustus himself the emperor could intervene directly in senatorial provinces by virtue of his *imperium maius* (see Chapter 3).

The distinction almost certainly mattered more to the Senate than to anyone else. The proconsulships of Africa and Asia particularly represented 'the crown of the public career' (Suetonius, *Vespasian* 4), and Pliny's careful praise of Arrius Antoninus (*Letters* iv.3) and Silius Italicus (*Letters* iii.7) for their conduct as proconsul of Asia exemplifies the importance attached to this annual post in the senatorial tradition. The Senate could think of it as 'all theirs,' even if no senator could get so far in his career as to have a chance at one of the two great prizes without the emperor's favour. The proconsul of Africa, down to the reign of Caligula, uniquely for the governor of a senatorial province, still had a legion under his command. Thereafter the legionary legate was independent of the proconsul, which might cause conflict at times of stress, as in the civil wars that followed Nero's death (see Chapter 7), until eventually the post of legate was combined with that of governor of the new imperial province of Numidia. The policy of not having legions in senatorial provinces is generally presented as intended to stop their governors getting above themselves. A more practical consideration was to avoid an annual change of command. The emperor had enough power, even in a senatorial province, to keep the governor in order.

An important piece of evidence to this effect is provided by an inscription from Cyrene, which contains four edicts of Augustus of the year 7/6 BC and a fifth of 4 BC promulgating a decree of the Senate (*SEG* ix.8 = *LR* pp.36–42). The first four relate to tensions in the province between Greeks and Romans, two of them regulating the composition of juries ('A Greek under indictment shall be given the right to decide the day before the prosecution opens its case whether he wants his jurors to be all Romans or half Greeks . . .'), one deals with a charge, apparently of *maiestas*, which has overtones of intercommunal rivalry, and one prescribes that 'persons from the province of Cyrene who have been honoured with [Roman] citizenship I order nonetheless to perform in their turn the personal compulsory services of the Greeks' (the expression translated here 'personal compulsory services' is in Greek *leitourgiai*, 'liturgies', equivalent to the Latin *munera*, a long-standing tradition and substitute for direct taxation in Greek cities; cf. page 256). The senatorial decree concerns a procedure for hearing extortion cases. The existence of social tensions and the concern of the Roman authorities to minimize them is interesting. Cyrene had a history of such problems, and was to suffer such damage in rioting, virtually amounting to civil war, between Greeks and

Jews under Trajan (115–117) that it never wholly recovered. But it is significant that in what was the nominally senatorial province of Crete and Cyrene, Augustus legislates by decree, and the first of the edicts specifically includes instructions to the governor of the province and his successors. There could be no clearer example of the emperor's use of his *imperium maius* (see Chapter 3), nor of the extent of his real power over the whole Empire, including the senatorial provinces.

To the scheme of senatorial and imperial provinces, all with governors of praetorian or consular status, there was one major exception. This was Egypt, which the emperor governed, not through a senatorial legate, but through an equestrian prefect. To begin with, this post was the crown of an equestrian's career. Sejanus's father, Seius Strabo, went on to Egypt from being praetorian prefect. Later, the path of promotion led in the other direction. Senators were not even allowed to visit the country without the emperor's special permission. The emperor in Egypt was the divine successor of the pharaohs, as the Ptolemies had been, and he inherited their highly developed system of taxation and lucrative monopolies. Egypt was of considerable strategic and economic importance. Its wheat, with that of Africa, fed Rome. It had a monopoly of papyrus production. It was the main starting point for trade with India, in which Strabo says that 120 ships a year took part, compared with very few under the Ptolemies (ii.118). This may be due to the discovery of the seasonal monsoons by a certain Hippalus (Pliny, *Natural History* vi.100–6). Excavations at the port of Quseir al-Qadim on the Red Sea, occupied into the second century, produced Chinese porcelain, Indian batik, spices, teak and potsherds inscribed in Tamil. A cave on the route from the Nile to the Red Sea has graffiti carved by men who sheltered here: 'Gaius Numidius Eros was here in the 28th year of Caesar's [i.e., Augustus's] reign on the way back from India in the month Phamenoth' (February-March, 2 BC), and eight years later 'Lysa, slave of Publius Annius Plocamus' took shelter in the same place (*AE* 1956, 55 = *EJ* 360a; *AE* 1954, 121 = *EJ* 360b). With all this, plus

Alexandria, second largest city of the Empire at this time, racked by communal strife, no wonder that Augustus wanted Egypt firmly under his own thumb.

Some of the lesser imperial provinces also had equestrian governors. Basically, until the time of Septimius Severus, only a senator might command a legion, except in Egypt. Therefore, if a province had a legionary garrison, it required a senatorial governor. But the province of Raetia for instance, which we know to have had a senator in charge right after it was conquered in 15 BC, subsequently came under an equestrian prefect (*praefectus*) when it ceased to have a legionary garrison. The first such prefect seems in fact to have been the senior centurion (*primus pilus*) of the legion that was leaving, promoted and left behind with a garrison of auxiliary troops (page 99). There are also several cases of tiny prefectures elsewhere in the Alpine regions, where a prefect would be responsible for a province comprising the valleys along which ran a particular line of communication, for instance the road across the Cols d'Izoard, de Vars and de la Cayolle (*CIL* xii.80). Another such prefecture was that of Cottius, whose arch at Susa, where the road going up into the western Alps from Turin (Augusta Taurinorum) divides to take either the Mont Cénis or the Mont Genèvre pass, has already been discussed (page 91). An equestrian province more important than any of these was however Judaea, which had been a client kingdom in Herod's day (see Chapter 3), and which was put under an equestrian prefect when Herod's son proved incompetent. There was of course no legionary garrison, and if the prefect needed reinforcements, as often happened in so turbulent a province, he had to appeal to the governor of Syria. When a major revolt broke out in 66, legions were brought in to suppress it and afterwards one was left as a permanent garrison, which entailed the replacement of the equestrian prefect by a senatorial legate.

In discussing legionary recruitment, we have already alluded to differences between the western and the eastern provinces. There was in fact a fundamental difference of language and culture. In the West, the language of administration, of business, of all educated people was Latin. It had no serious rival, although in the fields and in the streets other local languages proved tenacious. Oscan, the language of the central Italian highlands, was still being scribbled on walls in Pompeii in 79, and Irenaeus, Bishop of Lyon in the next century (see Chapter 10), writes that he is glad to have learned some Celtic back home in Galatia, because it is useful in his new diocese. In Africa both Punic and Berber survived to the time of St Augustine in the early fifth century, and later still of course Celtic ha ' such vitality that it has survived to the present day in Wale., and Brittany.

The language of the eastern half of the Empire, by contrast, was Greek. Here again, local languages survived, such as Coptic or Aramaic, but Greek not Latin was the *lingua franca,* and the Roman administrative machinery was bilingual. Official documents were promulgated in Greek as well as in Latin. Greek culture flourished. Even where it was not native, it had at least three centuries behind it, going back to Alexander the Great, and the Romans did not interfere any more than was necessary to maintain order. They favoured the ruling oligarchy in the cities, rich landed families who practised local benefactions like those of wealthy senators in Italy but who were slow to take their place in the Roman hierarchy (see Chapter 10). Senators from the western provinces are common before those from the Greek east accede to the rank and the offices for which their wealth and their standing in their own regions ought, according to normal Roman practice, to entitle them. We first find Greek senators in any number under the Flavians, and not until the second century do they commonly attain the consulship.

It seems clear that the provinces were better administered and the provincials better protected against abuse of power by Roman governors and officials than under the Republic. Even Tacitus admits as much (*Annals* i.2). Not that the situation was perfect: there are forty attested trials for maladministration and extortion in the period from Augustus to Trajan, and since almost all our knowledge of them comes from Tacitus or Pliny, it is reasonable to suppose that there were others in those parts of the period for which we do not have Tacitus or Pliny as a source. Nor was it easy for provincials to obtain redress. The Senate was inclined to close ranks and protect its own. Pliny for instance describes with much self-congratulation how he appeared for two successive governors of Bithynia, Julius Bassus and Varenus Rufus, who were accused by the provincials for misdeeds in office (note that the provincials had to wait until a governor's term of office was over before bringing a case against him). In Bassus's case, Pliny admits that he was guilty of taking presents, which was against the law, in fact a law of 59 BC which was still in force:

> What weighed heavily against him was the fact that in all innocence he had thoughtlessly accepted certain gifts from the provincials as their friend [he had been quaestor in the same province]. These his prosecutors called thefts and plunder, while he declared they were presents. (*Letters* iv.9)

Pliny spoke for five hours, his colleague for the defence for four, another senator

> made a forceful and well-reasoned reply, and then Theophanes [leading counsel for the province] spoke again. Here too he showed his lack of discretion, not only in claiming time to address the court after two accomplished speakers of consular rank, but also in continuing at length.

Since he was replying to nine hours of speeches for the defence, one wonders if Pliny's indignation is really justified.

The next day there were two more speeches for the defence, and then a day of cross-examination of witnesses. The consul-elect proposed to apply the law strictly, but another senator, Caepio Hispo, made a counter-proposal that Bassus pay a penalty but keeps his seat in the Senate:

Caepio, taking the view that the Senate has the power [as indeed it has] to reduce or increase the severity of the law, had reason to excuse an action which was illegal, strictly speaking, but not without precedent. Caepio's proposal was carried; in fact on rising to speak he was greeted with the applause which is usually given when a speaker resumes his seat. You can judge then how his actual speech was received ... Valerius Paulinus agreed with Caepio, but made the further proposal that the Senate should deal with Theophanes ... for it was clear that during his work for the prosecution he had committed a number of offences which came under the same law as that under which he had accused Bassus. But the consuls did not follow up the proposal, although it found great favour with the majority of the Senate ... When the court rose Bassus was met by crowds of people clamouring to demonstrate their delight.

Do you see what I mean about the Senate 'closing ranks'? Was Bassus really deserving of leniency, or was there a gross miscarriage of justice? Even if the Senate was impartial, it was not seen to be impartial, and Pliny himself records that some people outside the Senate called Caepio's proposal 'lax and illogical', and thought it wrong for someone 'who has had a penalty assessed against him to remain in the Senate'. And was Valerius Paulinus's proposal to prosecute Theophanes anything more than wanting to teach a lesson to an uppity provincial? As it happens, Pliny himself elsewhere provides us with damning evidence against Bassus, when he was himself governor of Bithynia later, writing to Trajan for advice:

A further type of case has also come to me for trial. A man was brought before me who had been sentenced to banishment for life by the governor Julius Bassus. *Knowing that all Bassus's acts had been annulled, and that the Senate had granted anyone sentenced by him the right to have a new trial,* so long as the appeal was made within two years ... (*Letters* x.56, my italics)

This particular letter and Trajan's reply contain other points of interest. The man whom Pliny is writing about had not gone into banishment, as sentenced, and had not appealed. What is to be done? Trajan rules that he must be punished for evading the sentence and is to be sent in chains to Rome to await trial. The strict law must be applied, even though there is a chance that the man had been unjustly condemned. Unfortunately we do not know whether he had ever learned of the decision granting him the right to a new trial. The fact that he did not apply for one might suggest that he had not; but possibly he was merely afraid of its coming out that he was still in the province when he ought to have left it.

In the same letter Pliny asks for a further ruling on another former governor's sentence of banishment:

A man has approached me with information that certain enemies of his, who had been sentenced to three years' banishment by the distinguished senator Publius Servilius Calvus, are still in the province. They on the other hand insist that their sentences were reversed by Calvus, and have quoted his edict of restitution. I therefore thought it necessary to refer the whole question to you, seeing that your official instructions [*mandata*] were that I should not recall anyone banished by one of the governors or myself, but I can find no ruling on the situation where a governor has passed sentence of banishment and subsequently reversed it.

Trajan replies that he will find out from Calvus why he reversed the sentence and let Pliny know his decision later.

We are struck by the very personal nature of the transaction: 'a man approached me with information that *certain enemies of his* . . .'. We get the impression that Roman justice is being used to pursue private feuds, and understand how easily an unscrupulous governor might find himself taking 'presents'. But the most important point is Pliny's reference to his official instructions. Each governor was given a set of official instructions on setting off for his province. Only if something is not covered in them does he need to refer back to the emperor. We hear about the cases mentioned in this letter because Pliny's instruction dealt with banishment, so that clearly it was considered an important issue, but did not cover these specific and rather unusual cases. It has been suggested that Pliny was constantly troubling Trajan about trivialities. Not a bit of it: where his instructions are clear, he decides for himself, and he refers back far less often than a British colonial administrator in the age of the telegraph would have been expected to do.

This was inevitable. The Empire was large and communications were slow. If we do not appreciate how slow, we cannot understand the constraints affecting both the government of the Empire and the strategy and conduct of military operations. Augustus had set up a system of posting stations for urgent dispatches:

> In order that what was happening in each province might be reported more quickly and without delay, he first of all stationed young men at frequent intervals along the military roads, but later replaced them by vehicles. It seemed more convenient that the same men who brought dispatches from a place should also be available for questioning if circumstances warranted it. (Suetonius, *Augustus* 49)

Dispatch carriers probably averaged fifty miles a day, or little more, on routine journeys, although in a crisis they might travel faster (the sign that a messenger bore urgent news was a feather tied to the spear which he carried, as if to symbolise the need for wings). The events of 68–9 provide us with some evidence for the speed with which dispatches might travel in an emergency. The news that the legions of Upper Germany had refused the oath of allegiance to Galba on 1 January 69, presumably on morning parade, reached Vitellius in Cologne while he was at dinner that night (this is just over 100 Roman miles), and reached Rome via the procurator of

Gallia Belgica at Rheims some time, it would seem, on 9 January. The total Mainz–Rheims–Rome distance by the shortest route over the Little St Bernard Pass is some 1280 Roman miles, but if the Pass was closed, as it almost certainly was in January, the route via the Mont Gènevre would have added an extra 100. This means that the courier probably covered some 1380 Roman miles in eight or eight and a half days, averaging about 160 miles a day.

Now if this calculation is right, it must represent the absolute maximum speed for the carrying of dispatches by land, since the greatest distance recorded as ever travelled in a single day is 200 miles (Tiberius hastening to his brother's deathbed, Pliny, *Natural History* vii.84), and it is regarded as worthy of comment that Julius Caesar once kept up 100 miles a day for eight successive days in a hired carriage, which Suetonius calls 'an incredible pace' (Suetonius, *Julius* 57). Obviously the longer the distance, the greater the chance of something going wrong, quite apart from the sheer fatigue. Rome to Antioch, capital of Syria and key to the eastern frontier provinces, was about 3000 miles. It is virtually inconceivable that the governor of Syria could hope to get a report to the emperor in Rome and have a reply back, using the posting service, in under two months, no matter how urgent the crisis, and routine dispatches might take that long in one direction only. If the Parthians crossed the frontier, or there were major riots in Antioch or Jerusalem, the governor was on his own. It made matters worse if the emperor was not in Rome; consider the extreme cases, Trajan campaigning in Mesopotamia or, a century later, Septimius Severus on Hadrian's Wall. And if a courier took so long, an army took much longer. To move reinforcements from the Rhine to the eastern frontier would mean five to six months' hard marching.

In some circumstances, times could be dramatically shortened by going by sea. Pliny gives a list of record times for certain voyages: Ostia to Africa (presumably Carthage or Utica) in two days, to Gallia Narbonensis in three, to Spain (presumably Tarraco) in four, to Gades (Cadiz) in seven, and

Puteoli to Alexandria in nine (*Natural History* xix.3–4). It was no doubt by sea in such favourable conditions that Galba's freedman Icelus brought Galba in 68 the news from Rome to Clunia in Spain that Nero was dead and that the Senate had recognized Galba. Icelus took only seven days, which means presumably four by sea from Ostia to Tarraco, and then three for the 332 miles from Tarraco to Clunia, beating the official courier by two days. On the other hand, in a season when the winds were favourable for a voyage in one direction, they were likely to be foul for the return, and navigation virtually ceased in the winter months. At best, sea voyages were unpredictable. Caligula sent a dispatch to Publius Petronius, governor of Syria, threatening his execution; it was delayed at sea for three months and arrived 27 days after the news of Caligula's death.

Even travellers on official business, unless they had high priority, had to submit to the normal chances and uncertainties of ancient travel. A centurion with a party of prisoners from Caesarea in Palestine to Rome first took ship in a coasting vessel which made Sidon in a day and from there, despite headwinds made a dash for Lycia (southwestern Asia Minor), where the centurion found a ship of the Alexandrian grain fleet that had been blown off course. They changed ships, but the wind was so consistently against them that it took 'a good many days' to make harbour on Crete, near Lasea. It seemed 'risky to go on with the voyage', because the season was so advanced, but 'the harbour was unsuitable for wintering', so the captain and the owner decided to go on, but they were caught in a northeasterly gale, had to run before it, were nearly driven ashore, 'jettisoned the ship's gear with their own hands', and at last, after fourteen days of storm, managed to put the ship aground on the island of Malta. We owe this vivid description to the fact that the apostle Paul was one of the centurion's prisoners (*Acts* 27). They spent three months on the island, before setting sail in another Alexandrian freighter which had wintered there. The grain ships were the largest freighters of their day. In the next century, when one was blown off course, it was 70 days at sea before it ended up in the Piraeus, which had been the main commercial harbour of the Mediterranean six centuries before, but was now a total backwater, and all Athens turned out to see it. If such ships were so at the mercy of the weather, we can see why winter navigation was generally avoided.

With the governor of a province so removed from any day-to-day contact with a superior or even with an equal, with an immense power of discretion to enforce what measures he judged necessary for public order, with arbitrary authority to compel provincials to obey his orders, no matter how unreasonable an individual might find them (*coercitio,* to which we shall return when discussing the position of the Christians in Chapter 10), it was of supreme importance to the province what sort of governor it had. The personality of the governor affected the administration of the province and the quality of life of the provincials more than the emperor's personality did. We have stressed the distinction between imperial and senatorial provinces, between legates and prefects, but, paradoxically, this mattered more at Rome than they actually did in the province. We have seen that emperors could intervene in nominally senatorial provinces. From the provincials' point of view, the biggest difference between imperial and senatorial provinces was probably that governors of imperial provinces stayed longer. They might also be less accessible, if engaged on active frontier warfare, like Agricola in Britain, and personal access to the governor in his legal capacity was important. But fighting, even for most imperial legates, was a minor part of their job. Most of their time went into the assizes, for which the governor travelled on circuit, into arbitrating disputes between the largely self-governing communities, and into financial administration and taxation.

Tax was crucial, and to this we shall return. For the moment, however, it is worth noting how little aware the reader is of the Roman authorities in those documents which more than any others that have come down to us show the Roman system from the point of view of its non-Roman subjects, that is to say, in the New Testament narratives.

There are the publicans, of course, the agents of the tax-collecting syndicates. And at moments of crisis we see the governor as judge: Jesus before Pontius Pilatus, prefect of Judaea, Paul before Gallio, proconsul of Achaea, brother of Seneca, Paul again before Felix and Festus, successive prefects of Judaea. But Paul travels all over the East, and in the cities it is the city magistrates and councils that he has to deal with, as at Philippi (*Acts* 16) and Ephesus (*Acts* 19). The Philippi episode is instructive. Paul and his companion Silas are mobbed, and the magistrates order them a flogging. The next day Paul reveals that they are Roman citizens and refuses to leave without an apology.

When Paul returns to Jerusalem after his extensive travels (at what other period of history could he have travelled as he did with so little difficulty?), Jews from Asia raise a riot against him and he is about to be lynched:

> While they were clamouring for his death, a report reached the officer commanding the cohort, that all Jerusalem was in an uproar. He immediately took a force of soldiers with their centurions and came down on the rioters at the double. As soon as they saw the commandant and his troops, they stopped beating Paul. The commandant stepped forward, arrested him, and ordered him to be shackled with two chains. (*Acts* 21)

Order must be restored; Paul is at the centre of the disturbance; therefore arrest him, and sort it out later. In fact, the commandant orders him to be examined under flogging; this is casually done and casually recounted, obviously a perfectly normal practice, although there is no charge against Paul (cf. page 278):

> But when they tied him up for the lash, Paul said to the centurion who was standing there, 'Can you legally flog a man who is a Roman citizen, and moreover has not been found guilty?' When the centurion heard this, he went and reported it to the commandant. 'What do you mean

to do?' he said. 'This man is a Roman citizen.' The commandant came to Paul. 'Tell me, are you a Roman citizen?' he asked. 'Yes', said he. The commandant rejoined, 'It cost me a large sum to acquire this citizenship.' Paul said, 'But it was mine by birth.' Then those who were about to examine him withdrew hastily, and the commandant himself was alarmed when he realized that Paul was a Roman citizen and that he had put him in irons. (*Acts* 22)

Again we see the importance attaching to citizen status, which protects the citizen from arbitrary flogging to extract information. There is then a plot to spring Paul from custody and lynch him. The commandant therefore sends him down under escort to the governor's palace at Caesarea. There is a hearing some days later when the High Priest comes down from Jerusalem, and the governor adjourns it for further evidence, putting Paul under open arrest and giving orders 'not to prevent any of his friends from making themselves useful to him'. Some days later the governor and his wife (Jewish, incidentally) send for Paul to ask about his teaching (one might guess that they had been making enquiries in the mean time), and the governor gets alarmed at what Paul has to say about 'morals, self-control and the coming judgement', and dismisses him. But 'at the same time he had hopes of a bribe from Paul; and for this reason sent for him very often and talked with him' (*Acts* 24). So, seen from below, it is perfectly natural to suspect the governor of expecting a bribe. We seem to be back to Julius Bassus again.

This is the governor as judge. He was also, as we have said, responsible for seeing that the taxes were collected. Taxation was not uniform throughout the Empire. The property tax and capitation tax which applied both to citizens and non-citizens were not levied in Italy or in colonies and certain other privileged communities outside Italy. Senators were probably exempt as well. Customs duties (*portoria*) were levied on external and internal trade, with internal rates between 2 per cent and 5 per cent, while the external rate was as high as 25 per cent at the Red Sea ports on luxury goods from India. Roman citizens also paid tax on inheritances and on the manumission of slaves. Dio alleges that Caracella's motive for making virtually all inhabitants of the Empire Roman citizens was to make them liable to these taxes (see Chapter 11).

In the provinces, cities were normally liable for collecting tax and remitting it to Roman officials. Only for land which lay outside any city's jurisdiction would tax-collecting syndicates (*publicani*) continue to be used, or government agents collect the tax directly. The *publicani* in fact became less and less important as officials took over their responsibilities, first in the imperial provinces and then in the senatorial ones. From Augustus onwards, there were regular censuses in each province to keep the tax rolls up to date, and territories organized for the first time as regular provinces promptly underwent a census. We have evidence for this procedure from Judaea under Augustus, Cappadocia under Tiberius, Dacia under Trajan, and we have already seen that it was probably this census as a prelude to regular taxation that Varus was conducting in Germany (see Chapter 3). Our knowledge, however, both of the fiscal system and of its real impact on the life of the provinces is singularly imperfect, and we may suspect that there was greater diversity from province to province than our sources allow us to document.

The survival of papyri gives us more information about Egypt than we have for most other provinces, but Egypt, as we have seen, had its own administrative norms, and we cannot generalize from Egyptian practice. The most famous of all Egyptian fiscal documents, dating from the middle of the second century, is the list of regulations of the official who administered the special account (*idios logos*) into which were paid the emperor's revenues from sources other than normal taxation (*Select papyri* 206 = *LR* pp.379–83). It reveals the minute attention with which the official tried to regulate inheritance, the registration of documents and various commercial transactions. Other papyri show that the authorities were worried about persons who abandoned everything and disappeared to avoid paying taxes. Extortion by officials in Egypt was a centuries-old tradition, despite attempts to check it. An edict from Galba's brief reign in 68, issued by the prefect Tiberius Julius Alexander, who was to be instrumental in securing the throne for Vespasian the following year (page 171), deplores 'recent abuses', obviously meant to be blamed on Nero's officials, and decrees:

> that persons not be forced against their will, contrary to the general practice of the provinces, into tax farming or other leases of imperial estate . . .
>
> that no one shall, under pretence of public obligations, have loans asigned from others which he did not originally make, and that no free persons shall ever be locked up in any jail whatsoever, except a criminal, or in the debtor prison, except those indebted to the *fiscus* . . .
>
> that native Alexandrians residing in the country for business reasons are not to be forced into any rural compulsory public service . . .
>
> that whenever a prefect has already decided to dismiss a case brought before him, it is not to be brought again before the assizes; and if two prefects have concurred in judgement, a state accountant who brings up the same matters before the assizes is also to be punished [i.e., as well as having the case thrown out], seeing that he does nothing but reserve for himself and the other civil officers a pretext for enriching themselves [i.e., presumably from bribes]; many persons have in fact preferred to abandon their private possessions, because they had spent more than their value through having the same matters brought up at each assize . . .
>
> I shall also establish the same rule for matters brought up under the special account (*idios logos*) . . . for there will be no end of vexatious denunciations if dismissed matters are brought up until someone decides to condemn . . .
>
> (II. G. Evelyn White and J. H. Oliver, *The Temple of Hibis in El Khargeh Oasis, Part II: Greek Inscriptions* [New York, 1938], no. 4 = *LR*, pp.375–9)

This document has been pressed into service to support theories of economic decline and official extortion in the Empire at large. That however it cannot do. Egypt *was* a special case. You could not even leave it without a pass, as Strabo tells us from personal experience (ii.101), and as numerous references in papyri confirm. The power of the local bureaucrats comes through strongly, as does the prefect's desire to keep them in check. The compulsory public service which is referred to took various forms and was a feature of life in other provinces too, particularly in the East. Provision of transport and accommodation for Roman officials might be the equivalent of a sizeable extra tax, and offered all too much scope for abuse. The earliest of numerous inscriptions regulating the practice comes from Pisidia under Tiberius and confirms that the people of Sagalassus must keep in readiness ten wagons and ten mules for the use of official travellers, while at the same time it defines what amount of transport each grade is entitled to, from the procurator and senators, who can have all ten wagons, down to centurions, who get only one wagon and specifies what shall be paid for the use of the service.

The central authorities in the East, apart from Egypt, where there was a long urban tradition, left the cities as much autonomy as they thought fit and laid upon the cities and especially on their councillors the responsibility for acting as agents of the Roman government in fiscal and other matters. Local pride bred a spirit of emulation which might cause competing cities to bankrupt themselves. Much of Pliny's business as governor of Bithynia under Trajan, reflected in book X of the *Letters*, was concerned with the cities' finances, as when, for instance, he writes to recommend that permission be given for rebuilding the public baths at Prusa, and Trajan agrees, 'provided that no new tax is imposed and that there is no further diversion of funds intended for essential services' (*Letters* x.23, 24).

In the West, certain areas also had a tradition of urban life dating back to pre-Roman times, and where no such tradition existed, we find the Roman authorities consciously fostering urban development, like Agricola as governor of Britain who 'privately encouraged and publicly subsidized the building of temples, forums, and houses' until the natives came to cultivate 'the allurements of vice, porticoes, baths and smart dinner-parties' (Tacitus, *Agricola* 21). In Gaul, the Rhineland and Britain, we can see this process at work throughout the first century. For the Danubian provinces the archaeological evidence is less complete, but the eventual result was the same.

The contrast is great between these areas and those parts of the western world where Greeks or Phoenicians had settled and founded cities centuries before, along the Mediterranean coastline of Gaul and Spain, in Baetica (southern Spain), and in Africa. Here there was as vigorous a municipal life as in the East, and the process of Romanization, operating through the towns, was correspondingly swifter. Latin, moreover, as we have already seen, took over from the earlier tongues, whereas it never replaced Greek in the East. 'Romanization' is a concept frequently used with no attempt to define what it means, but adoption of the Latin language is a fundamental part of it, along with Roman institutions and modes of thought, feeling and conduct consonant with those of Rome.

Baetica was well advanced on the path to Romanization even before Augustus. It produced the first provincial consul, Cornelius Balbus, consul 40 BC, from Gades (Cadiz), and a generation or so later was so rich as to have 500 Roman knights, a number which only Rome itself and Patavium (Padua) could match (Strabo iii.169). The contribution which Baetica and Tarraconensis, along the Mediterranean coast, make to Latin literature in the first century leaves no doubt as to the reality of Latin culture in their cities: the two Senecas were both born at Corduba, as was their kinsman Lucan; Columella was originally from Gades, and thought Italian landowners paid too little care to their estates. Quintilian and Martial came from Tarraconensis. The whole of Spain received Latin rights, half way to full citizenship, under Vespasian, and we are well supplied with documents illustrating Spanish municipal life, such as letters from Vespasian and

Titus to Sabora and Munigua respectively, or the municipal charters of Salpensa and Malaca. Spain appears to have adopted the imperial cult more spontaneously and more enthusiastically than other western provinces. The existing public monuments are as impressive as those of any province, even outside Baetica and Tarraconensis, as for instance at Merida, Segovia or Salamanca.

Narbonensis benefited especially from the favour of Augustus. To pre-Augustan colonies like Narbonne and Arles are added new ones, probably triumviral: Fréjus, Béziers, Orange. Nîmes and Vienne received Latin status. Everywhere there was building – theatres, temples, aqueducts. The Pont du Gard, carrying the aqueduct that supplied Nîmes, is 275 metres long and stands nearly 50 metres above the normal level of the stream, one of the most beautiful and most impressive of all Roman structures. Men from these cities soon came to take their place in Roman public life: Domitius Afer from Nîmes was praetor in 25, consul in 39, while Valerius Asiaticus from Vienne was consul twice, in 35 and 46. Narbonne and Arles became major trading centres, Arles supplanting Marseille as the main port for traffic up and down the Rhône, while Narbonne was the port from which the sigillata pottery from La Graufesenque and other south Gaulish centres was shipped. The elder Pliny can call Narbonensis 'more like Italy than a province', and, as we have seen, Narbonensis and the Spanish provinces are the first to produce significant numbers of recruits for the legions in the latter part of the century when Italian recruitment falls off. The old Greek towns along the coast and a little way inland shared in the general prosperity. Glanum (St Rémy de Provence) has notable monuments. But Massilia (Marseille), once the leader, remained a backwater, noted for its 'Greek charm and provincial simplicity' (Tacitus, *Agricola* 4).

Africa had an influx of Italian settlers and merchants in the late Republic. The Punic cities continued to flourish, and Punic cults and language persisted, even among the upper levels of urban society. Such major ports as Utica and Hadrumetum (Sousse) retained the economic importance

which was already well established before the Roman
conquest, the more so in the late Republic and under Augustus, before Carthage, destroyed in 146 BC, and refounded
by Caesar and Augustus, got back its former dominant
position. Carthage, which was eventually to overtake Alexandria in population, and Lepcis Magna, at the head of the
caravan routes into the Fezzan and hence the main outlet for
Transsaharan trade, both flourished exceedingly. Africa was
the main granary of Rome, and also had vast olive groves, as
it still does in some parts. You still drive south from Sousse
across rolling plains through an ocean of olive trees to where
the amphitheatre of Thysdrus (El Djem) stands out on the
horizon, like the distant sight of the cathedral at Chartres
over the wheatfields of northern France, and you understand
where the wealth came from that built an amphitheatre
seating 30,000 people in so remote a place (page 272).

The African towns exhibit a bewildering complexity of
municipal organization in the first century, and an interesting
mixture of Roman chequerboard planning and unplanned
native growth. We still find Punic magistrates called *sufetes*
and priests called *kohanim,* for instance at Mactar, where an
inscription set up in 88 by the young men's organization
shows a mix of Punic and Latin names, beginning with
Rogatus son of Addun and including Mufthum son of Samon
along with Faustus son of Sextus (*AE* 1959, 172; Picard,
Karthago viii (1957), p.77). Thugga (Dougga) still has
magistrates with Punic names in the middle of the first
century and shows in general a mixture of Latin, Punic and
Numidian influences. Almost everywhere the Punic gods are
still found, though identified, as was the Roman habit, with
deities of the Greco-Roman pantheon, Baal Hammon with
Saturn, Tanit with Juno, Eshmoun with Aesculapius, and so
on.

Side by side with the old Africa where Roman administration and Latin culture were grafted on to Punic stock was a
new Africa where the paramount influence was that of the
Roman army; and here we begin to rejoin northwest Europe.
We have seen that there was considerable fighting in Africa

down to 19 BC (see chapter 3), and the army continued to extend its influence and its lines of communication towards the south and the west thereafter. A milestone of AD 14 shows the 3rd Legion *Augusta* building a road from the port of Tacape (Gabès) via Capsa (Gafsa) to its camp, wherever that was (*CIL* viii.10018). Three years later began the revolt of Tacfarinas, which was not suppressed until 24. Tacfarinas, like Arminius in Germany, had served in a Roman auxiliary unit and was able to use his training against his former teachers. The cause of the outbreak was the fear and resentment felt by the nomadic and semi-nomadic tribes on the fringe of the area long settled and farmed under Punic influence, who saw the Roman army encroaching on their traditional grazing grounds and threatening their values and way of life. It is wrong to suppose that the Romans wished to sedentarize the nomads, or that they objected to nomadism as such. Indeed the supply of nomadic labour was essential to the farmer, just as the great estates in Italy relied on the labour of poor freeholders at harvest time (see chapter 8). But the extension of agriculture which went along with the extension of effective military patrolling inevitably affected the nomads' pastoral routine. The pattern of Roman centuriation (the division of the land into *centuriae* each of 200 *iugera*, roughly 700 mètres each way) is still visible over wide expanses of western and southern Tunisia up to the 500 metre contour line. The vast increase in the acreage devoted to olive cultivation and the establishment of new Roman towns in the interior based on the wealth thus created are a salient feature of Africa over the rest of the first century.

Romanization took a different form in Gaul, Germany and Britain. Especially in Germany and Britain, the role of the army was more important and more direct. Peace had to be imposed. This in itself was a gross interference in the Celts' and the Germans' value-system and lifestyle. Warfare had been to them a way of life, and to some extent the resistance to pacification was the natives' fighting for the right to go on fighting. With peace came trade, with trade the 'allurements of vice' already referred to. The army itself needed supplies, which had either to be brought in to the area where each unit was stationed, thus stimulating trade, or else obtained locally, thus stimulating local production. The soldiers' pay was largely spent locally, with the same effect. The eight legions on the Rhine in the Julio-Claudian period, with a similar number of auxiliaries, plus the Rhine fleet based on Cologne, represented between 85,000 and 90,000 men, not to mention their dependents — their women, their slaves, their hangers-on, together with the veterans and their families who chose to settle where they had served. This added up to a major economic factor in the development and subsequent Romanization of the area. We have some experience in the modern world of how military bases encourage or distort local economies.

Towns grew up to serve the needs of army bases, and often continued, even if the army moved away. Or the site of a legionary base would be used for a veteran colony. We find this happening as early as 25 BC at Aosta in northern Italy; it happens in Africa, with Ammaedara (Haïdra); it lay at the origin of Lincoln and Gloucester. And if the legion did not move away, there might still be founded a colony nearby, as at Cologne (Colonia Claudia Ara Agrippinensium) or Xanten, alongside the legionary base of Vetera. Along the whole length of the Rhine we trace back the modern cities to their roots in legionary bases or auxiliary forts.

The legions were builders as well as soldiers. When Agricola wanted to subsidize the construction of temples and forums, he could do so easily by supplying military architects and craftsmen. Army engineers built roads and bridges and aqueducts. The Pont du Gard may be the most impressive aqueduct in Gaul, but it is not the most sophisticated. That title must go to the Gier aqueduct serving Lyon, built under Hadrian, 75 km long, with four inverted siphons, that at Beaunant being 120 metres deep, more than twice as deep, in fact, as the Pont du Gard is high. The road systems of both Gaul and Britain were laid out with military needs foremost in their architects' minds, and both at the same time served the needs of trade. It used to be supposed that the Roman authorities compelled the native Gauls to abandon their hill-top *oppida* and descend to dwell in new Roman cities in the plain. The truth is that they did not have to. Once there was peace, so that a hill-top refuge was not necessary for security, and once the new trade routes and the new prosperity followed the new roads (and in Gaul especially the rivers), economic opportunity brought people down. So too in Britain, where a hill-top *oppidum* like Bagendon finds itself deserted to the profit of Cirencester in the valley below. Huge wine barrels have been found in the Roman bases along the Lippe valley; it is hard to imagine wine being imported on that scale by private initiative into so remote an area if it were not for the army. The army needed pottery and imported sigillata for its needs. Once a sigillata distribution network had been set up to supply those needs, the same network could supply civilians. Even where we cannot prove army involvement, we may suspect it, if only from the scale of some operation. So for instance the massive timber wharf recently excavated in the City of London and dating from around 80, which it is plausible to associate with Agricola's campaigns, but which no doubt will have served commercial purposes as well.

Spain, Narbonensis and Africa became so fully Romanized and their upper classes so successful, that each in turn provided Rome with an emperor. Neither Gaul, apart from Narbonensis, or Britain ever did, and despite Claudius's advocacy of opening the Senate to Gaulish notables, few of them made it. We find a large Berber landowner like Lollius Urbicus governing Britain and conquering the Scottish lowlands (see Chapter 10, page 246); we do not find a British counterpart in command in Africa or Asia. The Greek East had its own values: Romanization was uneven in its geographical spread as well as in its impact on different classes of society. We shall have occasion to consider this again in Chapter 10.

When Nero wanted a detachment of praetorians to go and kill his mother, their prefect, Burrus, declined to vouch for their obedience: their loyalty, he said, was to 'the whole house of the Caesars', not to Nero alone' (Tacitus, *Annals* xiv.7). Ninety years after Actium, the Julio-Claudian family had attained a seemingly unassailable hereditary position. Unworthy though Nero might be of his great-great-grandfather Augustus, no conspiracy could succeed as long as the troops stayed loyal to the family. Thus any conspiracy against him was dangerous, and the price for being suspected of conspiracy or disaffection was, as we have seen (Chapter 5), death. Those who, despite this, still hoped to get rid of Nero assumed that any replacement must come from a family with an ancestry rivalling that of the Caesars. Thus, Galba, who actually succeeded Nero, 'came from a very ancient aristocratic house ... and even had a tablet set up in the Palace forecourt, tracing his ancestry back to Jupiter on the male, and to Pasiphaë, Minos's wife, on the female side' (Suetonius, *Galba* 2). Nero shared this assumption: Vespasian, who finally came out of the civil wars after Nero's death as founder of a new dynasty, had been entrusted with the command in Judaea because he was 'an energetic commander, who could be trusted not to abuse his plenary powers ... nothing, it seemed, need be feared from a man of such modest antecedents' (Suetonius, *Vespasian* 4). Thus the events of 68–9 not only 'let out the secret, that an emperor could be made elsewhere than at Rome' (Tacitus, *Histories*, i.4), but showed that a senator of obscure Italian origin could reach the highest post of all.

The first overt move against Nero was taken by Gaius

Julius Vindex, governor of Gallia Lugdunensis and himself an Aquitanian chieftain whose family had acquired citizenship from Caesar, and whose father had been a senator. Vindex is a good representative of a class which had done well out of Roman rule in Gaul (page 139). His motive for rebellion has been much discussed. Ostensibly it was to replace Nero by a more worthy emperor. The slogan was 'freedom from the tyrant'. Vindex's candidate for the throne was Servius Sulpicius Galba, who had been for the past eight years governor of Hispania Tarraconensis. Vindex urged him to 'rescue the human race' (Seutonius, *Galba* 9); the phrase is echoed on Galba's coinage, SALUS GENERIS HUMANI, along with LIBERTAS RESTITUTA, ROMA RENASCENS, and the like. Galba staged a public demonstration where he allowed himself to be acclaimed as *imperator* and announced that he would henceforth govern in the name of the Senate and the people of Rome. Having one legion, 6th *Victrix*, under his command, he began raising further troops, including a new legion, 7th *Galbiana* (later *Gemina*), and 'called upon all Spanish provincials to unite energetically in the common cause of rebellion' (Suetonius, *Galba* 10). He also won over Marcus Salvius Otho, governor of Lusitania and erstwhile husband of Poppaea, and Aulus Caecina Alienus, quaestor of Baetica, whom he appointed to command 6th *Victrix*, while the former commander of that legion, Titus Vinius, was sent to look after Galba's interests at Rome.

The history of this period was written by the survivors. It is hard to know how much of what we are told is true, and how much was put around to justify the intrigues and the betrayals that rebellion and civil war produce. Suetonius represents Galba as hesitating whether to accept Vindex's summons, although we can scarcely imagine Vindex committing himself without having some prior assurance that Galba was willing. Galba is said to have intercepted orders from Nero for his own execution: perhaps so, or is this a convenient excuse for his breaking his oath of loyalty to Nero?

The immediate success of Vindex's rebellion depended not on Galba, but on the reaction of the nearest army, that of

Upper Germany, and its commander, Verginius Rufus. Vindex's first action was to try to seize Lyon, which closed its gates to him. While so occupied, he learnt that Verginius Rufus had invaded his province. Advancing to meet him near Besançon, he came to some agreement with Rufus himself, according to one story, but Rufus's legions insisted on fighting, cut Vindex's inexperienced troops to pieces, and Vindex committed suicide. Verginius Rufus was to die full of years and honours, three times consul, lauded by Pliny (*Letters* vi.10, ix.19). After Galba's success, was it convenient to agree on the story that Rufus had not given the order to massacre men who were after all fighting for Galba?

Vindex was dead, and nobody wrote his story. What were his motives? Some modern scholars have seen him as a Gaulish nationalist, aiming at 'more or less complete autonomy' for Gaul (the phrase is from the *Cambridge Ancient History*). This must surely be wrong. Not only is there no hint of it in our sources, but 'Gaul' was not a political entity and never had been. Vindex's own authority derived from Rome. If Rome's authority were destroyed, there is no reason to think that the rest of Gaul would have accepted Vindex's leadership because of his descent from Aquitanian chieftains. It is more likely that he saw himself as acting in the way a Roman senator should, resisting tyranny in the old Roman tradition whose appeal was no doubt all the more potent to a man adopted rather than born into it. Tacitus, himself coming from Narbonensis, could still, as we have seen (page 113), sneer at Sejanus for his 'municipal' origin. A provincial senator, not even of Italian descent, might well overcompensate. It would be interesting to know Vindex better.

Galba's emissaries were apparently already negotiating with the Senate. Nero, who was at Naples when he heard of Vindex's revolt on the ninth anniversary of his mother's murder (March 68), vacillated between sublime insouciance and the announcement of strong measures to meet the crisis which, however, were never carried out. Rufus, after Vindex's suicide, put himself at the disposal of the Senate; his troops

offered him the principate, and he refused it. On his tombstone, says Pliny, he claimed to have acted 'not for himself,
but for his country'. Galba, who despaired when he heard of
Vindex's defeat, recovered when he heard that the Senate and
the praetorians had accepted him as emperor. Nero was
dead: the praetorian prefect, Nymphidius Sabinus, had joined
in negotiations with the Senate and brought over the guard by
promising a donative of 30,000 sesterces per man in Galba's
name, Nero was proclaimed a public enemy and, already in
flight, killed himself (9 June 68). It was Galba's freedman
Icelus, he who took the news to Spain (page 152), who gave
permission for Nero to have a decent burial, and he was
buried in the Domitian family tomb, not the mausoleum of
Augustus, thanks to his two old nurses and his faithful con-
cubine, the freedwoman Acte.

Hated as Nero had been by the upper classes, and
although the Roman populace is recorded as celebrating his
death, he had friends who continued to put flowers on his
grave every year; Otho and Vitellius, Galba's successors,
found it expedient to appeal to his memory; at least three pretenders after his death claimed to be Nero, one of whom got
Parthian support; and some people were said to have been
influenced in backing Nerva for emperor by his friendship
with Nero thirty years before. Was this simply loyalty to the
last of the dynasty? Or did Nero have qualities to which the
senatorial tradition represented in our sources is blind?

Galba now proceeded to squander his opportunities. He
was slow in getting to Rome. On his way through Gaul he
rewarded the tribes which had supported Vindex and
punished those which had joined with the Rhine legions in
suppressing the revolt. The legions had offered the principate
to Verginius Rufus a second time on Nero's death, and he
had again refused. They swore allegiance to Galba reluctantly and only at Rufus's insistence. But Galba treated
Rufus coldly and replaced him in his command by the old,
lame and incompetent Hordeonius Flaccus. The legions
were not pleased. The governor of Lower Germany, Fonteius
Capito, suspected of plotting against Galba, was murdered

by two of his officers. Also murdered, on Galba's orders, was Lucius Clodius Macer, legate of the 3rd Legion *Augusta* in Africa, who refused to recognize Galba, raised another legion, and threatened to cut off Rome's grain supply.

Other new appointments which Galba made were ill-advised, none more so than that of Cornelius Laco to succeed Nymphidius Sabinus as praetorian prefect. Laco, whom Suetonius calls 'arrogant and stupid', was a former financial official who proved totally incapable of understanding or controlling his new command. Nymphidius, who had expected a better reward for bringing the praetorians over to Galba, was moved to unsuccessful rebellion. His own men killed him. Even so, Galba refused to pay them the donative that Nymphidius had originally promised on his behalf. Executions of men suspected of having supported Nymphidius or been too close to Nero caused alarm, and the subsequent disbanding of the emperor's German bodyguard upset the praetorians. Sailors from the Misenum fleet whom Nero had enrolled or promised to enrol in a legion petitioned Galba to keep this promise. He replied with a cavalry charge and had the survivors decimated. Economy measures, however necessary, were unpopular, especially among the Roman masses, whom Nero's extravagance had kept entertained. Disaffection was rife in the army. As 68 drew to its close, Galba had few supporters left.

On New Year's Day 69, Galba took office as consul for the second time. That same day, the army of Upper Germany refused to renew its oath of allegiance to him, and two days later joined the army of Lower Germany in proclaiming Aulus Vitellius, newly arrived governor of that province, as emperor. When the news reached Rome (page 150), Galba misguidedly adopted as his colleague and heir the thirty-year-old Lucius Calpurnius Piso Frugi Licinianus, of excellent family, a descendant of Pompey and Crassus, highly acceptable to the Senate, but unknown to the armies. This was a blow to Marcus Salvius Otho, who had been the first provincial governor to declare for Galba, and expected to succeed him. He now turned to the praetorian guard, and on

15 January, by pre-arrangement, slipped off to their camp and was proclaimed emperor. The praetorians lynched Galba in the Forum. Piso was also killed, and the Senate hastened to recognize Otho. There was now one new emperor in Rome and another on the Rhine.

For Galba, there is Tacitus's lapidary dismissal: 'By common consent worthy of Empire, if he had not been emperor.' Otho, whose record was bad (he had been Nero's boon companion and was heavily in debt), nonetheless began well, conciliating the Senate and generally winning support in Rome. Italy, the Danubian provinces, Africa and the East backed him. But the army in Germany was still committed to Vitellius, who soon received the support of the Spanish and Gallic provinces, Britain and Raetia. His generals invaded Italy, crossing the Alps with the winter snow still on the ground, and defeated Otho near Cremona before all of his Danube legions could join him (first Battle of Bedriacum, mid-April 69). Otho committed suicide, apparently to avoid further civil bloodshed, impressing everyone with the courage which they did not know he had. His troops surrendered, and the Senate voted Vitellius the usual honours.

Our sources depict Vitellius as cruel, gluttonous and corrupt. His victorious army is said to have treated Italy as if it were a conquered province, his lieutenants and favourites amassing fortunes, while Vitellius himself squandered one, largely on dinners. But this information comes from his victorious enemies. Otho's praetorian cohorts were disbanded and new ones recruited from the army of Germany. Vitellius's men, however, rapidly lost all semblance of discipline, and Vitellius had no money left to pay them the bonus they had been promised. The Danubian legions which had arrived too late to fight for Otho were sent back to their posts, but their leading centurions were put to death. This did nothing to strengthen the survivors' affection for Vitellius. His own Rhine legions seemed to be doing well out of his victory. No doubt the rest of the army wondered what was in it for them.

There were six legions in the Danubian provinces, and for

various reasons they had close ties with the legions in the East. At that time there were three in Syria, three more in Judaea, since the outbreak of the Jewish Revolt in 66, and two in Egypt. Although the East at first swore allegiance to Vitellius, intense behind-the-scenes activity led to the emergence of Vespasian as his challenger. Suetonius makes the first initiative come from troops of the Danubian army (*Vespasian* 6). Was this the official version, a spontaneous acclamation from below? It was probably more premeditated than that. The first overt move was the proclamation of Vespasian as emperor on 1 July by the prefect of Egypt, an Alexandrian Jew called Tiberius Julius Alexander. From this event Vespasian subsequently dated his reign. He was rapidly accepted by his own legions in Judaea, then by the Syrian and Danubian legions, the other eastern provinces and the main client kings. Gaius Licinius Mucianus, governor of Syria, was chosen to lead the invasion of Italy. The Danubian governors were not enthusiastic: the governor of Moesia warned Vitellius what was afoot, the governors of Dalmatia and Pannonia were 'rich old men', concerned only to stay out of trouble (Tacitus, *Histories* ii.86).

The invasion of Italy did not wait for Mucianus to arrive. The Danubian legions marched under the command of Antonius Primus, legate of that 7th *Gemina* which Galba had raised in Spain, himself a Gaul from Toulouse, and they defeated the Vitellians at the second Battle of Bedriacum in late October or early November 69. Nearby Cremona was sacked by the victors amid scenes of horror to which Tacitus devotes one of his purplest passages (*Histories* iii.32-4). The road to Rome was now open, and Vitellius' supporters were beginning to defect. But the new praetorian cohorts whom Vitellius had enrolled from his own former Rhine legions insisted on fighting it out. Vespasian's supporters in Rome itself were besieged on the Capitol, which the Vitellians proceeded to take by storm, burning the Temple of Jupiter and killing Vespasian's brother, Flavius Sabinus, city prefect since Otho's accession, whom Vitellius had not removed.

Primus's troops entered the city on 20 December. The

praetorians fought to the last. Vitellius was ignominiously killed. Rome for some days feared the fate of Cremona, until Mucianus arrived and restored order. The Senate recognized Vespasian, who was still in Egypt, and made him and his elder son, Titus, now commanding the army in Judaea, consuls for 70. Domitian, his younger son, aged nineteen, who had escaped from the storming of the Capitol, was appointed praetor with consular powers, and distinguished himself by 'playing the emperor's son' (*Histories* iv.2) and abusing his position. Mucianus, however, exercised effective power and neutralized all potential opposition. The hot-headed Primus was so skilfully stripped of all authority that he went off to complain fruitlessly to Vespasian, still at Alexandria (*Histories* iv.80) and in no hurry. He visited Asia and Greece on the way to Rome, where he arrived at the end of the summer, 70, to find peace and order prevailing.

Vespasian's legal position and authority were defined by a senatorial decree, the *lex de imperio Vespasiani*, one of our most important surviving epigraphic documents (*ILS* 244 = *LR* p.89):

> . . . that he shall have the right, just as the deified Augustus and Tiberius Julius Caesar Augustus and Tiberius Claudius Caesar Augustus Germanicus (i.e., Tiberius and Claudius respectively) had, to conclude treaties with whomsoever he wishes;
>
> And that he shall have the right, just as the deified Augustus and Tiberius Julius Caesar Augustus and Tiberius Claudius Caesar Augustus had, to convene the Senate, to put and refer proposals to it, and to cause decrees of the Senate to be enacted by proposal and division of the house; . . .
>
> And that at all elections especial consideration shall be given to those candidates for a magistracy, authority, *imperium*, or any post whom he has recommended to the Roman Senate and people or to whom he has given and promised his vote . . .

The same appeal to the precedents established by Augustus, Tiberius, and Claudius is also used to authorize Vespasian

> to transact and do whatever things divine, public and private he deems to serve the advantage and the overriding interests of the state ... to not be bound by those laws and plebiscites which were declared not binding upon the deified Augustus, etc. ...

Finally:

> That whatever was done, executed, decreed or ordered before the enactment of this law by the Emperor (*Imperator*) Caesar Vespasianus Augustus, or by anyone at his order or command, shall be as fully binding and valid as if they had been done by order of the people or plebs.

Tacitus sums it up in one phrase: 'At Rome the Senate decreed to Vespasian everything usual (*omnia solita*) for emperors' (*Histories* iv.3). In the last resort, if he chose to exercise all the powers conferred on him the emperor, as this law makes clear, was an absolute monarch. It is wrong to see in this law any new departure, nor is the Senate, as has been argued, asserting its own *auctoritas*. Vespasian had won the throne by force of arms. His troops occupied Rome. Vespasian continued to date his reign from his first acclamation at Alexandria. The Senate by this decree is not conferring power, but legitimizing it. It had done the same for four emperors in a year and a half, and had little *auctoritas* of its own left. The Senate, like the city of Rome, was one of the spoils of war.

Although order had now been restored in Italy, there were other parts of the Empire where fighting was still going on. In Judaea, after a lull while the fate of the Empire was settled elsewhere, Titus resumed operations in the spring of 70, besieged Jerusalem, stormed the outer walls in May, captured and destroyed the Temple in August, and put down the last resistance in the upper part of the city in September. Titus's staff included two pro-Roman Jews, Tiberius Julius Alexander, rewarded for his early support of Vespasian by promotion to the post of praetorian prefect, and the historian Josephus, whose eye-witness account, tendentious though it is, provides a vivid picture of the Roman army in action. He would have us believe that the burning of the Temple was an accident of battle and contrary to Titus's intentions (*Jewish War* vi.236–266). Titus, he claims, tried to have the flames put out, but in vain, and he just had time to see the inside before it was destroyed. Other sources more plausibly make it an act of deliberate policy. The Temple treasures were carried in the triumph which Titus and Vespasian celebrated in 71 (Josephus, *Jewish War*, vii.122–56), and subsequently depicted on the Arch erected to Titus at Rome after his death. Coinage celebrates IUDAEA CAPTA. This display of solid and authentic military success was a propaganda godsend for the new dynasty, and was made the most of, although the last rebels were not in fact subdued until the spring of 74, when Titus's successor, Lucius Flavius Silva, took the fortress of Masada after a seven-month siege. The surviving siege-works are an impressive monument to the Roman army's capacity to conceive and carry out large projects. The great rock of Masada was entirely surrounded by a wall to keep the defenders from breaking out, the Roman camps are still visible in the stony desert, and the most striking work of all is the great ramp built by Jewish prisoners up which the army brought a great battering ram to breach the defensive wall around the summit. According to Josephus, 960 defenders killed one another and themselves rather than surrender, the only survivors being two women and five children who hid in one of the underground cisterns (*Jewish War*, vii.399–401).

Minor actions were also fought to restore order in Pontus, in Moesia, where the Dacians and Sarmatians took advantage of the dislocation caused by civil war to cross the Danube in some force, and in Africa, where both Vitellius and Vespasian were remembered as proconsul, and where loyalties were confused by the rivalry between proconsul and legionary legate. Valerius Festus, commanding the 3rd

Legion *Augusta*, had the proconsul Lucius Calpurnius Piso murdered in Vespasian's interests, and then found himself obliged to put down a private war between two cities of the province, Oea (now Tripoli) and Lepcis Magna. The former had called in the Garamantes from the desert to their assistance; Festus's troops chasing them out again, discovered a new route into Garamantian territory which took only four days, whereas their territory had previously been considered inaccessible (Tacitus, *Histories* iv.50; Pliny, *Natural History* v.38). This may have been a major factor in the subsequent Roman penetration of the Sahara.

In northwest Europe, there was trouble in Britain and Germany. In both provinces over the next few years Vespasian deliberately set out to extend the limits of Roman-held territory. The garrison of Britain had been reduced from four to three legions in 67. Vitellius withdrew another 8000 men to join his Rhine army's march on Italy, but after the first Battle of Bedriacum sent back the 14th Legion which Nero had withdrawn. It went back to Germany for good the following year (70) to help suppress Civilis's revolt (page 176). Vitellius also replaced the governor, but neither Vitellius's nominee nor his predecessor could maintain discipline among their men in these unsettled times. The anti-Roman elements among the Brigantes, who occupied much of modern Yorkshire and Lancashire and extended even into the Scottish Lowlands, seized their chance to drive out the pro-Roman queen, Cartimandua. Her former husband, Venutius, replaced her. The Romans managed to rescue her, but could not do more. This left them with an active enemy rather than a client kingdom on their northern flank.

Even when Vespasian had consolidated his position in Italy, Britain still had to wait its turn. The Rhineland came first. Vitellius's army had included eight Batavian cohorts, whose indiscipline was a constant problem. After Bedriacum, they were sent back to the Rhine. When the Danube legions marched on Italy in Vespasian's name, emissaries tried to stir up trouble in Germany so as to prevent any troops left there from coming to Vitellius's help. A Batavian chieftain who had served in the *auxilia* and now had the Roman citizenship, Julius Civilis, threw himself enthusiastically into making trouble, ostensibly on Vespasian's behalf, using the eight Batavian cohorts and other fighting men from his own tribe and from other tribes on both banks of the lower Rhine. After Vespasian's victory at the second Battle of Bedriacum, the legionaries who were left in Germany swore allegiance to him, unenthusiastically, but with little choice. Civilis, however, continued to fight, with no pretence now of helping Vespasian, but openly in revolt against Roman authority. Other tribes joined in, notably the Treveri and Lingones. The native auxiliary regiments deserted *en masse*. Even the remnants of the legions swore allegiance to 'the empire of the Gauls' (*imperium Galliarum*, Tacitus, *Histories* iv.59). The Roman base at Vetera surrendered after a long siege. The whole Rhine valley from Mainz to the sea was in rebel hands. But the rebellion spread no further; in particular, the Sequani attacked and defeated the neighbouring Lingones, while the Mediomatrici, around the modern Metz, on the borders of the Treveri, also stayed loyal, and at a meeting of Gallic tribes held in the territory of the Remi (around Rheims) the Remi themselves took the lead in condemning the rebels. Inter-tribal rivalries and traditional enmities were still strong. Gaul was not a nation.

Meanwhile the success of Vespasian's cause in Italy left Mucianus with troops to spare. The Roman army returned to the Rhineland in overwhelming strength: five strong legions from Italy, the 14th from Britain, and two legions from Spain. Petillius Cerialis, set in command of Lower Germany, rapidly put an end to the rebellion. Tacitus's *Histories* break off in the middle of a sentence with Civilis suing for peace and all but the Batavian heartland, the *insula Batavorum*, once more firmly in Roman hands. What happened to Civilis, we do not know. Other ringleaders were executed, one of them, Julius Sabinus of the Lingones, after nine years in hiding. There were however no reprisals against the tribes concerned. Even the Batavi remained free from any other obligation than that of providing auxiliaries (Tacitus, *Germania* 29). Some

scholars have argued that the revolt caused the Romans
henceforth to cease recruiting auxiliary units in the areas
where they were to serve. It is true that some of the units
which had actually taken part in the revolt were either
disbanded or posted elsewhere, and their place on the Rhine
taken by units which had come in with the new legions sent to
suppress the revolt. But the evidence from tombstones and
discharge certificates (*diplomata*) makes it clear that local
recruitment continued to be the rule, except for certain highly
specialized units; for instance, a unit of Syrian archers, the
cohors I milliaria Hemesenorum, stationed at Intercisa
(Dunapentele) on the middle Danube for much of the third
century, went on receiving recruits from around Emesa
(Homs) in Syria, presumably because the locals could not
shoot. Where an auxiliary unit bears an ethnic or geographic
name, this records where it was first raised, but normally no
attempt was made to preserve the original ethnic composition. It does however seem that from now on the practice dies
out of having auxiliary units commanded by their own tribal
leaders, like Civilis or, at an earlier date, Arminius.
Henceforth, command of the auxiliary units is integrated into
the regular army career structure.

Petillius Cerialis himself, after putting down the rebellion,
was transferred to Britain, where he reinstituted a forward
policy in abeyance since Boudicca's revolt a decade earlier.
In that revolt he had commanded the 9th Legion. He now
moved forward into Brigantian territory and established his
old legion in a new base at York, a strategic location that
remained the key to northern England until modern times. He
may also have established a base at Carlisle. Certainly he
broke the power of the Brigantes and was rewarded with a
second consulship (74). His successor, Sextus Julius Frontinus, turned his attention to Wales, overrunning the south
and preparing for the subsequent invasion of the north by
establishing a legionary base at Chester. His work was to be
carried on by the next governor, Tacitus's father-in-law,
Gnaeus Julius Agricola. Petillius's arrival is in fact the
beginning of a series of campaigns designed to complete

the conquest, and extending through into Domitian's reign.

Meanwhile Vespasian also determined to advance the Roman frontier in Germany. Campaigns in 73 and 74 brought under direct control the Black Forest area, in the awkward re-entrant between the Rhine and the upper Danube, and new forts and roads were built, the beginning of the German *limes* system which was to be developed by Vespasian's successors (page 223). There was also fighting in the latter years of Vespasian's reign in the Lippe area, east of the lower Rhine, and Vespasian also strengthened the Roman hold on the Danube, building roads and increasing the garrison of the Danube provinces. He undertook a major reorganization of the eastern frontier region, where a minor war with the Parthians provided the future emperor Trajan with the chance to acquire some glory (Pliny, *Panegyric* 14). In Africa, the base of the 3rd Legion *Augusta* was moved forward to Theveste (now Tebessa, just west of the Tunisian-Algerian border), reflecting the progress made in extending westwards the area of settled agriculture; it was to move forward again to Lambaesis under Hadrian.

In his conduct of affairs, Vespasian showed great moderation and above all (not the most usual trait of emperors as a whole) common sense.

He was from first to last modest and restrained in his conduct of affairs, and more inclined to parade, than to cast a veil over, his humble origins ... he was not the sort of man to bear grudges or pay off old scores ... no innocent party was ever punished during Vespasian's reign except behind his back or while he was absent from Rome, unless by deliberate defiance of his wishes or by misinforming him about the facts in the case ... his one serious failing was avarice ... some claim that greed was in Vespasian's very bones ... still, the more credible view is that the emptiness alike of the Treasury [*aerarium*] and the Privy Purse [*fiscus*[forced Vespasian into heavy taxation and unethical business dealings ... certainly he spent his income to the best possible advantage, however questionable its sources. (Suetonius, *Vespasian* 12–16)

In two respects he notably departed from what had become established practice: he held the consulship every year of his reign, except two, and in 73 himself took the censorship with Titus as his colleague, thus underlining his control of the Senate in a manner which his recent predecessors had preferred to avoid. 'He reformed the senatorial and equestrian orders, now weakened by frequent murders and continuous neglect, replacing undesirable members with the most eligible Italian and provincial candidates available' (Suetonius, *Vespasian* 9). The Senate he treated with great respect, although he went so far as to put to death the obstructive Stoic, Helvidius Priscus, Thrasea Paetus's son-in-law. He gave the knights a greater role in the administration of the Empire than previously, while proportionally diminishing the role of freedmen. He restored discipline in the army and apparently tried to centralize and standardize its organization and procedures.

The legions were increasingly being recruited from the provinces, although Italians continued to form the praetorian cohorts. The virtual disappearance of Italians from the legions was not so much deliberate policy, as that social and economic conditions in Italy made legionary service no longer attractive (see Chapter 8). Vespasian paid particular attention to the provinces. He seems to have encouraged the spread of Roman citizenship and was generous with grants of money and colonial status to cities. No emperor since Tiberius had travelled so widely or knew the provinces so well, and probably none since Augustus had done so much good.

Vespasian was a shrewd man with a sardonic wit and the traditional virtues of the Italian countryside from which his family came. His portrait seems to suit his character. His death was unexpected and brought on partly by his refusal to treat seriously a fever and an attack of diarrhoea. Taken suddenly by an especially violent spasm, he said 'An emperor ought to die standing', and died as he struggled to his feet (Suetonius, *Vespasian* 24). The down-to-earth humour fits well with his character, as does his other attested deathbed remark, 'Oh dear, I think I'm becoming a god.' He was right, for he was hailed with genuine gratitude as *divus*. His son Titus succeeded automatically, being already 'partner in the Empire' and having held tribunician power since 71. He continued to number his years of tribunician power, his consulships, and his imperatorial salutations (for Agricola's victories in Britain) in the same series begun in his father's lifetime. It was all reminiscent of Tiberius's succession to Augustus.

Once he came into sole power, Titus, despite an earlier reputation for ruthlessness and profligacy, showed himself a reformed character, universally popular, 'the darling of the human race' (Suetonius, *Titus* 1). He sent away the Jewish princess Berenice, who had been his mistress, against the will of them both (*invitus invitam*, Suetonius, *Titus* 7). But he died after only a two-year reign, during which he made no great departure from his father's policies. His reign was marked by three major catastrophes in Italy: the eruption of Vesuvius in 79, which obliterated Pompeii and Herculaneum (see Chapter 8); a fire the next year in Rome which burned for three days, destroying temples, public buildings and thousands of dwellings; and a virulent outbreak of plague. Titus's liberality in relieving the distress caused by all three was a strong element in his popularity. His death was all the more regretted, in that people feared the arrogance of his brother and obvious successor, Domitian, who was only thirty, but had long been impatient for power.

Domitian succeeded his brother on 13 September 81. From the start, his autocracy was unveiled and his contempt for the Senate made manifest. Senators were exiled or executed. Domitian, unprecedentedly, had himself made censor in perpetuity, was addressed as 'Lord God', and appointed knights to sit in judgement on senators and to senior posts previously reserved for senators. His reign was marked by conspiracies, the most dangerous being the rebellion in 89 of

Lucius Antonius Saturninus, governor of Upper Germany. Domitian is credited with saying that nobody believes in conspiracies against the emperor until one of them succeeds. His suspicions led him to encourage informers, and his last years were a reign of terror for the Senate which showed its relief at Domitian's murder by damning his memory. While he was alive, writers like Statius and Martial practised Soviet-style sycophancy. After his death, the literary tradition, especially Tacitus and the younger Pliny, becomes uniformly hostile. But it should be noted that after Domitian's death his successors, especially Trajan, strengthened their own position by stressing Domitian's bad qualities, and those who had served under him, like Tacitus and Pliny, found it expedient to take the lead in damning him. Christian tradition too is against him, for reasons that we shall see.

In other respects, Domitian was a good administrator and a successful commander-in-chief. He undertook a considerable building programme in Rome (page 219). Like his father, he was an able finance manager. He showed concern for the grain supply, forbidding the further planting of vines in Italy and ordering half the acreage of vineyards in the provinces to be restored to grain production, though the edict was allowed to lapse. He was meticulous in administering justice, vigorously repressing corruption: 'He took such care to control city magistrates and provincial governors that their standard of restraint and justice was never higher; since his time we have seen many of them charged with all sorts of offences' (Suetonius, *Domitian* 8). He was strong for the maintenance of public order and morality, executing three unchaste Vestal Virgins in 83 and inflicting the archaic punishment of burial alive on the chief Vestal, Cornelia, in 91. He built extensively in Rome, as well as completing projects begun by Vespasian and Titus, including the Colosseum. There is less information about his work in the provinces, but the people of the Empire had much to thank him for, even though the Senate feared and hated him.

The soldiers on the other hand were devoted to him, and would have avenged his murder, if they had had a leader.

This was partly because Domitian raised their pay, the first increase since it was fixed by Augustus, but also because he was personally familiar to them. His first campaign was in Germany, where he led a successful campaign against the Chatti beyond the middle Rhine (83), broke their power, and took permanent possession of the Taunus region. Suetonius stigmatizes this campaign as 'quite unjustified by military necessity' (*Domitian* 6), but it gave the Romans a stronger frontier in the middle Rhine region, and after the suppression of Saturninus's revolt it proved possible to reorganize the frontier and permanently reduce the garrison. In Britain, the governor Julius Agricola, Tacitus's father-in-law, had been appointed by Vespasian, probably in 78. After consolidating the conquest of Wales and sending his auxiliaries swimming beside their horses across the Menai Straits to take Anglesey, he turned his attention to the north, thoroughly subdued the Brigantes, and conquered the Lowlands of Scotland, crossing the Forth and advancing up Strathmore to a great victory at Mons Graupius (Tacitus, *Agricola* 29–37, with the superb rhetorical exercise of the chieftain Calgacus's speech denouncing Roman imperialism: 'They make a desert and call it peace'). But Scotland could not be held; troops were more urgently needed elsewhere. 'Britain was wholly conquered and promptly given up', says Tacitus (*Histories* i.2), with considerable exaggeration on both counts. A new legionary base at Inchtuthil, near Perth, was however abandoned while still under construction, probably in or soon after 87, when the legion it was designed for was withdrawn, and all territory beyond the Forth was given up. Either now or within the next few years (certainly before 92) the 2nd Legion *Adiutrix* was transferred to the Danube front, which was coming under heavy pressure, and the garrison of Britain was permanently reduced from four to three legions.

On the Danube front, the Dacians, united under a strong new ruler, Decebalus (85–106), had invaded Roman territory in force (85), causing great damage. The governor of Moesia was killed, and when Domitian the following year sent a punitive expedition into Dacia, it met with disaster, and the praetorian prefect, its commander, perished. A second Roman invasion of Dacia in 88 avenged the defeat, but unrest among the Danube tribes normally subservient to Rome prevented the Romans from pushing home their advantage, and peace was concluded in 89 on terms which made Decebalus nominally a Roman client, receiving Roman subsidies. There was more fighting in 92, even though the Dacians stayed quiet, and a legion was annihilated. The Danube had now replaced the Rhine as the key frontier, requiring the heavier garrison, with nine legions stationed along its bank.

Domitian was assassinated by members of his own household (18 September 96). His wife Domitia was in the plot. So was at least one of the two praetorian prefects, the former governor of Egypt, Titus Petronius Secundus, who had been appointed, with a certain Norbanus as colleague, earlier in the year after Domitian had had the previous prefects executed. Domitia and others were particularly alarmed by Domitian's execution of his cousin, Flavius Clemens, 'a man of the most contemptible sloth' (Suetonius, *Vespasian* 15). If Clemens could be put to death, who was safe? The charge against Clemens was 'atheism, for which offence a number of others also, who had been carried away into Jewish customs, were condemned, some to death, others to confiscation of property' (Dio lxvii.14). Various passages suggest that the Romans at this date regarded Christianity as a Jewish sect (Sulpicius Severus, *Chronicles* ii.31, apparently based on a lost part of Tacitus, *Histories* v; cf. Suetonius, *Claudius* 25). Suetonius may possibly be referring to the Christians when he says that Domitian exacted the special tax on Jews from 'those who lived as Jews without professing Judaism' (*Domitian* 12). An early Christian cemetery at Rome was called 'the Cemetery of Domitilla' after Clemens's wife and was on ground which belonged to her. Another of Domitian's victims was Acilius Glabrio, consul in 91, also charged with 'atheism'; the Acilian family had a crypt in the first-century Christian Cemetery of Priscilla. 'Atheism' was a common charge against Christians, because they did not

worship the usual gods. It is therefore possible, though far
from certain, that Clemens and Domitilla, and also Glabrio,
were Christians. In any case, later Christian accounts
associate Domitian with Nero as the first two great per-
secutors of the church, although the extent of the persecu-
tions is undoubtedly much exaggerated.

The news of Domitian's death brought mixed reactions:
indifference on the part of the general public, anger from the
troops, wild delight from the Senate, who smashed his images
and voted that 'all inscriptions referring to him should be
effaced and all records of his reign obliterated' (Suetonius,
Domitian 23). With the praetorians lacking a leader, it was
indeed left for the Senate to nominate a successor, the elderly
and respectable Marcus Cocceius Nerva. How far he was
involved in the plot against Domitian is unknown. From now
on, we no longer have Suetonius to help us, and the sources
for Nerva's short reign (he died on 25 January 98) are scanty
and imprecise. His measures seem largely designed to win
support. He paid the usual donatives to army and people. He
took measures to relieve the burden on Italy: a law for
distributing state land, more generous exemptions from the
tax on inheritances, abolition of the charge on local communities for maintaining the public posting service (the
cursus publicus, page 150). He appointed Sextus Julius Frontinus, formerly governor of Britain and subsequently author
of a work on the Roman aqueducts, to take charge of Rome's
water supply system, which he reorganized. Nerva may also
have instituted the system of *alimenta* which Trajan developed further (see Chapter 8). The fact that he caused the
Senate to appoint a five-man commission to study how to cut
back on public expenditure does not necessarily mean that
there was a major financial crisis. Nerva's own measures had
increased charges on the treasury and diminished receipts,
some retrenchment was desirable, and Nerva and his
advisers, many of them elderly men like himself who had
already been in public life under Nero, will have seen a commission as preferable to the sort of ill-timed parsimony which
had made Galba so unpopular.

In the Senate's instant euphoria on Domitian's death, 'everyone had acted for himself, brought his personal enemies to trial (if they were not too powerful), and had them condemned amid the general confusion and chaos' (Pliny, *Letters* ix.13). Nerva tried to check this divisive thirst for vengeance. In some people's opinion he went too far. One of Domitian's most notorious informers was dining with Nerva, 'and was even leaning on his shoulder', when conversation turned to another notorious informer, now dead. Nerva wondered aloud what would have happpened to him if he had been still alive. 'He would be dining with us', replied one of the other guests (Pliny, *Letters* iv.22). Nerva had to conciliate the praetorians as well, bringing back as prefect Casperius Aelianus, who had served in that post under Domitian. Later in 97, Casperius led the praetorians in a demand that Domitian's murderers should belatedly be punished. Nerva gave in, and Petronius was amongst those executed, whereupon Casperius flaunted his power by forcing Nerva publicly to give thanks for the executions of his supporters. Faced with loss of control and the beginning of a situation that looked like 69 over again, Nerva swiftly adopted as his son and successor Marcus Ulpius Traianus (Trajan), an experienced soldier popular with the legions, born in Spain but the son of a man who had Leen consul, governor of Syria, and proconsul of Asia. Trajan was known to the Senate as a man of justice and moderation. What is more, he was governor of Upper Germany, and could have had his army rapidly in Rome, if the praetorians had continued to be obstreperous. He was immediately made co-emperor (October 97), and succeeded on Nerva's death three months later with so little fuss that he did not even think it necessary to come to Rome for over a year, until he had made sure that things were to his liking on the Rhine and Danube frontiers. Casperius, however, was quickly removed from his post as praetorian prefect and put to death. Trajan's appointment was ratified by the Senate. The army was content. Not the least of Nerva's services to the state was his choice of successor.

The Romanization of the western provinces of the Empire has already been discussed (Chapter 6). That the new emperor was born in Spain is a sign of how far it had gone. It has been shown that under Trajan and Hadrian only some thirty senators are known who still bore the names of the old Republican nobility, and few of these were among the leading men of the time. Trajan's consuls included Greeks from Asia Minor, the Moorish chieftain Lusius Quietus, Gaius Julius Alexander Berenicianus, the last known descendant of Herod the Great, and Gaius Julius Epiphanes Philopappus, grandson of Antiochus IV, last king of Commagene, and Athenian archon, whose wedding cake of a funeral monument still stands at Athens on the hill now named after him. The provinces provided many of the equestrian officials and the bulk of the legions. Trajan found it necessary to require senators by law 'to invest a third of their capital in [Italian] real estate, thinking it unseemly [as indeed it was] that candidates for office should treat Rome and Italy not as their native country, but as a mere inn or lodging-house for them on their visits' (Pliny, *Letters* vi.19). One result was a rise in the price of land, especially near Rome. Some of the new provincial senators, however, like Tacitus, were more Italian than the Italians, and almost excessively imbued with respect for Roman tradition, especially senatorial tradition.

Trajan treated the Senate with studied tact and affability. The Senate as a body had little power, but individual senators played an important role in the administration of the Empire. Trajan avoided numerous consulships (only twice after 101). His moderation was the more welcome by contrast with Domitian's arrogance. Where Domitian was 'Lord God', Trajan preferred to be called 'best of leaders' (*optimus princeps*). He paid close personal attention to the administration of the Empire. He intervened paternally in the affairs of municipalities and extended the responsibilities of the imperial bureaucracy. He showed special concern for Italy, developing the alimentary scheme for poor children, which also provided capital for Italian agriculture, and undertaking an impressive and expensive programme of public works (see page 219).

Some of the money for Trajan's vast expenditures came from the spoils of Dacia, which he reduced to a province in two hard-fought wars. We have seen how Trajan began his reign with a tour of the Rhine and Danube frontiers. Domitian's settlement with Decebalus was clearly not destined to be permanent. Decebalus may have been encroaching on his neighbours, forming alliances against Rome, even intriguing south of the Danube within the Roman province. During the winter of 98/9, which he spent on the Danube, Trajan began preparations for a Roman advance across the river. Forts were built, communications improved. After a necessary visit to Rome, Trajan set out again for the Dacian front on 25 March 101, and launched an invasion of Dacia. The details of the campaign escape us.

Communications along the Danube were impeded by the Iron Gate gorge, along which Roman army engineers had cut a spectacular road in 33/4 (*ILS* 2281 = *EJ* 267). Now in 101, as a newly found inscription shows, Trajan cut a canal: 'Because of the dangerous rapids he diverted the stream and made navigation on the Danube safe' (*JRS* lxiii [1973], 80–5). The campaign was afterwards commemorated by the erection of Trajan's Column (page 219), but the pictorial representation of events, like a strip cartoon, which winds around the Column, though useful for our knowledge of army equipment and activities, was never intended to convey precise chronological and topographical detail, and we are reduced to being grateful for such scraps of information as a citation by the late grammarian Priscian of a single phrase from Trajan's own account which suggests that the army, or one part of it, crossed the Danube at Lederata, near the legionary base at Viminacium. Trajan's Column appears to show legionaries crossing on one pontoon bridge and praetorians on another; dividing the force so that it meets again in a pincer movement would be standard textbook strategy, but everything else is conjecture.

The first Dacian War ended in autumn 102. Decebalus

was allowed to retain his throne, but had to accept a Roman garrison in his capital, Sarmizegethusa, and at other strategic points. A permanent bridge was built across the Danube, with twenty stone piers and a wooden superstructure, the work of Trajan's architect Apollodorus of Damascus. Dio saw only the piers still standing, but was vastly impressed (lxviii.13). Decebalus again prepared to make war. Trajan decided to finish with him. He left Rome once more (4 June, 105), spent the winter in military and diplomatic preparations, and once more marched into Dacia in the early summer of 106. There was less fighting than in the first war, Sarmizegethusa fell quickly, Decebalus committed suicide and his head was brought to Rome. The war was over (autumn 106; the date is confirmed by the *Fasti Ostienses*), and Dacia was incorporated as a province with a garrison of two or three legions, soon reduced to one, stationed at Apulum. A colony was founded at Sarmizegethusa, the Dacian gold mines were exploited with workmen brought in from Dalmatia, and the normal process of Romanization went forward.

The booty was enormous. A later writer asserts on the authority of Trajan's doctor, Titus Statilius Crito, who was in Dacia with him, that Trajan brought back five million pounds of gold and ten million of silver, plus other plunder and over half a million prisoners (Johannes Lydus, *On the magistracies* ii.28). Attempts have been made to save the credit of these figures, despite their obvious gross exaggeration, by dividing everything by ten. The figures have rather the look of vague immensity, as if to say 'Trajan brought back so much gold, you wouldn't believe it, and about twice as much silver ...'. It seems safe to conclude that the booty will have paid for the war and financed much of Trajan's extraordinary expenditure (public works, *alimenta,* donatives to the city populace, etc.); not for nothing did Trajan issue coins proclaiming LIBERALITAS.

Contemporary with the Second Dacian War were the minor operations undertaken by the governor of Syria beyond the Jordan, which led to the incorporation of the old

Nabataean kingdom as the new province of Arabia. Coins celebrate ARABIA ADQUISITA, new auxiliary units were recruited from among the Arab tribes, and milestones record the building of a great strategic road from Damascus to the Gulf of Aqaba via Bostra, the headquarters of the legion appointed to garrison the new province. There is no evidence linking these measures with preparations for a war against Parthia, but when that war broke out in 113, they were undeniably useful, and it is not impossible that Trajan, setting out for Dacia in 105 to eliminate the man whom he had unwisely allowed to remain as a client king three years before, might already have been planning to finish with client states and compromise measures on the eastern frontier as well. On the other hand, there is no evidence of troop movement to the eastern frontier until a change of ruler in Parthia and a consequent infringement on Roman rights in Armenia in or around 110 gave Trajan reason to intervene.

The chronology and topography of Trajan's Parthian War are as confused as those of his Dacian campaigns. Armenia was reduced to a province and by the summer of 116 Trajan had reached the Persian Gulf and carved two new provinces, Assyria and Mesopotamia, out of the Parthian empire. This was the high-water mark of Roman expansion. A revolt of the conquered areas and a Parthian invasion from the territory they still held caused concessions to be made and conquered territories returned to client rulers, including a Parthian prince, to whom Trajan handed over southern Mesopotamia and adjacent territories, including Dura on the Euphrates. Coins grandiloquently and misleadingly claim that Trajan had given the Parthians a king (REX PARTHIS DATUS). The Parthians never recognized him. Trajan himself was now in failing health. He returned to Antioch and thence set out for Rome, leaving Hadrian in command. He died *en route,* having allegedly adopted Hadrian on his deathbed (9 August 117). It was left for Hadrian to abandon Trajan's conquests in the East (see Chapter 9). Although the conquest of Dacia secured peace on the Danube for sixty years, the humiliation of Parthia had no lasting result.

Of the memory which Trajan left, we need no further evidence than the prayer of the Senate in the fourth century, that the new emperor might be 'more fortunate than Augustus and better than Trajan' (Eutropius viii.5), in parody of which the *Augustan History,* following Marius Maximus, records that the Senate acclaimed Commodus's murder with 'more savage than Domitian and filthier than Nero' (*Commodus* 19). The Middle Ages remembered him in legend as the type of the just king. Dante saw him released from hell, pagan though he was, through the prayer of Pope Gregory; not even Augustus had a longer or better posthumous innings.

*The State of Italy from
Petronius to Pliny*

By the time of Nero's accession, Italy had had almost a century of peace. The social and economic consequences of Augustus's policies had become well established. Italy as a whole was more prosperous than ever before. The gap between rich and poor was enormous, but the really rich from all over Italy were now fully integrated into Roman society. The great aristocratic families of the Ciceronian era had lost their political predominance, their social exclusiveness, and the overweening arrogance of which Cicero complained so bitterly. Society was more mobile. Great fortunes could be made by ex-slaves, not only, as we saw in Chapter 5, by the emperor's own freedmen like Pallas and Narcissus, but also by those who did well out of trade and commerce.

Of the latter group, the best known never actually existed. He is the first great fictional character in European literature, whom Helen Waddell called 'the only figure on whom Falstaff's belt would even slackly have hung', the egregious Trimalchio. His creator was Petronius, that Titus Petronius, consul in 61, who was Nero's 'Arbiter of Elegance', and of whom Tacitus says:

> He passed his days in sleep, his nights in business and in the pleasures of life. Just as others achieve fame by hard work, so did he by idleness, and he was considered not debauched and profligate, as are most of those who waste their own substance, but as a man of exquisite luxury . . . As proconsul of Bithynia, however, and later as consul, he proved himself energetic and competent. Then going back to his vices, or by pretending to vices, he was admitted to the inner circle of Nero's cronies as arbiter of elegance,

until the emperor thought nothing agreeable and truly refined unless Petronius had assured him that it was.

Falsely accused by his rival Tigellinus and ordered by Nero to commit suicide, Petronius opened his veins, had them bound up again, then opened again, all the time talking idly to his friends and listening to frivolous verses. Some slaves he rewarded, others punished. Going in to dinner, he fell asleep, making his death look natural. Moreover:

> He wrote out a list of Nero's lewdnesses, giving the names of male and female partners and the novel details of each act of lust, signed and sealed it, and sent it to Nero. Then he broke his seal-ring, lest it be used later to trap others. (Tacitus, *Annals* xvi.18–19)

A man of wit and audacity, it seems; also a writer of lyrics which rival Catullus for spontaneity, and the author of the first great European novel, the *Satyricon*. Trimalchio is only a minor character, but he dominates the one extensive fragment to have survived, which comes from Books 14–16 (there must have been twenty or more books originally), and which tells the story of a pretentious dinner party given by Trimalchio and attended by the disreputable trio, Encolpius (the narrator), Ascyltus and Giton, whose adventures, sexual and otherwise, around the seaports of Campania and southern Italy form the main narrative thread of the novel. Much nonsense has been written purporting to explain the meaning of this work. It is clearly satirical, but the narrator himself is also mocked, and it is hard to see what, if any, positive view of society Petronius wishes to espouse. The frame of reference is highly literary; parody and allusion abound, and the episode of the dinner party falls into the tradition of literary dinner parties going back to Plato's *Symposium* and beyond. But at the same time the satire would lose its point if it did not also recognizably reflect facets of contemporary Italian society.

What town was Trimalchio's dinner party held in? If any

one town is indicated, Puteoli has a stronger claim than Cumae. But Petronius and the other members of Nero's court whom the novel was no doubt meant to amuse knew the whole Bay of Naples area well. It was the most fashionable resort area, Nero and his mother both had villas there, as we have seen, and Petronius was at his villa at Cumae when he got the order to die. The subject matter of the *Satyricon* is life in that area a long way below the senatorial class. Ostensibly Petronius is the worldly courtier poking fun at his and his friends' social inferiors, a cheap form of humour permanently in vogue. But perhaps in his true estimation Nero and his entourage stood closer to the vulgar characters of the satire than they supposed. As for Trimalchio himself, we find his real life counterparts a few years later buried under the ashes of Pompeii, not many miles away (page 207).

Trimalchio is immensely rich, quite uneducated and monumentally vulgar. The adverb is literally true. Towards the end of the dinner party, drunk and maudlin, he insists on reading his will aloud from beginning to end and goes on to describe the elaborate monument he wants, with his pet dog carved on it, some wreaths, the fights of one of his favourite gladiators, ships in full sail, and Trimalchio himself 'sitting in the magistrate's seat in a purple-bordered toga wearing five gold rings and scattering coins to the people out of a bag' (*Satyricon* 71). There is more in the same vein, and then the epitaph:

Here lies Gaius Pompeius Trimalchio Maecenatianus. He was elected priest of Augustus in his absence. He could have had any office at Rome, but declined. Dutiful, brave and loyal, he started with little and left 30,000,000 sesterces, without ever listening to a philosopher.

By his own account, Trimalchio began as a slave boy from Asia who got his start by satisfying both his master's and his mistress's sexual needs. He was eventually left co-heir with the emperor (it was common practice to mention the emperor in one's will, and the various emperors' attitudes to such legacies figure prominently in our senatorial sources), and thus inherited a fortune sufficient for a senator, probably several million sesterces. So he went into business, built five ships, sent them to Rome loaded with wine when it was scarce, and lost the lot at sea; perhaps we are to assume that it was winter, when sailing was dangerous (page 152) and for that reason both risks and profits were higher. He estimates his loss (we must allow for deliberate exaggeration on Trimalchio's part or his creator's) at 30,000,000. So he tried again, with a cargo of wine, bacon, beans, perfume and slaves, and this time cleared a profit of 10,000,000 which he promptly put into land. His real estate and farming ventures prospered, and as soon as he could afford it, he retired from active involvement in business and began to finance freedmen. Now he has a house like a palace and estates so vast that we hear the following report of one day's events:

> 26 July: on the estate at Cumae belonging to Trimalchio, born, 30 boys, 40 girls; taken into the granary from the threshing floor, 500,000 measures of wheat; oxen broken in, 500. . . . On the same day, returned to the strongroom, because it could not be invested, 10,000,000 sesterces. (*Satyricon* 53)

Behind the blatant sneering at the *nouveau riche* we discern elements of a pattern borrowed from real life. It was probably easier for a slave than for a free man without money or education to make a fortune. Slaves were better placed to attract the attention of the rich, by Trimalchio's means or otherwise, and rich men would train and finance their slaves and ex-slaves in order to share in their profits, as Trimalchio did. Moneylending was practised by the most respectable men, and the return was fairly secure. The best investment of all was land, and in this respect Trimalchio is typical: having made his money, he buys land. It also conferred status. Trimalchio across the centuries shakes hands with the nineteenth-century Lancashire textile millionaire who buys his country estate and his baronetcy.

Trimalchio's wealth may be exaggerated (70 slaves born on a single day on only one of his numerous estates), but the disparity between rich and poor was enormous, and wealthy senators lived in a style that even the great eighteenth-century grandees would have found it hard to emulate. Our sources take for granted their houses in Rome, their villas in the hills or on the coast near Rome, their seaside villas at Baiae or other resorts on the Bay of Naples, their numerous estates elsewhere in Italy and especially where their family roots were, where they nourished their careers on political and dynastic alliances, and where they advertised their affluence, status, and power by their patronage of local municipalities. Nor were they limited to Italy. Although under the Republic senators had probably been forbidden to own land in the provinces, by Nero's reign not only were there senators of provincial origin, but Italian senators sometimes had vast provincial holdings. We do not know who the six men were who the elder Pliny says owned half the province of Africa (*Natural History* xviii.35). Nero however confiscated their estates, as he confiscated those of Rubellius Plautus in Asia (Tacitus, *Annals* xiv.22), and as Tiberius had confiscated the mines in Spain belonging to Sextus Marius (*Annals* vi.19, cf. Dio lviii.22).

Although there was a lively market in landed property, especially perhaps in the more fashionable areas, Cicero in his day, and the younger Pliny a century and a half later, both testify to the strength of their attachment to ancestral property. Pliny came from the area of Lake Como in northern Italy and maintained close ties with the region. When a friend wanted to acquire a property on the lake, he offered to sell her any of his own properties at her own price, except those inherited from his parents, 'for those I could not give up even to her' (*Letters* vii.11). This was despite the difficulty of ensuring that property stayed in the family, in the absence of primogeniture or of any clear legal system of entail. When the rich travelled, as they did quite a lot, they did not stay in hotels. Indeed there were no hotels in the modern sense, only low and sordid overnight lodging houses.

This is one reason why the rich tried to have a network of well-placed villas, which one also lent to travelling friends, thus putting them under an obligation that they could be expected to repay when called upon to do so.

A fashionable villa at Baiae might be kept for its amenity value alone and not expected to pay for itself, but many estates did, and it is clear that rich men derived much of their income from the land. Pliny complains of the hardships of being a landowner. He opted to let his farms out to tenants, instead of farming them himself through a slave manager (*vilicus*), as was often done. The choice between the two seems often to have depended on which was the more readily available. Columella in Nero's day assumes that the slave manager is the norm and the tenant the exception. The chief problem with tenants was getting them to pay their rent in bad years. The landlord could seize the tenant's goods, but then, as Pliny rightly observes, there was even less chance of his being able to pay in the future. This observation occurs in a letter (iii.19) where Pliny is asking a friend's opinion on whether to buy a property adjoining one of his own: the asking price is 3,000,000 sesterces, or three times the minimum property qualification for a senator, and Pliny, although not particularly rich by the standards of his contemporaries, and although he says he is short of ready cash, nonetheless assures his friend that he will have no difficulty at all in raising the money.

In a bad year, tenants could not pay the rent; in a good year, Pliny complains, there was a glut and prices were low. All the same, he did not do too badly. His estates in Umbria alone, which were not the main part of his property, made over 400,000 sesterces a year (*Letters* x.8). There is no real evidence, in Pliny's complaints or elsewhere, for a supposed crisis in Italian agriculture. The tenant's lot might be hard. The law was very much in the landlord's favour. The tenant had a five-year lease and no security thereafter, although Columella realised, as Pliny seems to have done also, that continuity of good tenants was in the landlord's interest. Tenants might be poor; landlords seem to have done pretty well.

(a) Coin of Augustus from the mint at Lyon, 10 B C , head of Augustus simply inscribed CAESAR PONT(ifex) MAX(imus), and Lyon altar ROM(a) ET AVG(ustus).

(b) Coin of Nero, Roman mint, A D 64, showing Nero with his full titles (NERO CLAVD(ius) CAESAR AVG(ustus) GER(manicus) P(ontifex) M(aximus) TR(ibunicia) P(otestate) IMP(erator) P(ater) P(atriae), and ships in new harbour at Portus inscribed AVGVSTI/PORT(us) OST(iensis), the last line flanked by S(enatus) C(onsulto) ('by authority of the Senate ').

(c) Coin of Vespasian, Roman mint, A D 71, head of Vespasian inscribed IMP(erator) CAES(ar) VESPASIAN(us) AVG(ustus) P(ontifex) M(aximus) TR(ibunicia) P(otestate) P(ater) P(atriae) CO(n)S(ul) III (i.e. for the third time), and a Jewish woman mourning under a palm tree, guarded by a figure in military dress, usually identified with Vespasian himself (*RIC* ii. 427, cf. *BMC* ii. 543).with the legend IVDAEA CAPTA ('Judaea captive') and S(enatus) C(onsulto) ('by authority of the Senate ').

The water supply of Nîmes

(a) The Pont du Gard

(b) The distribution basin where the aqueduct enters the city through the square channel at the back

The Roman army on campaign

(a) Masada from the west, the Dead Sea behind, and the Roman siege ramp in the centre.

(b) Scenes from the conquest of Dacia on Trajan's Column

Everyday life in the shadow of Vesuvius

(a) Pompeii: grain mills in a bakery

(b) Herculaneum: street scene

The heart of the empire

(a) Rome: the forum, with the Palatine on the right and the Arch of Titus on the left

(b) Ostia: an apartment building in brick-faced concrete, with shops on ground floor, Antonine

The army on Hadrian's Wall

(a) Housesteads fort: the latrine in the southeast corner

(b) Housesteads fort: granary, showing floor supported on pillars for under-floor ventilation

The towns of North Africa

(a) Castellum Tidditanorum: the forum, with statue bases and rooms, perhaps the Capitolium, opening to left

(b) Cuicul (Djemila): the theatre, with remains of the town on hill in middle distance

The third century

(a) IVLIA MAESA AVG(usta), grandmother of Elagabalus, and IVLIA MAM(m)AEA AVG(usta), mother of Severus Alexander, on coins of the period

(b) El Djem (Thysdrus): the amphitheatre, towering over its modern surroundings

The Cisalpine region, where Pliny's main estates lay, was and is extremely fertile. This was recognized already by Polybius in the second century BC, and Strabo refers to wine, millet, wool, pigs for the market at Rome, pitch (the extensive woods of antiquity have now disappeared), flax, wheat and barley. For wheat, Cisalpina was second only to Campania, while Raetian wine, grown especially around Verona, was first-class in Strabo's opinion (iv.206, cf. Pliny, *Natural History* xiv.16; Martial xiv.100). Livia drank nothing else; it was her recipe for longevity. Augustus liked it too, though it was not his favourite; Vergil too ranks it below the celebrated Falernian (Pliny, *Natural History* xiv.60–1; Suetonius, *Augustus* 77; Vergil, *Georgics* ii.95–6). Much of this produce was consumed locally. We have stressed elsewhere the difficulty of transporting bulk cargoes, especially grain, by land (page 59). There was, however, a considerable export trade in wine, much of it north of the Alps.

Our knowledge of different areas of the Italian countryside differs widely. Nowhere else has been so extensively surveyed as southern Etruria, which seems to have supported a large farming population in the first century. A distinction can be made between 'modest but fairly comfortable farmhouses', identified after ploughing by a surface scatter of tufa blocks, painted plaster and black and white mosaic tesserae, and more luxurious villas whose presence was revealed by column drums and mouldings, marble veneers, painted plaster and more complex mosaics. In the territory of Veii, for example, it is estimated that there was one rich villa every two square kilometres, with an even greater density further south around Rome. Often they occupied the site of a pre-Roman farmstead. We should not expect so great a density further away from the capital. Near Cosa, for instance, large estates developed in the later Republic, and excavation has revealed a villa at Settefinestre whose main central building was a perfect square with an area of 2000 square metres; the whole villa establishment, with gardens, porticoes and farm buildings, covered some 25,000 square metres. Before the end of the second century, however, it had been abandoned, perhaps because adjacent properties had been amalgamated.

Another grand villa lay in the Tiber valley near Lucus Feroniae. It belonged to the Volusii, as was attested by dedications in the household shrine by Quintus Volusius Saturninus, consul in 56, and his son Lucius, consul in 87. The villa was laid out in the late Republic with spacious and elegant rooms round a colonnaded atrium or enclosed courtyard. It had magnificent mosaics, both polychrome and black and white, gardens with colonnades and open areas, and a cryptoporticus or sunken gallery leading down to another set of rooms. After it was enlarged in the first century AD, it occupied a terrace measuring 180 × 120 metres, including an area behind the villa for agricultural use with a separate farmyard paved in heavy-duty basalt. The villa continued to be occupied into the third century, if not longer.

Much lower down the social and economic scale was a farmhouse at Monte Furco in the Ager Capenas, probably built under Augustus, which measured only 11 × 5 metres internally and sheltered people and animals under the same roof. It continued to be occupied into the second century, and was then turned into a barn. This suggests that the farm, like the Settefinestre villa, had been incorporated into a larger estate, a process that was becoming increasingly common. A similar building at Crocicchie on the Via Clodia some 14 km northwest of Rome went on into the third century when it must have been modestly prosperous, since a new bath-house was added. The overall evidence seems to indicate that by the end of the first century AD southern Etruria was being more intensively farmed than ever before. Even the more inaccessible areas had come under cultivation. Further north, new sites were still being developed; here marginal land was not cultivated until some time in the second century. Throughout the area, farming was mostly mixed, although the main emphasis was on vines and olives, both of which are crops requiring a considerable initial capital outlay. Some villas had very sophisticated arrangements for pressing and storage. In Campania, for instance, we find a farm at Posto near Capua laid out around the farmyard, with simple accommodation for the manager and his family on one side and farm buildings on two others. The fittings included cement-lined vats for oil and large storage jars (*dolia*) for wine. The owner had a separate villa nearby.

Campania was still, as it had been in Augustus's day (page 92), one of the wealthiest and most fertile areas of Italy. Writers of all periods vie with each other in superlatives: 'Campania, that most blessed of all plains' (Strabo v.242); 'that happy and blessed loveliness, bringing together in one place the work of rejoicing nature' (Pliny, *Natural History* iii.40); 'of all regions, not only of Italy, but of the whole world, the fairest is the region of Campania; nothing is balmier than its climate, indeed spring comes twice a year with flowers; nothing is more fertile than its soil, so that it is said to be a source of rivalry between Liber [vines] and Ceres [wheat] ... here are mountains clad with vines ... including Vesuvius, fairest of all ... on the coast the cities of Formiae, Cumae, Puteoli, Neapolis [Naples], Herculaneum, Pompeii, and the queen of cities, Capua herself' (Florus I.xi.3–6).

Vesuvius, though clearly volcanic, was reputed extinct (Strabo v.247). Vergil mentions the vines that covered its slopes, the olives, the good grazing, the arable land (*Georgics* ii.221–4). A mural painting from the House of the Centenary at Pompeii shows it clothed in vineyards. But it was not extinct. The catastrophic eruption of 79 which obliterated Pompeii and Herculaneum also buried farms and villas. On the flank of the mountain at Boscoreale it buried a particularly luxurious villa with splendid and uninterrupted views of the Bay, which had once belonged to Agrippa Postumus, had passed into the emperor's hands, and was in charge of an imperial freedman, Tiberius Claudius Eutychus, at the time of the eruption. Owners of other villas have also been identified. The properties range from the luxurious to the purely agricultural without accommodation for the owner or even a high-status manager. One dwelling had floors of beaten earth, another had bare walls and a set of stocks for slaves. There was one which functioned as an inn, another which incorporated a wineshop facing the road. One slave-run establishment included a large commercial bakery. But the vats and implements suggest that the staple products were wine and oil, and on the richer properties these might be the only large-scale activities, whereas those with a working farmer in residence tended to be less specialized.

The evidence from all the areas that we have considered points to an increasing rural population. There was considerable incentive to invest in agriculture. New land was brought into cultivation. Nor is evidence for rural prosperity and rural development limited to these areas. Even quite remote areas have yielded density figures of several sites per square kilometre, all of them apparently occupied in the same period. The evidence does not support the view of some modern scholars that Italy was passing through a major agricultural crisis in the latter part of the first century, though individuals, particularly tenant farmers and perhaps smallholders, will have had bad years, and smallholders may have lost their land to the large estates. But there is no evidence for declining productivity and certainly not for soil exhaustion, nor was there any lack of capital investment, rather the opposite.

The extent to which small peasant proprietors survived is indeed still a matter for debate. Certainly it varied from region to region. Large estates (*latifundia*) manned by slaves are attested primarily in central and southern Italy. Pliny thought that they had ruined Italy (*Natural History* xviii.35), but there are few references to slave labour on any scale in the north. Vergil in the *Georgics* does not even mention slaves and seems to presuppose the small farm as the norm, which may suggest that that was what he was familiar with in the Po valley and Campania in his day. Where large tracts of land were given over to sheep and cattle ranching, slave herdsmen could be used efficiently, as Cato realised in the second century BC, but estates which concentrated on vines and olives required a large supplementary labour force at harvest time. It would not be sound economics to maintain a staff of slaves throughout the year large enough to cope with all eventualities, including the harvest, if this meant that most of them would be unemployed or at least grossly under-employed most of the time. It was far more efficient to hire casual labour from the surrounding area as required at peak periods. Thus it was in the interest of the large proprietors to have a pool of labour available, in the form of smallholders and their families, themselves farming at or near subsistence level. These peasant smallholders will thus have provided the supplementary labour force for the large estates, as did the nomads and semi-nomads for the *latifundia* in Africa (page 162). Even today, the vine and the olive depend heavily on seasonal labour. Tunisian workmen cross over to southern Italy to work on the harvest, and a UN report alludes to the difficulty of developing olive cultivation because it creates 'periodic seasonal unemployment'.

Further evidence for the state of Italian agriculture comes from Trajan's *alimenta* programme, whereby money from the imperial treasury was lent to farmers through a non-repayable mortgage on part of their land, with the interest on the mortgage going to the local municipality or to imperial commissioners to support poor children. Two surviving inscriptions give details; one comes from Veleia in the north, the other from the territory of the Ligures Baebiani in the south, in the region of Beneventum (Benevento) (*ILS* 6675, 6509 = *LR* pp.345–7). The security required was land to the value of twelve and a half times the sum received, the rate of interest 5 per cent. At Veleia this produced 55,800 sesterces a year, distributed among 263 boys (16 sesterces a month each), 35 girls (12 sesterces) and 2 illegitimate children (12 sesterces to the boy, 10 to the girl). Nerva may have been the first to invest imperial funds in such a scheme, but private benefactors had undertaken similar measures in the past. We know of one such benefaction under Nero, and Pliny describes at some length a scheme which he set up at Comum (*Letters* vii.18), but there had been nothing on the scale organized by Trajan. He was proud of his achievement, which is commemorated on his arch at Beneventum, and coins celebrate ALIMENTA ITALIAE and 'the restoration of Italy', RESTITUTIO ITALIAE.

The purpose of the scheme was primarily to help the poor

to have and rear more children, rather than that the land-owners needed more money and could not otherwise have raised it. This is shown by several factors. Pliny, describing Trajan's parallel extension of the grain distribution at Rome to an extra 5000 children, emphasizes that 'from these the camp, from these the tribes [the citizens' voting units] will be filled up' (*Panegyric* xxviii.6). The excess of boys over girls among the recipients suggests a desire to increase the number of potential recruits. The reliefs on Trajan's arch at Bene-ventum, showing parents and children receiving the *alimenta*, point in the same direction. It has even been argued that, so far from landowners needing or even welcoming the loans, they had to be compelled to accept them. But this goes too far. The inscriptions suggest that the most prominent local families participated, no doubt from motives of public spirit and status obligation. Nor is it likely that Trajan would have resorted to compulsion in Italy, when he eschews it in the provinces, telling Pliny as governor of Bithynia that it was 'not in accordance with the justice of our age' (Pliny, *Letters* x.55).

The charges under Trajan's scheme were moreover less than Pliny burdened himself with. Pliny contracted to pay 30,000 sesterces a year on an estate worth 500,000, where a landowner at Veleia with a 500,000-sesterces estate would have got a loan of 40,000 for an annual payment of 2000, and he would actually have had the 40,000 to spend on improvements or extensions which would increase the value of the property and so compensate for the perpetual charge on it, whereas Pliny was not in fact getting any extra money at all. The system thus benefited landowners and poor children alike. It grew and flourished throughout the second century under a senatorial *praefectus alimentorum*, with in-scriptions from nearly fifty Italian towns. It should be accounted a measure of rare ingenuity and far-sightedness.

At the same time, however, it brings into the sharpest focus the vast differences between rich and poor. The first three landowners recorded on the Veleia inscription (and Veleia was not a particularly rich or noteworthy community, nor were individuals mortgaging all their property) put into the scheme estates worth 108,000 sesterces, 310,545 sesterces, and 843,879 sesterces respectively, this being in each case the valuation minus the annual rental. We remember that Pliny, though short of cash, saw no difficulty in raising 3,000,000. Although the legal minimum of capital for a senator was 1,000,000, a more realistic figure would be around 8,000,000. Pliny in his lifetime gave away something like 5,000,000; fortunately for us, his benefactions are well documented; he did not believe in doing good by stealth. The luxury and elegance of his villas and their grounds stand out from his own descriptions, which deserve to be read in full (*Letters* ii.17, for his villa on the coast near Rome; v.6, for one in Tuscany, in the Apennine foothills; both letters are very detailed). His main estates were near Comum in Cisalpina. But he describes himself as being of 'modest means' (*Letters* ii.4), and was certainly not rich by comparison with the real plutocrats, who counted in hundreds of millions. The two largest private fortunes recorded in our sources are in fact estimated at 400 million (not a precise amount, but clearly a lot of money), the men concerned being Gnaeus Cornelius Lentulus, consul in 14 BC, and Claudius's freedman Narcissus.

In sharp contrast, while an alimentary payment of 120 sesterces for a whole year was probably not enough for a child to live on, even for a girl who had the misfortune to be born a bastard, it was clearly not negligible. This was at a time when the ordinary legionary got 1200 a year (raised from 900 by Domitian), out of which he had to pay for food, clothes, equipment and other deductions, although it was supplemented by donatives on various occasions and a gratuity on discharge. In civilian life, an unskilled casual labourer might make 4 sesterces a day at most. This is what the labourers in the vineyard were paid in St Matthew's parable (Matthew 20), although even if Matthew is to be taken literally, he is really evidence only for Judaea. Other evidence suggests that 4 sesterces might be too much. A passage in the Babylonian Talmud implies that Rabbi Hillel earned only half that amount as a woodcutter in King

Herod's day. In Cicero's day at Rome, the normal wage was 3 sesterces a day (Cicero, *For Roscius the actor* 28, to my mind conclusive). In the previous century in rural Italy it was only 2 sesterces (Cato xxii.3). Cicero, incidentally, in the same speech, treats 50,000 sesterces as a sum too paltry for a gentleman to bother about (*For Roscius the actor* 22).

Further evidence, though from the year 164, comes from an inscription from Dacia, where a miner, apparently freeborn, contracts to work for 178 days, from 20 May to 13 November 164, seemingly without holidays, for 70 *denarii,* which is 280 sesterces, or just over $1\frac{1}{2}$ sesterces a day, plus his keep, the value of which is hard to estimate. For any day when he did not show up, he forfeited 5 sesterces, which was clearly intended to be a major deterrent (*CIL* iii, p.948, x = *LR* p.194). So, even allowing for fluctuations in wages and in the cost of living, we should regard 4 sesterces a day as an absolute maximum in the first century, and of course we cannot tell how many days' employment a casual labourer might hope to get in a year.

For the cost of living, our best source is graffiti from Pompeii. We find that a *modius* of wheat ($6\frac{1}{2}$ kilograms or rather more than 14 lb) cost 3 sesterces, and a loaf of bread weighing $\frac{1}{2}$ kilogram, or just over 1 lb, cost less than 1 *as* (0.25 sesterces). The same sum would buy a plate, a lamp or a measure of wine. It would also, by way of comparison with our last inscription, pay for a miner's admission to the baths at the mining centre of Vipasca near Aljustrel in modern Portugal (*ILS* 6891 = *LR* p.192). At such prices 4 sesterces a day was not too bad, at least outside Rome, where accommodation was much more expensive than elswhere. It is hard to tell whether the discrepancy between the really rich and the labouring poor was greater than in some third-world countries today, or in Victorian England, where the 3rd Marquess of Bute, a builder on a positively Roman scale (Cardiff Castle, Castell Coch, Mount Stuart, etc.) and a Pliny-like local benefactor, is credited with an income of £300,000 a year when he came of age in 1868, and the 1st Duke of

Grosvenor with £250,000 in 1874 (we note the round figures, like Narcissus's 400 million sesterces).

Pompeii and Herculaneum remain incomparably rich sources for our knowledge of daily life and small-town society. The great eruption of 79 was preceded by an earthquake in 62 which caused damage at both towns and in Naples, and Seneca records that fumes poisoned a flock of 600 sheep on the mountain (*Natural Questions* vi.27). Repairs were not yet finished seventeen years later when further tremors occurred, portending the actual eruption of 24 August 79, of which we have an eye-witness account. The elder Pliny happened to be commanding the naval base at Misenum, on the Bay, and his nephew, who was with him, later described what happened, in a letter to Tacitus:

> My uncle was stationed at Misenum in command of the fleet. On 24 August, in the early afternoon, my mother drew his attention to a cloud of unusual size and appearance . . . Its general appearance can best be expressed as being like an umbrella pine, for it rose to a great height on a sort of trunk and then split off into branches, I imagine because it was thrust upwards by the first blast and then left unsupported as the pressure subsided, or else it was borne down by its own weight so that it spread out and gradually dispersed. Sometimes it looked white, sometimes blotched and dirty, according to the amount of soil and ashes it carried with it.

The elder Pliny put to sea in one of the vessels under his command and had it steer 'straight for the danger zone', leading other ships to rescue the inhabitants:

> Ashes were already falling, hotter and thicker as the ships drew near, followed by bits of pumice and blackened stones, charred and cracked by the flames. Then suddenly they were in shallow water, and the shore was blocked by the debris from the mountain . . . [They landed at a friend's villa at Stabiae, four miles south of Pompeii, and

could not get off again because of a 'contrary wind' and 'wild and dangerous waves'. Although Vesuvius was shooting out 'broad sheets of fire and leaping flames', Pliny retired to sleep . . .] By this time the courtyard giving access to his room was full of ashes mixed with pumice-stones, so that its level had risen, and if he had stayed in the room any longer, he would never have got out . . . The buildings were now shaking with violent shocks, and seemed to be swaying to and fro, as if they were torn from their foundations . . . Elsewhere there was daylight by this time [i.e., it was now the morning of 25 August, but they were still in darkness, blacker and denser than any ordinary night . . . He (Pliny) stood leaning on two slaves and then suddenly collapsed, I imagine because the dense fumes choked his breathing. . . . (*Letters* vi.16)

The body was recovered next day, 'intact and uninjured'.

Every detail, the younger Pliny assures us, comes from eyewitnesses. The account illustrates the archaeological record. The wind was from the north, and the ashes blanketed Pompeii and Stabiae which lay south of the volcano. The streets and courtyards of houses filled up, as Pliny describes them, people were trapped, some escaped by climbing out of upstairs windows, only to choke in the street, the rain of pumice and ash continued until Pompeii was buried to an average depth of 6 metres, and some 2000 people are estimated to have died there. Herculaneum, which lay west of Vesuvius, escaped the fall-out but lay in the path of the mud flow which overwhelmed the town and thrust out into the sea – again, a phenomenon recognizable from Pliny's description. Less bodies have been found at Herculaneum than at Pompeii, perhaps because people saw the mud coming and fled, but recent excavations on what was the beach have revealed the skeletons of victims who were trying to get away by boat, unsuccessfully, including that of a soldier with his purse and his sword at his side. The houses and their furniture at Herculaneum are often better preserved than at Pompeii: wood was carbonized but not destroyed, the mud behaved capriciously, here sweeping things away, there seeping gently round them and preserving them as it set hard. But it set so hard that Herculaneum lies now beneath as much as 25 metres of rock, on which moreover is built the modern town of Resina. The site of Pompeii, on the other hand, is open countryside, and only about a quarter of the town still remains to be uncovered. Recent research has stressed the amount of open space within the town. Not only did many houses have quite large gardens, but space was given over to vineyards, for instance a large vineyard with facilities for wine production on a commercial scale in the area traditionally known as the Foro Boario and a small vineyard attached to a wineshop near the amphitheatre, and also to market gardens growing vegetables, fruits and nuts.

There are enough books on the town plan, domestic architecture and public buildings of Pompeii to make it unnecessary to describe them here. Together with the epigraphic record, they marvellously illustrate small-town society at a level which finds little place in the literature of the period, except for the *Satyricon*. We see the local landowning families dominating the social and administrative structure of the town in the Augustan period and the emergence of prominent new merchant families, often of freedman descent, in the next half-century. We are recognizably in the world satirized by Petronius when we meet the banker, auctioneer and municipal tax-collector (by contract), Lucius Caecilius Jucundus, whose business records were found in a chest excavated in the last century. It had been buried in the earthquake of 62 and never recovered. Jucundus had a sculptured relief in his household shrine showing the destruction of the town's chief temple, the Capitolium, in that earthquake. The sculptor humorously depicts the riders of equestrian statues throwing out their arms and legs as if to break their fall when the statue crumbled.

Also destroyed in the 62 earthquake was the Temple of Isis. This was restored at the expense of Numerius Popidius Celsinus. The Popidii were one of the oldest and most distinguished families in Pompeii. We might think Popidius Celsinus one of them, if we did not know that his father, Numerius Popidius Ampliatus, was a freedman, in fact a former slave of the Popidii. Not only that, but his son Celsinus was only six at the time he paid to restore the temple. Ampliatus himself, as a freedman, was not eligible for the town council, the *ordo decurionum,* but he could try to buy his son's way in. The *ordo* had a relatively high property qualification, and decurions were expected to spend their own money in public benefactions. So still more were the town's magistrates: the modernization of the large theatre at Pompeii under Augustus was undertaken by Marcus Holconius Rufus and his brother Celer, Rufus having been five times joint mayor (*duovir*), twice in the special fifth year, as *quinquennalis,* when the *duoviri* carried out a census and revised the list of the *ordo.* By the Neronian period, when the landowning families had lost their grip on the town's affairs, electoral competition was intense, as surviving inscriptions show. 'Marcus Holconius Priscus for *duovir*: all the fruit-sellers along with Helvius Vestalis support him' – but by now we cannot tell if this is a real Holconius or the descendant of one of their slaves.

The graffiti speak to us in the language of the streets, and men and women of the humblest classes live again: 'Yours for twopence [2 *asses*]', writes a prostitute. 'A copper pot is missing from this shop. 65 sesterces reward if anybody brings it back, 20 sesterces if he reveals the thief so that we can get our property back.' 'Apollodorus, doctor to the Emperor Titus, had a good crap here.' The graffito-writer's style does not change. Several inscriptions testify to the popularity of gladiatorial games (see chapter 10):

Twenty pairs of gladiators belonging to Decimus Lucretius Satrius Valens, priest [*flamen*] for life of Nero, son of Caesar Augustus, and ten pairs of gladiators belonging to Decimus Lucretius Valens his son will fight at Pompeii 8–12 April. There will be a full programme of wild beast combats and awnings [for the spectators].

Aemilius Celer [painted this], all alone in the moonlight. (*ILS* 5145 = *LR* p.359)

Pompeii had a large but old-fashioned amphitheatre, the scene of a disgraceful riot in 59 between the home crowd and visiting spectators from the rival city of Nuceria (Tacitus, *Annals* xiv.17); the riot is depicted in a wall-painting. Pompeii had its own gladiators' barracks, where skeletons were found of persons who had died in the eruption, including a woman with gold jewellery and an emerald necklace who surely had no respectable business there. The sex appeal of gladiators was notorious.

Pompeii then was a thriving city. It was well provided with bars and brothels, which did a good trade. Another particularly lively wall-painting shows two men quarrelling over their dice in a tavern and getting thrown out by the landlord: 'Get out, fight it out outside'. The Latin is the Latin of the streets, not often heard in literature, although again Petronius is an exception. There were several sets of baths, that fundamental Roman urban institution, some publicly owned, others private enterprise, like those advertised as follows: 'The Baths of Marcus Crassus Frugi. Sea water and fresh water bathing. Januarius, freedman' (*ILS* 5724). This presumably exemplifies the practice attributed to Trimalchio, of financing a freedman's business enterprise. Marcus Crassus Frugi, consul in 64, had another bathing establishment at Baiae (Pliny, *Natural History* xxxi.5). Senators in particular did not engage in trade, but they invested in it. Actually being a trader was socially degrading; making money by lending to traders, specially to one's own freedmen, was approved practice.

Italian trade and commerce were booming, despite some modern scholars' attempts to prove otherwise. One of Trimalchio's guests, a fellow immigrant from Asia named Ganymede, complains of inflation and municipal graft, but we should not regard his outburst as a serious piece of economic and political analysis:

You go on talking about things that don't matter in heaven or earth and all the time nobody cares how the cost of living pinches. For God's sake, today I can't even find a bite of bread. And how the drought goes on. We've had famine for a year now. Damn the magistrates, they're in league with the bakers, 'You scratch my back and I'll scratch yours.' So it's the little man that suffers . . . [then he talks about a peppery town-councillor from when he was a boy] and how graciously he returned your 'Good morning', he knew everybody's name, just as if he was one of us. So in those days food was dirt-cheap. For a penny you could buy a bigger loaf than you and the missus could eat . . . This town is going backwards like a calf's tail . . . Nobody any longer believes in Heaven, nobody keeps fast-days, nobody cares a straw for Jupiter, they all close their eyes and count what they've got. In the old days the married women in their best clothes used to climb the hill with bare feet and their hair down and their minds pure to pray Jupiter for rain, and of course at once it came down in bucketfuls, it was now or never, and they all went home like drowned rats. But as it is. . . . (*Satyricon* 44)

This is admirable fooling, and we have seen that there is some reason to think that there was mild inflation, and certainly there were many who had difficulty in making ends meet, but it does not add up to evidence for economic crisis, at least in the sense of general impoverishment, declining standards of living, and a shortage of money for developing new facilities and maintaining existing ones, which we find in the later Empire (page 243). Nor, if we turn to real life, does the state of the Italian or more specifically, what is often invoked in this context, the Arretine pottery industry. We have already noted the importance for the archaeologist of the red-gloss tableware known as terra sigillata (see chapter 2). The main Italian manufacturing centre from the Augustan period onwards was Arezzo (Arretium), although there were important workshops in Campania, for instance in the region of Puteoli. But the Arretine firms had established branches in

Gaul in the latter part of Augustus's reign, and by the middle of the first century AD the products of the south Gaulish centres were driving the true Arretine off the market, while the quality of the Arretine ware deteriorated. Hailed as a dramatic illustration of this was the discovery at Pompeii of a crate of pottery, still unpacked at the time of the eruption, probably a consignment from a wholesaler, containing lamps from north Italy and ninety decorated sigillata bowls from southern Gaul. Did not this show that Arezzo and Puteoli had lost even their own home market? Did not this imply that Italian industry, trade, and commerce were in decline, just like Italian agriculture?

Well, we have already seen that there is no reason to postulate an agricultural crisis; nor is there to postulate one in trade and commerce. That the Arezzo workshops were in decline is true. Their trade had dropped off and their standards of quality had gone down. But there are many possible explanations specific to Arezzo. Perhaps the best clay beds in the neighbourhood were exhausted. Perhaps fuel was running short (a subject about which too little is known). Arezzo was in any case an odd site to have become a major pottery exporting centre, lying as it does 150 km from the sea on a barely navigable river, yet exporting to Britain, it would seem, in one direction, and southern India (Arikamedu, near Madras) in the other. Sigillata required a clay with special firing properties, and that from Arezzo was clearly ideal. There may also have been a flourishing pre-sigillata pottery tradition there. My own suggestion, somewhat heretical, is that the major producer, Gaius Ateius, known from stamps bearing his and his slaves' and freedmen's names, was a large local landowner, a member of the senatorial family of that name, who established workshops to exploit the clay beds on his land, as other great landed proprietors around Rome are known to have used clay beds to produce bricks in great quantity (page 86). Exploitation of one's land in this way counted as an extension of agriculture, and so was perfectly respectable. If my theory were accepted, then the subsequent expansion of the Ateius workshops into Gaul would show the family financing freedmen, like Marcus Crassus Frugi with his baths at Pompeii. But whatever the explanation, there are reasons enough to explain the decline of Arezzo without our having to generalize from this to a supposed decline in Italian trade, which goes contrary to what other evidence we have.

In the balance of trade between Italy and the provinces, Italy was of course a net importer. The wealthy senatorial families with their swollen staffs of slaves were conspicuous consumers, drawing in luxury goods from all over the Empire and beyond, amber from the Baltic, for instance, silk from China, and spices from India. But still more, the city of Rome was a great parasite. We have had occasion in describing the work of various emperors, especially Augustus, Claudius and Trajan, to stress their concern for the grain supply of Rome, because the city would have starved without the imports from Africa and Egypt. The emperors also imported marbles for the embellishment of the city and wild beasts for its entertainment (pages 253, 276). What Aelius Aristides says in the time of Antoninus Pius must already have been true two or three generations earlier:

> Around lie the continents far and wide, pouring an endless flow of goods to you. . . . Whatever each people raises or manufactures is undoubtedly always here to overflowing. So many merchantmen arrive here with cargoes from all over at every season and with each return of the harvest that the city seems like the common warehouse of the world. . . . The arrival and departure of ships never ceases, so that it is astounding that the sea, not to mention the harbour, is sufficient for the merchantmen. (*To Rome* 11–13).

Here he is of course thinking especially of Portus, the artificial harbour which gradually supplanted Ostia as the main port of Rome. The outer basin, built by Claudius and completed under Nero, was 200 acres (80 hectares) in extent, with an inner basin added by Trajan of 81 acres (nearly

33 hectares). From here it took three days for boats to be towed up to Rome. Towing was necessary because the river was too winding for sailing to be possible, and congestion was a permanent problem.

Rome was like nowhere else, a city of over a million people. Pompeii, by contrast, had no more than 20,000, and no other city of the ancient world seems ever to have exceeded 300,000, which is the population conjectured for Carthage and Alexandria. For the ambitious, Rome *was* the world. Cicero had once written to a younger friend, and Petronius or Pliny, we may be sure, would have echoed the sentiment, 'The city, the city, my dear Rufus, stay in it and live in its sunlight. ... All foreign travel ... is skulking and paltry to men whose work could shine at Rome' (*To his friends* II.xii.2). Juvenal writes savagely of the squalor, the discomfort, the corruption of Rome, but it does not seem to have occurred to him to live anywhere else. Martial came there to make his reputation from the small Spanish town of Bilbilis, and at the end of his life returned home, famous and honoured in his own place, whence he writes to commiserate with Juvenal, still 'treading the thresholds of the great, fanned by your sweaty toga' (xii.18), but he has little good to say of small-town life otherwise. Better the humiliation of poverty at Rome than comfortable, boring obscurity elsewhere, despite the stock theme, so common in ancient literature, of the superiority of rural peace to the care and dangers of the city.

We have stressed Nero's role as patron of the arts. Rome continued to be the cultural magnet of the Latin-speaking half of the Empire under the Flavians. Vespasian, though himself without literary ambition, was a generous patron: 'He first paid teachers of Latin and Greek rhetoric an annual salary of 100,000 sesterces from the privy purse; he also gave prizes to leading poets and to artists as well' (Suetonius, *Vespasian* 18). He was also generous to actors and musicians, and must himself have been a constant reader with a good taste and memory, for Suetonius credits him with 'a knack of apt quotation from the Greek classics' (*Vespasian* 23), suggesting that, like a much more recent commander-in-chief in

Palestine, Field-Marshall Lord Wavell, he had often turned to poetry 'in the short leisures of a very busy life' (Wavell in the preface to *Other Men's Flowers*). Vespasian was also a decent orator in both Latin and Greek, and enough of a writer to produce his memoirs. Of his two sons, Titus 'could compose speeches and verses in Greek or Latin with equal ease' (Suetonius, *Titus* 3), while Domitian in his youth 'displayed a sudden devotion to poetry, which he would read aloud in public', and when he came to the throne, after a disastrous fire, he 'went to a great deal of trouble and expense in restocking the burnt-out libraries', although by this time he had given up 'bothering with either history or poetry' and 'now read nothing but Tiberius's notebooks and official memoirs' (Suetonius, *Domitian* 2, 20).

The attraction which Rome exercised led inevitably to gross overcrowding. Space was at a premium. For all but the rich, life at Rome meant, at best, living in an apartment block (*insula*). Martial, for instance, had an apartment up three flights of steep stairs, with a good view, but draughty and noisy, without running water. Many were worse off, with a whole family in one room and people sleeping in the stairwell or in the street. The well-built apartment blocks which survive at Ostia give us some idea of the layout of such blocks, but are more substantial than many of those which literary and legal sources attest at Rome. Juvenal complains of the danger of apartment blocks collapsing (*Satires* iii.190–6), and Aulus Gellius has an anecdote of a group of friends walking up the Cispian Hill when they see a multistorey apartment block and the neighbouring buildings on fire, and one of the group says, 'There is a high return from urban property, but the dangers are far higher. If there could be some way of stopping houses in Rome catching fire the whole time, I should certainly sell all my property in the country and buy urban property' (*Attic Nights* xv.1). Owning urban property to rent was in fact an established upper-class practice; there are slaves called *insularii* who managed an *insula* for their masters. There were also upper-class apartments, which even senators might rent in a crisis (Suetonius, *Vitellius* 7), or sons setting up on their own, or wealthy freedmen, whose apartment even Augustus might borrow for the night (Suetonius, *Augustus* 45).

Juvenal in particular writes so vividly of the horrors of life at Rome (read the third satire in its entirety) that we are carried away, and his exaggerations appear in textbooks as if they were the norm. One has to keep up appearances, he complains. The rich look after one another, nobody looks after the poor. The rich man has his private conveyance (in Juvenal, he has a 'huge Liburnian litter' (*Satires* iii.239–45), just as in a modern context it might be the company Rolls-Royce), where he can 'read on the way, or write or even sleep', whereas 'we in our hurry are impeded by the wave in front, while the crowd behind pushes us in the back as they press close'. It sounds like a tube station in the rush hour, and so much of the satire might be uttered by a London commuter in the pub after a bad day. Certainly there is no reason to think that things were worse for most people in first-century Rome than in eighteenth-century London, to which Dr Johnson adapted this satire, or the London of Dicken's novels.

Rome was clearly expensive, despite subsidized food and the possibility of handouts from one's patron or from the emperor. We turn, as always, to inscriptions to supplement the literary evidence, and there we find the common people of Rome, below Juvenal's social level, but at least able to afford to set up an inscription, even if only a gravestone. The real paupers could not even do that. The range of jobs recorded is extremely wide and attests a degree of specialization possible only in a city as large and complex as Rome. In certain trades women regularly worked alongside men, and often we can trace intermarriage between men and women in the same profession, the relationship quite frequently going back to a time when they were slaves together. The degree to which the artisan class appears to have been recruited from slaves who had learned their trade in the service of some great household or of a proprietor of an established business needs to be stressed.

Within the great households, there existed a variety of jobs and a status hierarchy which outdoes even the complexities of late Victorian England. Our best evidence comes from the communal tombs known as 'dovecotes' (*columbaria*), used for the burial of the ashes of slaves and freedmen of prominent persons or families, such as Livia, the widow of Augustus (still in use after her death), or the Volusii Saturnini, both on the Via Appia, or that of the Statilii, used from Augustus to Nero, on the Esquiline. We cannot tell how many household servants any one person or family may have had. Livia's *columbarium* had room for over 1000 dead, over a period of some thirty years, but it was not the only burial-place for her staff. The senator Pedanius Secundus in Nero's time is alleged to have had a staff of 400 in his town house (Tacitus, *Annals* xiv.43, where I take this to be the natural meaning, though in a very rhetorical context). Having a large household was clearly a status-symbol. Nearly eighty different job-titles are attested overall, and it has been conjectured that Livia must have had a staff of at least 150 persons, probably more, and no doubt could call on her husband's slaves too. Their quarters must have been as cramped as servants' quarters in many Victorian and Edwardian houses.

The household as a whole was run by a steward (*dispensator*), often a slave with slaves of his own. There were specialized staff responsible for admitting or keeping out callers, for knowing the precise treatment suitable for the rank of each, for looking after the comfort of guests. There were servants for the private apartments. The *cubicularii* or bedroom staff were numerous enough to need supervisory staff, and the head *cubicularius* was an influential figure who might be expected to have his master's ear. Women had their maids who were also often in their mistress's confidence, and whose high status is shown by the frequency with which they were given their freedom. Livia had a large staff solely to look after her wardrobe. There were hairdressers and masseurs (for men) or masseuses (for women). There were footmen and messengers. There were secretaries and accountants. There were numerous craftsmen, such as carpenters, masons, plumbers, glaziers, and the imperial family at least even had their own goldsmiths, silversmiths, jewellers and other skilled slaves. There were also slaves in what we should consider professional roles, as librarians, architects, doctors, and the like.

Slaves bred. There was no legal marriage for slaves, but they were commonly allowed or encouraged to contract permanent unions which might turn into marriage if both partners were freed. It was considered better to have slaves born within the household than to buy them; in this way, it was thought, they felt loyalty to the family. Slaves and freedmen show pride in having belonged to persons or families of importance (we can compare Jane Austen in *Persuasion:* 'nor could the valet of any new-made lord be more delighted with the place he held in society'), and the arrogance of rich men's slaves to humbler citizens was notorious, just as the hauteur, of, say, the duke's butler is a commonplace of English literature. We find among the slaves midwives to help fellow slaves and freedwomen give birth, wet-nurses, and teachers to instruct the slave children. Legal texts suggest that a female slave's child-bearing capacity was an important consideration. In all the households we have been referring to, male slaves outnumber female. There is some evidence that it was not uncommon for pregnant women slaves to be sent off to a country estate to have their children, but the disproportion among adult slaves suggests that boy slaves were kept more frequently than girls, who might be exposed and left to die, or sold, which, if there was a surplus of female slaves anyway in large households, would not be an attractive prospect – the girl could perhaps expect to end up in a brothel or at best as a poor man's drudge. This was one end of the scale, the other being represented by such slave women as Acte and Caenis, who finished up as freedwomen, the concubines and wives in all but name of Nero and Vespasian respectively, with their own household and a status which few women born free could have hoped for.

We should close this discussion of slavery with a word of warning. The complexity, legal and social, of the institution of slavery in the Roman world is surely clear, particularly if we bear in mind that we have in this particular discussion left out of account on the one hand the favoured and influential slaves and freedmen in public administration, and on the other the agricultural slaves and those members of urban households whose jobs were too menial to be recorded on inscriptions; there must after all have been slaves in Livia's household who cleaned the lavatories, but they do not appear in the *columbarium* with their higher-status fellows. The differences between Roman slavery and black slavery in the American South must be kept in mind. For a start, although there were some black slaves at Rome, there were not many, and generally there was no difference in colour, indeed no difference at all in physical appearance between master and slave. In most cases both came from the same Mediterranean stock. This meant that the descendants of freed slaves at Rome could blend into the free population as New World slaves set apart by their colour could not. For this and other reasons we must beware of importing into a discussion of Roman slavery intellectual analyses or emotional preconceptions derived from black slavery in the New World. We might also add that the Romans seem generally to have been free of colour prejudice, though there was something akin to it in the revulsion which they felt for the big, blonde, smelly barbarians, the Celts and still more the Germans, from the North.

The city of Rome itself, the physical setting in which the society we have been discussing operated, transformed by Augustus, underwent further striking changes under Nero and his successors. We have already alluded to Nero's influence on Roman architecture (see Chapter 5). The great fire of 64 and the troubles of the civil wars meant much rebuilding. Vespasian indeed authorized anyone to take over and build on abandoned sites, while he himself restored the Capitol, built a new forum adjacent to that of Augustus, and gave back the 300 acres (120 hectares) which Nero had confiscated for his Golden House and park, undertaking the construction of the Flavian Amphitheatre (the Colosseum) on the site of Nero's artificial lake. It was completed by Domitian, who was another great builder. He further expanded the area of the imperial forums with his Forum Transitorium, which Nerva was to complete; he built the Arch of Titus in his brother's honour between the Forum and the Colosseum, with reliefs showing the spoils from the Temple at Jerusalem; he was responsible for a new circus, whose outline is still preserved in the Piazza Navona; but his greatest monument was the new palace on the Palatine, architecturally in the forefront of its period, conventionally rectilinear outside, but all curved shapes and dramatic spatial effects inside.

The Flavian period also saw a transformation of the residential and commercial quarters. Private houses, apartment buildings, stores and warehouses were largely rebuilt in concrete and brick, like those at Ostia already referred to. Concrete was coming into its own as *the* Roman building material, and architects were beginning to realise its possibilities for innovation in the use and shaping of interior space, possibilities that were to be triumphantly realised in Hadrian's Pantheon (page 225). The water supply was thoroughly overhauled, as Frontinus testifies, and Trajan was responsible for extensive wharves and warehouses along the Tiber bank, which did something to ease the congestion on the river.

Trajan also built the last of the imperial forums, one of the great tourist sights of late antiquity. To get the level ground required, the Quirinal hill was cut back 125 feet (nearly 40 metres), which was the height of Trajan's Column. The Column, decorated with the reliefs recording the conquest of Dacia, was the centrepiece of the scheme and was flanked by two libraries. One side of the forum was occupied by the great Basilica Ulpia, conservative in style, rich in ornament, the inspiration for other such buildings in provincial cities, such as Carthage. Against the flank of the Quirinal was built a shopping centre, with access on three levels, over 150 shops, and a market hall, all of brickfaced concrete, as modern and innovative as the Basilica was conventionally classical. If the poor and the slaves lived in cramped and often sordid conditions, they nonetheless had their public entertainments, such as the circus and the amphitheatre (see Chapter 10), with a universal appeal like that of football today; they had the public baths, on a scale to which there is no modern parallel; and the ubiquity of bars serving drink and often food in Pompeii and Ostia and no doubt in Rome itself, if we had the same amount of evidence, suggest that they played somewhat the same role as public houses in run-down working-class areas of Victorian London. Life was lived in the streets, as it is to a large extent in the Mediterranean today, and the streets and public places of the city provided buildings and surroundings of considerable splendour. The public areas and buildings of Rome worthily reflected the stability of Roman order and the prosperity of Italy.

When the news of Trajan's death reached Antioch (11 August 117), the troops there acclaimed Hadrian as his successor. Hadrian promptly wrote off to the Senate, asking for Trajan's deification and the ratification of his own succession. He claimed to have been adopted by Trajan on his deathbed. Whether this formally took place, or whether Trajan's wife Plotina forged the official documents, as some alleged, is unimportant. Hadrian had in any case been Trajan's ward ever since his father, Trajan's first cousin, died when he was ten; he was married to Trajan's great-niece; and his career, even though not marked by the sort of special favours and accelerated honours that would have marked him unequivocally as the destined heir, nonetheless left him on Trajan's death in an unassailable position. He had held the consulship, though as suffect only, in 108; he was now consul designate for the second time, for 118, and legate of Syria, in command of the army assembled for the eastern campaigns. Either Hadrian had to succeed, or there would have been civil war.

We have already considered how unsatisfactory the sources are for the legislative and administrative activity of Hadrian and his successors. Again and again, they show us a procurator here or a military unit there, some piece of legislation, some administrative structure, without the evidence to show when the disposition was made or the institution put in place. Bearing in mind this disadvantage, we shall nevertheless try in this chapter to sketch chronologically the work of Hadrian, Antoninus Pius and Marcus Aurelius, completing the picture by sketching thematically in the following chapter some of the salient features of the period.

Hadrian himself, born Publius Aelius Hadrianus, came from a family long settled in Spain, although it traced its origins back to Picenum and claimed, perhaps with some exaggeration, to have been senatorial for five generations. Relations with the Senate, however, proved one of Hadrian's problems. They never in fact recovered from the initial crisis of his reign, when four ex-consuls, including Trajan's great Moorish general, Lusius Quietus, were tried at Rome *in absentia* (in Hadrian's absence too, be it noted), condemned on a charge of conspiracy, hunted down, and summarily executed wherever each happened to be caught. The circumstances are obscure. Hadrian is said to have disclaimed responsibility in his autobiography, and to have blamed Attianus, his praetorian prefect, whom shortly afterwards he dismissed. The four men, alleged to have plotted Hadrian's assassination, may have opposed his policy of abandoning Trajan's eastern conquests. Hadrian took an oath for the future never to put a senator to death without a vote of the Senate, but the damage was done.

Hadrian did in fact immediately withdraw from Trajan's new provinces beyond the Euphrates, returning to a policy of supporting client kings, rather than direct rule. Elsewhere in the Empire he inherited disturbances which had broken out during Trajan's absence in the East: tribal uprisings in Britain, on the lower Danube, and in Mauretania, and a widespread revolt among the Jewish communities throughout the eastern provinces, which caused great damage:

The Emperor Caesar Traianus Hadrianus Augustus, son of the deified Traianus Parthicus, grandson of the deified Nerva, *pontifex maximus,* holding the tribunician power for the third time, thrice consul, ordered the restoration for the city of Cyrene of the baths together with the porticoes and ball courts and other appurtenances, which had been torn down and burned in the Jewish revolt. [*AE* 1928, 2 = *LR* p.413; the year is 119. Another inscription, *AE* 1928, 1, mentions the restoration of a road which had been 'ripped up and ruined in the Jewish revolt']

Hadrian promptly restored order, remitted arrears of taxes, and emphasized the continuity of the regime by the honours which he paid to Trajan's memory. Propaganda stressed the 'eternity' of Rome. Coins were issued celebrating 'the Golden Age' (SAECULUM AUREUM). There were no new wars. Hadrian set himself to reorganize and consolidate the administrative machinery of the Empire. He spent two or three years in Rome, until he was sure of his hold on the reins of power, and then devoted some five years to a tour of the provinces, beginning with Gaul, where he gave much attention and numerous benefactions to the urban communities, and then going on to Germany, where he tightened up army discipline, lived rough and trained with the soldiers, and put in hand further road building and other frontier works. To Hadrian's reign belongs the first continuous barrier, a wooden palisade, along the *limes* in the angle between the Rhine and the Danube.

From Germany he sailed to Britain, perhaps early in the spring of 122. Nearly forty years had elapsed since Agricola's recall; they have left virtually no record in the literary sources. We have noted that one legion was removed soon after Agricola left (page 182); the territory north of the Forth-Clyde isthmus had been given up, but the Lowlands south of that line were strongly held until about 105, with a key fort at Newstead in the Tweed valley, garrisoned by a mixed force of legionaries and auxiliary cavalry. Roman coins and pottery at native sites attest the beginning of contact with the occupying forces. But around 105 southern Scotland was abandoned and troops withdrawn to the line of the future Hadrian's Wall along the Tyne-Solway isthmus, perhaps because Trajan's Dacian Wars had made him call on further reinforcements from Britain. The three legionary bases were already at York, Chester and Caerleon; the governor's headquarters were at London; and the former legionary bases at Lincoln and Gloucester had become colonies under Domitian and Nerva respectively. This was how Hadrian found the province when he arrived.

Hadrian may have initiated the building of a forum at both

Wroxeter and Leicester; no doubt in Britain, as in Gaul, he paid special attention to the towns. But the great monument to his visit is Hadrian's Wall, 80 miles long, dividing the still imperfectly pacified Brigantians to the south from the more hostile tribes to the north. With its forts and its westward extension down the Solway shore, it took at least six years to build and required well over a million cubic yards of stone. Nothing like it exists on other frontiers; few Roman structures have been so comprehensively studied or so passionately argued about.

Later in 122 Hadrian returned to Gaul and thence to Spain where he passed the winter. His time was not spent wholly on business. He was an avid sightseer (the Christian Tertullian describes him as 'a seeker-out of all curiosities', *Apology* 5), and keen on hunting. His favourite horse, Borysthenes, is buried at Apt in southern France, and an inscription preserves the rather doggerel epitaph Hadrian wrote for him. From Spain he crossed the Straits of Gibraltar into Mauretania, where he conducted military operations of some sort, and then before the end of 123 sailed through the Mediterranean to the Greek-speaking east (he never again visited the western European provinces), where he spent a couple of years, bestowing benefactions on cities and indulging his taste for Greek culture and antiquities.

By 126 he was again in Italy. The following year, games celebrated the tenth anniversary of his accession. Hadrian accepted the title of *pater patriae*. Coins stressed CONCORDIA. Hadrian set off again, going first to Africa, where his landing at Carthage coincided with the breaking of a five-year drought. By July 128, he had travelled inland to visit the new legionary base at Lambaesis, where an inscription preserves his speech to the troops whom he had watched on manoeuvres (page 254). His concern for discipline and training is readily apparent; with no wars it will not have been easy to stop the army growing slack. From Africa he returned very briefly to Rome, before going on to Athens; thereafter he remained until 134 in Greece and the eastern provinces. Coins and inscriptions celebrate his visits and lavish benefactions to the towns along his route, but do not permit us to establish his precise itinerary. In October 129, however, he was in Egypt, where his favourite, a Bithynian youth called Antinous, was drowned in the Nile. Some suspected suicide. Hadrian's grief was very public and memorials to Antinous included a city, Antinoopolis, founded in his honour. It was probably earlier that same year, while visiting Palestine, that Hadrian decided to found a colony to be called Colonia Aelia Capitolina on the site of Jerusalem, with a temple to Jupiter replacing the Jewish Temple which Titus had destroyed (page 174). This sparked off another great Jewish revolt (132–5), led by Simon Bar-Kochba. Dio may exaggerate when he alleges that 50 fortresses and 985 villlages were destroyed and over half a million men killed in battle, but the war was a serious one and the repression merciless (Dio lxix.14). Jews were thereafter 'strictly forbidden even to set foot on the land around Jerusalem' (Eusebius, *Ecclesiastical History* iv.6).

All his life, in fact, Hadrian was an enthusiastic builder, both at Rome and in the provinces. He founded new cities, embellished old ones: temples, baths, theatres, amphitheatres, a whole new suburb at Athens, harbour works at Ephesus, roads and aqueducts, including the aqueduct, one branch 132 km in length, the other over 90, which provided Carthage with 32 million litres of water a day, and the vast complex of cisterns which the aqueduct fed (page 252). The scale of his operations and the scope of his imagination are alike impressive. Few surviving monuments of antiquity strike the imagination more powerfully than the Pantheon, rebuilt by Hadrian as a rotunda 142 feet (43.2 metres) high and the same in diameter, lit by a single opening 30 feet across in the roof. The span of the dome exceeds that of St Peter's, and was unmatched until modern times. The interior was embellished with coloured marbles, and the bronze doors which are still in place led in from a massive portico fronting on to a narrow piazza. Other buildings in Rome include Hadrian's own mausoleum on the right bank of the Tiber, rivalling Augustus's. It was converted in the Middle Ages into the papal fortress of Castel St Angelo. Outside Rome lay

Hadrian's villa at Tibur (Tivoli), sprawling over 160 acres (65 hectares), a pastiche of styles, crammed with works of art, begun early in his reign, intermittently enlarged, and due to become the passion of his old age.

No emperor since Augustus had left his mark so strongly on the physical appearance of the Empire. Marguerite Yourcenar in her novel *Memoirs of Hadrian* hits it off beautifully:

> In a world still largely made up of woods, desert and uncultivated plain, a city is indeed a fine sight, with its paved streets, its temple to some god or other, its public baths and latrines, a shop where the barber discusses with his clients the news from Rome, its pastry shop, cobblers' and perhaps a bookshop, its doctor's sign, and a theatre, where from time to time a comedy of Terence is played. Our men of fashion complain of the uniformity of our cities; they suffer in seeing everywhere the same statue of the emperor, and the same water pipes. They are wrong: the beauty of Nîmes is wholly different from that of Arles. But that very uniformity, to be found on three continents, reassures the traveller as does the sight of a milestone; even the dullest of our towns have their comforting significance as shelters and posting stops.

In one other way, Hadrian changed the face of the Roman world: he grew a beard, allegedly to hide scars (*Augustan History, Hadrian* 26), or possibly in imitation of the fashion of Greek philosophers, who traditionally went bearded. The Roman upper classes had been clean shaven for centuries. Henceforth they grow beards like the emperor.

Hadrian's last years were marred by painful illness and by the problem of the succession. Ancient gossip and modern speculation often give the impression that we know more than in fact we do. Dio has the story, not necessarily true, of a dinner-table conversation which named ten possible successors (Dio lxix.17), of whom Hadrian appeared to single out Lucius Julius Ursus Servianus. What, if anything, lies behind this? Servianus was over ninety, but had married Hadrian's sister, and their grandson, Gnaeus Pedanius Fuscus Salinator, then aged eighteen, was Hadrian's only blood-relation. But there is no evidence that Hadrian ever considered making him his heir, and Servianus was clearly too old. What happened next, genuine conspiracy or not, we cannot tell, but both Servianus and Fuscus were put to death in circumstances which reminded many senators of the affair of the four ex-consuls at the start of the reign. Hadrian then adopted one of the consuls for 136, Lucius Ceionius Commodus, who took the name Lucius Aelius Caesar. Again, we cannot tell what specially commended him to Hadrian. In any event, he died first, on the last night of 137, and Hadrian's new choice was a certain Titus Aurelius Fulvius Boionius Arrius Antoninus, who in his turn adopted both Lucius Aelius Caesar's young son (who became Lucius Aurelius Commodus), and his own wife's nephew (to be known as Marcus Aurelius Verus, the future emperor Marcus Aurelius, at this time a youth of seventeen whose qualities seem to have attracted Hadrian's attention). It is indeed possible that what singled out Antoninus from other possible senatorial candidates was precisely his relationship to Marcus Aurelius, whom Hadrian perhaps already saw as his ultimate successor.

Antoninus himself, aged fifty-one, consul back in 120, from a family that traced its roots back to Nîmes in southern Gaul, was wealthy, competent, moderately distinguished, not apparently outstanding in any way, acceptable to the Senate, highly respectable, perhaps a bit dull. When Hadrian died (10 July 138), Antoninus succeeded without further incident, except that he had to defend Hadrian's memory against a vindictive Senate which would have refused him the customary divine honours. It is probably for this that Antoninus himself was honoured with the addition to his name of Pius. As for Hadrian, he remains for us in many respects, as he was for his contemporaries, an enigma. On his deathbed he is said to have composed lines to his 'little, charming, wandering soul', now going to a place where 'you will not make jokes as you used to'. It is a fitting and haunting epitaph for a complex and haunted man.

In most fields of internal policy and administration, it is likely that Hadrian continued and developed policies and trends already established by his predecessors. The Empire had never been more prosperous, and Hadrian, despite his largesses and his expensive building programme, does not seem to have lacked for money. Perhaps, however, financial considerations underlay, at least in part, the abandonment of Trajan's eastern conquests, since to retain and garrison them would have required considerable expenditure, although on the other hand the new provinces might have been expected to pay for themselves through increased revenue. That Hadrian interested himself in the financial administration of the Empire seems clear, but it is not clear that new developments or new appointments first attested during his reign were in fact initiated then, still less that Hadrian himself bore personal responsibility for them. For instance, he has been credited by modern scholars with a wide extension of the system of equestrian procurators and with fixing definitively the equestrian career structure. But as was pointed out earlier (Chapter 2), epigraphic evidence, especially for men of equestrian rank, gets fuller from now on, and a procuratorial post first attested under Hadrian may go back much earlier. The career structure had become clear. At the top, the 200,000-sesterces-a-year men (*ducenarii*) included the top officials of the emperor's own staff, the procurators governing minor provinces, and some others, such as the chief librarian of the city of Rome. Lower grades received 100,000 or 60,000 a year. But this structure had developed over the years, and Hadrian's role has probably been overstated.

Two areas where Hadrian's own interest and initiative were, however, especially involved were the army and the law. We have already referred to his concern during his travels for military discipline and training. A passage in the *Augustan History* ascribes to him the qualities traditionally ascribed to good generals, such as a willingness to share the soldiers' rough food and labours, and to this extent it may be merely a conventional eulogy, but some details are less familiar, and may be based on contemporary evidence, the more so in that the passage goes on to record Hadrian's responsibility for Hadrian's Wall, a fact undoubtedly true and not found elsewhere in extant literary sources. Specifically, Hadrian is said to have 'rooted out of the camp dining rooms, porticoes, covered arcades and ornamental gardens' (*Augustan History, Hadrian* 10), a detail which suits his interest in architecture, as well as his concern for discipline. Moreover,

> he made an effort to get to know all about military stores and skilfully examined provincial revenues, so that if there was a deficiency anywhere, he could make it up. More than any other emperor, however, he strove never to buy or to keep up anything unnecessary. (*Augustan History, Hadrian* 11)

This, if true, supports the view that Hadrian took a personal interest in the financial administration of the Empire. It is moreover an archaeological commonplace that Roman military equipment tends to be more standardized in the second century than in the first. Perhaps Hadrian, if he interested himself in such matters, helped along the trend towards centralization and standardization.

Hadrian is also commonly credited with actively encouraging more intensive recruitment in the frontier provinces and especially among soldiers' sons. If so, he was again merely encouraging a process that was already well established. The more Romanized provinces, like Italy itself, provide a smaller and smaller proportion of recruits throughout the second century. The *Augustan History* has a story, expressly attributed to Marius Maximus, of Hadrian's summoning a meeting at Tarraco (Tarragona), where the Spanish representatives laughed at the idea of conscription (12.4). Voluntary recruitment was clearly insufficient. In theory, legionaries had to be citizens, and since soldiers could not marry (page 137), their sons were not citizens, and were therefore, strictly speaking, ineligible for the legions. But as we saw in Chapter 6, examples are attested from the time of Augustus onwards of soldiers who receive citizenship on enlistment, so that they will qualify, and this becomes commoner in the second century. Hadrian may have encouraged the practice. One sign that it spread during his reign is the number of men with the name Aelius, who turn up in succeeding decades on inscriptions listing veterans; the name suggests that they or their fathers got the citizenship from Hadrian.

Hadrian was certainly responsible for other legal changes which improved the soldier's status and thus no doubt favoured recruitment. Take the question of wills. The recognition of a soldier's will as valid even if not made in due form goes back at least to Flavian times, but Hadrian extended this to veterans and provided that a will was not invalidated by execution or, in most cases, by suicide. A soldier had long been recognized as having full control of the money and property accruing to him from his military service, even if his father was alive and the soldier would otherwise legally have been under his father's authority (page 137). Hadrian extended this privilege by ruling in the soldier's favour on certain doubtful issues. Perhaps most important of all these reforms was a ruling that soldiers' sons, naturally illegitimate since soldiers could not legally marry, might nonetheless inherit their father's property. This ruling is set out in a letter of Hadrian's to the Prefect of Egypt preserved on papyrus:

> I know, my dear Rammius, that those whose fathers begat them during their military service have hitherto been forbidden to inherit their fathers' property . . . I now make them a gift of this opportunity which I take of interpreting more humanely the somewhat severe regulations of the emperors my predecessors. To whatsoever extent therefore sons begotten on military service are not lawful heirs of their fathers, I decree that these also may now claim possession of their fathers' property in accordance with that section of the Edict which grants possession to

blood-relations. (*Select Papyri* 213 = *FIRA* i.78 = *LR* p.519)

Dio notes that military regulations established by Hadrian remained in force a century later (lxix.9), and some of his enactments survive in the *Digest*. But his influence was by no means confined to military law. In other fields of law also, Hadrian is the first emperor whose legislation and rulings are preserved to any considerable extent. The *Digest*, for instance, contains little pre-Hadrianic material, and the earliest rescript, or authoritative imperial ruling on a point of law, preserved in Justinian's *Code* is Hadrianic. Our sources stress the personal interest which Hadrian took in the administration of justice, and among his undoubted achievements was that he set the lawyer Salvius Julianus to edit the praetor's so-called Perpetual Edict and publish it in definitive form. The date is a matter of some dispute. Julianus, who came from the small town of Pupput (Souk el-Abiod, near the modern tourist resort of Hammamet in Tunisia), was paid a double salary as quaestor (*ILS* 8973, from Pupput), perhaps for his work on the edict, but the details of his early career remain obscure. Most modern scholars, however, would place the publication of the new edict in the last years of the reign, although it may have been in preparation for some time before that. Julianus, we may note, went on to be consul in 148 and to hold provincial governorships culminating in that of his native province of Africa early in Marcus Aurelius's reign, but the post of prefect of the city and a second consulship are ascribed to him only by the *Augustan History* in the life of Didius Julianus, and the supposed relationship of the two men may itself be wholly fictitious, suggested by their sharing the name Julianus. This serves as a good example of how the *Augustan History* mixes fact and deliberate fiction, and how careful we must be in using it.

The precise scope of Julianus's revision of the edict is not wholly clear, and appears to stop short of what would be implied by calling it codification. But its influence was enormous. Not only did it stimulate a vast effort of exegesis

(Ulpian alone wrote more than eighty books of commentary on it, much used in the compilation of Justinian's *Digest*), but it strongly reinforced the tendency to make the emperor himself the sole source of law. The preamble to the *Digest* makes this clear:

> Julianus himself, that most acute framer of laws and of the Perpetual Edict, laid it down in his own writings that whatever was found to be defective should be supplied by imperial decree, and not he alone but the deified Hadrian as well in the consolidation of the Edict and in the decree of the senate which followed it most clearly prescribed that where anything is not found set out in the Edict it shall be provided for in accordance with the rules of the Edict, and by inferences from and analogies to the rules, by more recent authority. (*Digest*, Constitution '*Tanta ...*' 18)

Such authority was, increasingly, solely that of the emperor, until Ulpian can write simply, 'What has pleased the emperor has the force of law.'

We note in the passage just cited from the *Digest* that the revised edict, referred to as the Perpetual Edict, was obviously brought before and confirmed by a decree of the Senate. Again there is no certainty about the part Hadrian himself played, but some modern scholars credit him with the initiative in giving senatorial decrees force of law. The first such decree which we know to have directly altered the civil law is in fact Hadrianic, but there may have been earlier ones, and the distinction is perhaps important only to the specialist in legal history. By the end of the first century AD, the popular assemblies were no longer convened to pass laws, and the Senate's decrees filled the vacuum. By Hadrian's day, moreover, nobody doubted that the emperor's authority was sovereign, and he might make law by his own edicts and other enactments. The various forms became confused. It may, as we have seen, be under Hadrian that the rescript assumes its later importance, that is to say, the emperor's ruling on a point of law submitted for his advice. Certain legal scholars were also authorized to give binding rulings in the emperor's name, and this procedure too, which in fact goes back to Augustus's day, attracted Hadrian's systematizing attention, causing him to rule that such opinions, when unanimous, had the force of law, but recognizing the possibility of disagreement, in which case the judge must decide (Gaius, *Institutes* i.7). The most likely explanation is that Hadrian intended to make it clear beyond doubt that, where the authorized experts agreed, their unanimous opinion *must* be followed, but the recognition that several authorities might disagree may well be linked with the parallel development under Hadrian of the imperial rescript, issued under the emperor's own direct authority.

Hadrian's concern for efficiency in the administration of the law is also shown by his creation of four judicial districts for Italy, each entrusted to a judge of consular rank, who would go round holding assizes, as provincial governors did, instead of leaving all Italy dependent on the courts at Rome. But this measure was seen as derogating from Italy's privileged status and was so unpopular that it was dropped, although reintroduced under Marcus Aurelius, with judges of praetorian rank bearing the same title of *iuridici* already used in the provinces. Hadrian's basic humanity is attested in anecdotes and in legal enactments which reveal a disposition towards generosity in the fields of marriage and inheritance and in the treatment of slaves. On the other hand, he was strong on upholding social distinctions and public decorum. According to the *Augustan History* he 'ordered senators and Roman knights always to wear the toga in public except when returning from a banquet' (*Hadrian* 22), and always wore it himself in Italy. This is plausible, but is it true? It might be invented on the analogy of one of Suetonius's anecdotes of Augustus (Suetonius, *Augustus* 40). But if so, it is nonetheless significant. It shows the sort of thing judged to be in character for Hadrian. The story would not have been told of all emperors.

When we pass on to the reign and the achievements of Antoninus Pius, we meet again the same problems as with

Hadrian, but in a more acute form. There are no great
dramas in his life, at least that we know of: no execution of
the four ex-consuls, no travels, no Antinous. His biography in
the *Augustan History* is less than half the length of Hadrian's.
The epigraphic record is impressive, but does not help us very
much to reconstruct a chronology or a narrative of policy
decisions. Antoninus did not have Hadrian's interest in
building; the one significant surviving monument of his reign
in Rome is the Temple of Antoninus and his wife Faustina in
the Forum, now the Church of St Lorenzo in Miranda, with a
1602 baroque facade, while the Temple of the Deified
Hadrian is represented by a wall and eleven slender columns
near the Pantheon.

Along the frontiers, the only serious fighting was in
northern Britain, undertaken perhaps as a sop to military
opinion. Here the African, Quintus Lollius Urbicus from
Tiddis (see Chapter 10), governor of Britain 139–45, reconquered the Lowlands of Scotland and built a new frontier
barrier, the Antonine Wall, from the Forth to the Clyde.
After a serious rebellion in 154 the new Wall was abandoned,
then reoccupied, and finally abandoned for good, probably a
year or two after Antoninus's death. Other frontiers were
strengthened, especially the German *limes*. There was trouble
in Mauretania. But most people in the Empire heard of these
distant operations 'as if they were myths', says Aelius
Aristides (page 256).

In the general administration of the Empire, and particularly in the field of law, Antoninus generally followed
Hadrian's policies, and there were no dramatic changes. It
has for instance been suggested that Antoninus was the first
to give formal recognition in law to the distinction between
the upper classes (*honestiores*) and the rest (*humiliores*), a
distinction expressed in the different penalties to which the
classes were liable. But this distinction goes back, in essence,
to the previous century. We see a tendency to subject the
lower orders of society, even Roman citizens, to punishments
which were mostly reserved under the Republic for slaves,
and although some emperors might apply these punishments

even to knights and senators, such incidents arouse the unfailing indignation of Tacitus and other upper-class writers. Hadrian certainly recognized the distinction, as in a notable rescript on the penalties for moving boundary stones, which prescribes relegation for men of standing ('relegation' was a form of banishment without loss of civil rights), but a beating and two years' hard labour for the rest (*Digest* XLVII.xxi.2). That Antoninus permitted further development of this system is clear. We need only cite the following text from the *Digest*: 'Whoever steals gold or silver from the imperial mines is punished, according to an edict of the Divine Pius, with exile or the mines, depending on his personal status' (XLVIII.xiii.8). But there is no evidence that he made any great innovation.

Similarly we find Antoninus Pius continuing in Hadrian's tradition of leniency and humanity in interpreting the law, for instance in testamentary cases, in the use of torture, and in the condition of slaves, although we also find him stressing that 'the power of masters over slaves must remain intact and no man must have his rights diminished' (*Digest* I.vi.2). Roman law was always strong on the rights of property owners.

Aelius Aristides stresses above all the stability of the period. Happy are those who enjoy the *pax Romana*, wretched those outside the Empire who are denied its blessings. The administration of the Empire moves with the regularity of the universe. Justice and order prevail. All this is due to the emperor's watchfulness, but not to his presence: 'he can stay quietly where he is and govern the whole world by letters which arrive at their destination almost as soon as they are written' (*To Rome* 33). This last phrase, as we have seen (page 151), is a gross exaggeration. No doubt Aelius Aristides said what he knew his hearers would want to hear, although he is not necessarily the less sincere for that; but the climate of opinion where such a speech was welcome was not one to encourage innovation. Antoninus got through an enormous amount of work. Inscriptions reveal his concern for the provinces. Communications were improved, public works continued, particular attention paid to repair and maintenance. Antoninus was a careful steward. He was also a skilled financial manager, with a reputation for personal frugality, if not downright parsimony, as several stories suggest, and he is reputed to have left the public treasury with an enormous capital reserve.

Antoninus then reaped the fruits of his predecessors', and especially of Trajan's and Hadrian's, sound government and attention to detail. He left the Empire at the apparent height of security and prosperity, ripening to its fall. It was 'the Indian summer of the Antonines', the period when for Gibbon 'the condition of the human race was most happy and most prosperous' (page 244). The next reign was to reveal the stresses and weaknesses, to show how far this happy state of affairs (happy above all, let us remember, for the upper classes, the *honestiores*, the men of property) depended on continued peace. It is however appropriate that Antoninus was to have the calmest deathbed of any emperor to date, dying quietly on 7 March 161, and succeeded, according to the long-matured plan, by Marcus Aurelius, who had married Antoninus's daughter and had several children by her. The whole family was very close, and a model of domestic propriety.

There is no evidence that Antoninus intended Marcus to share the imperial power with his adoptive brother, Lucius Commodus. Our sources suggest that this was Marcus's own decision, and that it caused some surprise. We must however admit that we do not have enough information to judge what happened, and why. Dio thought that Marcus saw in Lucius a physical robustness which he himself lacked, hoping apparently to leave any warfare to Lucius and to have more time himself for philosophy, but this has all the earmarks of a pure conjecture to try to explain what was not understood (Dio lxxi.1). Marcus dropped his own name Verus and gave it to his brother, henceforth known as Lucius Verus, both took the name Augustus, and they held all offices jointly, except that of *pontifex maximus*, which could not be shared and belonged to Marcus alone. There was in fact no doubt who was the senior partner and the stronger character. Lucius Verus, while amiable and frank, was idle and dissolute, although we are not to believe all the stories which the *Augustan History* tells about him. The author enjoyed exercising his imagination on fantasies of extravagance.

The reign began with a major war against Parthia, breaking the uneasy peace which had endured since Trajan's day. The extent to which Parthia at any moment posed a threat to Rome's eastern frontier depended to a large degree on Parthia's own internal unity and stability. Parthia had been ruled since 148 by Vologaeses III, who was to remain king until 193 or thereabouts. He had consolidated his power and the unity of his kingdom, and seized the opportunity of the change of emperors at Rome to invade both Armenia and Syria, defeating two Roman armies and placing a Parthian prince on the Armenian throne. Marcus sent Lucius Verus to take command, apparently choosing his staff for him, and it seems clear, even if we allow for the bias of our sources and the fictions of the *Augustan History*, that Verus took little interest in the fighting, which went on until the early months of 166 and ended in Roman victory and a strengthening of the Roman position on the frontier. In August, Rome witnessed the first triumph for nearly fifty years, since Trajan's posthumous triumph in 118. Marcus and Lucius were adorned with honorific titles. More significantly, in October, Marcus gave the title of Caesar to his sons, five and four years old. It was a sign that the hereditary dynastic principle had not been abandoned.

The eastern war, though successfully concluded, had two immediately disastrous consequences. Firstly, the returning army brought back plague, which ravaged the Empire and brought on a serious famine. Secondly, the northern frontier had been weakened to find troops for the East, and there was a mass breakthrough of tribes from beyond the Danube. The chronology is uncertain. Throughout 167 Marcus probably stayed in Rome, supervising measures to deal with the plague. In 168 he took command in person on the Danube. Lucius unwillingly went with him. By the end of the summer the situation was under control, and new measures had been taken to strengthen the defences of northern Italy. Early in 169, both emperors set out to return to Rome, and on the way Lucius died of a stroke, which precluded Marcus's return to the front that summer. But fighting continued, Roman reinforcements were summoned, and the following year (170) a massive offensive was launched across the Danube. It seems to have met with disaster, and the barbarians invaded Italy, besieging Aquileia, while the lower Danube frontier was also breached, the barbarians invading Greece and penetrating as far as Eleusis.

The tide turned in Rome's favour in 172. The Marcomanni accepted an unfavourable peace, and coins proclaimed, somewhat optimistically, 'the subjection of Germany', GERMANIA SUBACTA. Fighting however continued until 175, when Marcus patched up peace on hearing that the governor of Syria, Avidius Cassius, had proclaimed himself emperor, but the usurper was killed by his own troops, and although Marcus made a precautionary tour of the East, by 178 he was again campaigning successfully on the Danube. The previous year he had invested his only surviving son, Commodus, as joint emperor. When Marcus died in camp at Vienna, on 17 March 180, the war was going well, and Dio records a garrison of 20,000 men in the territory of the Marcomanni and Quadi north of the Danube where Marcus planned to establish two new provinces. It was not to be. Commodus's automatic accession to sole power, aged 18, proved unfortunate in this, as in other respects (see Chapter 11). He made peace with the tribes all along the front and withdrew the advanced garrisons which Marcus had established beyond the river. By so doing, he sacrificed the peace and security on this frontier which Rome might perhaps otherwise have had.

Marcus was the first emperor since Vespasian, 101 years before, to have left a son to succeed him. Each previous emperor's propaganda had made much of adoption, the choice of the best man for the job (Trajan's slogan of *optimus princeps*). But this was merely making the best of necessity.

The alacrity with which Marcus abandoned the 'principle' of adoption suggests that traditional family sentiment would have reasserted itself earlier, if Trajan or Hadrian had had a son. Commodus was weak, and rapidly became vicious and debauched as well, the antithesis of his philosopher father, who drew strength from the Stoics' emphasis on duty. Marcus indeed was a noble character, especially in his own eyes, but somewhat cold, self-sufficient and joyless, 'the fine flower of paganism' running to seed. In administering the Empire, he displayed a rigid conservatism, especially in maintaining and strengthening social and class distinctions. We see him not only through his own eyes in the *Meditations* and through his correspondence with Fronto (page 268), but also through the eyes of the lawyers, who esteemed him for the scrupulous care with which he carried out his judicial duties. His rulings show him continuing in particular cases the trend to greater leniency and humanity which we have already remarked on in Hadrian and Antoninus. But it has been pointed out that in his *Meditations*, when he lists those who have most influenced him, the name of Maecianus, his law teacher, is not there, and that the subjects on which he meditates do not appear to include ways of improving the administration of the Empire and the condition of its inhabitants. He was scrupulous in carrying out his duty as he understood it, but not imaginative.

His reign, through no fault of his own, had exposed some of the weaknesses of the Empire. The frontiers had been stabilized, thoughts of further expansion given up, and the legions had settled down into their permanent bases, often forming close ties with the local population (page 136). But when there was severe pressure on one frontier, it could only be met by weakening another. There was no effective strategic reserve. Response to crisis was inevitably slow, given the slowness of communications (page 151). The fighting and still more the plague in Marcus's reign hurt economically. There are increasing signs of debasement of the coinage, although not on the ruinous scale of the Severan period. Depopulation led to the settlement of barbarians within the Empire, particularly in the Danube provinces, apparently to provide agricultural labour. This was not a wholly new phenomenon, but it seems to have been on a new scale, and fraught with disastrous possibilities. Other social or economic weaknesses which the modern eye discerns, but which contemporaries had not developed the concept to analyse, or which they simply overlooked, include the enormous differences of wealth, with overconsumption at one end of the scale, grinding poverty at the other, technical stagnation, no new markets, increasing taxation, a growing bureaucracy.

There is no one simple explanation for the Empire's growing problems and the eventual collapse of the Empire in the West: certainly not widespread lead poisoning (Vitruvius already knew all about lead poisoning and warned that 'water ought by no means to be conducted in lead pipes, if we want to have it wholesome,' viii.6.II); not climatic change, for the scientific evidence is heavily against it; not soil exhaustion, for the symptoms of economic decline became as potent in Egypt, where the Nile flood renewed the soil each year, as elsewhere; not manpower shortage, despite the ravages of plague under Marcus Aurelius and again in the middle of the third century; not miscegenation and the dilution of some supposedly pure Roman stock, although many cities, especially Rome, must have been as much of racial melting pots as North American cities in the present century – but New Yorkers are not noticeably effete or lacking in the skills needed to survive. What is more, and commonly overlooked, is that any explanation of why the western half of the Empire disintegrated, politically, militarily, and to some extent culturally, in the fourth and fifth centuries must also account for the fact that the eastern half did not. The conventional Marxist explanation stresses weaknesses supposedly arising from the slave-owning structure of ancient society, but the great flaw in this theory is that, if this were a fundamental reason for the Empire's collapse, according to the supposed laws of historical inevitability, it ought to have applied equally to East and West, and it clearly did not.

Slavery, moreover was never common in some of the most prosperous provinces, such as Gaul and Egypt. It probably diminished in the later Empire, and is not to be blamed for the technological conservatism of the Roman world, which is rooted in attitudes going back to early Greece and in the great division between the rich and the poor who actually did the work, slave or free. A famous story about Vespasian shows him opposed to technological innovation, precisely because he wishes to create work for the free poor at Rome (Suetonius, *Vespasian* 18).

The Empire did not just fall apart, it was riven asunder by a combination of civil war in pursuit of power and personal advantage, and of attack from outside, by Germans, Parthians, and in the seventh century by the Arabs, who decisively shattered the unity of the Mediterranean world. Economic weakness there was, and the basic injustice of Roman society meant that, when things got bad, the burden on the less favoured was literally intolerable. So you get the men who abandon their land because they cannot pay their taxes, while the powerful magnate lives like a prince on his estates. This is part of what the impoverishment of the curial class meant (page 293). You find Septimius Severus on his deathbed telling his sons that all that matters is keeping the soldiers happy (page 290). It may be that, as we have said, the signs of these weaknesses were there to be seen by Marcus Aurelius's day. It remains equally true that many men, even somewhat later, failed to see them. It was after Marcus's death that Tertullian wrote:

The world is every day better known, better cultivated and more civilized than before. Everywhere roads are traced, every district is known, every country opened to commerce. Smiling fields have invaded the forests, flocks and herds have routed the wild beasts, the very sands are sown, the rocks are broken up, the marshes drained ... Wherever there is a trace of life, there are houses, human habitations and well-ordered governments. (*On the Soul* 30)

To most of the inhabitants of the Empire, it seemed stable enough. 'Rome eternal' was not just a slogan on the coinage, but a concept deeply rooted in men's minds, so potent that St Augustine, writing the *City of God* after the fall of Rome to the Goths in 410, tried to turn men's minds from the earthly Rome to 'that city in which alone life is eternally happy' (iii.17).

Gibbon, with whom we start the next chapter, has imposed upon us by sheer intellectual authority the concept of 'decline and fall'. What, if anything, does decline mean in this context? 'The Late Antique period', it has been said, 'has too often been dismissed as an age of disintegration . . . No impression is further from the truth. Seldom has any period of European history littered the future with so many irremoveable institutions. The codes of Roman Law, the hierarchy of the Catholic Church, the idea of the Christian Empire, the monastery. . . .' Our own intellectual tradition makes us judge Late Antiquity by the standards of the early Empire (what the French call, revealingly the 'Haut-Empire'). The late Empire is judged to be in decline because it does not come up to the same standards. Although Paulinus of Nola writes one of the loveliest lyrics of all antiquity ('I, through all chances that are given to mortals' – *ego te per omne quod datum mortalibus*), and the first Latin hymns of the Christian Church trample across the centuries to the rhythm of the marching songs of the legions (*pange, lingua, gloriosi proelium certaminis,* like the song about Julius Caesar, the 'bold adulterer,' which his soldiers sang at his triumph *ecce Caesar nunc triumphat . . .*, Suetonius, *Julius* 49), nevertheless they are not part of the classical canon. The towns 'decay' – the baths fall out of use, temples are deserted, the forum ceases to be the centre of civic and commercial activity, and we assume that the cause is economic. The bars so frequent in Pompeii and Ostia seem to disappear. But in fact many of the changes are caused by changed values. The Christian Church opposed the amphitheatre, the theatre, the baths, the bars, which often served as brothels, and obviously the pagan temples, for moral and religious reasons. The rich ceased to spend their money on the beautification of their cities, as they would have done in the Antonine age, and gave it instead to the Church; Paulinus can serve as an example, who sold estates 'like a kingdom' and retired to be a simple parish priest at Nola. The rich lived far more on their estates, and if the town property that they left vacant was sub- and sub-sub-divided for the poor, we should not forget that in eighteenth- and nineteenth-century London the slums were largely made up of middle- and upper-class houses, sadly decayed, in which many poor families lived. Indeed the familiar contemporary problem of the decline of the inner city, which is what the late antique city also suffered from, is not caused by an absolute decline in the economic health of our society, but by a shift in the distribution of economic resources. In 1881 Brixton was peculiarly 'genteel', 'a suburb for the wealthy tradesman'. If it is 'genteel' no longer, that is because the wealth is now invested elsewhere.

This is not to deny that the later Empire suffered from a genuine economic crisis, in the sense in which we discussed it earlier (page 200), but the concept of 'decline' requires closer examination. Paradoxically, we might have found ourselves more at home in the early Empire, pagan though it was, than in the Christianized late Roman or Byzantine city. The influence of 'classical' culture, its values as represented in literature, the visual images of its art and architecture, even the tone of its conversation and its jokes, to judge from the examples given by Macrobius, for instance, all this affects us and is more familiar to us than the wholly different value-system and social environment of Late Antiquity. This is why Gibbon was so successful for so long in imposing his own conceptual framework on the study of the relationship between the early and the later Empire, and why his judgement on the Antonine Age, with which we start the next chapter, has had so long a run.

The elder Pliny had spoken of 'the immeasurable majesty of the Roman peace' (*Natural History* xxvii.3). Over the next two or three generations, in the mouths of panegyrists like his nephew or, later, Aelius Aristides, the idea of the Empire as the model of peace and stability became a commonplace. Never had the Roman world seemed so ordered and so prosperous. A century later, Tertullian sees it becoming 'every day . . . more civilized' (page 241). Gibbon tried to pin down the happy moment in a judgement that shaped the imagination of his successors (page 242):

> If a man were called to fix the period in the history of the world, during which the condition of the human race was most happy and prosperous, he would, without hesitation, name that which elapsed from the death of Domitian to the accession of Commodus. The vast extent of the Roman Empire was governed by absolute power, under the guidance of virtue and wisdom. The armies were restrained by the firm but gentle hand of four successive emperors, whose characters and authority commanded involuntary respect. The forms of the civil administration were carefully preserved by Nerva, Trajan, Hadrian and the Antonines, who delighted in the image of liberty, and were pleased with considering themselves as the accountable ministers of the laws . . . A just, but melancholy reflection embittered, however, the noblest of human enjoyments. They must often have recollected the instability of a happiness which depended on the character of a single man . . . The ideal restraints of the Senate and the laws might serve to display the virtues, but could never

correct the vices, of the emperor. The military force was a blind and irresistible instrument of oppression; and the corruption of Roman manners would always supply flatterers eager to applaud, and ministers prepared to serve, the fear or the avarice, the lust or the cruelty, of their masters.

How much truth is there in Gibbon's rhetoric? From 'the vast extent of the Roman Empire' we can call up people and places to see what life could be like. Let us for this chapter concentrate especially on Africa and Asia, the two wealthiest provinces, the centres of Latin and Greek cultural and intellectual life, outside Rome. From them we can in some sort judge the other provinces. We begin with a place of no importance or fame then or now, Castellum Tidditanorum, or Tiddis. Tiddis lies about 16 km northwest of Cirta (Constantine) in what is now eastern Algeria. From the site at the present day you see no human habitation, except at night, when the lights of Cirta on its crag overlooking the River Rhumel shine across the plain to Tiddis on its own rocky hill upstream. The area around Cirta in the early Empire retained an unusual form of municipal administration, based no doubt on pre-Roman tribal patterns, in which the small towns ringed round Cirta, once its own outlying defensive strong-holds (*castella*), long formed a federation governed from Cirta, although Tiddis had attained some degree of municipal autonomy by the mid-second century. The hill on which it stood had been a strong point since neolithic times. The town of the Roman period occupied the eastern slope. This is quite steep. Houses and other structures are tunnelled into the rock. Roads follow the contours. At some points they are replaced by stairways cut into the hillside. Everything is red, the colour of the rock. A primitive, archetypal, Mediter-ranean hilltown, you would say; the setting, and no doubt the way of life, are not so different from Minoan Gournia in Crete, at the other end of the Mediterranean and a millenium and a half earlier.

And yet Tiddis has all the trappings of Romanized urban

life. You enter the town through an arch which records that 'Quintus Memmius Rogatus, son of Publius, of the tribe Quirina, aedile, constructed the arch with its gates at his own expense.' The street inside which climbs the hill has paving stones laid over the rock. On the right is a sanctuary of Mithras, a grotto carved from the rock, with an inscription, 'To the invincible Mithras his worshippers built this at their own expense from the ground up.' Facing the Mithraeum, as excavated, is a Christian chapel of the late Empire, transformed from an earlier building of unknown purpose. Up the hill is a little irregular square flanked by cisterns, over fifty of which are known from the town in all, with buildings on one side used for a bimonthly market, which an inscription tells us was held on the 12th or 14th and on the last day of each month. An inscription from a neighbouring *castellum* tells us that the market there was held the previous day. The markets would be served by itinerant vendors going from one to the other, like the weekly *souks* which are still so important in North Africa.

On the next terrace up stands the forum. It is approached by an arch, like the forum of any self-respecting town, but measures only 10 metres by 30, and the three rooms which open off it are cut into the hill for lack of space. Are they the Capitolium, the threefold sanctuary to Jupiter, Juno and Minerva, which is a standard feature of forums, generally a single temple, but elsewhere in Africa, for instance at Sufetula (Sbeïtla), three separate ones? The open space of the forum was adorned with statues of members of the imperial house or distinguished citizens, of whom the most distinguished was Quintus Lollius Urbicus. His statue is gone, but the base reads:

To Quintus Lollius Urbicus, son of Marcus, of the tribe Quirina, consul, legate of Augustus for the province of Lower Germany, *fetial* [priest], legate of the emperor Hadrian in the campaign in Judaea, in which he was presented with the spear of honour and a golden crown, legate of the 10th Legion *Gemina,* praetor as Caesar's candidate, tribune of the *plebs* as Caesar's candidate, legate of the proconsul of Asia, urban quaestor, tribune with the broad stripe [i.e., as a potential senator] of the 22nd Legion *Primigenia*, member of the Commission of Four for the maintenance of roads, patron [of Tiddis], by decree of the town councillors [decurions] at public expense. (*CIL* viii.6706 = *ILS* 1065)

This inscription gives his career in reverse order. Subsequently, as we know from other sources, he went on to be governor of Britain, in which capacity he conducted the advance into Scotland which led to the establishment of a new frontier along the line from the Forth to the Clyde, the so-called Antonine Wall (page 234), and ended his public career as prefect of the city of Rome (*praefectus urbi*). This is a case of 'local boy makes good' – very good indeed! The family mausoleum which he built still stands on a hillside amidst rolling wheatfields just north of Tiddis, no doubt on the family estate which provided the wealth that made this meteoric career possible. It is a castellated tower tomb of standard Roman type with an inscription commemorating Urbicus, 'prefect of the City', his parents, two brothers and an uncle (*CIL* viii.6705). None of them figures otherwise in history. Apart from Urbicus, the family seems to have been content to cultivate its estates and live the lives of country landowners.

It need hardly be pointed out that at no other period of history could the second or third son of a Berber landowner from a very small town in the interior enjoy a career which took him to Asia, Judaea, the Danube (where the 10th *Gemina* was stationed), the lower Rhine and Britain, culminating in a position of great power and honour in the capital of the Empire to which all these regions belonged. Nor does it seem likely that the Tidditani and their descendants, of whatever class, have ever since been more 'happy and prosperous'. Nor was the prosperity of Tiddis at its height in Urbicus's day: still to come in the next century were public baths above the forum, which necessitated considerable works of excavation and hydraulic engineering. Not that life at all levels was equally rosy, or all inhabitants of the Empire equally contented: but we must go at least part of the way with Gibbon's judgement.

The wealth of Africa was primarily agricultural. We have referred already to the importance of grain and olives (page 161). Irrigation extended the area of cultivable land. In what is now western Libya, Roman olive presses are found 80 km south of the present-day limit of olive cultivation. Sufetula (Sbeïtla), a Vespasianic foundation in the pre-desert zone of Tunisia, owed its existence and its later prosperity to the olive. It was sending recruits to the legion at Lambaesis in the second century. The extent of the remains and the magnificence of the forum show what it once was. Remains of barrages and water leats in the bed of the Oued Sbeïtla, and Roman sites scattered among the hills round about, suggest the source of its wealth. And Sufetula was only one of many new centres. Cillium (Kasserine) yields the epi-graphic boast of the veteran Flavius Secundus that he was the first man in the area to grow grapes. Ammaedara (Haïdra), the headquarters of the 3rd Legion *Augustus* from Tiberius's day to Vespasian's, then became a colony with extensive territory and with several large estates in the area. On the imperial estate known as the Saltus Massipianus the tenants are found erecting buildings at their own expense. The Saltus Beguensis in 138 belonged to the senator Lucius Africanus. Another large landowner was a certain Valeria Atticilla. All this territory must once have belonged to the local tribe, the Musulamii, and had been alienated for the benefit of the Roman state, either for the support of the legion while it was at Ammaedara, or for individuals. Further east, Lucius Claudius Honoratus was a member of the council both at Cirta and at Cuicul (Djemila) and presented the latter with an assembly room fitted out with statues and columns (*AE* 1964, 225). Examples could be multiplied.

The most fertile land in the province of Africa was in the valley of the Medjerda, the ancient Bagradas. Here there was a great concentration of imperial land, possibly originating in

Nero's confiscations (page 129). Inscriptions of Trajan's reign cast light on how these estates were exploited. The first of these inscriptions is a regulation set out by imperial freedman procurators responsible for the administration of the estates and is said to based on 'the Mancian Law' (*lex Manciana*), of which nothing is known except what can be inferred from such texts. The procurators rule as follows:

> Anyone living within the estate of Villa Magna Variana, that is, in the village of Siga, is permitted to bring those fields which are unsurveyed under cultivation under the terms of the Mancian Law, whereby anyone who brings such land under cultivation acquires a personal usufruct. Of the crops produced on such land they must in accordance with the Mancian Law deliver shares to the owners, or to the chief lessees or bailiffs of this estate as follows . . . (*CIL* viii.25902 = *LR* pp.179–80)

They go on to define the 'shares . . . customary under the Mancian Law' which must be paid to owners, chief lessees, or bailiffs by tenant farmers:

> one third of the wheat from the threshing floor, one third of the barley from the threshing floor, one fourth of the beans from the threshing floor, one third of the wine from the vat, one third of the oil extracted, one *sextarius* of honey per hive.

New fig orchards and new vineyards pay no contribution for the first five harvests, while an olive grove on previously uncultivated land pays nothing for ten harvests. There are regulations governing fields laid down to grass, the pasturing of cattle, responsibility for the destruction of crops (the clause is too mutilated for the full meaning to be recoverable), the forfeiture of land left uncultivated for two years, and finally the obligation on all tenant farmers to give six days' labour a year to the owners, chief lessees or bailiffs. Two further clauses on obligatory labour are obscure.

Another inscription by procurators acting in Hadrian's name states that it is the emperor's wish 'that all parts of the land suitable for olives and vines as well as for grains be brought under cultivation' and extends squatters' rights even to 'those parts among the leased-out surveyed parcels of the ... estates which are not being exploited by the chief lessees' (*LR* pp.182–3). The scales were nonetheless weighted in the chief lessee's favour, and another inscription records a petition early in Commodus's reign complaining of the lessee's brutality and exactions contrary to the law but in collusion with the emperor's own procurators, with whom the chief lessee 'stands very high in their favour because of his lavish gifts and is well known to each of them in succession because of the lease' (*LR* p.184). This produces a ruling confirming that the tenants may not be required to perform more than six days' work a year for the chief lessee, which was the abuse they were most indignant about. The law, as we have seen earlier (page 196), tended to be written with the landlord's interests in mind, and poor men might have their rights abused, but the provision for squatters' rights and the ruling that even the emperor's own chief lessee and his procurators must observe the law suggest that the poor were better served than at many periods and in many places even today.

Africans, not surprisingly, are well attested in the administration of the wheat supply to Rome, the *annona*. Marcus Vettius Latro from Thuburbo Maius, priest of Ceres at Carthage, after army service became *procurator annonae* at Ostia and Portus, before going on to procuratorships in Sicily, the Cottian Alps and Mauretania Caesariensis (*AE* 1939, 81). Titus Flavius Macer, who owned property and held a priesthood at Ammaedara (Haïdra), was the imperial administrator (*praefectus gentis*) of the tribe of the Musulamii, whose lands bordered those of Ammaedara, and in some emergency, perhaps that of 99, when the Egyptian harvest is known to have failed, he was put in charge of gathering in extra grain supplies (*curator frumenti comparandi in annonam urbis*), a job which presumably he did well, because he was then appointed procurator of imperial estates in the regions of Hippo (Annaba) and Theveste (Tebessa), from where he was promoted to be procurator of Sicily, itself an important grain-growing area (*ILS* 1435). His name, Titus Flavius, suggests a recent award of citizenship from one of the Flavian emperors, and it is an attractive suggestion that he may himself have belonged to the tribe of the Musulamii which he was appointed to administer. Vespasian in 75 joined Hippo and Theveste by road (*CIL* viii.10119), another index of development.

Let me take one more example, a couple of generations later. Sextus Julius Possessor came from Mactar (page 161), did military service, and around 167 became assistant to the *praefectus annonae*, with responsibility for 'verifying the quantity of oil from Africa and Spain, transporting emergency supplies, and paying the shippers' accounts', after which he was procurator for the bank of the River Baetis (the Guadalquivir, which flows into the Atlantic at Gades) (*ILS* 1403). It is not clear what his duties will have been, but possibly to do with docking and warehousing facilities. His subsequent career included a spell in Egypt, as procurator in charge of the Mercurium district of Alexandria, which had great granaries where the grain was stored while awaiting shipment to Rome; and we also know that his daughter married a man making his career too in the service of the *annona*. This is quite a career, from a small town in Africa to Ostia, to Spain, and then to Egypt, not counting the military service in his youth. People like this, middle-class in our terms, had a considerable stake in the way the Empire worked. Their equivalents and descendants probably suffered more than the upper-class landowners like Lollius Urbicus when the system broke down.

If Africa's wealth came above all from agriculture, agriculture was not the sole economic activity of the province. During the second century, the production of red-slip tableware developed to a point where Africa challenged Gaul as an exporter, and in succeeding centuries was to become the main producer for much of the Mediterranean world. Not enough is yet known about the centres of production and the means of distribution, but Hadrumetum (Sousse) is one important centre. Sousse and Carthage were the two chief ports of the province. Carthage in the second century was growing rapidly and becoming endowed with buildings worthy of its importance. Hadrian was responsible for a great aqueduct and the vast cisterns which received and stored its water (page 225). Antoninus built the baths on the seashore now called by his name, the largest to have survived from the ancient world except for those of Caracalla and Diocletian at Rome. The amphitheatre was enlarged, a theatre and an odeon were constructed, the circus was second in size only to Rome's Circus Maximus. The summit of the Byrsa, the acropolis of Punic Carthage, had been levelled in Augustus's day and turned into a great esplanade supported by massive retaining walls. Now, after a disastrous fire, it was remodelled, probably at the same time as the Antonine Baths were built, on the lines of one of the imperial forums of Rome, with a massive basilica inspired by Trajan's Basilica Ulpia in his forum to Rome. Both the baths and the basilica were decorated with marbles, not only African, but Greek and eastern as well, which suggests an official involvement, sparing no expense. The palace of the proconsul of Africa, on the site, it seems, of the present Hôtel Reine Didon, enjoys one of the world's great views. Carthage was clearly marked out as the second city of the Latin-speaking West, rivalled in the East only by Alexandria and Antioch.

Marble was in fact another of Africa's exports. Carthage itself lacked good stone. Even good utilitarian building stone had to be brought from some distance, most commonly from the El Haouria quarries at the tip of Cap Bon. But inland there were marble and other fine stones, none more prized than the veined yellow and red marble from Simitthu (Chemtou) on the upper Bagradas. Simitthu had its forum, constructed over the buried remains of Numidian royal tombs, it had its theatre, its amphitheatre, its impressive aqueduct, a Trajanic bridge over the river, and, a little away from all of this, the massive quarries and buildings which provided accommodation for the workmen and workshops in which the marble was fashioned into bowls and other objects. The marble was widely exported. It became fashionable at Rome; we find it for instance used in Hadrian's Pantheon. Some of the monolithic columns were up to 50 feet long and were transported over a high mountain range on their way to the port of Thabraca (Tabarka) on the north coast, from where they were shipped. The earliest recorded road along this route was built under Hadrian in 129 (*CIL* viii.22199), but Pliny records that the marble was being used in Rome in his day (*Natural History* xxxvi.49). The feat of transportation is as impressive as the remains of the quarries, on which Roman inscriptions lie beside more recent ones recording that one of the galleries was converted into a hospital for Algerian troops operating from inside Tunisia in the Algerian war of independence.

The demand for marble was such during the days of prosperity and ambitious building projects that marble was shipped in large blocks to be stored until needed and then cut to size, or in columns of certain standard dimensions, in multiples of the Roman foot. Blocks can be dated by masons' and storekeepers' marks on them. Hundreds of blocks from the first and second centuries were found in store, still unused, in the Marmorata quarter of Rome, beside the Tiber, when it was cleared in the nineteenth century, and a block of Chemtou marble, quarried in Domitian's reign under the supervision of the imperial slave Felix, and marked with another inscription in 132, probably in the course of stocktaking at Rome, was just being cut up and used for paving and veneering in a building at Ostia in 394, when the building was destroyed before it was finished and this block and another were left to await the twentieth-century archaeologist. Rome was the most prolific consumer of marble (pages 87–8), but we have already referred to the extensive use of marble in the Antonine building programme at Carthage, and even a smaller city, Sabratha, the forum, the basilica, the main baths, the theatre, various fountains, and six out of the seven known temples in the city were all rebuilt in the course of the second century. These few examples suggest the scale and complexity of the organization required.

Africa had no serious external enemy to be guarded against, and its one and only legion was largely concerned with internal security, with controlling the movement of the nomads, and with helping to develop both agriculture and urbanization. The spread of cultivation, as we have seen, was linked with the extension of army control, and Hadrian, in his Lambaesis address after reviewing the garrison in 128, points out that they man 'many widely scattered posts', as well as having one cohort in rotation always on duty in Carthage (*ILS* 2487 = *LR* p.508). An amusing sidelight on the use made of army specialists in civilian contexts is cast by an inscription, the Latin of which is far from perfect, dating from some time about 153, and set up by a retired surveyor of the 3rd *Augusta* called Nonius Datus. He was called in to correct something that had gone dreadfully wrong with the construction of an aqueduct for the city of Saldae (formerly Bougie, now Bejaia) on the north coast. Nonius Datus had carried out the original survey, but had not been in charge of subsequent work. Saldae was in Mauretania Caesariensis, and it is the procurator of that province who writes to the legate of the 3rd *Augusta* asking to have Nonius Datus sent to help. Let Nonius Datus take up the story:

I set out and on the way endured an attack by bandits. Although stripped and wounded, I got away with my team and reached Saldae. I met Varius Clemens [the procurator]. He took me to the mountain where they were crying over a tunnel of doubtful workmanship, which they thought had to be abandoned because the penetration of the digging of the tunnel had been carried further than the width of the mountain. It was apparent that the digging had strayed from the line, so much so that the upper tunnel turned right, to the south, and likewise the lower tunnel turned north, to its right. So the two ends were out of line and had gone astray ... When I assigned the work, so they knew who had what quota of digging, I set up a work competition between the marines and the auxiliary troops. And so they linked up where the mountain was pierced . . . When the water flowed, Varius Clemens the procurator dedicated the completed work . . . . (*CIL* viii.1812; the tunnel is 428 metres long)

The reference to bandits is interesting. It reminds us that even at the height of the Antonine Age law and order out in the countryside could not be taken for granted. It is interesting too that the army lends not only Nonius Datus's specialist services, but also a working party of troops – not, however, legionaries. We note the civilians' dependence on the army-trained technician. The whole episode warns us not to think of the whole empire working like clockwork. In many small towns the level of education and technical competence would not be high. Pliny's letters from Bithynia provide parallels to the Saldae debacle, for instance the unfinished and abandoned aqueduct at Nicomedia and the unfinished theatre at Nicaea which is already 'sinking and showing immense cracks' (x.37, 39). Pliny too, fired with enthusiasm to build a canal, is told to get a surveyor from the nearest legion, 'someone who has experience of this kind of work' (x.41, 42).

If we have spent so long on Africa, it is because the evidence is particularly rich and Africa itself was just moving into prominence (see page 281). Asia provides both similarities and differences. Except for the Punic settlements on the coast, like Carthage, Utica and Sousse, most of the towns of Africa were either native centres or new Roman foundations, but in either case they soon adopted Roman institutions, as we have seen at Tiddis. The cities and towns of Asia, however, had a history and tradition quite independent of Rome. The common council of the cities of Asia existed from the late Republic and represented the interests of the cities in their dealings with Rome and with the emperor. Numerous embassies are recorded. Individual cities enjoyed a great measure of internal autonomy. Their culture was Greek, their leading citizens mostly content with honours in their native city and province. Not until the second century do we find the territorial magnates of the Greek half of the Empire beginning to take their place alongside their western counterparts in the consular *fasti*. Attachment to Greek culture was tenacious: 'Although I was an Arcadian of Messene, my father did not give me a Greek education, but sent me here [to Rome] to learn jurisprudence,' says a boy disgustedly in Philostratus (*Life of Apollonius* 42).

The second century saw the efflorescence of Greek culture usually referred to as the Second Sophistic, a term favoured by Philostratus himself, who in addition to his novel based on the life of Apollonius of Tyana also wrote, in the early third century, the *Lives of the Sophists*. 'Sophist' has of course none of the pejorative sense which attaches to it in English. The second-century sophists were professional orators and teachers of rhetoric. Rhetoric and philosophy were the twin cornerstones of higher education. What sophists did can best be defined in the terms of Aelius Aristides's attack on philosophers for failing to do it: they spoke and wrote, adorned festivals, honoured the gods, advised cities, comforted those in trouble, settled disputes, and educated the young. Aelius Aristides himself, whose speech in praise of Rome we have already noticed (page 235), was a distinguished sophist, responsible for other speeches in praise of Cyzicus, Corinth, Athens, Rhodes and Smyrna. Rome gets special treatment, but is not unique; apart from Rome, the other cities are all Greek. Smyrna (Ismir) became Aristides's adopted home; along with Athens and Ephesus it was one of the main centres of the sophistic movement. Despite almost constant ill-health, Aristides was much travelled. Most sophists were. He was also rich, but devoted much energy and many appeals to Roman governors, as he himself tells us at length, to avoiding his share of public duties, which normally devolved upon the rich. The Greek cities had for centuries relied on their wealthiest citizens to assume expensive burdens ('liturgies'). Way back in fifth-century Athens, the putting on of plays and the fitting out of warships were liturgies. Augustus had ruled in the case of Cyrene that men receiving citizenship were still bound to fulfil liturgies for the city (page 143). Not only literary, but also second-century legal texts reveal how eagerly sophists and other intellectuals sought exemption from liturgies, and how concerned emperors were that not too many should be granted. The fuss that was generated suggests how many wealthy sophists there were: if all were to be exempt, the cities would be seriously hampered.

Although Aristides visited Rome only once, he was on close terms with successive Roman governors of Asia and enjoyed influence even at Rome. In 178 Smyrna was devastated by an earthquake. Aristides, who had always refused to serve his adopted city officially, wrote this time to the joint emperors Marcus Aurelius and Commodus (it cost him nothing) and secured their help in rebuilding before the city's official embassy on the subject had even arrived. Aristides is by this time a leading sophist, but not the most distinguished or the most influential. He does not, for instance, rival Antonius Polemo, who had settled at Smyrna in the previous generation and had the finest house in the city. His family can be traced back into the late Republic, it produced men of note in successive generations, and finally, in 148, a consul, Marcus Antonius Zeno. Polemo was on Hadrian's staff when Hadrian toured Asia Minor in 123. His influence with the emperor is commemorated in an inscription (*IGRR* iv.1431), and he is said to have persuaded Hadrian to give Smyrna forty million sesterces originally intended for Ephesus. The reaction of the Ephesians is not recorded.

The most distinguished and apparently the richest of all these sophists, however, was Polemo's contemporary and rival, Aristides's teacher, the Athenian Herodes Atticus, whose full name was Lucius Vibullius Hipparchus Tiberius Claudius Atticus Herodes. What a blend of cultures is in that name! Again, the family was of great antiquity and distinction. Although his grandfather's estate had been confiscated, Herodes's father and Herodes himself were both exceedingly rich. Herodes built a stadium for the Panathenaic games and an odeon or concert hall, still in use, although the roof of expensive cedar wood has gone. Corinth had to thank him for a theatre, Delphi for its stadium, Thermopylae for baths, Olympia for an aqueduct. Herodes was one of the Greeks who achieved, or accepted, the consulship, in 143. He was a friend of Marcus Aurelius, having grown up in the house of Marcus's maternal grandfather. Marcus's tutor, Fronto, unaware of the connection and about to appear on the other side to Herodes in some trial, is preparing to accuse him 'of free men cruelly beaten and robbed, and one indeed killed'; he is 'an undutiful son, mindless of his father's prayers' (he had in fact cheated the citizens of Athens out of money left to them in his father's will). And so on. Philostratus, no enemy to Herodes, also speaks of his harsh treatment of freedmen and slaves. As with Aristides refusing his liturgies, it is a milieu where the rich are very privileged. It is also a milieu where Greek-speaking sophist and African-born tutor to the emperor (Fronto came from Cirta, the metropolis of Tiddis) meet on equal terms.

The third of the great sophistic centres along with Smyrna and Athens, was Ephesus. Its impressive ruins today are largely those of the second-century city. And again we find a munificent sophist. Titus Flavius Damianus gave generously to the poor and to the restoration of public buildings. He built a marble portico from the city to the Temple of Artemis, the 'Diana of the Ephesians' of *Acts* 19 (page 154). He built a marble dining hall in the actual sanctuary. His father-in-law was responsible for a concert hall and one, possibly two, gymnasia. This is wealth, inherited from generation to generation, secured by prudent marriages, backed by family tradition and culture, on the scale of senatorial fortunes in Italy. Hardly any sophists were poor: Philostratus records only three from relatively humble backgrounds.

These wealthy men, however, chose to stay in their own world, *domi nobiles* in the late Republican sense (page 11). They competed for honours, secure in the knowledge that their Roman masters would always support them against the lower classes, would maintain their status, and would keep their competition within acceptable limits, without finding them a threat. Plutarch's treatise, the *Precepts of Statecraft*, is almost wholly on this theme. What had destroyed the leading families of Republican Rome was contention for real political power. The sophists had everything but that, and were satisfied. They may also have despised the Romans as uncultured. Perhaps Hadrian's philhellenism helped to bring more Greeks into the Roman political career. By the early third century, a Greek like Cassius Dio sees no incompatibility. But when in the course of the second century these wealthy local potentates transferred their ambitions to Rome, rather than being content with priesthoods and magistracies and competitive benefactions within their own sphere, it fatally impoverished the cities and left the rest of the curial class with a financial burden which they found literally intolerable (page 293).

From what we know of senatorial origins, we can see that the proportion of Italian senators declines markedly in the Flavian period (I use this as a chronological marker, not to suggest that the Flavian emperors were biassed against Italians). By the time of the Severi, the proportion of senators known to be of Italian origin falls below half. Only one senatorial family still survived which could trace its ancestry back to the Republic; they were the Acilii Glabriones. The great patrician clans were almost extinct by Vespasian's day, and of the 26 families whom Augustus and Claudius had elevated to patrician status, we know of only six still surviving under Trajan. By the time of Septimius Severus, few senators had more than one or two generations of senatorial ancestors at the most, and the Senate had come to be largely recruited from equestrians of provincial origin. The first non-Italian senators, as we have seen, were mostly westerners, with Africans becoming prominent from Hadrian onwards. This is the context in which Greeks start to appear in the Senate and the *fasti*. Their scarcity relative to the Africans is not so much because of any Roman prejudice against them, whatever Juvenal may have thought of the lower class Greek immigrants in the streets of Rome (*Satire* iii.58–125), but because the Greek magnates themselves had other outlets and ambitions. If Lollius Urbicus from Castellum

Tidditanorum and Salvius Julianus from Pupput could reach
the very highest offices of state, could Antonius Polemo of
Smyrna, so influential with emperors, have been excluded?

The statistics quoted, although based, as usual, on fragmentary evidence, do suggest a rapid turnover of senatorial
families, and further recent study confirms this. Rich families
limited the number of their children in order to keep the
family property together. The Augustan laws on marriage
and on the number of children in a family were designed to
discourage this (page 96), but the evidence shows that they
did not succeed. Not all sons of senatorial families necessarily
entered the Senate, because they lacked the ability, the
ambition, or the money. Being a senator involved conspicuous display, and the ostentation of large houses, large
staffs, and a way of life to match will have dilapidated all but
the largest fortunes, unless they were renewed by inheritance
from outside the direct line of descent, by marriage to an
heiress, by the emperor's bounty, or by the profits, legal or
corrupt, of office-holding, especially as governor of a
province. The ideal strategy for perpetuating and aggrandiz-
ing the family will have been to leave one surviving son on
one's own death (and not to defer that until the son is too old
to make a successful career on his own account); to have
married a rich heiress or a rich widow, so that the son will
inherit two family fortunes; and for the son in his turn to
marry an heiress. This model is perhaps a *reductio ad
absurdum,* but there is enough evidence to show both restric-
tion of the birthrate and fervent pursuit of heiresses (and
legacies). To aim at leaving a single heir when so many died
before their time was to risk leaving no heir at all.

What I hope comes out clearly from this chapter so far is
the unimportance of geographical divisions in comparison
with those of class and economic status. By the second
century, the upper classes shared a common culture and a
common set of economic and status interests sufficiently
powerful to outweigh other distinctions. This applies, not
only to Italy, Africa and Asia, but to the fringe provinces as
well. There was also an Empire-wide diffusion of ideas at

levels which transcended the class structure. This is particularly noticeable in the field of religion. Eastern religions, for instance, had a considerable appeal in the West. We can look at one very specific instance where the imperial system contributed to the spread of eastern cults. We find a regiment of archers from Emesa (Homs) in Syria stationed on the middle Danube at Intercisa, south of Aquincum (Budapest), from about 180 onwards. They were sent there to guard the frontier against raiding horsemen. Because the locals were not trained to archery from childhood, the regiment continued to recruit from its homeland, contrary to normal recruiting practice (page 177). They attracted a settlement of Syrian traders and others, and introduced eastern cults. There is even a synagogue.

Of the eastern cults, that of Mithras, which was just beginning at this time, became one of the most widespread. We have already referred to the Mithraeum at Tiddis. Mithraism as we know it developed within the Roman Empire from concepts of Persian origin. In Britain, for instance, it is represented by the rather grand temple excavated in the 1950s on the banks of the Walbrook in the City of London, and by the simple shrine, holding only a handful of worshippers, outside the fort of Carrawburgh on Hadrian's Wall. Another widespread eastern cult was that of Isis. Egyptian in origin, known at Rome, and generally held in disrepute by the more respectable, since the late Republic, it enjoyed imperial patronage under the Flavians. Vespasian, who cultivated Isis and her fellow Egyptian deity Serapis, probably did so out of personal conviction, because it is hard to see what political advantage there was in it.

The cult of Isis brings us back to Africa. Apuleius (we do not know his full name) was born at Madauros (Mdaourouch, just west of the Tunisian-Algerian frontier), where St Augustine later went to school. He was rich, well educated, had lived at Rome and in Greece, but spent his later life in Africa. He married a wealthy widow and was accused by her disappointed relations of having gained her affections by magic. Brought to trial at Sabratha in 158/9, he defended himself in a speech which comes down to us as the *Apology*, in which he makes it clear that, though not himself guilty, he firmly believes in the power of magic, and he seems to take it for granted that so did everyone else. Apuleius also wrote the only other ancient novel worthy to stand beside the *Satyricon*: this is the *Metamorphoses* or *The Golden Ass*. The hero, mixing magic spells with sex, is inadvertently transformed into an ass. It is Isis who saves him, Isis who subsequently guides his life. Isis saves him from his sexual appetites. She required purity of her worshippers. She did not however require their exclusive worship. Membership of an Isiac community was quite compatible with participation in the official cults of the state or the local municipality, including that of the emperor.

With two other cults of eastern origin this was not the case. The exclusiveness of the Jewish religion has already been sufficiently emphasized. After the Bar Kochba rebellion, however, and the banning of Jews from Jerusalem (page 225), the Jews figure less prominently in our sources. Some at least had made their accommodation with the Roman authorities. The Talmud shows us Rabbi Judah ha-Nasi, known as Judah the Prince, a wealthy Jewish landowner with an estate in Syria, very interested in agriculture, holding his morning levee for his clients like a Roman landowner, close friend of one of the Severan emperors, accepted by Rome as the patron of all Jews everywhere. He is a figure not unlike a Polemo or a Herodes Atticus, without the rhetorical fame.

Also exclusive were the Christians: as exclusive as the Jews, as widely diffused as the devotees of Mithras or Isis, and better organized. Irenaeus, Bishop of Lyon for the last two decades or so of the century, was born in Asia Minor, possibly at Smyrna, where he studied under Polycarp, the Bishop. Irenaeus was born about 130, which makes him roughly contemporary with Aelius Aristides. He might as a child have heard Polemo. His ambitions lay elsewhere. Towards the age of fifty, he was a priest at Lyon. Absent on a mission to Rome, he missed the execution of 48 or more Christians at Lyon in 177, in which Bishop Pothinus died.

Irenaeus succeeded him. He records, as we have mentioned elsewhere (page 146), how useful it was to have learned some Celtic in Galatia, because it stood him in good stead with the peasants around Lyon.

The martyrs of Lyon and at Vienne nearby are known to us from a letter sent by those two churches to the churches of Asia and Phrygia and preserved by Eusebius in his *Ecclesiastical History* (v.1). The letter is in Greek, Bishop Pothinus and several of the other martyrs have Greek names, and two are specifically stated to come from Asia. The new bishop, Irenaeus, was also Greek. It looks as if the Christian church in Lyon had its roots among Greek immigrants. The martyrs were arrested by the tribune of the urban cohort stationed at Lyon, acting together with the city magistrates. Popular feeling was whipped up against them, disgusting allegations were made, some were betrayed by members of their own household, torture was used, and they were kept in prison to await the governor, who condemned most of them to death. The Roman citizens amongst them were beheaded, the governor having written to the emperor to get the sentence confirmed, the others killed in the arena by wild beasts.

This was a familiar pattern. Irenaeus's teacher, Polycarp, Bishop of Smyrna, had been betrayed by a servant, arrested on the order of a municipal officer, and brought before the proconsul of Asia in the stadium, where the spectators were assembled for the games. When asked to abjure his religion, Polycarp replied, 'I have served him [Christ] for eighty-six years and he has done me no wrong. How can I blaspheme my king and my saviour?' The people were crying for his execution, Polycarp launched into an eloquent defence addressed to the proconsul, and the proconsul told him, 'Persuade the people' – that is to say, they are the ones who want your blood, not me! Polycarp was burnt alive, and the church at Smyrna described it in a letter to the church at Philomelium in Pisidia, which has survived. Polycarp was a central figure in the transmission of Christian teaching, because of his long life, his personality, and the fact that, as

Irenaeus tells us, he had 'known John and others who had seen the Lord'. Smyrna was an important cultural centre for the Christians, just as much as for the sophists, and their contacts, on their own level, were just as wide.

Christianity had also taken firm root in Africa, and again there is some evidence at Carthage, as at Lyon, to suggest that the church there was at least partly based in the Greek community. The distinction between the Latin West and the Greek East was of course not absolute and Carthage was a cosmopolitan city with a large Jewish community, as well as inhabitants who chose to write Greek. The surrounding countryside spoke Latin, if not Berber or neo-Punic. A group of Christians from a small town near Carthage so obscure that we do not know the correct form of its name, Scilli or Scillis or Scillium, were put to death in 180 by the proconsul Vigellius Saturninus. We have what appears to be part of the official transcript of their trial, known as the *Acts of the Scillitan Martyrs*. As in the other cases we have met, the defendants proclaim their faith; they deny any wrongdoing; one of them says, 'Honour to Caesar as Caesar, but fear to God', as if remembering Christ's 'Render to Caesar the things that are Caesar's . . .'; their spokesman Speratus has in a satchel 'books and letters of Paul, a just man'. They refuse an adjournment, and the proconsul passes sentence: the defendants, 'having confessed that they live according to the Christian religion, since they obstinately persisted when given the opportunity of returning to Roman ways, are to be executed by the sword'. The reply is, 'We give thanks to God'. Twelve persons are named, seven men and five women. The names suggest humble status; two are native African. That Christianity had adherents in all social classes is however clear. We need only look at the account of the martyrdom of Vibia Perpetua and her companions in the Carthage arena to celebrate the birthday of Geta, Septimius Severus's younger son, probably in 203. Perpetua was 'of good birth, well educated, and respectably married' (*Martyrdom of Perpetua and Felicity* 2); her companions were members of her household, including slaves.

We begin to discern the strength of Christianity. The care taken to record and circulate records of martyrdoms suggests not only the wide diffusion of the faith, but also its cohesiveness. The church in Lyon reports back to the churches of Asia, perhaps like a missionary church reporting back to the mother church. Tertullian, who belonged by birth and upbringing to literary circles in Carthage, takes it for granted that his readers will know of the ex-Christian Peregrinus, who killed himself at the Olympic Games in 165 (*To the Martyrs* iv.4). Addressing Julius Scapula, proconsul in 212/13, he warns him of the consequences of persecution of Christians at Carthage, everyone losing friends and relations, even senatorial families, even the proconsul's own entourage affected (*To Scapula* v.2).

By the end of the second century, Christianity had become a phenomenon unlike any other. There was no specific law against it. The legal position was unchanged from what it had been at the start of the century, when Pliny found himself having to deal with accusations that some people in Bithynia were Christians and wrote to Trajan, 'I have never been present at an examination of Christians, and so do not know the nature or extent of the punishments usually given to them'. Like other governors whom we have seen in action, he asked the accused if they were in fact Christians and gave them every chance to renege. Then, he says, 'if they persist, I order them to be led away to execution; for whatever it is that they believe, I am convinced that their disobedience and inflexible obstinacy should not go unpunished.' On the other hand, he has examined them under torture and found them not guilty of any specific crime, but only of a 'detestable superstition'. He is worried, because it affects 'a great many people of every age and class, both men and women', and 'not only the towns, but villages and rural districts too' (*Letters* x.96). Quite right, replies Trajan, we cannot lay down a fixed rule, and Christians are not to be hunted out, but 'if they are brought before you and the charge is proved, they must be punished'. On which Tertullian was to comment, not unjustly, 'What inconsistency in pursuit of expediency'.

Clearly the Roman authorities wished that Christianity would just go away. Pliny's attitude, finding Christian beliefs incomprehensible and repulsive, is typical of Roman male upper-class values. On the other hand, Christianity could not in fact be ignored. Where it was sufficiently strong, it could harm the local economy. The opposition to Paul at Ephesus was led by men who made a living from pilgrims coming to the temple of Artemis (page 154), and Pliny's letter records that as a result of his deterrent action against the Christian community 'the flesh of sacrificial victims is on sale everywhere, although until recently hardly anyone could be found to buy it' (most meat on the market would come from sacrifices, and Paul shows that Christians had a crisis of conscience over whether they might eat it, I *Corinthians* 8–10). Christians also threatened public order. Some actively courted martyrdom by ostentatious defiance of authority. In any case, they were widely unpopular, perhaps because their communities were so exclusive and their rituals private. The eucharist was misunderstood to involve, quite literally, cannibalism. The records show that it was usually the crowd or the local authorities who wanted the Christians executed. The Roman governor gives them the chance to deny their religion and thus be saved; their 'inflexible obstinacy' forces him, by his own standards, to preserve public order and his own dignity by executing them for failing to respect his power of *coercitio* (page 56).

Nor should we underestimate the strength of religious feeling among the pagans. Dio, for instance, makes it clear that omens were taken seriously, for instance those foretelling the deaths of Commodus and Didius Julianus, whom the Senate hated. Aristides, that dedicated valetudinarian, believed that his life was directed by Aesculapius, in whose sanctuary at Pergamum he lived for some years. Inscriptions also attest belief in cures worked by Aesculapius (e.g., *IGRR* i.41 = *LR* p.571, from Rome). Eastern cults we have already referred to; Christian writers do not make the mistake that some modern sceptics have done of assuming that paganism was dead or dying. For Minucius Felix in the *Octavius* and

Tertullian in the *Apology*, the pagans were all too sincere in their beliefs. The belief in the numinous, the association of certain places with the holy, was very powerful. The Christian church was later to try to capture such places for itself by promoting the cult of some appropriate saint in place of the pagan divinity. In cultures as different from each other as the Celtic and the Berber, as indeed in Greek and Roman belief, springs were accounted holy. There is the example of the hot spring at Hamman Sayala near Beja in Tunisia, where miraculous cures are attributed to the intervention of a holy woman, Lella Sayala, to whom candles and incense used to be burnt within living memory (perhaps they still are). Work on the spring early this century revealed Roman baths with a dedication by an imperial freedman to the *genius* or presiding spirit of the place, named Aquae Traianae. It is this spirit who is still invoked under the name of the Moslem holy woman Lella Sayala.

Paganism was alive at this level of popular belief, as well as in the great cults. Sacrifice and ritual formed part of almost every activity of daily life, from the offering in the family shrine of even the most humble home to the great state ceremonial accompanying or preceding every act of emperor or magistrate. Even in the fourth century, with Christianity officially triumphant, the removal of the altar of Victory from the Senate-house moved the pagans to passionate protest, inspired, it would seem, by genuine religious sentiment, not mere antiquarianism. A third-century calendar of religious festivals and sacrifices to be celebrated by the garrison of the fort at Dura-Europus on the Euphrates shows how difficult it was for a Christian or a Jew to serve in the army (*LR* p.567). Even emperor worship, which it has been said 'would have collapsed under the weight of its own absurdity, if it had not been for imperative social need', and which many moderns, in fact, find it hard to take seriously, not only provided a focus for and an expression of loyalty, like toasting the Queen and standing for the National Anthem, or the equivalent in other countries, but probably aroused the feelings of genuine religious awe in simple folk.

The Antonine Age has been called 'an age of anxiety' when people seem often to have worried both about their condition in this world and their prospects in the next. Despite their riches, their unassailable social position, their network of friends, their culture, their possibilities of travel, many of the second-century grandees, for instance, seem somewhat arid, preoccupied, lacking in joy. Aristides is not the only one constantly fussing about his health. No wonder that Galen, the physician from Pergamum who became doctor to three emperors and most of Roman society, was one of the success stories of the age. The correspondence between Marcus Aurelius and his tutor Fronto is full of their bowels and their assorted aches and illnesses. Fronto writes two whole letters, one to inform Marcus that he has a severe pain in his private parts and a second to let him know that the pain is still there, but has moved to the other side (Loeb ed., I, p.224). There is a strong sense of foreboding, an anxiety that one's own and one's family's health is in the hands of supernatural powers, and there is no doubt of the fervour and sincerity with which they are invoked in prayer.

Marcus's *Meditations* are deeply pessimistic. Life is compared to dirty bathwater: oil, sweat and scum (viii.24). There is barely any point in doing anything. At his noblest, Marcus has the bleak grandeur of Ecclesiastes; 'Vanity of vanities, saith the preacher, all is vanity'. In a more trivial mood, he sounds like Eeyore. And this was the master of the world:

> Consider, for the sake of argument, the times of Vespasian. You will see all the same things: men marrying, begetting children, being ill, dying, fighting wars, feasting, trading, farming, flattering, asserting themselves, suspecting, praying for the death of others, grumbling at their present lot . . . coveting a consulate, coveting a kingdom. Then turn to the times of Trajan: again everything is the same, and that life too is dead . . . (*Meditations* iv.32)

The style is elegant, as befits a pupil of Fronto and a

contemporary of the great sophists. But for men with something new to say, and men who thought that what they were doing was building for posterity, we go at this same period to the great Roman lawyers or to the Christians.

That the Empire was based on class- or status-distinction is clear. Equally clear is the extent to which the intellectual, social and architectural development of the towns and cities was based on the agricultural surpluses of the countryside. And if in a given year, or for several years, because of drought or disturbances or for whatever reason there was no surplus, the townsfolk still took what they required. Doctor Galen describes the consequences of several successive bad years:

Immediately summer was over, those who live in the cities, in accordance with their universal practice of collecting a sufficient supply of corn to last a whole year, took from the fields all the wheat, with the barley, beans and lentils, and left to the rustics only those annual products which are called pulses and leguminous fruits; they even took away a good part of these to the city. So the people in the countryside, after consuming during the winter what had been left, were compelled to use unhealthy forms of nourishment. Through the spring they ate twigs and shoots of trees, bulbs and roots of unwholesome plants, and they made unsparing use of what are called wild vegetables, whatever they could get hold of, until they were surfeited; they ate them after boiling them whole like green grasses, of which they had not tasted before even as an experiment. I myself in person saw some of them at the end of spring and almost all at the beginning of summer afflicted with numerous ulcers covering their skin, not of the same kind in every case, for some suffered from erysipelas, others from inflamed tumours, others from spreading boils, others had an eruption resembling lichen and scabs and leprosy. (*On wholesome and unwholesome foods* i.1–7, tr. G.E.M. de Ste Croix, *The Class Struggle in the Ancient Greek World*. p.14)

Philostratus records how the leading men of Aspendos were keeping all the wheat for export, while the poor were reduced to vetches 'and whatever else they could get' (*Life of Apollonius* i.15). Libanius of Antioch, though later than our period, puts the matter in words equally applicable to the second century; addressing the emperor of the day, Theodosius I, on the subject of freed labour, he not only stresses the dependence of the town on the country for all its sustenance, but catalogues the immense hardships and injustices inflicted on the poor peasants (*Orations* I, 'On Forced Labour', Loeb ed. vol. II).

Thus, whether or not one was 'most happy and prosperous' in the Antonine Age would seem to depend largely on one's position in society. On the whole, the upper classes, the men of property, were united in support of the system, and one need not be a Marxist to recognize that lawyers and, one might add, administrators thought 'in terms of the interests of the class to which they themselves and their clients belonged'. This is shocking only to those who think that most people ever behave differently. Horizontal stratification of society was more important than regional divisions. Of nationalism in the modern sense there is little trace. Rome was the 'common fatherland' (*communis patria*) of the propertied classes, and of all those engaged in the imperial service, while even those who felt no great sentiment of loyalty to Rome might look on the emperor or on the local governor as their protector against local and immediate oppression. We have seen examples earlier in this chapter. There was always opposition. Nonius Datus on his way to Saldae, despite his accompanying troops, no less than the solitary traveller of Christ's parable, 'fell among thieves'. Thieves, brigands, *latrones,* might be many things, from mere robbers to men with a rooted grievance against the established order, whether religious, as among the Jews of Judaea, or economic, or both, since both seem to come together, after our period, in the Circumcelliones of North Africa. Often they were driven to it by desperation. One brigand, Bulla, otherwise known as Felix, plundered parts of

Italy for two years at the head of 600 men, until he was captured and sentenced to the arena. Dio preserves two significant sayings, one a message to the authorities, 'Feed your slaves, to stop them becoming brigands', the other a retort to the praetorian prefect Papinian who was interrogating him and asked, 'Why did you become a brigand?' Bulla answered, 'Why are you prefect?'

This chapter, indeed this book, has mostly dealt with men. It was essentially a man's world. Individual women come to our attention, as heiresses, as the wives or widows of great men, or occasionally as personalities in their own right. Vibia Perpetua, in the story of her martyrdom at Carthage, aged 22, stands out. We do not even know who her husband was. It was one of the attractions of Christianity that it gave women an assured place, where other religions, such as Mithraism, might exclude them, even if the place which Christianity gave them was a subordinate one. In the secular world, women might be great heiresses. Second-century women, however, even of the upper class, make less mark in our sources than some of their first-century predecessors. It was part of the trend towards greater circumspection and sedateness: no more flaunting women like Lollia Paulina (Pliny, *Natural History* ix.117), not to mention Messalina or Agrippina. Pliny was shocked at the luxury and excesses of an earlier period. Ummidia Quadratilla died at the age of 78, game to the last. Pliny's disapproval is extreme; he prefers her priggish grandson:

> He lived in his grandmother's house, but managed to combine personal austerity with deference to her sybaritic tastes. She kept a troop of mime actors whom she treated with an indulgence unsuitable to a lady of her high position, but Quadratus [the grandson] never watched their performances either in the theatre or at home. Once ... she told me that as a woman, with all a woman's idle hours to fill, she was in the habit of amusing herself playing draughts or watching her mimes, but before she did either, she always told Quadratus to go away and work. (*Letters* vii.24)

Her frivolity is excused by her earlier life: she, like the Montanus to whom Juvenal applied the phrase, 'had known the old luxury of the Empire and the nights of Nero' (*Satires* iv.137). In comparison, even the women of the imperial house in the second century are shadowy figures. It was to be the Severan dynasty that gave Rome empresses who were virtually its rulers (see Chapter 11).

Moderns find it hard to reconcile the positive aspects of Roman civilization with the gladiators, the wild beasts, the savage executions. These were not however a mere aberration. They were fundamental to the culture and to the social system. The Flavian Amphitheatre (Colosseum) at Rome seated some 50,000 spectators. The very largest amphitheatres included in addition those at Capua, Verona and Milan in Italy, Pola in Yugoslavia, Augustodunum (Autun) in Gaul, Carthage and Thysdrus (El Djem) in Africa. None of these can have held less than 30,000 people. Amphitheatres holding 20,000–25,000, like the well-preserved ones of Nimes and Arles, used today for bull fighting, were numerous. Even small towns in the western provinces had their own, often quite small. In Tunisia alone, which is only a part of the Roman province of Africa, a recent list enumerates over twenty. They came in all sizes, down to the little arenas hollowed out of the hillside beside military camps, which served the garrison for weapon drill, as well as for the occasional gladiatorial show. There is just such a one beside the remote Welsh fort of Tomen-y-mur, and similarly there was an amphitheatre for the garrison at Dura-Europus on the Euphrates. This too was part of the spread of Roman civilization.

The resources put to the building of the great amphitheatres were considerable, in materials, in manpower, in engineering skill, which the story of Nonius Datus and the aqueduct at Salsae warns us could be hard to come by. The Flavian and post-Flavian designs are very sophisticated in terms of crowd control, ease of access and evacuation for so many people, drainage and discharge of rainwater, provision of awnings against the sun, and arrangements for the delivery and storage of props and performers, animal and human. From service galleries under the arena itself, in the grander structures, lifts could hoist the wild beasts into the arena 'untouched by human hand,' so to speak. The arrangement can be well studied in the amphitheatre of the legionary base at Lambaesis. The humbler establishment at Mactar in central Tunisia still preserves the arrangement whereby beast cages could be slotted into openings around the arena and the cage opened from above. At El Djem, which has the best-preserved underground installations of any surviving amphi-theatre, there were lifts like those at Lambaesis and a gallery running lengthwise under the arena was prolonged beneath the seating at each end to give access to the underground storage through doors big enough to admit large wagons, quite divorced from the arrangements for spectator access on a higher level.

'Where your treasure is, there will your heart be also,' said Christ, and the converse is also true: by how a society invests its resources you can tell where its real priorities are. In most towns and cities, the amphitheatre was the biggest building (its only rival would normally be the circus, if there was one, or the public baths). It dominated its surroundings like a Gothic cathedral (I have already compared the visual impact of the amphitheatre at El Djem to Chartres, page 161), or with the effect of a great mediaeval castle, like Harlech or Windsor, or a cluster of modern skyscraper office blocks, at the same time the citadel and the secular temple of wealth and power, rising from the lakeside at Toronto or Chicago, or diminishing St Paul's and the Wren churches of the City of London. The Romans did not develop the office block, and no Roman temple was ever as impressive as the amphitheatre. Public slaughter was clearly for the Romans a fundamental institution, a social, if not a religious, ritual which had to be properly housed and to which society was prepared to devote extensive resources. How far there was a conscious religious element is unclear, but slave attendants were sometimes costumed as gods, Mercury, Pluto or Charon, and Christian victims might be paraded as pagan priests and priestesses (*Martyrdom of Perpetua and Felicity* 18).

The intellectual justification for gladiatorial shows was that they 'inspired a glory in wounds and a contempt of death, since the love of praise and desire for victory could be seen, even in the bodies of slaves and criminals' (Pliny, *Panegyric* 33). It was said that they started as funeral games: 'Once upon a time, men believed that the souls of the dead were propitiated by human blood, and so at funerals they sacrificed prisoners of war or slaves of poor quality bought for the purpose' (Tertullian, *On the Shows* 12). Tacitus complains of their popularity: 'How often will you find anyone who talks of anything else at home? And when you enter the lecture halls, what else do you hear the young men talking about?' (*Dialogue on Orators* 29). Intellectuals often deplored them, not out of sympathy for the victims, but because of their effect on the spectators. They recognized the danger of addiction, but for the most part they themselves still attended (the passage most commonly cited is Seneca, *Letters* vii.2).

It is often claimed that such shows were confined to the West or that, when given in the East, they were for the benefit of Italian immigrants. The evidence proves otherwise. Amphitheatres were less common in the East and virtually confined to the major cities. A second-century magistrate at Antioch in Pisidia 'promised a contest and within two months constructed a wooden amphitheatre' (Robert, Gladiateurs . . . 92) – and this at a date when any town of similar size in the West would have had its permanent stone-built amphitheatre. The Greek towns generally made do with their theatre alone. This suggests that gladiatorial and wild beast shows were less firmly rooted, less institutionalized in the East, and other evidence supports this conclusion. But of the general enthusiasm, East as well as West, there is no doubt. Plutarch and others condemn them, but Dio Chrysostom accuses the Athenians of 'crazy infatuation' for gladiatorial shows which they actually staged in the Theatre of Dionysus (Dio Chrysostom xxxi.121), and Polemo, the great sophist, 'seeing a gladiator running with sweat and terrified of fighting for his life, said "You are suffering as much as if you were going to deliver a speech" ' (Philostratus, *Lives of the Sophists* 541, ed., Kayser). Such off-hand joking (or is it a joke? Polemo does not elsewhere show much sense of humour) suggests how casually gladiatorial contests were now accepted in the Greek world. Libanius, the very mirror of Greek culture, enthuses over gladiators, whom he compares to the heroes of Thermopylae (*Life* 5). Could a Greek go further?

Most gladiators were slaves or condemned criminals, some were free men who enlisted for a fixed term. Often slaves continued to fight after being freed: it was the only trade they knew. Before the contest there was a last dinner, as depicted on the cover of this book, where someone is ironically warning the diners not to make too much noise: 'Quiet, let the bulls sleep'. The person giving the show gloried in the cruelty: a magistrate at Minturnae has on the base of his statue, 'Over four days he showed eleven pairs: from these eleven of the best gladiators in Campania were killed, with ten bears killed cruelly' (*CIL* x.6012). From the other side, it looked different:

> To the spirits of the dead. Glauco, born at Mutina, fought seven times, died in the eighth. He lived 23 years and 5 days. Aurelia set this up to her well-deserving husband, together with those who loved him. My advice to you is to find your own star. Don't trust Nemesis. That is how I was deceived. Hail and farewell. (*CIL* v.3466)

Bulls and bears were among the less exotic fauna on display. Pliny records the appearance of tigers, crocodiles (risky – Symmachus in the fourth century had some which refused to eat for fifty days and barely survived till needed), giraffes, lynxes, rhinoceroses, ostriches, hippopotami (*Natural History* viii.65). Lions were commonplace – six hundred in a single show as long ago as the first century BC (Pliny, *Natural History* viii.53, Dio xxxix.38). Elephants were also seen, and slaughtered, in the late Republic, and by Nero's day were being bred in Italy (Columella iii.8). Commodus, who prided himself on his marksmanship, once killed five hippopotami in a single show; after Roman times, no hippopotamus was seen in Europe again until 1850. The scale of operations, from the capture of such beasts to their transport, their nourishment in captivity, and their eventual delivery to the arena, was enormous. It figures in many African mosaics, and the mosaics of the Bardo museum in Tunis, and elsewhere, record, as do innumerable inscriptions, the competition for prestige involved in laying on a show and the care taken to specify how many animals were provided – and with some of the animals, it is clear that they were veteran performers, known by name as a successful gladiator might be. It is hard to imagine any activity less productive than the capture and shipment of wild animals for mass slaughter, and the resources devoted to it demonstrate not only the importance attached to the amphitheatre, but also the sheer wealth of the Empire, and the extent to which this wealth might be unproductively squandered.

The amphitheatre played a fundamental role in Roman life. Gladiatorial motifs are common on everyday household objects. Advertisements and graffiti at Pompeii are as common as football slogans today in public lavatories. All classes met in the amphitheatre, hierarchically separated. The presiding magistrate, which in Rome itself meant the emperor, had the power of life and death over the contestants. Emperors, when they attended the 'games' (*ludi*) at Rome, manifested themselves to their people. The people, secure in collective anonymity, could demonstrate their wishes. Under Caligula, they called for a tax cut. Caligula sent in the soldiers. The demonstration of Caligula's unpopularity encouraged the conspirators who were plotting to kill him (Josephus, *Jewish Antiquities* xix.24–7, cf. Dio lxix.13). Dio has several amphitheatre stories from his own day, as an eyewitness. Commodus ordered the senators to acclaim him with chants of, 'You are Lord, the foremost and most blessed of men' (lxxii.20). He was present in 195 when the crowd, not in the amphitheatre, but in the circus, followed the conventional cheer of 'Immortal Rome' by shouting in unison 'like a well-trained choir,' 'How long are we to be at war?' (lxxv.4).

We have already remarked on the Romans' 'highly developed and theatrical sense of public ceremonial' (page 53). Herodian's account of the public dramatization of an emperor's apotheosis seems to outdo any cinematic 'Caligula,' 'Quo Vadis' or 'Satyricon.' (iv.2). Josephus's description of Vespasian's and Titus's triumph shows military and religious pageantry mixed with frightfulness: vivid depictions of all war's horrors, and a halt in the proceedings while the chief prisoner, 'who had just figured in the procession amongst the prisoners was dragged with a noose around him and scourged by his escorts to the place near the forum where Roman law requires that criminals condemned to death should be executed.' The news that the execution has been completed is greeted with 'shouts of universal applause,' and the ceremonial proceeds (*Jewish War* vii.5).

The amphitheatre was part of this theatre of terror. It was a lesson in pain and death, in the uncertainty of life, in the stratification of society and the arbitrariness of power. 'It is expedient that one man should die for the sake of the people', said Pontius Pilate. Those who died in the arena died for the established social order. It was not just entertainment to keep people quiet, though it was that as well: Juvenal's 'bread and circuses' (*Satires* x.81), Fronto's 'wheat supply and public shows' (*Letters,* Loeb ed., II, p.216). More importantly, it was a terrifying demonstration of what could happen to those who failed to please their masters, who failed to conform to the established order: slaves, criminals, Christians, and not these alone. A spectator who was witty at Domitian's expense was dragged out and thrown to the dogs in the arena (Suetonius, *Domitian* 10). Commodus walked towards the senators' seats holding in one hand the head of an ostrich which he had just sacrificed and in the other the sacrificial knife. The threat was blatant..Dio records how he himself chewed on a laurel leaf from the wreath on his head to stop himself giggling, presumably from sheer terror.

The Roman order was based partly on consent, partly on custom, partly on institutionalized terror. There was a ruthless logic about it. When Sejanus fell (page 115), his children were to die as well, partly to add to the terror of his fall, partly to stop them growing up to avenge him. One was a little girl. Custom forbade the execution of a virgin. So the executioner raped her before he strangled her. The Christian accounts of martyrdoms reveal. a casual and familiar acquaintance with torture and routine brutality which reminds one of Nazi concentration camps. The implements of torture are mentioned – 'the claws', 'the iron seat' – with no explanation. Christian readers needed none. At Perpetua's trial, her aged father tries the proconsul's patience by going on too long pleading with his daughter. He is knocked down and set upon with whips. Gibbon writes of the emperors from Trajan to Marcus Aurelius that their 'characters and authority commanded involuntary respect'. We saw them in Chapter 10 as men honest in their generation, using their position for the common good, as they saw it, 'pleased with considering themselves as the accountable ministers of the laws', to use once more a Gibbonian phrase. So they were. They were also stern upholders of the established order. Their reward was and is to be praised by those who consider that without order there is no security, no scope for culture and learning, no chance for people to lead their own lives and bring up their children in peace and security; that without order we risk returning to the state which Hobbes described, 'wherein every man is at war with every man, and the life of man solitary, poor, nasty, brutish and short'. The price paid for the Antonine order, however, by the outcast, the dispossessed, or simply by those, like the Christians, who subscribed to a different set of values, was institutionalized terror on a scale unknown to the modern world, except in Soviet Russia.

When Marcus Aurelius died in 180, his eighteen-year-old son Commodus already possessed all the imperial powers. For the last two and a half years he had been with his father on the Danube front. For some months his father's death meant little change. Commodus was the seventeenth emperor, and the first ever to have been born to a reigning emperor. He was the sixth emperor of the dynasty founded by Nerva, which thus went one better than the Julio-Claudians. Commodus's father had been generally popular and had enjoyed excellent relations with the Senate. Commodus himself was a brilliant athlete and outstandingly good-looking, with blonde, curly hair that shone in the sunlight, as if powdered with gold. He inherited his father's advisers, and every possible step had been taken to ensure a smooth succession and the continuation of established policies. Everything augured well for the new reign. But within a few months Commodus had abandoned the war on the Danube to return to the pleasures of Rome, without securing a lasting frontier settlement. He rapidly gave over enormous power and influence to his chamberlain (*cubicularius,* page 216), the Bithynian Saoterus, thus alienating the Senate and members of his own family. Within two years came the first plot to assassinate him, and his sister Lucilla, widow of Lucius Verus, was one of the prime movers. This was to be the pattern of the reign, with Commodus devoting himself to pleasure, abandoning power to a succession of favourites, and falling at last, after surviving a number of inefficient conspiracies, to a well-executed palace plot on the last day of 192.

The successful conspirators put it about that Commodus's murder was unpremeditated, done to forestall his own insane plan to murder the new consuls, other leading senators, and members of his household the next day. This is the version of Dio and Herodian (Dio lxxii.22; Herodian i.17). But the *Augustan History* alleges long premeditation, and a number of minor details suggest that this is right. The throne was offered to Publius Helvius Pertinax, who had been deeply involved in the politics of the last few years, and who was Commodus's colleague in the consulship for 192, as well as being City Prefect. The *Augustan History,* no doubt following Marius Maximus, records him as having been implicated in the plot from the start (*Pertinax* 4); the official version makes the offer of the throne a surprise. But somebody had made haste to inform the aged Claudius Pompeianus of what was happening, and to get him to come to Rome before the night was over. Pompeianus had been one of Marcus Aurelius's trusted advisers, and was Commodus's mentor when he came to the throne. Superseded and disgusted by Commodus's conduct, he had for the past ten years lived in retirement on his country estates. Pertinax had been taken to the praetorian camp before midnight, and somewhat half-heartedly acclaimed emperor. He went straight on to a hastily summoned meeting of the Senate. While waiting for the meeting to begin, he was approached by Pompeianus, to whom he offered the throne. Pompeianus refused. By being there to receive the offer, and refuse it, he had played his destined part in the building of Pertinax's image. When the Senate meeting opened, Pertinax announced that he had been chosen emperor by the soldiers, but did not wish to serve. This too was a necessary part of the image. His unwillingness was not taken seriously. He was unanimously acclaimed and the usual titles and powers were voted. The praetorians were clearly restive, but Pertinax took measures to conciliate them, as well as to please the Senate and restore order to administration and finance. Among those designated for the following year's magistracies was Cassius Dio, as praetor (Dio lxxiii.12). Pertinax's reign, however, lasted less than three months. The praetorians staged two abortive coups, followed by one that succeeded. Pertinax was cut down in the palace portico. There was no obvious successor.

What followed has become notorious, but there is no reason to doubt the basic truth of the account. Two men claimed the vacant throne. One was Pertinax's father-in-law, Flavius Sulpicianus, whom Pertinax had appointed City Prefect; the other was an elderly senator, Didius Julianus, perhaps the senior consular then living, apart from Claudius Pompeianus. They bid against each other for the support of the praetorians, Julianus winning with a bid of 25,000 sesterces per man. Later that day, he was confirmed by the Senate. But he had no real support anywhere. The provincial armies and their commanders were not likely to accept a new emperor just because he had bought the support of the praetorians.

The first provincial governor to move was Lucius Septimius Severus, governor of Pannonia Superior and commander of three legions. His earlier career had been generally undistinguished, and his appointment to Pannonia Superior seems to have owed less to outstanding merit or to his having served previously in the posts which would naturally lead up to so important a command, than to his African connections. He came from a leading family of Lepcis Magna, and owed his advancement to another African, Aemilius Laetus, Commodus's last praetorian prefect. Africans were strongly entrenched in positions of influence at this period, and providing mutual support, like Scotsmen in London in Dr Johnson's day. Septimius could count on well-placed supporters. Twelve days after Pertinax's murder, he staged a ceremony whereby he was proclaimed emperor by the legion stationed at Carnuntum, declared his intention of avenging Pertinax, and added Pertinax's name to his own, styling himself Imperator Caesar Lucius Septimius Severus Pertinax Augustus. Of the western governors, the one whose potential reaction caused Septimius most concern was Decimus Clodius Albinus, governor of Britain. Albinus was another African, from Sousse, which was also the home of Didius Julianus's mother. He had formerly governed Lower Germany, where he might therefore still have support, and if he crossed the

Channel, he might pose a serious threat. Septimius therefore offered him the title of Caesar, which he accepted, and which marked him out as Septimius's potential successor. Meanwhile he remained in Britain, and bided his time.

It was AD 69 all over again. Septimius had the Rhine and Danube armies on his side, notionally those of Britain also, and the support of the legions in Spain and Africa. But popular demonstrations had already been organized at Rome on behalf of Gaius Pescennius Niger, governor of Syria, who could count on the support of the eastern armies. Ignoring this threat, however, Septimius marched on Rome, taking Aquileia and Ravenna without resistance. Julianus's authority melted away, his efforts at conciliation came to nothing, Septimius's agents were active in Rome, and finally the Senate met to condemn Julianus to death and to proclaim Septimius emperor, before he had even arrived in the city. Julianus had reigned for 66 days, an even shorter time than Pertinax. A deputation of one hundred senators went out to meet Septimius, and were received by him armed and surrounded by armed guards. The source of his power was thus made obvious. Of the two new praetorian prefects, one was another African. They were to command a new guard, for one of Septimius's first actions on arriving in Rome, and one of his most dramatic, was to trick the old guard into parading unarmed outside the city, where they could be surrounded by armed men of Septimius's Danubian legions, whereupon Septimius ignominiously disarmed and disbanded them. The praetorians had remained preponderantly Italian over two centuries, while the legions were now almost wholly recruited from the provinces. The new guard was chosen from the men of Septimius's own legions. The old guard had exercised a disproportionate influence on the Empire's affairs, and the change was symptomatic of Italy's decline.

Septimius's entrance into Rome was spectacular (Dio lxxiv.1). The next day he addressed the Senate. Again his armed guard was in evidence. Again he declared himself the avenger of Pertinax; he also asked for a decree that no senator be put to death without the Senate's approval. The soldiers received a donative, and Pertinax a most magnificent funeral. Coins were struck in the name of Septimius and of Albinus, who were designated to hold the consulship jointly for 194. Then, after less than a month in Rome, Septimius left for the East, and after hard fighting Pescennius Niger was killed (spring 194). His eastern supporters suffered deprivation and confiscation, and some cities were punished, notably Antioch, while the province of Syria was divided into two. Early in the spring of 195, Septimius crossed the Euphrates and invaded Parthia. Dio says his motive was glory; another motive will have been to unite Niger's legions with his own in a campaign against a common enemy. Septimius may also have harboured long-term ambitions in this area. He had served here earlier in his career as legate of one of the Syrian legions, and had married Julia Domna, a very capable woman from the old royal stock of Emesa (Homs), who accompanied him on this campaign. Septimius gained three imperatorial salutations, took the titles Arabicus and Adiabenicus, accepted a triumphal arch, but refused a triumph. Part of the territory which he had conquered became a new province, the first significant accretion of territory since Trajan's day.

Septimius now proceeded to dispense with his temporary ally and erstwhile potential successor, Albinus, making it clear that he was designating his own son to succeed him. Albinus had supporters in the Senate. Herodian and the *Augustan History* suggest that Septimius now sent agents to assassinate Albinus; the story may be fiction. Septimius himself put out propaganda against Albinus, alleging that he had been behind the murder of Pertinax. Albinus decided to fight. The chronology is obscure, but before the end of 195 Albinus had proclaimed himself emperor and had been declared a public enemy by the Senate. The Senate had little choice, but Dio reports a popular demonstration in the Circus Maximus against renewed civil war (page 277). Septimius returned from the East with admirable speed, visited Rome, where coins record his generosity to the people and his holding of lavish games, and then marched through

Pannonia, Noricum, Raetia, and Upper Germany to attack
Albinus's forces, which were based on Lyon. Two battles
brought Septimius victory. His army entered Lyon, sacked
and burnt it. Albinus committed suicide. Septimius behaved
with a notable lack of generosity in his victory. Albinus's
body was mutilated and thrown into the Rhône, his wife and
sons were put to death, and his supporters hunted down.
Extensive confiscations increased the imperial holdings; for
instance, much Spanish oil production seems to have passed
under imperial control, and it has been suggested, though
with too little evidence, that Gaulish production of terra
sigillata was seriously affected. Septimius returned to Rome,
where he appalled the Senate by demanding the deification of
Commodus, his 'brother', since Septimius now called himself
'son of Marcus'. He is said to have praised cruelty, decried
clemency, and attacked the senators for their hypocrisy and
loose living (Dio lxxv.8, an eye-witness). Twenty-nine
senators were put to death, over a third of whom had links of
birth or property to Africa; were these Albinus's connections? Septimius's son Antoninus, better known as Caracalla,
was proclaimed emperor-designate. The usual largesse was
distributed to the urban populace. Septimius then set out
again to resume his campaigns in the East.

The struggle between Septimius and Albinus was notable
for the use both made of coinage. This gives us a truer picture
of where both men stood than what the writers say about
them. Septimius is known to have struck at least three
hundred and forty-two different issues in the first three years
of his reign. They advertise his military successes, his
generosity, the loyalty of the legions (a theme that had a habit
of appearing on the coinage whenever their loyalty was in
doubt), and, as the break with Albinus approached, the
dynastic pretensions of Septimius's family. Coins struck for
Caracalla (it is convenient to call him by this name to avoid
confusion) celebrate 'perpetual security' and 'perpetual hope'.
Septimius made no attempt to conceal the real bases of his
power, which were military might and the favour, or at least
acquiescence, of the urban populace. Albinus on the other
hand used the mint at Lyon to proclaim his confidence in the

result of the coming struggle, and to lay claim to the virtues which might endear him to the Senate, notably 'clemency' (CLEMENTIA) and 'fairness' (AEQUITAS). The Senate might well have preferred Albinus, but it was the army which decided the issue.

Before returning to the east, Septimius raised three new legions. In a significant break with tradition, all were placed under equestrian prefects instead of senatorial legates, and one of them was left behind in Italy, stationed only twenty miles from Rome. The downgrading of the Senate's importance and the loss of Italy's privileged position were thus made obvious. Septimius moved with his usual speed, established himself at Nisibis by late summer 197, built a fleet on the Euphrates, launched an amphibious operation down the river, found Seleucia and Babylon abandoned, marched on the Parthian capital, Ctesiphon on the Tigris, and took it by storm on 28 January 198, the centenary of Trajan's accession. Septimius assumed the title of Parthicus Maximus, Caracalla became Augustus, Septimius's younger son Geta was named Caesar. Septimius did not try to annex all of the new territory which he had overrun. The army withdrew, laden with booty. It stopped to lay siege to Hatra, between the Tigris and the Euphrates, but failed to take it. There were heavy casualties, and some disaffection in the army. A purge of possible rivals brought several of the emperor's close associates to death, including Julius Laetus, the general to whom he owed most but who had now become so popular with the soldiers that they 'used to say that they would not go on another campaign unless Laetus led them' (Dio lxxv.10).

A second attempt to take Hatra in the autumn 198 also failed; Dio blames Septimius for failing to press home the attack (lxxv.11–12). The war may have dragged on thereafter, but Septimius himself left for Egypt, organising part of his conquered territory as a new province of Mesopotamia under an equestrian prefect instead of a senator. In Egypt Septimius indulged in sightseeing, carried out a number of religious rites, and overhauled the administration. In particular, he allowed Alexandria and other major cities to have a council, like cities elsewhere in the Empire, and rectified another anomaly by permitting Egyptians to enter the Senate, which had previously been forbidden to them. Egypt was becoming a province like the others. Papyri record numerous legal rulings made by Septimius, but the account in the *Augustan History* of his supposed edict against proselytising by Jews or Christians is fictional.

From Egypt Septimius went to Syria, where he assumed the consulship for 202 with Caracalla as his colleague. Caracalla was only thirteen, and never before had two co-emperors assumed the consulship together. It was not unusual for a consul to enter office while away from Rome, but still rare for both ordinary consuls to be away. Septimius and Caracalla celebrated their inauguration with due pomp at Antioch. No opportunity was lost of bringing Caracalla into prominence. It strengthened Septimius's own position to have a recognized successor. The conspiracies in which Caligula, Nero, Domitian and Commodus had met their ends would have been hampered, had there been a co-emperor possessed already of the necessary powers to assume sole authority.

The new consuls returned to Rome overland through Asia and the Danubian provinces. Dio relates anecdotes connected with the journey which illustrate the enormous power and growing arrogance of Plautianus, the praetorian prefect. Like Septimius a native of Lepcis Magna and a boyhood friend, he had been constantly at Septimius's side since his accession. On their arrival in Rome, Plautianus's daughter was married to Caracalla with vast ostentation, although Caracalla loathed his new wife and father-in-law. There were spectacular shows and lavish donations to the praetorians and the people. But once again Septimius left Rome after only a few weeks there, this time for his native Africa. He spent the winter of 202–3 at Lepcis, which he embellished with a vast building programme, and where the first signs of estrangement between Septimius and Plautianus became apparent, apparently because Septimius saw Plautianus getting too much of the hometown adulation which Septimius felt should be his. There were visits to other parts of the province and a campaign against the desert tribes. Lepcis, together with Carthage and Utica, was granted the *ius Italicum,* or immunity from provincial taxation. For the past five years the legate of the 3rd Legion *Augusta* at Lambaesis had been extending and strengthening frontier works along the edge of the desert. Septimius now created the province of Numidia out of what had been *de facto* since Caligula's time the independent military command of the legionary legate (page 143), and inscriptions show him to have visited Lambaesis, probably on a tour of inspection of the new frontier works.

Septimius's return to Rome was marked by fresh celebrations, including the dedication of his great arch in the forum, between the Senate House and the Rostra. Preparations were also set on foot to celebrate the Secular Games in the following year (204), calculated to be two *saecula* of one hundred and ten years apiece since the Augustan celebration of the Games. This was to be the seventh and, as it proved, the last celebration. For the year after (205), Caracalla and Geta were to share the consulship. Plautianus's position was weakened. Details are obscure. None of our sources is as satisfactory as for the earlier part of the reign. Dio, however, continues to record significant anecdotes and scenes of which he was often an eyewitness. His account of Plautianus's fall is detailed enough, and no doubt true in substance, although it leaves a number of questions unanswered. Caracalla set up an apparent plot by Plautianus against himself and Septimius, and when Plautianus appeared to answer the accusation, Caracalla had him killed on the spot, Septimius not interfering (Dio lxxvi.2). Herodian's version smacks of official apologetics. Plautianus's confiscated wealth was so enormous that a special procurator was appointed to administer it.

Two new praetorian prefects were appointed, one a soldier, formerly Prefect of Egypt, the other the distinguished jurist, Papinian (Aemilius Papinianus). The *Augustan History* records that 'some say' that he was related to Septimius through his second wife (*Augustan History, Caracalla 8*), which would imply that he was from the east, if the second wife was Septimius's. But the passage is ambiguous, and may in any case be fiction. Certainly the other two great jurists of the age, Ulpian (Domitius Ulpianus) and Julius Paulus, were both easterners. Septimius himself gave much time and care to administering the law, as Dio records; he himself was one of Septimius's legal advisers. To Ulpian we owe the definitive formulation of the principle that the emperor is above the law, (page 232), but Septimius and Caracalla nonetheless declared their intention to live in accordance with the laws. This did not however prevent them from putting senators to death without trial, and Dio's stories vividly attest the terrorized attitude of the Senate as a whole. Septimius's position was secure, but the arrogant behaviour of his two sons and their evident mutual hostility augured badly for the future. When news arrived from Britain in the course of 207 that 'the barbarians there were rebelling, overrunning the country, taking away booty and creating destruction' (Herodian iii.14), Septimius took the chance to get himself and his sons away from the demoralizing atmosphere of Rome.

The governor of Britain was yet another African, Lucius Alfenus Senecio from Cuicul (Djemila), that most beautiful and idyllic of Roman sites; he had been governor of Syria Coele and was therefore presumably a man of proved military talent. Albinus had stripped Britain of troops in 196, and the northern tribes had seized their opportunity to plunder and destroy. Archaeology suggests that the destruction was widespread, involving even the legionary base at York, although the dating of some of the evidence is controversial, and restoration work in the Pennines had still not been finished as late as 205 (*AE* 1963, 281, from Bainbridge). Senecio took over in that year, and had some military success over the next two years, but something more was needed if the situation was to be fully restored. So he asked for 'reinforcements . . . or a visit from the emperor' (Herodian iii.14). Septimius decided to bring the reinforcements himself, although his health was no longer good, and for most of the journey he had to ride in a litter. Commemorative coins naturally portray him on a horse, like David's portrait of

Napoleon crossing the Great St Bernard Pass on a prancing white charger, familiar from Courvoisier brandy advertisements. In fact Napoleon rode a donkey. Septimius's mind was still active, and he still struck like lightning. The rebellious tribes sued for peace at his approach, but their overtures were rejected. Septimius was aiming at a signal and decisive victory.

The campaign cannot be reconstructed in detail. Dio's account is fragmentary, Herodian's is vague. Archaeology reveals something of the careful logistical preparation. The fort at South Shields, for instance, on the Tyne estuary, was transformed into a massive supply base, and there is evidence of great new building at Corbridge, perhaps with the same end in view, perhaps to create a new legionary headquarters. Marching camps revealed by air photography extend through the Lowlands and up the east coast of Scotland almost to the Moray Firth. Those in the Lowlands are some 165 acres (67 hectares) in extent, and those north of the Firth of Forth fall into two series, of 120 and 63 acres (49 and 26 hectares) respectively, perhaps representing two separate divisions of the army, or possible two successive campaigns. In any case the scale of operations is impressive, and the construction of a permanent base at Carpow on the south bank of the Tay suggests that Septimius intended to advance the Roman frontier to the Antonine Wall once more, and indeed beyond.

Caracalla shared with his father the front-line command, Geta was left in charge of the lines of supply. Caracalla's hatred of his brother was unconcealed, and Dio has a story, scarcely credible, but for that reason unlikely to be altogether untrue, that Caracalla once threatened to kill his father in full view of the army. (Dio lxxxvi.14). Septimius had no illusions about Caracalla's character, and Dio alleges that he even thought of putting him to death while there was still time, as he claimed Marcus Aurelius ought to have done with Commodus, but he could not bring himself to do it. He made Geta co-emperor, belatedly, it might be thought, since he was less than a year younger than his brother; but perhaps it might have been thought that it would cause practical problems to have three co-emperors at once. Now it did not matter. Septimius knew he had not long to live. During the winter of 209–10 he returned to York, where he continued to attend to the routine business of the Empire, such as legal rulings and embassies (how long did it take to get a despatch from Antioch to York and back? cf. page 151). When rebellion broke out again, Caracalla went north alone to deal with it, and allegedly used the opportunity to ingratiate himself with the army. Septimius died at York on 4 February 211. His last words, which Dio claims to give *verbatim,* were to his sons: 'Do not disagree with each other, enrich the soldiers, despise everyone else' (Dio lxxvi.15).

Caracalla tried to get the army to accept him as sole emperor, but failed. Geta was popular, partly because he looked very like his father. Caracalla then made peace, abandoned the territory that had been won, including the new and as yet unfinished base at Carpow, and returned to York, where he and Geta acquiesced in a show of reconciliation, on the urging of their mother Domna. Then they left for Rome, where they made little attempt to conceal their mutual hostility. Geta appears to have been the more cultured and was preferred by the Senate. It did him little good. Before the end of the year Caracalla had had him murdered, and proceeded to obliterate his portraits and inscriptions. He himself reigned for just over five years, until murdered in April 217 by one of the Praetorian Prefects, Opellius Macrinus. Dio hated him, and neither his nor Herodian's account of the reign is reliable.

It is ironical that an emperor so little loved and who achieved so little should nonetheless be responsible for one of the landmarks of Roman history, the issuing of an edict granting Roman citizenship to virtually all free inhabitants of the Empire. This edict, the so-called *constitutio Antoniniana,* dating from 212 (attempts to prove another date do not succeed), may have been the idea of one of Caracalla's legal advisers, rather than his own. Papinian had died in the purge of Geta's presumed supporters, but Ulpian and Paulus were still active. It has proved a gold mine for modern scholarship.

Dio claims that its purpose was to raise money by making everyone liable to taxes on citizens, such as inheritance taxes, which were doubled, and taxes on the manumission of slaves (Dio lxxviii.9). It may seem more significant to posterity than it seemed at the time. It is not even mentioned on the coinage. The distinction between citizen and non-citizen had already been replaced in practice by that between *honestiores* and *humiliores* (page 234). The precise scope of the edict is unclear, particularly the meaning of *dediticii*, who were excluded from its provisions. Nor is it clear that it really promoted popular identification with Rome in a sort of supra-national patriotism, as is sometimes claimed. The upper classes already knew where their interests lay, and to the lower classes it no longer made much difference.

Macrinus did not last long. He was the first emperor from outside the Senate, and Dio is predictably horrified by his disregard for established custom. But he was also incompetent, and lost the respect of the troops. Julia Domna had been ousted by Macrinus from any position of influence, and committed suicide, but her sister, Julia Maesa, who was at Emesa, did not give up so easily. The eldest of her grandchildren, aged fourteen, had succeeded to the hereditary priesthood of Elagabalus in that city. He closely resembled his cousin Caracalla. He was proclaimed to be Caracalla's illegitimate son and acclaimed emperor under the name Marcus Aurelius Antoninus, although he is always known to posterity by the name of his god, Elagabalus. Macrinus was defeated in battle near Antioch on 8 June 218, and the Senate accepted the new emperor. He proved to be a religious fanatic with bizarre sexual proclivities. We must disallow most of the stories in the *Augustan History,* but they show what a fertile imagination could invent when presented with so suggestive a subject. Elagabalus forfeited any support, and to preserve her own position his grandmother prudently had him murdered (12 March 222), having previously arranged for him to adopt his cousin, another grandson, who succeeded under the name Marcus Aurelius Severus Alexander.

Severus Alexander reigned for thirteen years. His

grandmother Maesa soon died, but his mother, Julia Mammaea, became his adviser. Details of the reign cannot be recovered. The *Augustan History* life of Severus Alexander is one of the most fictional. In fact, the most important event of the reign happened outside the Empire. In 226, after a dynastic struggle, Ardashir (Artaxerxes) was crowned king, not of Parthia, but of the Persian Empire. Dio records the alarm inspired by the prospect of a newly expansionist power beyond the Euphrates. In 230 Ardashir invaded the province of Mesopotamia and threatened Syria. Severus Alexander took the field, and apparently restored the *status quo*. But in the meantime the Germans were making trouble. Alexander returned to Rome and thence went on to take command on the Rhine. By early 235 he was ready for war, but tried to avoid it by negotiation and the offer of subsidies. The troops refused to accept this, and murdered him. His successor, the Thracian Maximinus, had risen from the ranks. Physically enormous, he was brutal and uncultured, a sort of Idi Amin. He did not last long, and the next fifty years of military anarchy were the nadir of the Empire, with the different provincial armies making and murdering emperors and pretenders virtually at will. The reforms of Diocletian, emperor 284–305, created what was virtually a new order, although the changes were more gradual and the precedents for Diocletian's reforms more extensive than scholars have commonly assumed.

The Severan dynasty had lasted for almost forty-two years, with the brief interlude of Macrinus's rule. What had it achieved? Septimius had been the greatest expander of the Empire since Trajan a century earlier. Perhaps he was lucky not to have to deal with strong attacks on the eastern and northern frontiers simultaneously; perhaps his own aggressive measures forestalled such attacks. It has been argued that by weakening Parthia he facilitated the rise of the new Sassanid dynasty that was to prove so difficult a neighbour to his successors. But his achievements suggest that Rome was not yet militarily or economically enfeebled to the point of being unable to defend her frontiers. It was the military anarchy of the half century from the death of Severus Alexander to the accession of Diocletian that so fatally weakened the defences of the Empire by turning the legions from their task of facing external foes to the more profitable pastime of civil war. The way that Albinus stripped Britain of its defences to serve his own ambition had already given a foretaste of what was to come, on a larger scale and at points on the frontier far more vital than Hadrian's Wall.

Economically, it is true, Severus's policies imposed a strain on the Empire's resources. He was, as we have seen, lavish with donations. His building activity was considerable, including major buildings at Rome, and Dio criticizes it as wasteful (lxxvi.16). He increased the size of the army and the soldiers' pay. Significantly, Ulpian defines the word *tributum* (tribute, taxes) as what is 'paid [tributum] to the soldiers' (*Digest* LV.xvi.27). The upkeep of the army was the most conspicuous form of government expenditure. Coinage, progressively debased, was issued primarily to pay the troops. But the Empire was still relatively prosperous: it was in the half-century of anarchy following the Severan dynasty that inflation became chronic, that taxes drove men to abandon their property, that the curial class found their responsibilities an unbearable burden (page 241).

Severus's contempt for the Senate is the chief impression left by his deathbed advice to his sons, and the Senate repaid him with dislike. This still redounds to his discredit with most modern historians, who unconsciously assume that they would have been senators if they had lived in Roman times. But did the Senate deserve respect? Individual senators may have been men of worth, but the Senate as a body was consistently servile and self-seeking. Dio, moreover, himself a leading senator, praises Septimius's intellect, though being rather patronizing about his lack of education; he recognizes also his loyalty to his friends, his foresight, his generosity and skilled financial management (lxxvi.16). Less can be said of his successors. Caracalla was a bad lot, Elagabalus worse, and Severus Alexander remains a vague figure for want of evidence. The women, after Septimius's death, were the backbone of the dynasty. It would be interesting to see what Tacitus would have made of them. Domna and her sister Maesa in particular were women of guts and resource. Domna had intellectual interests, and it was she who encouraged Philostratus to compose his *Life of Apollonius*, though the extent of her 'circle' has been much exaggerated. Maesa's determination to secure her own and her family's position by ruling through a grandson suggests a grasp of political reality and a ruthlessness that in the outcome are impressive if not wholly admirable. The next generation, Maesa's daughters Soaemias and Mammaea, are more shadowy figures, partly for want of evidence.

Two trends that did not begin with the Severans reach new heights under their rule: one is the development of Roman law, the other the power and influence of the provincials. Nothing better illustrates the importance which lawyers had acquired than their appointment, beginning with Papinian, as praetorian prefect. Papinian is often regarded as the greatest of all Roman lawyers. Papinian and the other two great lawyers of the Severan age, Ulpian and Paulus, between them account for over half the entries compiled three centuries later into Justinian's *Digest*, and it can plausibly be argued that they have had more influence on posterity than any other Latin writers, even Vergil, Cicero or Ovid. Their view of law, transmitted through Justinian's compilers, has shaped European law and society since the revival of legal studies in the twelfth century and still underlies the European legal tradition in its various national guises today.

As for the growing power and influence of the provincials, which naturally implies a reduction in the special privileges of Italy, we have already mentioned the number of Africans prominent in public life. Septimius's rise to the throne is part of the African surge, not a cause of it. It has been calculated that out of 106 men most prominent in the reign of Septimius Severus, and of whom 76 can be identified with at least some probability as to their place of origin, 35 were African (nearly half). But Italians continue to be found in positions of authority, along with men from the other western provinces.

We should not attribute to Septimius a conscious policy of 'provincialization' of the Senate, nor did he set out deliberately to favour provincials and exclude Italians elsewhere in the public service. Similarly, it has been calculated that the Severan period saw a striking increase in the number of provincials holding procuratorships, equestrian posts in the army and centurions' rank, but again it cannot be shown that this was deliberate policy rather than the continuation of a trend already begun. It is true that more centurions now come from the more backward areas of the Empire, particularly from the Danubian provinces, and that equestrian commissions were now more freely given to men risen from the ranks, so that army officers in general were of lower social standing and less allied to the propertied classes of the Empire than before. It is also true, as we have seen, that Septimius disbanded the old Praetorian Guard, which had been largely the preserve of the Italians. This foreshadows the total eclipse of Italy and the split between army and civilian in the later Empire. The Severan age, in this as in so many respects, is one of transition, carrying on trends already well established over the preceding centuries, and at the same time pointing the way towards the Empire of Diocletian, Constantine and their successors, which even after the West was irretrievably lost, endured and flourished, restricted in territory and based on Byzantium, for well over a millenium.

The Roman Empire in the West eventually fragmented under the impact of the barbarian invasions. It retained its power over men's minds. Celtic warriors rode out from Edinburgh, which had been but briefly under Roman rule, to confront Germanic invaders in Yorkshire when there was no longer any Roman authority in the whole island, and felt and called themselves Roman. Charlemagne had himself crowned emperor in Rome on Christmas Day 800, and founded what was to become, by a perverse twist of terminology, the Holy Roman Empire of the German Nation. Three monarchs who survived into the twentieth century still rejoiced in the title of Caesar: the German Kaiser, the Tsar of Russia and the

Shah of Persia. None ruled a country that had been part of the Empire. So strong was the imprint of Rome's authority and the magic of her name, even beyond her borders: 'What wert thou, Rome, unbroken, when thy ruin Is greater than the whole world else beside?' (Hildebert of Lavardin, Archbishop of Tours, [1056–1133], trans. Helen Waddell, *More Latin Lyrics*, 263.

Latin remained for centuries the common tongue of Europe and for longer still the language of the Catholic Church, which took over from the secular Empire the ideal of 'eternal Rome'. 'The great Age of the Augustans', wrote Helen Waddell, 'is to us a thing set in amber, a civilization distinct and remote like the Chinese ... To the mediaeval scholar, with no sense of perspective, but a strong sense of continuity, Virgil and Cicero are but the upper reaches of the river that still flows past his door'. It was the persecuted Christians who finally preserved and transmitted what remained of Rome's heritage. Although the Church had a wholesome fear of the power of pagan literature, 'and not only pagan literature, but the whole sensible appearance of things', as Paulinus of Nola warns us, yet it remains true 'that the Church continued to teach the classics; that but only for the Church, the memory of them would have vanished from Europe.'

Maps

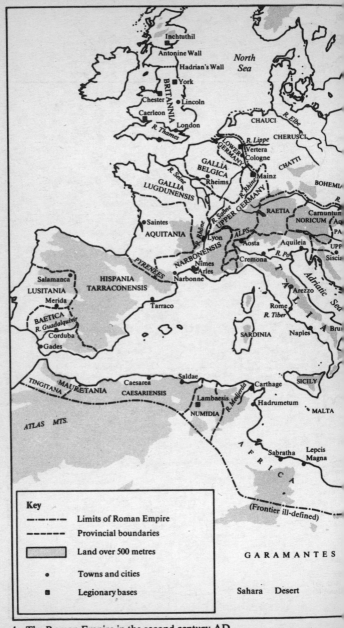

1. The Roman Empire in the second century AD

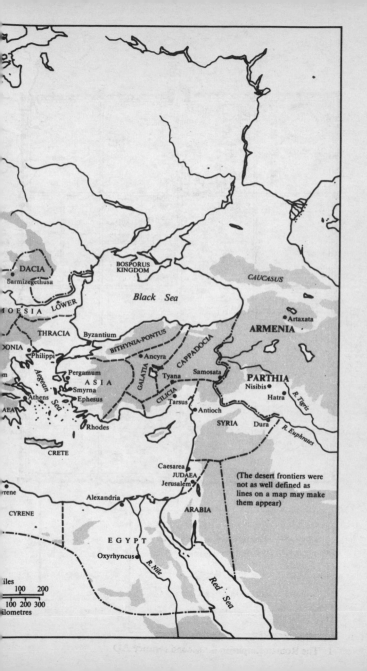

DACIA
Sarmizegethusa

MOESIA LOWER
THRACIA
DONIA
Philippi
m
Pergamum
Athens
AEA
Smyrna
Ephesus
Rhodes
CRETE

BOSPORUS
KINGDOM

Black Sea

CAUCASUS

Artaxata

ARMENIA

Byzantium
BITHYNIA-PONTUS
Ancyra
GALATIA
CAPPADOCIA
Tyana
Samosata
CILICIA
Tarsus
Antioch

PARTHIA
Nisibis
Hatra

R. Tigris

SYRIA
Dura

R. Euphrates

Aegean Sea

rene

CYRENE

Alexandria

Caesarea
JUDAEA
Jerusalem

ARABIA

(The desert frontiers were
not as well defined as
lines on a map may make
them appear)

E G Y P T
Oxyrhyncus
R. Nile

Red Sea

iles
100   200

100 200 300
kilometres

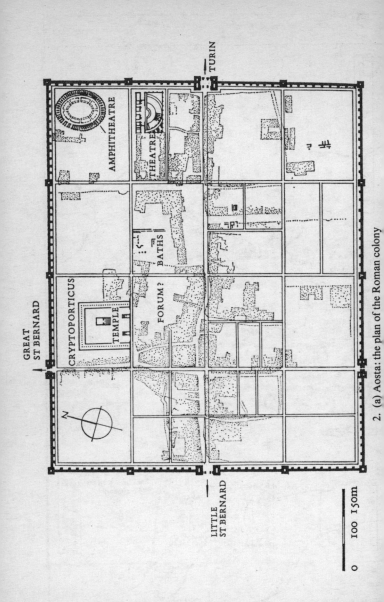

2. (a) Aosta: the plan of the Roman colony

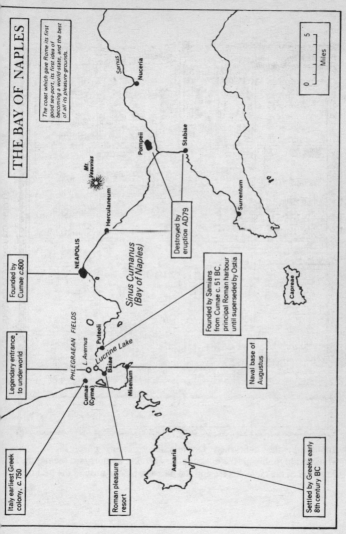

THE BAY OF NAPLES

The coast which gave Rome its first good sea-port, its first idea of becoming a world-state, and the best of all its pleasure grounds.

Founded by Cumae c.500

Legendary entrance to underworld

Italy earliest Greek colony, c.750

Roman pleasure resort

Founded by Samians from Cumae c. 51 BC, principal Roman harbour until superseded by Ostia

Naval base of Augustus

Settled by Greeks early 8th century BC

Destroyed by eruption AD79

Sinus Cumanus
(Bay of Naples)

PHLEGRAEAN FIELDS

Cumae (Cyme)
L. Avernus
Lucrine Lake
Puteoli
Baiae
Misenum

NEAPOLIS

Herculaneum

Mt. Vesuvius

Pompeii

Stabiae

Surrentum

Nuceria

Sarrus

Aenaria

Capreae

0   5
Miles

(b) *Vesuvius, Herculaneum and Pompeii*

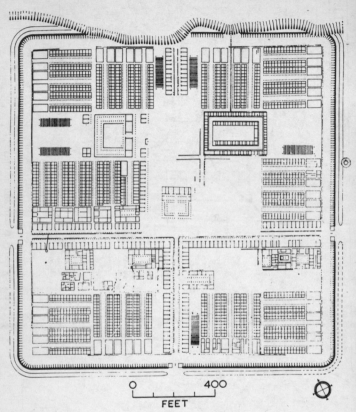

3. Inchtuthil: the unfinished Domitianic legionary base, showing the standard layout, with the headquarters around a courtyard facing the T-junction of the main streets and the barrack blocks around the perimeter

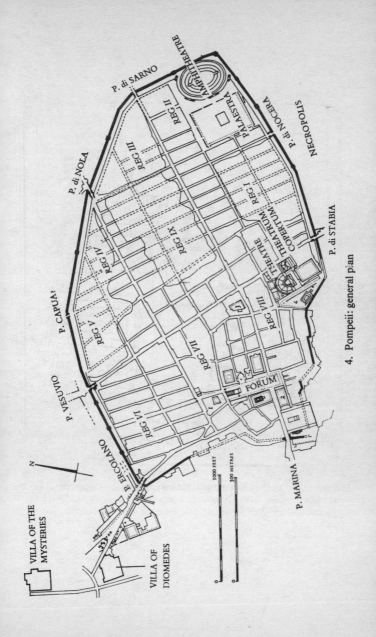

4. Pompeii: general plan

VILLA OF THE MYSTERIES

VILLA OF DIOMEDES

N

P. ERCOLANO

P. VESUVIO

P. CAPUA?

P. di NOLA

P. di SARNO

REG VI

REG VII

REG V

REG IV

REG IX

REG III

REG II

FORUM

REG VIII

REG I

AMPHITHEATRE

PALAESTRA

P. di NOCERA

NECROPOLIS

THEATRE

THEATRUM
TECTUM

P. di STABIA

P. MARINA

1000 FEET

300 METRES

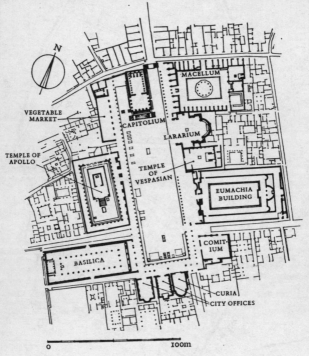

N

VEGETABLE
MARKET

TEMPLE OF
APOLLO

MACELLUM

CAPITOLIUM

LARARIUM

TEMPLE
OF
VESPASIAN

EUMACHIA
BUILDING

COMIT-
IUM

BASILICA

CURIA
CITY OFFICES

0   100m

5. Pompeii: the forum area

ROME IN THE TIME OF THE EMPERORS

——	Walls of Aurelian and Honorius
····	'Wall of Servius Tullius'

1 Forum of Trajan
2 Forum of Augustus
3 Forum of Julius Caesar
4 Forum of Vespasian
5 Forum Romanum

0   1
Mile

From Augustus onwards, who boasted he had found Rome of brick and left it of marble, successive emperors left their imposing marks on the buildings of the city.

6. The city of Rome

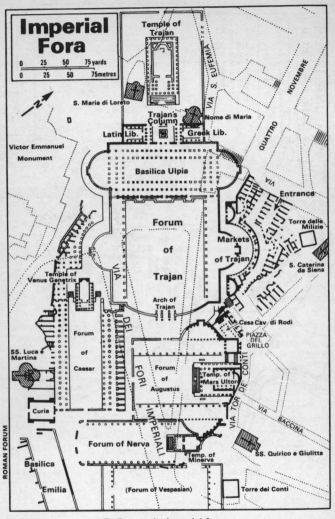

7. Rome: the imperial forums

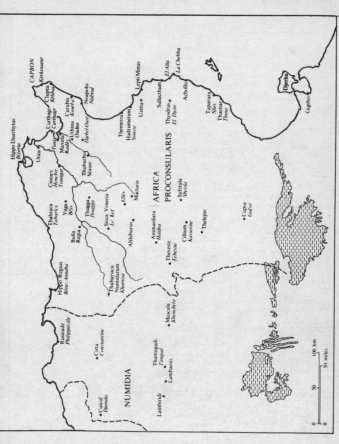

8. Roman Africa (Saldae, page 254, is on the coast, just off the map to the west)

Map labels:

Hippo Diarrhytus
Bizerta

CAPBON
Kerkouane

Clupea
Kélibia

Carthago
Carthage
Curubis
Utica
Tunis
Uthina
Maxula
Oudna
Radès
Djebel Oust

Neapolis
Nabeul

Cincari
Tooreur

Thuburbo
Maius

Themetra
Hadrumetum
Sousse

Lepti Minus
Uzitta

Sullecthum

El Alia
La Chebba

Thysdrus
El Djem

Acholla

Taparura
Sfax

Thaenae
Thina

Thabraca
Tabarka

Vaga
Béja

Thugga
Dougga

Bulla
Regia

Sicca Veneria
Le Kef

Elles

Mactaris

Hippo Regius
Bône, Annaba

Thuburscu
Numidarum
Khamisa

Althiburos

AFRICA
PROCONSULARIS

Ammaedara
Haidra

Sufetula
Sbeitla

Rusicade
Philippeville

Cirta
Constantine

Thevesta
Tébessa

Cillium
Kasserine

Capsa
Gafsa

Thelepte

Djerba

Gigthis

Cuicul
Djemila

Thamugadi
Timgad
Lambaesis

Masrula
Khenchela

NUMIDIA

Lambiridi

0   50   100 km
0   50 miles

Reigns of ROMAN EMPERORS from Augustus to Diocletian

27 BC–AD 14	Augustus	⎫
AD 14–37	Tiberius	the Julio-
37–41	Gaius (Caligula)	Claudian
41–54	Claudius	dynasty
54–68	Nero	⎭
68–9	Galba	
69	Otho	⎫
69	Vitellius	69, 'the year of the
69–79	Vespasian	four emperors'
78–81	Titus	the Flavian
81–96	Domitian	dynasty
96–8	Nerva	
98–117	Trajan	each emperor
117–38	Hadrian	chosen and
138–61	Antoninus Pius	adopted by
161–80	Marcus Aurelius	his predecessor
161–9	Lucius Verus (co-emperor)	
178–93	Commodus (178–80, co-emperor with his father)	
193	Pertinax	
193	Didius Julianus	
193–211	Septimius Severus	⎫
198–217	Caracalla (198–211, co-emperor with his father)	
209–12	Geta (209–11, co-emperor with father and brother; 211–12, with brother alone)	the Severan dynasty (excluding Macrinus)
217–18	Macrinus	
218–22	Elagabalus	⎭
222–35	Severus Alexander	
235–8	Maximinus	⎫ 'fifty years of
238–84	(about twenty emperors)	⎭ military anarchy'
284–305	Diocletian and colleagues	

GREEK AND LATIN AUTHORS

This list contains the full name and dates, where known, of all Greek and Latin authors mentioned in this book, chronologically by date of birth. Sometimes this is pure guesswork, as for instance when we know from allusions in the book itself roughly when it was written, but nothing further of the author's life. The accounts of the Christian martyrdoms are an extreme example. But it is interesting to range authors with their coevals, to realize that St Luke must have been much of an age with Petronius, and also to speculate on what some of those who died young might have written in their old age.

Authors who wrote wholly or mostly in Greek are given in italics. Those whose works are no longer extant, but whom we have referred to as sources for other writers, are marked with an asterisk. Dates marked *c.* (*circa*) are approximate, those with a question mark are frankly conjectural.

c. 455–*c.* 400 BC	*Thucydides*
234–149 BC	Cato the Elder (Marcus Porcius Cato)
106–43 BC	Cicero (Marcus Tullius Cicero)
86–34 (?) BC	Sallust (Gaius Sallustius Crispus)
84 (?)–54 (?) BC	Catullus (Gaius Valerius Catullus)
70–19 BC	Vergil (Publius Vergilius Maro)
85–8 BC	Horace (Quintus Horatius Flaccus)
64/3 BC–after AD 23	*Strabo*
63 BC–AD 14	Augustus (Imperator divi f. Augustus)
(dates unknown, writing 20s (?) BC)	Vitruvius (Vitruvius Pollio)
(poem written 31–27 BC)	Anon., *Panegyric on Messalla*
59 BC–AD 17	Livy (Titus Livius)
c. 55 BC–between AD 37 and 41	Seneca the Elder (Lucius Annaeus Seneca)
43 BC–AD 17	Ovid (Publius Ovidius Naso)
c. 30 BC–AD 45	*Philo Judaeus*
c. 20 BC–after AD 30	Velleius (Gaius Velleius Paterculus)
(writing AD 20s–30s)	Valerius Maximus
(writing *c.* AD 45)	Pomponius Mela
c. 4 BC–AD 65	Seneca the Younger (Lucius Annaeus Seneca)
3 BC (?)–AD 67	*Domitius Corbulo (Gnaeus Domitius Corbulo)

All dates henceforth AD

15–19	*Agrippina (Julia Agrippina, mother of Nero)
c. 15–c. 50	Phaedrus
before 18–after 65	Columella (Lucius Junius Moderatus Columella)
20 (?)–66	Petronius (Petronius Arbiter, probably to be identified with Titus Petronius Niger, consul in 61)
(dates unknown)	*Various authors, including St Paul and St Luke, the New Testament*
(writing after 69)	*Cluvius Rufus
(writing after 69)	*Fabius Rusticus
23/4–79	Pliny the Elder (Gaius Plinius Secundus)
c. 30–104	Frontinus (Sextus Julius Frontinus)
34–62	Persius (Aulus Persius Flaccus)
c. 35–100 (?)	Quintilian (Marcus Fabius Quintilianus)
37/8–after 100 (?)	*Josephus (Flavius Josephus)*
39–65	Lucan (Marcus Annaeus Lucanus)
c. 40–after 112	*Dio Chrysostom (Dio Cocceianus)*
c. 40–c. 104	Martial (Marcus Valerius Martialis)
before 50–after 120	*Plutarch (Lucius (?) Mestrius Plutarchus)*
c. 55–c. 135	*Epictetus*
c. 56–after 112/13	Tacitus (Publius (?) Cornelius Tacitus)
60 (?)–after 127	Juvenal (Decius Junius Juvenalis)
c. 61–c. 112	Pliny the Younger (Gaius Plinius Caecilius Secundus)
c. 69–well after 121	Suetonius (Gaius Suetonius Tranquillus)
(writing under Hadrian)	Florus (probably Publius Annius Florus)
c. 88–144	*Polemo (Marcus Antonius Polemo)*
(writing 127–48 & later)	Ptolemy (Claudius Ptolemaeus)
before 100–after 165	*Appian (Appianus)*
c. 100–65	*Justin Martyr*
c. 100–c. 166	Fronto (Marcus Cornelius Fronto)
c. 100–c. 169	Salvius Julianus (Lucius Octavius Cornelius Publius Salvius Julianus Aemilianus)
c. 101–77	*Herodes Atticus (Lucius Vibullius Hipparchus Tiberius Claudius Atticus Herodes)*
(perhaps born under Trajan)	Gaius (fuller name unknown)
115 (?)–180 or later	*Pausanias*
117–c. 187	*Aelius Aristides (Publius Aelius Aristides)*
c. 120–after 180	*Lucian (Lucianus)*

121–80	M. Aurelius (*Imperator Caesar Marcus Aurelius Antoninus Augustus*)
c. 123–after 158	Apuleius
129–99 (?)	Galen (*Galenus*)
c. 130–*c.* 180	Aulus Gellius
c. 130–*c.* 202	*Irenaeus*
(written 180 or soon after)	Anon., *Acts of the Scillitan Martyrs*
c. 160–*c.* 240	Tertullian (Quintus Septimius Florens Tertullianus)
c. 170–between 244 and 249	*Philostratus (Flavius Philostratus)*
(written 203 or soon after)	Anon., *Martyrdom of Perpetua and Felicity*
(killed 223)	Ulpian (Domitius Ulpianus)
(died after 229)	*Cassius Dio (Cassius Dio Cocceianus)*
(writing early 3rd cent.)	*Marius Maximus
(writing early 3rd cent.)	*Herodian*
(writing early 3rd cent.)	Minucius Felix (Marcus Minucius Felix)
c. 200–58	Cyprian (Thascius Caecilius Cyprianus)
c. 240–*c.* 320	Lactantius (Lucius Caelius or Caecilius Firmianus, also called Lactantius)
c. 260–340	*Eusebius*
314–*c.* 393	*Libanius*
(writing late 4th cent.)	Aurelius Victor (Sextus Aurelius Victor)
(writing late 4th cent.)	Eutropius
(writing late 4th cent.)	Anon., the *Augustan History*
353/4–431	Paulinus of Nola (Meropius Pontius Paulinus)
354–430	Augustine (Aurelius Augustinus)
c. 360–*c.* 420	Sulpicius Severus
(writing early 5th cent.)	Macrobius (Ambrosius Theodosius Macrobius)
(writing early 5th cent.)	Orosius (Paulus Orosius)
6th century	*Johannes Lydus (Joannes Laurentius Lydus*
11th century	*Xiphilinus (Joannes Xiphilinus)*
12th century	*Zonaras (Joannes Zonaras)*

Further Reading

The criteria of selection for this list are explained in the Preface, pages 3–4. Through the works listed here you will be able to find further references to more specialized works and to older works and works in other languages. *Titles marked with an asterisk contain particularly valuable bibliographies*. The General Works are not normally referred to specifically under the different chapters, but will often be relevant. Where books have appeared in both a British and American edition, I must ask readers to accept my apologies if only one is given.

General Works

A more detailed account of the period will be found in the *Cambridge Ancient History*, vols. X-XII (1934–9)*, still useful, though dated; a new edition is in preparation. The later Republic and the first part of our period are also covered in H. H. Scullard, *From the Gracchi to Nero* (3rd ed., London, Methuen, 1970), generally reliable, with useful references to modern discussions in the notes. A. Garzetti, *From Tiberius to the Antonines* (London, Methuen, 1974)*, ending in AD 192, is chiefly useful for the 266 pages of notes and bibliography; the translation from the Italian is often misleading, especially on proper names, technical terms, and family relationships. Paul Petit, *Pax Romana* (London, Batsford, 1976)*, takes too much for granted, but is valuable for its account of Marxist, especially Russian, scholarship.

On the economic history of the period, the fundamental work is still M. Rostovtzeff, *Social and Economic History of the Roman Empire*, 2 vols. (2nd ed., rev. P. M. Fraser, Oxford U.P., 1957). There is a mass of data, though the treatment of individual provinces is uneven, in Tenney Frank (ed.), *An Economic Survey of Ancient Rome*, 6 vols. (Johns Hopkins U.P., 1933–40, reprinted Octagon, 1975). I have got many ideas from Fernand Braudel,

Capitalism and Material Life 1400–1800 (Fontana, 1974), dealing with another pre-industrial society. Other works on the economy are cited below under Chapters 6 and 8. For travel, see below under Chapter 6, and on trade routes see M. P. Charlesworth, *Trade Routes and Commerce of the Roman Empire* (2nd ed., 1926, reprinted Ares, 1974), and Mortimer Wheeler, *Rome beyond the Imperial Frontiers* (London, Penguin/Bell, 1954, reprinted Greenwood, 1971). Sture Bolin, *State and Currency in the Roman Empire to 300 AD* (Stockholm, Almqvist and Wiksell, 1958), is interesting on the devaluation and debasement of the coinage, though probably overestimates the sophistication of the coiners. On coinage, politics and propaganda, read C. H. V. Sutherland, *Coinage in Roman Imperial Policy 31 BC–AD 68* (London, Methuen, 1951); also, full of ideas, but often wrong, Michael Grant, *From Imperium to Auctoritas* (Cambridge U.P., 1946).

Literature in its social context is discussed by R. M. Ogilvie, *Roman Literature and Society* (Brighton, Harvester; Totowa, N. J., Barnes and Noble; Penguin, 1980). Excellent in parts, but uneven, is the *Cambridge History of Classical Literature* II: *Latin Literature* (Cambridge U.P., 1982)*, also useful for individual biographies and lists of works.

On town-planning, architecture and art, brilliantly related to social history, see Mortimer Wheeler, *Roman Art and Architecture* (London, Thames and Hudson, 1964). More detailed treatments are to be found in two Pelican History of Art books: J. B. Ward-Perkins, *Roman Imperial Architecture* (2nd ed., 1981)*, and Donald Strong, *Roman Art* (1976)*. Brief but valuable is J. B. Ward-Perkins, *Cities of Ancient Greece and Italy: Planning in Classical Antiquity* (New York, Braziller, 1974) (good plans and photographs, especially air photographs, and especially on Italy itself)

On Roman law, the best introduction is Barry Nicholas, *An Introduction to Roman Law* (Oxford U.P., 1962), together with H. F. Jolowicz and Barry Nicholas, *Historical Introduction to the Study of Roman Law* (3rd ed., Oxford U.P., 1972). The relationship of law to society is the theme of J. A. Crook, *Law and Life of Rome* (London, Thames and Hudson, 1967). The basic work of reference is W. W. Buckland, *A Text-book of Roman Law from Augustus to Justinian* (3rd ed., rev. P. Stein, Cambridge U.P., 1963).

Various aspects of administration and policy are discussed by Fergus Millar, *The Emperor in the Roman World (31 BC–AD 337)* (London, Duckworth, 1977), and *The Roman Empire and its*

Neighbours (2nd ed., London, Duckworth, 1981); A. N. Sherwin-White, *The Roman Citizenship* (2nd ed., Oxford U.P., 1973); J. S. Reid, *The Municipalities of the Roman Empire* (Cambridge U.P., 1913), still useful despite its age. A series of articles by A. H. M. Jones, *Studies in Roman Government and Law* (Oxford, Blackwell 1960), discusses aspects of legal and financial administration, and Jones returns to the theme in *The Criminal Courts of the Roman Republic and Principate* (Oxford, Blackwell, 1972); see too J. A. Crook, *Consilium Principis: Imperial Councils and Counsellors from Augustus to Diocletian* (Cambridge U.P., 1955).

On the army, the standard work in English is Graham Webster, *The Roman Imperial Army of the First and Second Centuries AD* (2nd ed., London, Black; New York, Barnes and Noble, 1979)*, on which see my review in *American Journal of Philology* cii (1981), 465–9. For the soldier's life and conditions of service, see G. R. Watson, *The Roman Soldier* (London, Thames and Hudson, 1969), together with articles cited below under Chapter 6. Essential documents discussed and translated in Robert O. Fink, *Roman Military Records on Papyrus* (American Philological Assoc. Monograph 26, Case Western Reserve U.P., 1971). For the history of the legions, refer to H. M. D. Parker, *The Roman Legions* (Oxford U.P., 1928, reprinted with new bibliography, Cambridge, Heffer, 1958), and for the auxiliaries to G. L. Cheesman, *The Auxilia of the Roman Imperial Army* (Oxford U.P., 1914, reprinted Ares, 1975), supplemented but not superseded by P. A. Holder, *Studies in the Auxilia of the Roman Army from Augustus to Trajan* (British Archaeological Reports S70, Oxford, 1980).

On everyday life, see J. Carcopino, *Daily Life in Ancient Rome* (Yale U.P., 1940; London, Routledge, 1941; also in Penguin), mostly about the city of Rome itself. Wider in scope, and highly entertaining, is J. P. V. D. Balsdon, *Life and Leisure in Ancient Rome* (London, Bodley Head, 1969); his *Romans and Aliens* is full of additional recondite information (London, Duckworth, 1979). Other aspects of social history are to be found in Ramsay MacMullen, *Roman Social Relations 50 BC to AD 284* (Yale U.P., 1974); Jean Gagé, *Les classes sociales dans l'Empire romain* (Paris, Payot, 1971); Stanley F. Bonner, *Education in Ancient Rome* (U. of California Press, 1977)*. J. P. V. D. Balsdon, *Roman Women: Their History and Habits* (London, Bodley Head, 1969), is mostly concerned with the upper classes, while Sarah B. Pomeroy, *Goddesses, Whores, Wives and Slaves: Women in Classical Antiquity* (New York, Schocken, 1975)* has more on Greece than on

Rome. See further the articles by S. M. Treggiari listed below under Chapter 8.

On geographical and climatic factors affecting Roman history, see M. Cary, *The Geographical Background of Greek and Roman History* (Oxford U.P., 1949). The most complete and up-to-date atlas is N. G. L. Hammond (ed.), *Atlas of the Greek and Roman World in Antiquity* (Park Ridge, N.J., Noyes, 1981), while the best of the cheaper atlases is Michael Grant (ed.), *Ancient History Atlas 1700 BC to AD 565* (rev. ed., London, Weidenfeld and Nicolson, 1974).

Preface

The quotation on page 2 is from Theodor Mommsen, *The Provinces of the Roman Empire: the European Provinces*, ed., T. R. S. Broughton, (U. of Chicago Press, 1968), 4–5. That on pages 2–3 is from Peter Brown, *Religion and Society in the Age of St Augustine* (London, Faber and Faber, 1972), 16. Of the books referred to, P. A. Brunt and J. M. Moore, *Res Gestae Divi Augusti: the Achievements of the Divine Augustus* (Oxford U.P., 1967), provides Latin text, translation, and an invaluable commentary. N. Lewis and M. Reinhold, *Roman Civilization, Sourcebook* II: *the Empire* (Columbia U.P., 1955; rev. ed. Harper Torchbooks, 1966), is particularly useful for its translations of inscriptions and papyri: judicious selection, brief but helpful notes. Michael Crawford, *The Roman Republic* (Fontana, 1978), precedes this present work in the Fontana History of the Ancient World; Crawford's Epilogue sets the scene for my Chapter 1. On legal and constitutional terminology, see further the relevant articles in the *Oxford Classical Dictionary* (2nd ed., Oxford U.P., 1970). On the *novus homo*, see T. P. Wiseman, *New Men in the Roman Senate 139 BC–AD 14* (Oxford U.P., 1971); on nobility, H. Hill, 'Nobilitas in the imperial period', *Historia* xviii (1969), 230–50. On the citizen's right of appeal, see A. H. M. Jones, 'I appeal unto Caesar', *Studies in Roman Government and Law* (above, General Works), 51–65, and A. N. Sherwin-White on St Paul's specific case, *Roman Society and Roman Law in the New Testament* (Oxford U.P., 1963), 57–70. On the *equites*, see T. P. Wiseman, 'The definition of "Equus Romanus" in the late Republic and early Empire', *Historia* xix (1970), 67–83. The most complete compilation of evidence on prices and values is R. P. Duncan-Jones, *The Economy of the Roman Empire: Quantitative Studies* (Cambridge U.P., 1974).

I The New Order

On Octavian's rise to power and the political and social changes which it occasioned, see above all R. Syme, *The Roman Revolution* (Oxford U.P., 1939). On political allusions in Vergil's earlier poems, see Colin Hardie, 'Octavian and Eclogue I', in Barbara Levick (ed.), *The Ancient Historian and his Materials: Essays in Honour of C. E. Stevens on his Seventieth Birthday* (Farnborough, Gregg International, 1975), 109–22; L. P. Wilkinson, *The Georgics of Virgil: a Critical Survey* (Cambridge U.P., 1969), ch. 7; and Chester G. Starr, 'Virgil's acceptance of Octavian', *American Journal of Philology* lxxvi (1955), 34–46. On Cremona and Mantua, L. J. F. Keppie, 'Vergil, the confiscations, and Caesar's Tenth Legion', *Classical Quarterly* xxxi (1981), 367–70. On the Herodian dynasty, see A. H. M. Jones, *The Herods of Judaea* (Oxford U.P., 1938), and on all aspects of Jewish history, E. Schürer, *The History of the Jewish People in the Age of Jesus Christ (175 BC–AD 135)*, rev. ed. by Geza Vermes and Fergus Millar, 2 vols. to date (Edinburgh, Clark, I 1973, II 1979); also E. M. Smallwood, *The Jews under Roman Rule from Pompey to Diocletian* (Leiden, Brill, 1976). That Octavian's Illyrian conquests were limited in extent was proved conclusively by R. Syme in papers of the 1930s reprinted with additional material in his *Danubian Papers* (Bucharest, Assoc. Internat. d'Etudes du Sud-Est européen, 1971), 13–25, 135–44. On the importance of client kingdoms in Roman policy, see E. N. Luttwak (below, under Chapter 6). On Antony's dispositions in this regard, see G. W. Bowersock, *Augustus and the Greek World* (Oxford U.P., 1965), ch. 4). I have not yet seen A. N. Sherwin-White, *Roman Foreign Policy in the Near East* (London, Duckworth, 1983).

II The Sources

Most authors quoted are available in the Loeb series and many in Penguin translations (see my comments, page 4). On the Brunt and Moore edition of the *Res Gestae* and the Lewis and Reinhold *Sourcebook*, see above under Preface. For the Augustan Age, with its chronological limits generously interpreted, there is an extensive collection of source material in Kitty Chisholm and John Ferguson, *Rome: the Augustan Age* (Oxford U.P./Open University Press, 1981).

M. L. W. Laistner, *The Greater Roman Historians* (U. of California Press, 1947) sets Tacitus in the tradition of ancient historiography; R. Syme, *Tacitus*, 2 vols. (Oxford U.P., 1958), brilliant and fundamental, puts him in the context of his own time. The commentary on the *Annals* by H. Furneaux (Oxford U.P., 1896) is still unsurpassed and contains introductory chapters of great value on Tacitus's methods and treatment of key figures, e.g., Tiberius. The best general treatment is B. Walker, *The Annals of Tacitus* (Manchester U.P., 1952). On the *Histories*, see G. E. F. Chilver, *A Historical Commentary on Tacitus' Histories* I and II (Oxford U.P., 1979; commentary on III–V in press). On Suetonius see A. Wallace-Hadrill, *Suetonius* (London, Duckworth, 1983); for Dio there is Fergus Millar, *A Study of Cassius Dio* (Oxford U.P., 1964), good on Dio's own views and on how the history was written. A. N. Sherwin-White, *The Letters of Pliny* (Oxford U.P., 1966), is a commentary with an excellent introduction, while Betty Radice's introduction to the Penguin translation, *The Letters of the Younger Pliny*, could scarcely be bettered. For a bibliography of recent work on other Latin authors, see the *Cambridge History of Classical Literature* (above, General Works). On Jewish sources, see Schürer (above, Chapter 1).

Except in collections of source material, such as those already cited, inscriptions are not readily accessible in translation, but they are often easy to translate for anyone with a rudimentary knowledge of Latin, once certain conventions and abbreviations have been mastered. The best introductory manual in English is J. E. Sandys, *Latin Epigraphy: an Introduction to the Study of Latin Inscriptions* (2nd ed., Cambridge U.P., 1926, reprinted Ares, 1974). The standard collection of Latin inscriptions is the *Corpus Inscriptionum Latinarum*, which began to appear in 1863 and is now inevitably outdated, even with various supplements. Hermann Dessau, *Inscriptiones Latinae Selectae*, has some inscriptions found since the relevant volume of *CIL* appeared, and has invaluable indexes. New inscriptions are collected annually in *L'Année épigraphique*. Greek inscriptions of the Roman Empire are in *Inscriptiones Graecae ad res Romanas pertinentes*. Both *ILS* and *IGRR* have been reprinted by Ares (1979, 1975 respectively).

The modern trend is towards individual volumes for the inscriptions of a single country, which may or may not coincide with a Roman province. So we have R. G. Collingwood and R. P. Wright, *The Roman Inscriptions of Britain* (Oxford U.P., 1965); J. Vives, *Inscripciones latinas de la España romana* (Barcelona, 1971–2); L.

Barcóczi and A. Mócsy, *Die römischen Inschriften Ungarns* (3 vols. to date, Budapest, 1972–81). North Africa, epigraphically very rich, has A. Merlin, *Inscriptions latines de la Tunisie* (Paris, 1944), a sequel to R. Cagnat, A. Merlin and L. Chatelain, *Inscriptions latines d'Afrique (Tripolitanie, Tunisie, Maroc)* (Paris, 1923), itself a sequel to *CIL* viii. For Algeria, there is S. Gsell, H.-G. Pflaum, and others, *Inscriptions latines de l'Algérie*, starting in 1922 and still going strong. The first fascicule of L. Chatelain, *Inscriptions latines du Maroc*, appeared in 1942, and no more since. Then there are collections of the Greek, Berber, Punic and neo-Punic inscriptions. Tripolitania, part of Roman Africa but never under French rule, has its own collection: J. M. Reynolds and J. B. Ward-Perkins, *The Inscriptions of Roman Tripolitania* (Rome and London, 1952). And so on.

There are also collections of inscriptions arranged by subject matter, such as M. J. Vermaseren, *Corpus Inscriptionum et Monumentorum Religionis Mithriacae* (The Hague, 1956–60), or L. Robert, *Les gladiateurs dans l'Orient grec* (Paris, 1940, reprinted Amsterdam, Hakkert, 1971). There are collections for students' use, like Victor Ehrenberg and A. H. M. Jones, *Documents Illustrating the Reigns of Augustus and Tiberius* (2nd ed., Oxford U.P., 1955). There are also inscriptions of such importance that they are the subject of a detailed monograph; these will be referred to below, in the appropriate place.

Papyrological studies are equally daunting. Fortunately there is an excellent guide: E. G. Turner, *Greek Papyri: an Introduction* (Oxford U.P., 1968). This contains among other things a list of the main collections of papyri that have been published, with their customary abbreviations. Useful discussion and further references in A. K. Bowman, 'Papyri and Roman Imperial History, 1960–75', *JRS* lxvi (1976), 153–73. For the Vindolanda tablets, see A. K. Bowman and J. D. Thomas, *Vindolanda: the Latin Tablets* (Britannia Monograph no. 4, 1983).

Archaeological reports commonly appear in a variety of national journals, such as *Britannia*, *Gallia*, *Germania*, *Antiquités Africaines*, etc.; or in local journals, often difficult to obtain outside the country of origin, such as the *Transactions of the Architectural and Archaeological Society of Durham and Northumberland*; or in the journals of societies or institutions, such as the *Antiquaries Journal*, *Papers of the British School at Rome*, *Comptes-Rendus de l'Académie des Inscriptions et Belles-Lettres*, etc.; and so on. There is no regular up-to-date bibliography. Numerous archaeological atlases or encyclopaedias exist, mostly popularizing and somewhat superficial. Not to be confused with these is Richard Stillwell (ed.), *Princeton Encyclopaedia of Classical Sites* (Princeton U.P., 1976), with summaries and bibliographies for each site, an invaluable work of reference.

For the study of Roman pottery, the best introduction is now D. P. S. Peacock, *Pottery in the Roman World: an Ethno-archaeological Approach* (London, Longman, 1982)*. On the implications of the transfer of pottery workshops from Italy to Gaul, see C. M. Wells, 'L'implantation des ateliers de céramique sigillée en Gaule: problématique de la recherche', *Figlina* ii (1977), 1–11, and review of S. von Schnurbein, *Die unverzierte Terra Sigillata von Haltern* (Münster, 1982), in *Antiquaries Journal* (forthcoming).

On archaeological air photography there is now an extensive literature. Outstanding results have been obtained by, e.g., Jean Baradez, *Fossatum Africae: Recherches aériennes sur l'organisation des confins sahariens à l'époque romaine* (Paris, 1949), and more recently by Roger Agache in northern France and by J. K. St Joseph in Britain. Outstanding as an introduction is John Bradford, *Ancient Landscapes: Studies in Field Archaeology* (London, Bell, 1957); see especially ch. 4 on Roman centuriation. Superb photographs and commentary in S. S. Frere and J. K. St Joseph, *Roman Britain from the Air* (Cambridge U.P., 1983). Reflections on the variations in the epigraphic record by Ramsay MacMullen, 'The epigraphic habit in the Roman Empire', *American Journal of Philology* ciii (1982), 233–46.

III The Work of Augustus

As for Chapter 1, R. Syme, *The Roman Revolution*, is fundamental for both personalities and concepts (e.g., *amicitia*, *clientela*, *auctoritas*). An excellent and well-illustrated general account is Donald Earl, *The Age of Augustus* (London, Elek/Toronto, Ryerson, 1968). No recent account in English is as complete as Dietmar Kienast, *Augustus: Prinzeps und Monarch* (Darmstadt, Wiss. Buchgesellschaft, 1982)*. Salutary reflections on the settlement of 27 BC by Fergus Millar, 'Triumvirate and Principate', *JRS* lxiii (1973), 50–67; more scepticism by E. A. Judge, 'Res Publica Restituta: a Modern Illusion?' in J. A. S. Evans (ed.), *Polis and*

Imperium: Studies in Honour of Edward Togo Salmon (Toronto, Hakkert, 1974), 279–311, and sound common sense from W. K. Lacey, 'Octavian in the Senate, January 27 BC', *JRS* lxiv (1974) 176–84. On 23 and the conspiracy of Murena, many articles since 1960, especially in *Historia*, mostly dating the conspiracy to 23, but see now, restating the case for 22, E. Badian, '"Crisis Theories" and the beginning of the principate', in G. Wirth (ed.), *Romanitas – Christianitas (Festschrift Johannes Straub)* (Berlin and New York, de Gruyter, 1982), 18–41, with references to earlier articles (I did not see Badian's article until this chapter was finished). On Augustus's name and on Roman names generally, see R. Syme, 'Imperator Caesar: a study in nomenclature', *Roman Studies* I (Oxford U.P., 1979), 361–77; A. N. Sherwin-White discusses 'The emperor and his virtues', *Historia* xxx (1981), 298–323; and on tribunician power, see W. K. Lacey, 'Summi fastigii vocabulum: the story of a title', *JRS* lxix (1979), 28 34. On the vitally important topic of the grain supply, discussed here and in later chapters, little need be added to Geoffrey Rickman, *The Corn Supply of Ancient Rome* (Oxford U.P., 1980)*, but see also P. D. A. Garnsey, 'Grain for Rome', in Peter Garnsey, Keith Hopkins and C. R. Whittaker, *Trade in the Ancient Economy* (London, Chatto and Windus, 1983)*. A. H. M. Jones, *Studies in Roman Government and Law* (above, General Works) contains important work on Augustus's legal position. For the dating of Horace, *Odes* IV, later than 13 BC, see Gordon Williams, *Horace* (*Greece and Rome*, New Surveys in the Classics 6, Oxford U.P., 1972); I propose to develop the argument further in a forthcoming article. Horace's portrayal of Augustus is discussed by Eduard Fraenkel, *Horace* (Oxford U.P., 1957), especially 239–97, 353–6, 383–99, 432–53; the quotation on page 63 is from Fraenkel, 395. On Graves's portrayal of Livia, see P. B. Harvey, *Classical Outlook* lvii (1979) 11–13. The quotation about the British general on page 66 comes from A. J. Smithers, *Toby: a Real Life Ripping Yarn* (London, Gordon and Cremonesi, 1978), 112. For the notion that the two Julias were guilty of conspiracy as well as adultery, see R. Syme, *History in Ovid* (Oxford U.P., 1978), 193–8, 206–11. On the Cornelii, R. Syme, 'Piso Frugi and Crassus Frugi', in his *Roman Studies* II (Oxford U.P., 1979), 496–509. On Marcus Crassus in the Balkans and the refusal of his claim to receive the *spolia opima*, awarded for killing the enemy commander in battle, see R. Syme, 'Livy and Augustus', *Roman Studies* I, 400–54. Augustus's campaigns in Europe are discussed at length in C. M. Wells, *The German Policy* *of Augustus: an Examination of the Archaeological Evidence* (Oxford U.P., 1972)*. Articles cited therein are not repeated here. Further reading to do with Augustus's army reforms will be found below under Chapter 6. On Spain, see R. Syme, 'The conquest of north-west Spain', *Roman Studies* II, 825–54; on the Germans, the best account in English is Malcolm Todd, *The Northern Barbarians 100 BC–AD 300* (London, Hutchinson, 1975), and see also my review of R. Nierhaus, *Das swebische Gräberfeld von Diersheim* (Berlin, 1966) in *JRS* lix (1969), 303–5, together with *The German Policy of Augustus*, ch. 2. The absence of an up-to-date commentary in English on Tacitus's *Germania* is much to be regretted. On the beginnings of Romanization between Rhine and Elbe, C. M. Wells, 'The Impact of the Augustan Campaigns on Germany', in *Assimilation et Résistance à la Culture gréco-romaine dans le Monde ancien: Travaux du VIe Congrès International d'Etudes Classiques (Madrid, Septembre 1974)*, ed., D. M. Pippidi (Bucharest and Paris, 1976), 421–31. On Varus's marriage to a daughter of Agrippa, see M. Reinhold, 'Marcus Agrippa's son-in-law, P. Quinctilius Varus', *Classical Philology* lxvi (1972), 119–21, based on a new papyrus (*Zeitschrift für Papyrologie und Epigraphik* v [1970], 217–83). For a fuller statement of the argument on pages 83–4, see my *German Policy of Augustus*, ch. 1. I cannot accept the arguments of Josiah Ober, 'Tiberius and the political testament of Augustus', *Historia* xxxi (1982), 306–28, that Tiberius invented Augustus's advice to keep the Empire within existing boundaries.

IV Italy under Augustus

For all buildings in Rome, the standard work of reference is Ernest Nash, *Pictorial Dictionary of Ancient Rome*, 2 vols. (rev. ed., London, Thames and Hudson, 1968). On brick production, see Tapio Helen, *Organization of Roman Brick Production in the First and Second Centuries AD: an Interpretation of Roman Brick Stamps* (Helsinki, 1975), and Päivi Setälä, *Private Domini in Roman Brick Stamps of the Empire: a Historical and Prosopographical Study of Landowners in the District of Rome* (Helsinki, 1977). On senators in trade, see below under Chapter 8. On etiquette for emperors, see A. Wallace-Hadrill, 'Civilis princeps: between citizen and king', *JRS* lxxii (1982), 32–48. On the *ara Pacis*, see J. M. C. Toynbee, 'The Ara Pacis reconsidered',

Proceedings of the British Academy xxxix (1953), 67–95, and 'The "ara Pacis Augustae"', *JRS* li (1961), 153–6. On the Roman aqueducts, see Thomas Ashby, *The Aqueducts of Ancient Rome* (Oxford U.P., 1935); construction techniques in E. B. Van Deman, *The Building of Roman Aqueducts* (Washington, Carnegie Inst., 1934, reprinted McGrath, 1973); see also H. B. Evans, 'Agrippa's water plan', *American Journal of Archaeology* lxxxvi (1982), 401–11. On the Lyon aqueduct and siphons, see below under Chapter 6. On the development of building techniques, see M. E. Blake, *Ancient Roman Construction in Italy from the Prehistoric Period to Augustus* (Washington, 1949); *Roman Construction in Italy from Tiberius through the Flavians* (Washington, 1959; and with D. Taylor-Bishop, *Roman Construction in Italy from Nerva through the Antonines* (Philadelphia, 1973). W. V. Harris, *Rome in Etruria and Umbria* (Oxford U.P., 1971), 316–18, lists Augustan buildings as an index of prosperity in those areas. For Augustan street layouts still visible in air photographs, see Ward-Perkins, *Cities of Ancient Greece and Italy* (see above, General Works). On rural discontent, see P. A. Brunt, 'The army and the land in the Roman revolution', *JRS* lii (1962), 69–86. See also below under Chapter 8. Population estimates in P. A. Brunt, *Italian Manpower 225 BC–AD 14* (Oxford U.P., 1971). On the 'demi-monde', see the brilliant article by Jasper Griffin, 'Augustan poetry and the life of luxury', *JRS* lxvi (1976), 87–105, supplemented by his 'Genre and real life in Latin poetry', *JRS* lxxi (1981), 39–49. The patron-client relationship is discussed by R. P. Saller, *Personal Patronage under the Early Empire* (Cambridge U.P., 1981). Social mobility has been much studied: see Keith Hopkins, 'Elite mobility in the Roman Empire', and P. R. C. Weaver, 'Social mobility in the early Roman Empire: the evidence of the imperial freedmen and slaves', in M. I. Finley (ed.), *Studies in Ancient Society* (London and Boston, Routledge, 1974), 103–20, 121–40; B. Dobson, 'The Centurionate and social mobility' in C. Nicolet (ed.), *Recherches sur les structures sociales dans l'antiquité classique* (Paris, 1970), 99–115. Further references to publications relevant to this chapter appear below under Chapters 6 and 8.

V The Consolidation of the Principate

The circumstances of Tiberius's accession and the death of Agrippa Postumus have generated much modern controversy and speculation, naturally inconclusive. The discussion by B. Levick, *Tiberius the Politician* (London, Thames and Hudson, 1976)*, is judicious and helpful. See also Robin Seager, *Tiberius* (London, Eyre Methuen, 1972). On the bases of popular acceptance of Tiberius's and his successors' power, see Ch. Wirszubski, *Libertas as a Political Idea at Rome during the Late Republic and Early Principate* (Cambridge U.P., 1968), and Z. Yavetz, *Plebs and Princeps* (Oxford U.P., 1969)*. On treason (*maiestas*), see R. A. Bauman, *The Crimen Maiestatis in the Roman Republic and Augustan Principate* (Johannesburg, 1967), followed by his *Impietas in Principem: A Study of Treason against the Emperor with Special Reference to the First Century AD* (Munich, 1974). Evidence for treason trials in R. S. Rogers, *Criminal Trials and Criminal Legislation under Tiberius* (American Philological Assoc. Monograph 6, Middletown, Conn., 1935), criticised by C. W. Chilton, 'The Roman law of treason under the early principate', *JRS* xlv (1955), 73–81, with Rogers's reply, 'Treason in the early Empire', *JRS* xlix (1959), 90–4. On emperor worship, see L. R. Taylor, *The Divinity of the Roman Emperor* (American Philological Assoc. Monograph 1, 1931, reprinted Scholar's Press, no date); see also Duncan Fishwick, 'The development of provincial ruler worship in the western Roman Empire', *ANRW* ii.16 (1978), 1201–53. There has been no book on Caligula in English since J. P. V. D. Balsdon, *The Emperor Gaius* (Oxford U.P., 1934). The same year saw the first edition of A. Momigliano, *Claudius: the Emperor and his Achievement* (2nd ed., Oxford U.P., 1961)*, which popularized a more favourable interpretation than that of Tacitus and Suetonius. On the palace at Fishbourne, see Barry Cunliffe, *Fishbourne: a Roman Palace and its Garden* (London, Thames and Hudson, 1971). For the Claudian-Nero campaigns in Britain, see D. R. Dudley and Graham Webster, *The Roman Conquest of Britain AD 43–57* (London, Batsford, 1965), and Graham Webster, *Boudica: the British Revolt against Rome AD 60* (London, Batsford/Totowa, N.J., Rowman and Littlefield, 1978). The material from Llyn Cerrig Bach is in Cyril Fox, *A Find of the Early Iron Age from Llyn Cerrig Bach, Anglesey* (Cardiff, National Museum of Wales, 1946). Policy on citizenship and the Lyon plaque are discussed by A. N. Sherwin-White, *The Roman Citizenship* (above, General Works), ch. 9. On the new harbour at Portus, see Rickman, *Corn Suply* (above under Chapter 3), 73–9, and Tenney Frank, *Economic Survey* (above, General Works), 236–42. On relations with the Senate, D. McAlindon, 'Senatorial Opposition to Claudius and Nero', *American Journal of Philology* lxxvii (1956),

113–32, and 'Claudius and the Senators', *ibid.*, lxxviii (1957), 279–86, together with 'Entry to the Senate in the Early Empire', *JRS* xlvii (1957), 191–7, and 'Senatorial advancement in the age of Claudius', *Latomus* xvi (1957), 252–62. Claudius's role in developing the system of equestrian administrators is discussed by A. N. Sherwin-White, 'Procurator Augusti', *PBSR* xv (1939), 11–26. On financial administration and the blurring of the distinction between the public treasury (*aerarium*) and the emperor's own finances (*fiscus*), see Fergus Millar, 'The fiscus in the first two centuries', *JRS* liii (1963), 29–42, and P. A. Brunt, 'The fiscus and its development', *JRS* lvi (1966), 75–91. There are also relevant articles on adminstration and finances in A. H. M. Jones, *Studies in Roman Government and Law* (above, General Works). For Nero's reign we have B. H. Warmington, *Nero: Reality and Legend* (London, Chatto and Windus, 1969). Miriam T. Griffin, *Seneca: a Philosopher in Politics* (Oxford U.P., 1976)*, is excellent. Important articles include F. J. Lepper, 'Some Reflections on the "Quinquennium Neronis"', *JRS* xlvii (1957), 95–103; on Claudius's policy in the East and on Corbulo's campaigns, see D. Magie, *Roman Rule in Asia Minor to the End of the First Century after Christ* (Princeton U.P., 1950), I, 540–61. On the position of the Christians, see below on Chapter 10. On Nero's Golden House, see Axel Boëthius, *The Golden House of Nero: Some Aspects of Roman Architecture* (U. of Michigan Press, 1960).

VI The Army and Provinces in the First Century AD

On the size of the army, Ramsay MacMullen, 'How big was the Roman imperial army?', *Klio* lxii (1980), 451–60. On recruitment, P. A. Brunt, 'Conscription and volunteering in the Roman imperial army', *Scripta Classica Israelica* i (1974), 90–115. See also J. C. Mann, *Legionary Recruitment and Veteran Settlement during the Principate*, ed., M. M. Roxan (U. of London Inst. of Archaeology, Occasional Publications vii, 1983). Marriage in Brian Campbell, 'The marriage of soldiers under the Empire', *JRS* lxviii (1978), 153–66. On soldiers' pay, the basic study is by P. A. Brunt, 'Pay and superannuation in the Roman army', *PBSR* xviii (1950), 50–71, supplemented by M. Speidel, 'The pay of the auxilia', *JRS* xiii (1973), 141–7. Soldiers' duties and daily life in G. R. Watson, 'Documentation in the Roman army', *ANRW* ii.1 (1974), 493–507, and R. W. Davies, 'The daily life of a Roman soldier under the principate', *ANRW* ii.1 (1974), 299–338. On food, see R. W. Davies, 'The Roman military diet', *Britannia* ii (1971), 122–42. On awards for valour, Valerie A. Maxfield, *The Military Decorations of the Roman Army* (London, Batsford, 1981). For Gaul, see J. F. Drinkwater, *Roman Gaul: the Three Provinces 58 BC–AD 260* (London and Canberra, Croom Helm, 1983); ownership of land in E. M. Wightman, 'Peasants and potentates: an investigation of social structure and land tenure in Roman Gaul', *American Journal of Ancient History* iii (1978), 97–128. The importance of client kings is stressed by E. N. Luttwak, *The Grand Strategy of the Roman Empire* (Johns Hopkins U.P., 1976)*. Further discussions of the development of Roman frontier policy by Fergus Millar, 'Emperors, frontiers, and foreign relations 31 BC–AD 378', *Britannia* xiii (1982), 1–23; A. R. Birley, 'Roman frontiers and Roman frontier policy', *Trans. of the Architectural and Archaeological Soc. of Durham and Northumberland*, n.s. iii (1974), 13–25; J. C. Mann, 'The frontiers of the principate', *ANRW* ii.1 (1974), 508–33. The Cyrene edicts are in F. De Visscher, *Les édits d'Auguste découverts à Cyrène* (Louvain, 1940). On trade with the East, see M. G. Raschke, 'New studies in Roman commerce with the East', *ANRW* ii.9 (1978), 604–1378. My information on Quseir al-Qadim comes from the Toronto *Globe and Mail*, 17 Sept., 1982. On Punic and Berber, see Fergus Millar, 'Local cultures in the Roman Empire: Libyan, Punic and Latin in North Africa', *JRS* lviii (1968), 126–34, and compare Ramsay MacMullen, 'Provincial languages in the Roman Empire', *American Journal of Philology* lxxxvi (1966), 1–17. On maladministration, see P. A. Brunt, 'Charges of provincial maladministration under the early principate', *Historia* x (1961), 189–227; see also G. P. Burton, 'Proconsuls, assizes, and the administration of justice under the Empire', *JRS* lxv (1975), 92–106. On governors' *mandata*, see Fergus Millar, *The Emperor in the Roman World* (above, General Works), 314–17, modified by G. P. Burton, 'The issuing of mandata to proconsuls and a new inscription from Cos', *Zeitschrift für Papyrologie und Epigraphik* xxi (1976), 63–8. On the speed of travel by sea, see Lionel Casson, *Ships and Seamanship in the Ancient World* (Princeton U.P., 1971), and by land, A. M. Ramsay, 'The speed of the Roman imperial post', *JRS* xv (1925), 60–74. More generally, Lionel Casson, *Travel in the Ancient World* (London, Allen and Unwin, 1974)*. On the New Testament narratives, A. N. Sherwin-White, *Roman Society and Roman Law in the New Testament* (above under Preface). On taxation, P. A. Brunt, 'The revenues of Rome', *JRS* lxxi (1981), 161–72, including a summary of the evidence for provincial censuses. Keith Hopkins, 'Taxation and trade in the Roman Empire (200 BC–AD 400)', *JRS* lxx (1980), 101–28, argues that the need to raise money for taxes stimulated trade. On maritime trade, see Jean Rougé, *Recherches sur l'organisation du commerce maritime en Méditerranée sous l'empire romain* (Paris, 1966). On Egypt, we now have Naphtali Lewis, *Life in Egypt under Roman Rule* (Oxford U.P., 1983), especially valuable for its discussion of economic and financial matters, e.g., ch. 8 on 'census, taxes and liturgies'. The Pisidian inscription referred to is analysed by Stephen Mitchell, 'Requisitioned transport in the Roman Empire: a new inscription from Pisidia', *JRS* lxvi (1976), 106–31. Romanization in Britain and Gaul can best be studied in A. L. F. Rivet, *Town and Country in Roman Britain* (London, Hutchinson, 1958)*, and J. F. Drinkwater (cited above). On Spain, see Leonard A. Curchin, 'Personal wealth in Roman Spain', *Historia* xxxii (1983), 227–44. On provincial building, especially in Gaul and Africa, see J. B. Ward-Perkins, 'From Republic to Empire: reflections on the early provincial architecture of the Roman West', *JRS* lx (1970), 1–19. The best introduction to the province of Africa is still T. R. S. Broughton, *The Romanization of Africa Proconsularis* (John Hopkins U.P., 1929; reprinted Greenwood, 1968). On the Tacfarinas revolt, see R. Syme, 'Tacfarinas, the Musulamii and Thubursicu', *Roman Studies* I, 218–30; brief further reflections by C. M. Wells, 'The Defense of Carthage', in J. G. Pedley (ed.), *New Light on Ancient Carthage* (U. of Michigan Press, 1980), 47–65, esp. 49–51. On the role of the nomad and semi-nomad, see C. R. Whittaker, 'Land and Labour in North Africa', *Klio* lx (1978), 331–62; also Brent D. Shaw, 'Fear and loathing: the nomad menace and Roman Africa', in C. M. Wells (ed.), *L'Afrique romaine: les Conférences Vanier 1980* (U. of Ottawa Press, 1982), 29–50; see also the following article in that work, Michel Janon, 'Paysans et soldats', 51–67. There are useful modern parallels in *Nomades et nomadisme au Sahara* (UNESCO, Recherches sur la zone aride xix, Paris, 1963), e.g., the article by B. Sarel/Sternberg on seasonal nomadism, 'Les semi-nomades du Nefzaðua'. Importance of casual labour for ancient agriculture stressed by Ramsay MacMullen, 'Peasants, during the principate', *ANRW* ii.1 (1974), 229–52. There is a useful introduction to modern research in Eric R. Wolf, *Peasants* (Foundations of Modern Anthropology, Englewood Cliffs, N.J., Prentice-Hall, 1966), with a selection of articles in George Dalton (ed.), *Tribal and Peasant Economies* (American Museum Sourcebooks in Anthropology, Garden City, N.Y., Natural History Press, 1967). Further references below on Chapter 10. On centuriation, see O. A. W. Dilke, 'Archaeological and epigraphic evidence of Roman land surveys', *ANRW* ii.1 (1974), 564–92. For the role of the army, the seminal paper is Ramsay MacMullen, 'Rural Romanization', *Phoenix* xxii (1968), 337–41. His book, *Soldier and Civilian in the later Roman Empire* (Harvard U.P., 1967)*, contains much documentation relevant to our period also. See further A. R. Birley, 'The economic effects of Roman frontier policy', in Anthony King and Martin Henig (eds.), *The Roman West in the Third Century: Contributions from Archaeology and History* (British Archaeological Reports, S109, Oxford, 1981), 39–53. The Lyon aqueducts are discussed in an important paper by A. T. Hodge, 'Siphons in Roman aqueducts', *PBSR* li (1983). On the abandonment of the *oppida*, see P.-A. Février, 'The origin and growth of the cities of southern Gaul to the third century AD', *JRS* lxiii (1973), 1–28, with further references to works, mostly in French, there and in Drinkwater, *Roman Gaul*. The link between army supply and trade is stressed by P. S. Middleton, 'Army supply in Roman Gaul: an hypothesis for Roman Britain', in B. C. Burnham and H. Johnson (eds.), *Invasion and Response* (British Archaeological Reports, 73, Oxford, 1979), 81–98, and in a Cambridge PhD thesis, as yet unpublished. The London wharf was reported in *The Times*, 20 July 1981.

VII 'Emperors Made Elsewhere than at Rome'

On the revolt against Nero, see G. E. F. Chilver, 'The Army in Politics, AD 68–70', *JRS* xlvii (1957), 29–35; and P. A. Brunt, 'The revolt at Vindex and the fall of Nero', *Latomus* xviii (1959), 531–59. See also K. R. Bradley, 'A *publica fames* in AD 68', *American Journal of Philology* xciii (1972), 451–8; and R. Syme, 'Partisans of Galba', *Historia* xxxi (1982), 460–83. The events of 69 are vividly related by Kenneth Wellesley, 'The Long Year AD 69' (London, Elek, 1975). Rival emperors' propaganda is reflected in the coinage of these years, but we have no comprehensive study from this point of view, as we should have if Sutherland's *Coinage in Roman Imperial Policy 31 BC–AD 68* (above, General Works) continued after the fall of Nero; see however Colin M. Kraay, 'The Coinage of Vindex and Galba, AD 68, and the continuity of the Augustan Principate', *Numismatic Chronicle* (series vi) ix (1949), 129–49; also to some extent relevant is Barbara Levick, 'Concordia at Rome', in R. A. G. Carson and Colin M. Kraay (eds.), *Scripta Nummaria Romana: Essays Presented to Humphrey Sutherland* (London, Spink, 1978), 217–33, esp. 226–7; the standard catalogue of Roman coins is H. Mattingly and E. A. Sydenham, *The Roman Imperial Coinage* (London, 1923–), along with H. Mattingly, *Coins of the Roman Empire in the British Museum*, 5 vols. (London, 1923–50). On the *Lex de imperio Vespasiani*, there is much modern literature, but it is necessary to cite only P. A. Brunt, 'Lex de imperio Vespasiani', *JRS* lxvii (1977), 95–116. The date of the fall of Masada (74, not 73, as generally supposed) is given by two newly discovered inscriptions, see Schürer (above under Chapter 1) for details. I. A. Richmond, 'The Roman Siege-works of Masada, Israel', *JRS* lii (1962), 142–55, is fundamental. The excavations are described by Y. Yadin, *Masada: Herod's Fortress and the Zealots' Last Stand* (London, Weidenfeld and Nicolson/New York, Random House, 1966). On the penetration of the Sahara, see E. W. Bovill, *The Golden Trade of the Moors* (2nd ed., Oxford U.P., 1968), ch. 3; R. G. Goodchild, 'Oasis forts of Legio III Augusta on routes to the Fezzan', and Olwen Brogan, 'The camel in Roman Tripolitania', *PBSR* xxii (1954), 56–68 and 126–31 respectively. On Britain under the Flavians, see A. R. Birley, 'Petillius Cerialis and the conquest of Brigantia', *Britannia* iv (1973), 179–90; V. E. Nash-Williams, *The Roman Frontier in Wales* (2nd ed., rev. M. G. Jarratt, U. of Wales Press, 1969); and W. S. Hanson, 'The first Roman occupation of Scotland', in W. S. Hanson and L. J. F. Keppie (eds.), *Roman Frontier Studies 1979* (British Archaeological Reports, S71, Oxford, 1980), 15–43*. The so-called 'Stoic opposition' to Vespasian is handled by P. A. Brunt, 'Stoicism and the Principate', *PBSR* xliii (1975), 7–35. J. A. Crook, 'Titus and Berenice', *American Journal of Philology* lxxii (1951), 162–75, tries to examine the political implications of the relationship. The trend towards rehabilitating Domitian begins with R. Syme, 'The imperial finances under Domitian, Nerva and Trajan', *Roman Studies* I, 1–17 (calling Domitian 'this able and intelligent Emperor'), and is continued by K. H. Waters, 'The Character of Domitian', *Phoenix* xviii (1964), 49–77; see also H. W. Pleket, 'Domitian, the Senate, and the provinces', *Mnemosyne* xiv (1961), 296–315, and E. Birley, 'Senators in the Emperor's service', *Proceedings of the British Academy* xxxix (1953) 197–214. For Britain, see Tacitus, *Agricola*, eds., R. M. Ogilvie and I. A.

Richmond (Oxford U.P., 1967), esp. Introduction, section 6. Mons Graupius may now have been identified by air photography, see J. K. St Joseph, 'The camp at Durno, Aberdeenshire, and the site of Mons Graupius', *Britannia* ix (1978), 271–87. For Inchtuthil, consult brief annual reports in *JRS* xliii (1953), to lvi (1966). There is not much recent work in English on the Rhine and Danube under Domitian, but see H. Schönberger, 'The Roman frontier in Germany: an archaeological survey', *JRS* lix (1969), 144–97, esp. for the Flavian period 155–64; and on the Danubian campaigns, A. Mócsy, *Pannonia and Upper Moesia* (Provinces of the Roman Empire, London, Routledge, 1974), ch. 4. On Trajan, see K. H. Waters, 'Trajan's character in the literary tradition', in *Polis and Imperium* (above under Chapter 3). R. Syme, *Tacitus*, 2 vols. (Oxford U.P., 1957) is necessary reading. On the composition of the Senate, see M. Hammond, 'Composition of the Senate, AD 68–235, *JRS* xlvii (1957), 74–81, and the very important new study by Keith Hopkins and Graham Burton, 'Ambition and withdrawal: the senatorial aristocracy under the emperors', in Keith Hopkins, *Death and Renewal: Sociological Studies in Roman History* II (Cambridge U.P., 1983)*, 120–200. On Trajan's campaigns, R. Syme, 'The lower Danube under Trajan', *Danubian Papers* (above under Chapter 1), 122–34, is largely devoted to problems of chronology. On Trajan's canal, see J. Sasel, 'Trajan's canal at the Iron Gate', *JRS* lxiii (1973), 80–5. For Trajan's Column as a source of information on the army, the fundamental study is by I. A. Richmond, 'Trajan's army on Trajan's column', *PBSR* xiii (1935), 1–40; Lino Rossi, *Trajan's Column and the Dacian Wars* (London, Thames and Hudson, 1971), discusses also the monetary and epigraphic evidence, as well as the reliefs on the Adamklissi monument, on which see also I. A. Richmond, 'Adamklissi', *PBSR* xxii (1967), 29–39, though Richmond's dating is doubtful. On the East, see G. W. Bowersock, 'A report on Arabia Provincia', *JRS* lxi (1971), 219–42, and F. A. Lepper, *Trajan's Parthian War* (Oxford U.P., 1948). On the view that some favoured generals passed more rapidly through the magistracies to the consulship, see Brian Campbell, 'Who were the "viri militares"?', *JRS* lxv (1975), 11–31.

VIII The State of Italy from Petronius to Pliny

The quotation from Helen Waddell is from *The Wandering Scholars* (Penguin, 1954; first published London, Constable, 1927),

p. 23. On the Bay of Naples, see J. H. D'Arms, *Romans on the Bay of Naples* (Harvard U.P., 1970), and 'Puteoli in the second century of the Roman Empire: a social and economic study', *JRS* lxiv (1974), 104–24. Also, full of common sense as well as learning, J. H. D'Arms, *Commerce and Social Standing in Ancient Rome: a Social and Cultural Study of the Villas and their Owners from 150 BC to AD 400* (Harvard U.P., 1981), to be read along with H. W. Pleket, 'Urban elites and business in the Greek part of the Roman Empire', in Peter Garnsey, Keith Hopkins and C. R. Whittaker (eds.), *Trade in the Ancient Economy* (London, Chatto and Windus, 1983)*, from which work note also the introduction by Keith Hopkins, discussing and going beyond the work of A. H. M. Jones, *The Roman Economy: Studies in Ancient Economic and Administrative History*, ed., P. A. Brunt (Oxford, Blackwell, 1974), and M. I. Finley, *The Ancient Economy* (U. of California Press, 1973), on the deficiencies of which as applied to Rome, see the review by M. W. Frederiksen, *JRS* lxv (1975), 164–71. On senatorial attitudes to property, see Elizabeth Rawson, 'The Ciceronian Aristocracy and its properties', in M. I. Finley (ed.), *Studies in Roman Property* (Cambridge U.P., 1976), 85–102, amplified by S. M. Treggiari, 'Sentiment and property: some Roman attitudes', in A. Parel and T. Flanagan (eds.), *Theories of Property: Aristotle to the present* (Waterloo, Ont., 1979), 53–85. On Cisalpina, see G. E. F. Chilver, *Cisalpine Gaul: Social and Economic History from 49 BC to the Death of Trajan* (Oxford U.P., 1941). In general, K. D. White, *Roman Farming* (London, Thames and Hudson, 1970). Pliny's affairs in R. P. Duncan-Jones, 'The Finances of the younger Pliny', *PBSR* xxxiii (1965), 177–88, and, on agricultural wealth in general, 'Some configurations of landholding in the Roman Empire', in Finley, *Studies in Roman Property*, 7–34, to which add Finley's own paper therein, 'Private farm tenancy in Italy before Diocletian', 103–21. The evidence from Etruria is assembled by T. W. Potter, *The Changing Landscape of South Etruria* (London, Elek, 1979)*, with his further comments on 'Villas in South Etruria: some comments and contexts', in K. S. Painter (ed.), *Roman Villas in Italy: Recent Excavations and Research* (Brit. Mus. Occasional Papers 24, London, 1980), 73–81; this volume also contains an interim report on Settefinestre, 1975–9, by A. Carandini and T. Tatton-Brown, 9–43. On Crocicchie, see T. W. Potter and K. M. D. Dunbabin, 'A Roman villa at Crocicchie, Via Clodia', *PBSR* xxxiv (1979), 19–26. There are several important contributions based on recent survey and excavation in Italy in G. Barker and R. Hodges (eds.), *Archaeology and Italian Society: Prehistoric, Roman and Medieval Studies* (Papers in Italian Archaeology II, British Archaeological Reports S102, Oxford, 1981). Villas around Vesuvius in R. C. Carrington, 'Studies in the Campanian "villae rusticae"', *JRS* xxi (1931), 110–30. On peasants and small proprietors, see P. D. A. Garnsey, 'Where did Italian peasants live?', *Proceedings of the Cambridge Philological Society* xxv (1979), 1–25; John K. Evans, 'The peasantry of classical Italy', *American Journal of Ancient History* v (1980), 19–47, 134–73; C. R. Whittaker, 'Agri deserti', in Finley, *Studies in Roman Property*, 137–65. On casual labour and tenant farmers, P. D. A. Garnsey, 'Non-slave labour in the Roman world', in Garnsey (ed.), *Non-Slave Labour in the Greco-Roman World* (Cambridge Philological Society, 1980), 34–47. On the *alimenta*, P. D. A. Garnsey, 'Trajan's alimenta: some problems', *Historia* xvii (1968), 367–81, is basically right. On the arch at Beneventum, see I. A. Richmond,. 'The arch of Beneventum', *Roman Archaeology and Art: Essays and Studies by Sir Ian Richmond*, ed., Peter Salway (London, Faber and Faber, 1969), 229–38. Books on Pompeii and Herculaneum are innumerable; the best of recent years is Wilhelmina F. Jashemski, *The Gardens of Pompeii, Herculaneum, and the Villas Destroyed by Vesuvius* (New Rochelle, Caratzas, 1979); also Michael Grant, *Cities of Vesuvius: Pompeii and Herculaneum* (London, Weidenfeld and Nicolson, 1971), and, for its illustrations, Theodor Kraus, *Pompeii and Herculaneum: the Living Cities of the Dead* (English trans., New York, Abrams, 1975). Recent work summarized by R. Ling, 'Pompeii and Herculaneum: recent research and future prospects', in H. McK. Blake, T, W. Potter, D. B. Whitehouse (eds.), *Papers in Italian Archaeology I: the Lancaster Seminar*, 2 vols. (British Archaeological Reports S41, Oxford, 1978), i 153–73*. On the position of freedmen, see P. D. A. Garnsey, 'Descendants of freedmen in local politics: some criteria', in B. Levick (ed.), *The Ancient Historian and his Materials* (above under Chapter 1), and 'Independent freedmen and the economy of Roman Italy under the principate', *Klio* lxiii (1981), 359–71. The crate of Gaulish pottery at Pompeii is discussed by D. Atkinson, 'A hoard of Samian ware from Pompeii', *JRS* iv (1914), 26–64. On Arikamedu, most recently, Vimala Begley, 'Arikamedu reconsidered', *American Journal of Archaeology* lxxxvii (1983), 461–81. On pottery and 'crisis', see Giuseppe Pucci, 'Pottery and Trade', in Garnsey *et al.*, *Trade in the Ancient Economy*, 105–17. On Ostia, we have the comprehensive study by Russell Meiggs, *Roman Ostia* (2nd ed., Oxford U.P., 1973), and on living conditions, Gustav Hermansen, *Ostia: Aspects of Roman City Life* (U. of Alberta Press, 1982). On property at Rome, see B. W. Frier, *Landlords and Tenants in Imperial Rome* (Princeton U.P., 1980); P. D. A. Garnsey, 'Urban Property Investment', in Finley, *Studies in Roman Property*, 123–36. See also Helen Jefferson Loane, *Industry and Commerce of the City of Rome (50 BC–AD 200)* (Johns Hopkins U.P., 1938, reprinted Arno, 1979). On the condition of the poor at Rome, it is worth comparing Henry Mayhew, *London Labour and the London Poor* (London, 1851). For women working alongside men, see Ramsay MacMullen, 'Women in public in the Roman Empire', *Historia* xxix (1980), 208–18. More generally, on jobs in Rome, see the excellent articles by P. A. Brunt, 'Free labour and public works at Rome', *JRS* lxx (1980), 81–100; S. M. Treggiari, 'Urban labour in Rome: *mercenarii* and *tabernarii*', in Garnsey, *Non-Slave Labour*, 48–64. Slave households discussed by S. M. Treggiari in a series of articles: 'Domestic staff at Rome in the Julio-Claudian period, 27 BC to AD 68', *Histoire sociale/Social History* vi (1973), 241–55; 'Family life among the staff of the Volusii', *Transactions of the American Philological Association* cv (1975), 393–401; 'Jobs in the household of Livia', *PBSR* xliii (1975), 48–77; 'Jobs for women', *American Journal of Ancient History* i (1976), 76–104; 'Questions on women domestics in the Roman West', in *Schiavitù, Manomissione e Classi Dipendenti nel Mondo Antico* (Rome, 1979), 186–201; 'Concubinae', *PBSR* xliv (1981), 59–81; 'Women as property in the early Roman Empire', in D. Kelly Weisberg (ed.), *Women and the Law: a Social Historical Perspective* (Cambridge, Mass., Schenkman, 1982), 7–33. On slaves' opportunities for advancement, P. R. C. Weaver, *Familia Caesaris: a Social Study of the Emperor's Freedmen and Slaves* (Cambridge U.P., 1972). On slavery in general, William L. Westerman, *The Slave Systems of Greek and Roman Antiquity* (Philadelphia, American Philosophical Society, 1955), is valuable for its compilation of evidence, but the most important book of recent years is M. I. Finley, *Ancient Slavery and Modern Ideology* (London, Chatto and Windus/New York, Viking, 1980; Penguin, 1983)*, reviewing earlier treatments and stressing the central importance of slavery in the ancient world. See further Keith Hopkins, *Conquerors and Slaves: Sociological Studies in Roman History* I (Cambridge U.P., 1978), esp. sections 1–3, with the review by E. Badian, *JRS* lxxii (1982), 164–9. The argument that slaves were better off than the free poor was common in the American South, see the collection by Eric L. McKitrick (ed.), *Slavery Defended: The Views of the Old South* (Englewood Cliffs, N.J., Prentice-Hall, 1963). On racial prejudice, see A. N. Sherwin-White, *Racial Prejudice in Imperial Rome* (Cambridge U.P., 1970); Frank M. Snowden, Jr, *Before Color Prejudice: the Ancient View of Blacks* (Harvard U.P., 1983). On the bars, see G. Hermansen, 'The Roman inns and the law', in J. A. S. Evans (ed.), *Polis and Imperium* (above under Chapter 3), 167–82. For a Victorian parallel, Michael Young and Peter Willmott, *Family and Kinship in East London* (rev. ed., Penguin, 1962), ch. 1, esp. p. 23, quoting Mayhew (cited above).

IX The Orderly Government of the Empire

On Hadrian, see R. Syme, *Tacitus*, 2 vols. (Oxford U.P., 1957), 236–52, 481–503. Still useful is P. J. Alexander, 'Letters and speeches of the Emperor Hadrian', *Harvard Studies in Classical Philology* xlix (1938), 141–77. For Britain, the fort at Newstead was published by James Curle, *A Roman Frontier Post and its People: the Fort of Newstead in the Parish of Melrose* (Glasgow, Maclehose, 1911). For the towns, see John Wacher, *The Towns of Roman Britain* (London, Batsford, 1975). The best introduction to Hadrian's Wall is D. J. Breeze and B. Dobson, *Hadrian's Wall* (2nd ed., Penguin, 1978). Relations with the local people in Peter Salway, *The Frontier People of Roman Britain* (Cambridge U.P., 1967). Of general histories of Roman Britain, the most complete is Sheppard Frere, *Britannia: a History of Roman Britain* (2nd ed., London, Cardinal, 1974)*; also to be recommended are Malcolm Todd, *Roman Britain 55 BC–AD 400* (Fontana, 1981); John Wacher, *Roman Britain* (London, Toronto and Melbourne, Dent, 1978); and Peter Salway, *Roman Britain* (Oxford History of England, 1a, Oxford U.P., 1981). For the background to the Jewish revolt, drawn largely from Jewish sources, we have S. Safrai, 'The relations between the Roman army and the Jews . . .', in *Roman Frontier Studies 1967: Proceedings of the Seventh International Congress held at Tel Aviv* (Tel Aviv, 1971), 224–9; N. R. M. de Lange, 'Jewish attitudes to the Roman Empire', in P. D. A. Garnsey and C. R. Whittaker, *Imperialism in the Ancient World* (Cambridge U.P., 1978), 255–81; and important studies by Shimon Applebaum, *Prolegomena to the Study of the Jewish Revolt (AD 132–135)* (British Archaeological Reports S7, Oxford, 1976), and 'Judaea as a Roman province: the countryside as a political and economic factor', *ANRW* ii.8 (1978), 355–96. There is a popular account of the finding of Bar-Kochba's letters by Y. Yadin, *Bar-Kokhba* (London, Weidenfeld and Nicolson/New York, Random House, 1971). On the Pantheon at Rome, see William L. MacDonald, *The Pantheon: Design, Meaning and Progeny* (Harvard U.P., 1976). The quotation from Marguerite Yourcenar, *Memoirs of Hadrian*, is from the Book Society edition (London, 1955), 136–7 (also available from Penguin). Beards are discussed by Gilbert Bagnani, 'Misopogon, the beard hater', *Echos du monde classique/Classical News and Views* xii (1968), 73–9. On Antoninus's succession and titles, including 'Pius', see Mason Hammond, 'Imperial elements in the formula of the Roman emperors...', in *Memoirs of the American Academy at Rome* xxv (1957), 17–64. On the administration of the Empire, Mason Hammond, *The Antonine Monarchy* (American Academy at Rome, 1959)*; see also the General Works on law and administration listed above. On the working of the rescript system, the theory of Tony Honoré, *Emperors and Lawyers* (London, Duckworth, 1981) is highly controversial. On the legal distinction between upper and lower classes, see P. D. A. Garnsey, *Social Status and Legal Privilege in the Roman Empire* (Oxford U.P., 1970). For the fighting in Britain, see the works cited above, plus G. S. Maxwell, 'The native background to the Roman occupation of Scotland', and D. J. Breeze, 'Roman Scotland during the reign of Antoninus Pius', in *Roman Frontier Studies 1979* (see above on Chapter 7), 1–13 and 45–60* respectively. On Aelius Aristides, see below on Chapter 10. A. R. Birley, *Marcus Aurelius* (London, Eyre and Spottiswoode, 1966) is a useful biography. Valuable insights into court life are found in Edward Champlin, *Fronto and Antonine Rome* (Harvard U.P., 1980). The emperor's own self-portrait is analysed by P. A. Brunt, 'Marcus Aurelius in his *Meditations*', *JRS* lxiv (1974), 1–20. Garzetti, *From Tiberius to the Antonines* (see above, General Works) is particularly copious in his treatment of Hadrian, Antoninus, and especially Marcus. J. F. Gilliam, 'The plague under Marcus Aurelius', *American Journal of Philology* lxxxii (1961), 225–51, corrects earlier scholarly exaggerations. On barbarian settlement within the Empire, see the comprehensive treatment by G. E. M. de Ste Croix, *The Class Struggle in the Ancient Greek World from the Archaic Age to the Arab conquests* (London, Duckworth, 1981)*, app. 3. It is not possible to give a comprehensive reading list on the causes of the Empire's decline. The two most important contributions are by N. H. Baynes,

'The decline of the Roman power in Western Europe: some modern explanations', *JRS* xxxiii (1943), 29–35, and F. W. Walbank, *The Awful Revolution: the Decline of the Roman Empire in the West* (Liverpool U.P., 1969). More recently, Ste Croix, *Class Struggle*, ch. 8, offers 'a Marxist analysis on class lines', which, like much else in that great book, contains brilliant insights and vast learning, but is also curiously uneven; his analysis certainly fails the criterion that 'any explanation of why the western half of the Empire disintegrated ... must also account for the fact that the eastern half did not' (see above, page 240). On points of detail, for the impoverishment of the curial class, see P. D. A. Garnsey, 'Aspects of the decline of the urban aristocracy in the Empire', *ANRW* ii.1 (1974), 229–52; on the fall of Rome and St Augustine, see T. D. Barnes, 'Aspects of the background of the *City of God*', in Wells (ed.), *L'Afrique romaine* (above on Chapter 6), 69–85. The quotation on page 242 is from Peter Brown, *Religion and Society in the Age of Saint Augustine* (London, Faber and Faber, 1972), 13, a brilliant introduction to the differences between the classical and late Roman world. Two other books by Peter Brown place a salutary emphasis on change rather than on 'decline', continuity instead of 'fall': *The World of Late Antiquity: from Marcus Aurelius to Muhammed* (London, Thames and Hudson, 1971), and *The Making of Late Antiquity* (Harvard U.P., 1978), in which see page 49 on urban change related to. changed values. The parallel with Brixton is taken from Donald J. Olsen, *The Growth of Victorian London* (London, Batsford, 1976; Penguin 1979), 241. On 'the classical canon', see Helen Waddell, *The Wandering Scholars* (above under Chapter 8). Further documentation on the later period in A. H. M. Jones, *The Later Roman Empire 284–602: a Social, Economic and Administrative Survey*, (3 vols., Oxford, Blackwell/2 vols., U. of Oklahoma Press, 1964). I was first set to thinking about many of the problems discussed in this section by Jane Jacobs, *The Death and Life of Great American Cities* (New York, Random House, 1961).

X 'The Immeasurable Majesty of the Roman Peace'

Work on Roman Africa is mostly in French, and many sites are poorly published (e.g., Tiddis). There is an excellent bibliography in Paul MacKendrick, *The North African Stones Speak* (London, Croom Helm/U. of North Carolina Press, 1980)*, though on the book as a whole see my review in *Classical Review* xxxii (1982),

29–30. Tunisian sites are discussed in the recent book by A. Mahjoubi, *Les cités romaines de Tunisie* (Tunis, no date), brief but very useful; see also the summary of recent archaeological work in J. H. Humphreys (ed.), A. Ennabli, 'North African News Letter iii.1: Tunisia, 1956–80', *American Journal of Archaeology* lxxxvii (1983), 197–206. On local markets, see Brent D. Shaw, 'Rural markets in North Africa and the political economy of the Roman Empire', *Antiquités Africaines* xvii (1981), 37–84. Evidence from Libya in Barri Jones and Graeme Barker, 'Libyan valleys survey', *Libyan Studies (11th Annual Report . . . 1979–80),* 11–36. Evidence for imperial estates assembled by Dorothy J. Crawford, 'Imperial estates', in M. I. Finley (ed.), *Studies in Roman Property* (Cambridge U.P., 1976), 35–70; see also John Percival, 'Culturae Mancianae: field patterns in the Albertini Tablets', in B. Levick (ed.), *The Ancient Historian and his Materials* (see above on Chapter 1), 213–27; C. R. Whittaker, 'Rural labour in three Roman provinces', in Garnsey, *Non-Slave Labour* (above under Chapter 8). On the wealth of Africa, see R. P. Duncan-Jones, 'Costs, outlays, and summae honorariae from Roman Africa' and 'Wealth and munificence in Roman Africa', *PBSR* xxx (1962), 47–115, and xxxi (1963), 159–77 respectively. African careers in Michael G. Jarrett, 'An album of the equestrians from North Africa in the emperor's service', *Epigraphische Studien* ix (1972), 146–232. The importance of the pottery trade in A. Carandini, 'Pottery and the African economy', in Garnsey *et al.*, *Trade in the Ancient Economy* (see above on Chapter 8), 145–62. The rebuilding of the Byrsa at Carthage is described by Pierre Gros, 'Le forum de la haute ville dans le Carthage romaine . . .', *Comptes rendus de l'Académie des Inscriptions et Belles-Lettres* (1982), 636–58. On the marble trade, J. B. Ward-Perkins, *Quarrying in Antiquity: Technology, Tradition and Social Change* (London, British Academy, 1972, offprinted from the *Proceedings of the British Academy* lvii). On Africa in general, P. D. A. Garnsey, 'Rome's African empire under the principate', in P. D. A. Garnsey and C. R. Whittaker, *Imperialism in the Ancient World* (Cambridge U.P., 1978), 223–54. For the survival of non-Roman elements, the fundamental study is M. Bénabou, *La résistance africaine à la romanisation* (Paris, Maspero, 1976), more briefly illustrated by the same author, 'Les survivances préromaines en Afrique romaine', in Wells, *L'Afrique romaine* (above under Chapter 6). Turning to Asia, we begin with A. H. M. Jones, *The Greek City from Alexander to Justinian* (Oxford U.P., 1940), still fundamental. On the Second Sophistic, see above all G. W. Bowersock, *Greek Sophists in the Roman Empire* (Oxford U.P., 1969)*. Greek attitudes to Rome, especially as revealed by Aelius Aristides, in James H. Oliver, *The Ruling Power: a Study of the Roman Empire . . . through . . . Aelius Aristides* (American Philosophical Society, reprint, 1980, of a work originally published in the *Transactions of the APS*, n.s., xliv (1953), 871–1003); so too V. Nutton, 'The beneficial ideology', in Garnsey and Whittaker, *Imperialism in the Ancient World*, 209–21; R. Syme, 'The Greeks under Roman rule', *Roman Studies* II, 566–81. Also relevant is C. P. Jones, *Plutarch and Rome* (Oxford U.P., 1971). On Herodes Atticus, see Paul Graindor, *Un milliardaire antique: Hérode Atticus et sa famille* (Cairo, 1930, reprinted Arno, 1979). On Athens and Corinth at this period, see D. J. Geagan, 'Roman Athens: some aspects of life and culture I, 86 BC–AD 267', and J. Wiseman, 'Corinth and Rome: 228 BC–AD 267 in *ANRW* ii.7 (1979), 371–437 and 438–548 respectively. Archaeological evidence for the Asian and Syrian cities, e.g., Antioch, Ephesus, Pergamum, Smyrna, can best be consulted in the *Princeton Encyclopedia of Classical Sites*; on Antioch, see Glanville Downey, *A History of Antioch in Syria from Seleucus to the Arab Conquest* (Princeton U.P., 1961), and on Ephesus Clive Foss, *Ephesus after Antiquity: a Late Antique, Byzantine and Turkish City* (Cambridge U.P., 1979)*, which, like J. H. W. G. Liebeschuetz, *Antioch: City and Imperial Administration in the Later Roman Empire* (Oxford U.P., 1972)*, contains insights valuable for our earlier period also. Articles already cited, especially Garnsey, 'Aspects of the decline of the urban aristocracy in the Empire' (above under Chapter 9), and Hopkins and Burton, 'Ambition and withdrawal' (above on Chapter 7), are highly relevant here. On the special case of the Syrian archers on the Danube, see J. Fitz, *Les Syriens à Intercisa* (Brussels, Collection Latomus cxxii, 1972). On religion, E. R. Dodds, *Pagan and Christian in an Age of Anxiety*. (Cambridge U.P., 1965) is stimulating and fundamental. The best recent general works are John Ferguson, *The Religions of the Roman Empire* (London, Thames and Hudson, 1970)*, and Ramsay MacMullen, *Paganism in the Roman Empire* (Yale U.P., 1981)*. J. H. W. G. Liebeschuetz, *Continuity and Change in Roman Religion* (Oxford U.P., 1979)*, covers a wider range of topics than the title suggests and is an important contribution to social history. On eastern religions, Franz Cumont, *Les religions orientales·dans le paganisme romain* (Paris, 1929), though some of his views are no longer accepted, remains indispensable. On Mithraism, see M. J. Vermaseren, *Mithras, the Secret God* (London, Chatto and Windus, 1963), and on Isis, Friedrich Solmsen, *Isis among the Greeks and Romans* (Harvard U.P., 1976). On eastern cults in Roman London, and especially the Mithras Temple, see Ralph Merrifield, *The Roman City of London* (London, Benn, 1965), 60–4; Hadrian's Wall *mithraea* in R. G. Collingwood and Ian Richmond, *The Archaeology of Roman Britain* (London, Methuen, 1969), 160–3. On Isis and Apuleius, see Fergus Millar, 'The World of the *Golden Ass*', *JRS* lxxi (1981), 63–75. On the Christians, out of an immense literature, see Henry Chadwick, *The Early Church* (Pelican History of the Church; Penguin, 1967); and W. H. C. Frend, *Martyrdom and Persecution in the Early Church: a Study of a Conflict from the Maccabees to Donatus* (Oxford U.P., 1965). On the martyrs of Lyon, see the seminar papers published in *Les Martyrs de Lyon (177)* (Paris, 1978). The *Acts of the Scillitan Martyrs* and the *Martyrdom of Perpetua and Felicity* are to be found in H. Musurillo, *Acts of the Christian Martyrs* (Oxford U.P., 1972). On the legal position of Christians, see the articles by A. N. Sherwin-White and G. E. M. de Ste Croix in Finley, *Studies in Ancient Society* (above under Chapter 4), 210–62, and by Z. Yavetz and D. L. Stockton in Levick, *The Ancient Historian and his Materials* (above under Chapter 1), 181–212. Also T. D. Barnes, 'Legislation against the Christians', *JRS* lviii (1968), 32–50, and *Tertullian: a Historical and Literary Study* (Oxford U.P., 1971), covering more ground than the title suggests. See now P. A. Brunt, 'Marcus Aurelius and the Christians', in Carl Deroux (ed.), *Studies in Latin Literature and Roman History* I (Brussels, Collection Latomus clxiv, 1979), 483–520. Provincial attitudes to Rome in A. N. Sherwin-White, *The Roman Citizenship* (see above, General Works), part 4. Opposition to the established order is most comprehensively treated by Ramsay MacMullen, *Enemies of the Roman Order: Treason, Unrest and Alienation in the Empire* (Harvard U.P., 1966)*. On the semantic possibilities of 'bandit', see Eric Hobsbawm, *Bandits* (London, 1961). Actual fighting in Stephen I. Dyson, 'Native revolts in the Roman Empire', *Historia* xx (1971), 239–74, and 'Native revolt patterns in the Roman Empire', *ANRW* ii.3 (1975), 138–75. On gladiatorial games, my debt is clear to Keith Hopkins, 'Murderous games', in his *Death and Renewal* (above under Chapter 7), 1–30. See also Georges Ville, *La gladiature en occident des origines à la mort de Domitien* (Ecole française de Rome, 1981). The sub-arena structures at Lambaesis in J.-C. Golvin and Michel

Janon, 'L'amphithéâtre de Lambèse . . .', *Bulletin archeologique* xii/
iv (1976/78), 169–93, esp. 178–80. For El Djem, see the *Princeton
Encyclopedia of Classical Sites*. On the development and prosperity
of the surrounding countryside, see P. Trousset, 'Nouvelles observa-
tions sur la centuriation romaine à l'est d'El Jem', *Antiquités
Africaines* xi (1977), 175–207. Gladiators in the East in Louis
Robert (see above under Chapter 2); the quotation on page 274 is
from Robert, no. 92. On the circus and theatre demonstrations, like
those in the amphitheatre, and for some indication of how 'sport',
whether of gladiators or chariot-racing, might play a similar part in
antiquity to football today, see Alan Cameron, *Circus Factions:
Blues and Greens at Rome and Byzantium* (Oxford U.P., 1976),
brilliant and incisive. On the supply of animals for the games, see G.
Jennison, *Animals for Show and Pleasure in Ancient Rome* (Manchester U.P., 1937); see also J. M. C. Toynbee, *Animals in Roman
Life and Art* (London, Thames and Hudson, 1973). The North
African mosaic evidence is collected by K. M. D. Dunbabin, *The
Mosaics of Roman North Africa* (Oxford U.P., 1978)*.

XI An Age of Transition

The two English biographies of Septimius Severus are Maurice
Platnauer, *The Life and Reign of the Emperor Lucius Septimius
Severus* (Oxford U.P., 1918, reprinted Greenwood, 1970), and A.
R. Birley, *Septimius Severus, the African Emperor* (London, Eyre
and Spottiswoode, 1971). Michael Grant, *The Climax of Rome*
(London, Weidenfeld and Nicolson, 1968; Cardinal, 1974) covers
this period and on to the death of Constantine (337). Geoffrey
Turton, *The Syrian Princesses: the Women Who Ruled Rome
AD 193–235* (London, Cassell, 1974), is a lively and popular
account, but insufficiently sceptical where the *Augustan History* is
concerned. Fergus Millar, *A Study of Cassius Dio* (Oxford U.P.,
1964) is explicitly 'a contribution to our understanding of the
Severan period' (Preface, vii), and valuable as such. Articles of value
include E. Birley, 'Septimius Severus and the Roman army', *Epigraphische Studien* viii (1963), 63–82, and A. N. Sherwin-White,
'The *tabula* of Banasa and the *Constitutio Antoniniana*', *JRS* lxiii
(1973), 86–98. On the aftermath, see, for the Celtic warriors from
Edinburgh, Nora Chadwick, *The British Heroic Age: the Welsh
and the Men of the North* (U. of Wales Press, 1976); Richard
Hodges and David Whitehouse, *Mohammed, Charlemagne, and the*

Origins of Europe: Archaeology and the Pirenne Thesis (London, Duckworth, 1983), for the latest evidence on the final transition from Roman to medieval Europe; I am personally indebted, for opening my eyes to much that is true on this phenomenon, to Hugh Trevor-Roper, *The Rise of Christian Europe* (London, Thames and Hudson, 1966). The lines from Hildebert of Lavardin quoted on page 296 are translated by Helen Waddell, *More Latin Lyrics from Virgil to Milton* (London, Gollancz, 1976), 263, and the final quotations from her great book, *The Wandering Scholars* (above under Chapter 8), 11, 16–17. On the transmission of classical texts, see L. D. Reynolds and N. G. Wilson, *Scribes and Scholars: a Guide to the Transmission of Greek and Latin Literature* (2nd ed., Oxford U.P., 1974).

Index

Fontana Press

Fontana Press is the imprint under which Fontana paperbacks of special interest to students are published. Below is a selection of titles.

You can buy Fontana Press books at your local bookshop or newsagent. Or you can order them from Fontana Paperbacks, Cash Sales Department, Box 29, Douglas, Isle of Man. Please send a cheque, postal or money order (not currency) worth the purchase price plus 22p per book (maximum postal charge is £3.00 for orders within the UK).

NAME (Block letters) _____

ADDRESS _____

_____

_____